HOW TO MANAGE WITH A UNION

BOOK TWO

Jules J. Justin

HOW TO MANAGE WITH A UNION

BOOK TWO

The Rules of Seniority, Past Practice, Overtime, Technological Changes, Subcontracting, and Labor Arbitration

Industrial Relations Workshop Seminars, Inc.

NEW YORK

For information write the Publisher:
Industrial Relations Workshop Seminars, Inc.
21 East 40th Street, New York, N. Y. 10016

Published simultaneously in Canada

Library of Congress Catalog Card Number: 68-13936

FIRST EDITION

Printed in the United States of America

Contents

Contents

Contents

SECTION TWO

The Rules of Past Practice

SECTION   THREE

The Rules of Overtime

SECTION   FOUR

The Rules of Labor Arbitration

Contents

SECTION FIVE

Rules for Handling Technological Changes and Improved Production Methods

xiv

S E C T I O N   S I X

Rules for Handling the Subcontracting Case

Preface

To assure order, there is a clear procedural line drawn: the company directs and the union grieves when it objects . . . That challenge is made through the grievance procedure, not through rebellion.

Arthur J. Goldberg

This book makes up the second part of my work *How To Manage With A Union* and deals with the rules of seniority, past practice, overtime, technological changes, subcontracting and labor arbitration. The first book dealt with the rules of collective bargaining, grievance handling and corrective discipline. Although each section in each book stands on its own feet, I will do what I do at the beginning of the second day of my workshop seminars before dealing with the sections in this book: summarize the rules of collective bargaining, grievance handling, and corrective discipline covered in Book 1.

We began with the first two rules of collective bargaining: The supervisor never grieves under the labor contract; and management never initiates arbitration to enforce its order. Why not? Because the union's political structure compels it to leave the job of managing to management, retaining for itself the job of defending its own rights and the rights of the employees it represents under the contract. The union cannot join with management in managing the workers. The shop steward will not join with you, Mr. Supervisor, in supervising your employees. You and you alone have the burden of managing—initially interpreting each contract clause, applying the contract benefits, enforcing the contract's set of working conditions, and initiating disciplinary action. That's the supervisor's right of administrative initiative: to direct and control the work force without asking, consulting with, or getting the shop steward's prior approval. The shop steward reserves to himself his administrative right to protest and appeal through the grievance procedure, including arbitration if provided for, any action the supervisor initiates but not the supervisor's right to initiate that action.

In bargaining out grievances and disciplinary cases the shop steward follows the rules of collective bargaining, grounded in the customs of the marketplace—*Caveat emptor* (let the buyer beware) coupled with the professional's credo, never give a sucker an even break—with its wheeling, dealing, deuces wild and one-eyed jacks strategy, along with the competitive rule of the marketplace, what will the traffic bear.

Next we found that the worker joins a union for four primary reasons: (1) to compel recognition and respect for the dignity of his person and his acquired skills, (2) to protect his job security, (3) to secure promotional opportunity, and (4) to improve his standard of living. The pressures of the labor market constrain management to satisfy the economic needs of its employees. Satisfy those first three reasons that motivate workers to organize, Mr. Manager, and you'll be managing along lines of excellence without the help of a union or of an arbitrator to monitor your employee relations.

The labor contract sets up the law of the shop for the contract term. It represents a compromised package settlement of wages, hours, and working conditions that the negotiators agreed upon. In administering the contract's set of working conditions, Mr. Supervisor, take care that you don't compromise that compromised settlement! You don't have the authority to give the employees in your department more and the shop steward doesn't have authority to accept less than the contract stipulates. The contract decides what's fair, proper, and correct for your employees. Each supervisor administering one labor contract serves as one member of his management's team and not as a subcontractor running his own department as a separate independent business. Twenty-seven supervisors operating under one labor contract don't administer twenty-seven separate contracts!

The labor contract doesn't give management its management's rights; it only regulates the exercise of management's rights insofar as the contract's set of working conditions stipulates. The contract gives management only one contractual right—the no-strike pledge, by either an expressed no-strike clause or an implied agreement not to strike over grievances and disciplinary cases that the negotiators agreed the parties would finally settle by binding arbitration or by both. The "agreement to arbitrate grievance disputes," said the U.S. Supreme Court, "is the quid pro quo for an agreement not to strike." By giving the no-strike pledge the union guarantees that it will respect the supervisor's right to initiate action in administering the contract and maintaining employee discipline. By agreeing to binding arbitration management guarantees that it will respect the shop steward's right to protest any action the supervisor initiates that he believes violates the employees' or the union's rights under the contract.

What backs each of those guarantees? For the union, retroactive adjustment, by undoing management's violation and making the employees or the union "whole." For management, retroactive adjustment, by assessing money damages against the union for violating its no-strike pledge and making management "whole" for the losses it suffered. That's the way the collective bargaining contract balances the supervisor's responsibility to manage according to the contract's set of working conditions against the shop steward's responsibility to honor the union's no-strike pledge and protest the supervisor's action in the orderly way provided for by the grievance and arbitration machinery.

The shop steward polices the contract. He doesn't police employees' job performance, attendance, or conduct. That's the supervisor's job. The shop steward polices only the contract, and he performs his job by filing a grievance protesting the supervisor's action and processing it through the steps of the grievance procedure according to the specified conditions and time limits. A late grievance can be a lost grievance. A late answer, the grievance goes to the next step.

The law does not give the union the right to decide when to take up grievances. The supervisor initially sets the time in his step depending upon production and personnel needs prevailing in his department; and management's representatives initially set the time for conferring on grievances in the higher steps. If management's representatives frustrate the union by bottling up grievances in any step, the shop steward has the right to file a grievance protesting such dilatory action.

The law does not obligate management to pay for grievance time, although most contracts count a reasonable time spent in grievance handling during working hours as time worked. If the shop steward abuses his representative office, he subjects himself to disciplinary action.

What makes a legitimate grievance—a rightful grievance? The contract! The set of working conditions agreed to by the negotiators determines a legitimate grievance. Only a grievance the contract makes the supervisor responsible for constitutes a rightful grievance. The contract decides the right or wrong of a grievance. The contract decides whether a grievance has any merit. The contract decides the justice of a grievance. The contract tells how to settle a grievance on its merits. The contract decides the arbitrator's delegated authority to make a final and binding settlement of a grievance. Bargaining out or arbitrating every grievance raises the material issue: Did the supervisor's action violate the contract?

In a borderline case the supervisor gives himself the benefit of doubt, leaving it to his representatives in the higher steps to fill in any loopholes in the contract. In settling a grievance the supervisor avoids setting new precedents or new policies or starting restrictive practices. In denying a grievance that has no merit under the contract the supervisor writes short, specific answers and to the point: Grievance denied. The action protested has not violated the contract. Thus, the supervisor avoids giving his representatives in the higher steps wet powder in his written answer.

In every case in which the shop steward claims that the supervisor's action or refusal to act violated the contract, management has the burden of proof. The union has the burden of proof in the one case when management claims that the shop steward violated the union's no-strike pledge. He who initiates action bears the burden of justifying his action.

Three social rules prevail in the work unit: (1) self interest, which motivates employees and union representatives alike; (2) equality of treatment, which requires each employee to share equally the responsibilities as well as the benefits of the job and (3) social pressure, the unwritten code of the shop that says, don't be an informer!

Plant rules assure equality of benefit and equality of responsibility for all. Workers do not regard plant rules as punitive measures but as accepted standards of personal conduct and job responsibilities. Plant rules tell each employee where he stands in relation to his job and to his fellow workers. In drafting plant rules avoid qualifying or restrictive words such as "repeated," "continuous," "excessive," "wilful," "intentional," or other words that express conclusions. Just state the rule of conduct required or prohibited, such as no unexcused or unauthorized lateness or absence, no fighting, no horseplay, no gambling. Avoid setting forth the penalty or a schedule of graduated penalties for any infraction of a rule. Let the supervisor decide the penalty to fit each case and each employee.

Corrective discipline satisfies the social rule of equality of treatment by enforcing equally among all employees established plant rules, job responsibilities, safety practices, and personal standards of conduct. Corrective not punitive discipline encourages the wrongdoer to correct himself, deters others from doing wrong, and leads to self discipline. The job of maintaining discipline rests with the supervisor. The shop steward cannot join with the supervisor in managing the employees. The shop steward reserves to himself the role of defending the employees he represents.

The standard of just cause or any other comparable standard justifying disciplinary action obligates the supervisor to take into account extenuating circumstances that may excuse the offense or mitigate the penalty. The burden rests on the supervisor to show cause for the penalty as well as cause for the discipline imposed. Having initiated discipline, the supervisor must prove the wrongdoing charged and the justness of the penalty. In reviewing the supervisor's total disciplinary action, including the penalty, the arbitrator does not usurp management's right to manage. The standard of just cause or other comparable one authorizes the arbitrator to review the cause for the penalty imposed as well as the cause for disciplinary action.

When a supervisor disciplines one employee in the group he supervises, he disciplines all. Corrective discipline serves equally the interests of management, the union, and the employees, because corrective discipline satisfies the rule of equality of treatment. Employees respond to oral warnings, which they consider friendly advice. Oral warnings, unless communicated to the union, carry little weight as disciplinary action under the labor contract. Only disciplinary action communicated to the union with an opportunity for it to protest binds the union.

Criticizing a wrongdoer in writing and publishing that criticism by making his misconduct known to others creates the social pressure that induces self discipline as no other form of punishment can do. Economic detriment—loss of money or job benefits—hardly substitutes for public censure of misconduct. That's just the punishment the offender expected—being charged for lateness or unexcused absences or having the hours counted against him when he refuses to work overtime without a reasonable excuse. The price paid substitutes for the feeling of shame without which a wrongdoer hardly ever mends his ways.

If an employee fails to correct himself after oral warnings or if the gravity of his misconduct warrants immediate disciplinary action rather than friendly advice, start the steps of corrective discipline by (1) sending him a letter of reprimand setting forth in black and white the facts of his misconduct and (2) publishing that written reprimand by mailing a copy of the letter to the union's office and delivering a copy to the shop steward or union committee chairman.

If the written reprimand stands and within an approximate twelve month period thereafter the employee commits the same or comparable misconduct, proceed with the next steps of corrective discipline by (3) imposing a disciplinary suspension without pay of not less than three working days and not more than ten working days. (When you read the section on corrective discipline in Book 1 you'll see the need for this rule.) Then, (4) publish that disciplinary suspension letter by mailing a copy to the union and delivering a copy to the shop steward or union committee chairman.

The employee who fails to mend his ways discharges himself. If the disciplinary suspension stands and within approximately twelve months thereafter the employee commits the same or comparable offense, terminate his employment by (5) a letter of discharge, and (6) publish that letter of discharge by sending copies to the union's representatives.

A shop steward fills a dual role. As an employee the plant rules, job duties, and standards of personal conduct required of all employees apply equally to him. As a union representative his office compels him to defend the rights under the contract of the union and the employees he represents. If a shop steward abuses his representative office or engages in personal misconduct he subjects himself to disciplinary action. If he fails to respond to oral warnings or if the gravity of his misconduct warrants immediate disciplinary action, the supervisor follows the steps of corrective discipline but disciplines him with a second written reprimand before the step of disciplinary suspension.

Why two written reprimands? To neutralize any claim that the shop steward's legitimate union activities motivated the supervisor in disciplining him or that the supervisor discriminated against him because he exercises, perhaps too zealously, his right of advocacy in defending the employees he represents. Not through fear or favor but to show that he respects the shop steward's dual role as an employee and a union representative, the supervisor accords him preferential treatment in applying the steps of corrective discipline by disciplining him with a second written reprimand before imposing a disciplinary suspension.

On the other hand, if the shop steward violates the union's no-strike pledge by leading, encouraging, or participating in a concerted action, then the supervisor accelerates the steps of corrective discipline and instead of any written reprimands initially imposes a disciplinary suspension of not less than three nor more than ten working days.

In some cases of personal misconduct the gravity of the offense may warrant accelerating the penalty and instead of a written reprimand imposing a disciplinary suspension. In the unusual case in which the supervisor discharges for the first offense, where the employee has maintained a normally satisfactory record during the preceding year, the burden rests on the supervisor to justify such extreme penalty by facts that would lead to the reasonable finding that the supervisor could not chance the misconduct happening again.

The steps of corrective discipline put the union and all employees on notice of anyone's wrongdoing, and if the employee fails to mend his ways, the final step of discipline takes effect—discharge and termination of employment. In Book 1 you will find representative letters of reprimand, disciplinary suspension, and discharge in full text, dealing with a variety of disciplinary cases.

In Book 2, which deals with the rules of seniority, past practice, overtime, technological changes, subcontracting and labor arbitration, I cover:

> How to apply ability, qualifications and length of service in promotions, layoffs, recalls and transfers. Five ways to improve the quality of the work force. How to eliminate restrictive or inefficient past practices. How to assign and distribute overtime work and avoid pyramiding of premium pay. How to maintain operational efficiency and reduce costs of production, by consolidating jobs, reducing crews, eliminating idle time, and reevaluating work loads, and job and incentive rates because of technological changes and improved production methods. How to subcontract production or maintenance work during the contract term and how to use the arbitration process.

Applying the rules of labor relations set forth in these two books will help every member of management's team manage with a union along lines of excellence.

JULES J. JUSTIN

SECTION ONE

The Rules of Seniority

I

What Makes Up Seniority?

The Case of the Laid-Off Senior Employees

The company bought the business of another firm and transferred the manufacture of certain types of knitting machines it had not previously made to its own plant. The company also hired a number of employees of the former company, experienced in the work, to assemble the new type of machines. The company then reduced the assembly work on its own operations and laid off, among others, two assemblers who had greater seniority than the newly hired assemblers.

Article VII, Section 4 of the contract provided:

It is understood that in all increases or decreases of working forces the following factors shall be considered:

(a) Length of continuous service or seniority.
(b) Ability, efficiency, training, skill and cooperation.

Seniority or continuous service will govern the selection under all conditions, unless outweighed by the factors under (b).

The union filed a grievance protesting the company's action in laying off assemblers who had acquired seniority in the bargaining unit while retaining the newly hired employees to do the assembly work.

The company denied the grievance, claiming that the changeover in assembly work had created unusual circumstances requiring employees with more technical skills and that it had the right under the seniority clause to retain the newly hired assemblers because they possessed greater ability, efficiency, training and skill than the two senior employees whom the company had laid off. The union then appealed to arbitration.

I sustained the union's grievance, finding that the two laid-off employees qualified for the assembly work and that under the seniority clause the company did not have "the right to measure the factors of ability, efficiency, training, skill and cooperation competitively between or among employees qualified for the job in an occupational group—but only to measure those factors against the objective requirements of the job."

I held that under the seniority clause as written the parties did not intend to judge competitively the relative abilities of employees but only their abilities with reference to the requirements of the job. In my award I said:

> This is the modified type of seniority clause. The factors under (b) modify length of service or seniority. In other words, the operation of seniority or continuous service is contingent upon the employee first satisfying the factors under (b). Length of service or seniority does not come into play—does not govern the selection—until the factors under (b) are satisfied.
>
> How do the parties intend, under this modified type of clause, to measure, to judge, the factors under (b)? By reference or in relation to the requirements of the job. The standards against which the factors under (b) of each employee are to be measured are the job requirements as established by the company and practiced in the plant by the employees. Not mere ability to do the job, as is implied under the strict or straight type of seniority, where the factors under (b) are not expressed in the contract.

Noting that under this type of modified seniority length of service alone doesn't determine the senior employee's priority to the job because "he must meet the factors under (b) of the job requirements, before he can exercise his seniority preference," I said:

4

This type of clause does not set up two standards or measuring rods against which the factors under (b) are to be judged. It does not specify that employees be measured not only by:

(1) ability, efficiency, training, skill and cooperation required by the job; but also

(2) competitively, as between two or more employees, each of whom meets standard (1). The competitive type of clause permits the company to measure employees relatively to each other, as well as with respect to the requirements of the job.

The language of the seniority provision itself, as well as the way the parties had in the past applied this clause on layoffs, showed that the company did not have the right to retain the relatively better qualified employee but had to retain the senior qualified one; and in my award I said:

> The proof establishes that in all the years past, during which this clause had been in operation, the parties applied it, as the union claims in this case, so that senior in length of service employees who met the factors under (b) with respect to the requirements of the occupation had been retained. The fact that the instant seniority clause covers both increases and decreases—layoffs and promotions—of the working forces, in the absence of express language or proof showing a contrary intent, the way the parties themselves applied this clause in the past constrains the arbitrator to resolve any ambiguity in language in favor of upholding that past practice. Otherwise, the seniority protection that the parties intended to provide by their seniority clause would be rendered illusory.

You will note, Mr. Foreman, that seniority means more than length of service. It encompasses ability, skill, and other qualifying factors and in some cases judges the qualifying factors competitively among qualified employees. Now let's see what makes up seniority under the labor contract.

Defining Seniority: the Ten Factors
That Make Up Seniority

Seniority under the labor contract constitutes a contractual right of preference or priority of a qualified employee, as between two or more employees in the bargaining unit or covered by the contract, to an available job, based on the qualifying factors defining or governing the preference or priority in the work unit agreed upon under your contract.

Now, let's break that definition down into its ten component parts: Seniority under the labor contract constitutes:

1. a contractual right of
2. preference or priority of a
3. qualified employee, as between
4. two or more employees in the
5. bargaining unit or
6. covered by the contract, to an
7. available job, based on the
8. qualifying factors defining or governing the preference or priority, in the
9. work unit agreed upon under
10. your contract.

Now, let's see what makes up each of those ten standards of seniority.

Contractual Right

First, you will note, Mr. Foreman, that seniority arises by virtue of the labor contract—and only by the labor contract you administer. The law or special statutes, such as those dealing with military service, veterans, union membership or union activity, and fair employment practices, may circumscribe the contractual rights of seniority; but except for those overriding legal limitations, the labor contract creates and governs all seniority rights of the employees you supervise in the bargaining unit covered by that contract.

Preference or Priority

Next, you will note that seniority gives an employee only a preference or priority to a job by setting up a relative status or condition of employment. Seniority establishes only a relative status or condition of employment that regulates the relationship among employees to avail-

6

able work or employment. The seniority status of one employee conditions and subjects the seniority rights of other employees to an available job. Since the labor contract creates the preference or priority as a contractual condition of employment, the parties, signatories to the contract, retain the power to change this relative condition of employment during the contract term by mutual agreement.

Qualified Employee

Next, you will note that length of service alone does not create or even necessarily improve an employee's ability and qualifications to perform a job. Therefore, seniority implies that an employee must possess at the time the ability and qualifications to meet the duties, responsibilities, and requirements of the job, if he asserts his priority.

What makes up the duties, responsibilities, and requirements of a job? Meeting all the required standards of job performance, including attendance, conduct, safety practices, care of equipment and materials, quantity and quality of production—all these make up the duties, responsibilities, and requirements of every job.

Between Two or More Employees

During the contract term the seniority system agreed upon by the parties governs the relative status between and among employees—not between management and an employee or between the union and an employee, or between management and the union—unless the parties mutually change that relative status of employment set up by that seniority system.

Bargaining Unit

The preference or priority extends only to those employees in the bargaining unit, as certified by law or as agreed to by the parties, and as expressly set forth in the contract, unless the contract provides otherwise.

Covered by the Contract

Unless your contract provides otherwise, the preference or priority as a relative status or condition of employment does not apply to employees or jobs outside that bargaining unit or to transfers out of or back to that bargaining unit. Therefore, if the parties want that relative status to extend to other employees or to regulate conditions of employment outside that bargaining unit, the contract must so provide.

Available Jobs

Seniority does not create jobs or work. The preference or priority extends only to an available job or work that exists at the time the employee asserts his right of priority.

Qualifying Factors Defining or Governing the Preference or Priority and Work Unit Agreed Upon

Here we have to consider standards eight and nine together because these two standards make up every seniority system. When you know, Mr. Foreman, the seniority system your labor contract sets up, you'll be better able to select the qualified or the better qualified employee and defend your selection in settling the seniority grievance.

But first, let me define the final factor of seniority—standard ten.

Your Contract

The contract you administer, Mr. Foreman, creates the priority as a contractual right and governs that contractual right. No other contract, nor any past practice under any other contract, governs the preference or priority rights of employees in the bargaining unit or outside the bargaining unit, if covered by your contract.

Now, for standards eight and nine, which together make up every seniority system.

The Seniority System

All seniority systems consist of two separate but interdependent parts:

Part I   Sets forth the content—the qualifying factors—defining or governing seniority.

Part II   Establishes the operational group—the work unit within which the qualifying factors operate.

Now let me illustrate those two separate but interdependent parts that make up all seniority systems.

ALL SENIORITY SYSTEMS CONSIST OF

Part I—CONTENT

The qualifying factors defining or governing seniority:

HOW DOES YOUR CONTRACT DEFINE SENIORITY?

That is:

WHAT FACTORS MAKE UP SENIORITY?

That is:

WHAT TYPE OF SENIORITY CLAUSE DOES YOUR CONTRACT SET UP?

O

C

E

A

N

PART II—OPERATIONAL

The work unit agreed upon:

WITHIN WHAT WORK UNIT DO YOUR FACTORS OR TYPE OF SENIORITY OPERATE?

An ocean lies between those two separate but interdependent parts because one is as unlike the other as a man is unlike a woman.

We can liken a seniority system to a family. By definition, a family consists of a man and a woman—a husband and a wife—or at least must start off with them. The surviving descendants of a family may consist of two brothers or two sisters, but at the beginning, a man and a woman start the family. And you know how a woman differs from a man—physiologically, psychologically, and in all other ways! But, to have a family, "you can't have one without the other."

So too, with any seniority system.

Part I sets forth the content, the qualifying factors defining seniority.

Part II, on the other side of the ocean, describes the work unit, the structural base within which Part I operates. You see, Part I defines, and Part II sets up the unit within which Part I functions. To have a seniority system, "you can't have one without the other." Though they differ from each other, together they make up a seniority system dependent on each other.

ONLY THREE WAYS TO DEFINE SENIORITY

The negotiators can define seniority in only three ways; they can express seniority by only three types of clauses:

Type I   Strict or straight seniority

Type II   Modified or contingent seniority

Type III   Relatively equal in ability seniority

ONLY TWO WORK UNITS

Negotiators can set up Part II, the work unit within which one of the three types operates, in only two ways:

1. *Geography or area:* Plant-wide, company-wide, multiple plant, department, yard, floor, or other area.
2. *Job or craft:* Classification, occupation, operating group, family of jobs, grouping or bailiwick of related jobs, skills or crafts.

These are the only two ways to set up the work unit within which Type I, II or III operates.

DISTINGUISHING BETWEEN THE DEFINITION OF SENIORITY AND THE WORK UNIT

In preparing, presenting, and arguing the seniority grievance—in the grievance steps or before the arbitrator—you must first consider,

Mr. Foreman, how your contract defines seniority: Type I—strict or straight, Type II—modified or contingent, Type III—relatively equal in ability. Then you must deal with that part of your seniority system first, keeping it separate from the work-unit part.

Unless you clearly keep in mind that Part I defines the type of seniority under your contract and that Part II only describes the work unit within which that type operates, you will confuse the issue in dispute. You must keep them apart, as if an ocean separated them, and handle them separately. If you mix them up by starting to argue "plant-wide seniority" or "seniority by job classification," you may be taken to concede that your contract limits seniority only to length of service (Type I) when, as a matter of fact, your contract may define seniority as Type II or Type III. Unless you distinguish Type I from Types II and III, you may end up losing the grievance.

Now then, let's see how each of the three types defines seniority and what distinguishes each type from the other.

Type I—Strict or Straight Seniority

To illustrate:

Seniority shall govern or determine layoffs and recalls, promotions and transfers.

Increases or decreases in the work force shall be by seniority.

Layoffs and recalls after layoffs shall be in order of seniority, i.e., the last hired shall be the first laid off and recalls shall be in reverse order.

Note that Type I uses the word "seniority" alone, meaning essentially length of service. This type, strict or straight seniority, implies passage of time—length of service—as the sole qualifying factor defining seniority. But how about other qualifying factors, such as ability, job qualifications, skills, experience, or physical fitness? Does Type I imply these other qualifying factors? Do these other ability qualifications constitute material factors in deciding the priority between two or more employees?

Yes! Length of service alone does not create the qualifying factors

11

of ability, skills, experience, and job performance, including attendance, production and conduct records, that every job requires. Passage of time alone does not necessarily improve those qualifying factors that you, Mr. Foreman, must first inquire into in determining the seniority priority among your employees to an available job.

Does Type I, strict or straight seniority, necessarily imply that the senior employee possesses such qualifying factors as ability, skills and experience at the time he claims priority to a job? Yes! Length of service alone does not assure the presence of these ability factors.

Take the case where the company automates its freight elevators or substitutes escalators. Would you say the negotiators intended under Type I to give an elevator operator with twenty years of service whom the change displaced the seniority right to displace a punch-press operator with, say, seven years of service even though the punch-press job may be in the same or lower labor grade in the wage structure? No, unless the contract otherwise provided and the displaced elevator operator then possessed the ability factors to qualify for the punch-press operator's job.

But in promoting employees under Type I, have foremen considered those ability factors?

Generally no! Foremen have interpreted or have applied strict or straight seniority without considering the ability factors of skills, experience, attendance, production, and conduct records. Foremen generally have applied strict or straight seniority with reference only to length-of-service. They have often ignored the ability factors because no one told them that "seniority" encompasses ability to perform the available work. And from this narrow concept of strict or straight seniority flowed so-called trial periods—not to break-in on the new job or to demonstrate qualifications for the job—but as training periods to learn the necessary skills.

Type II—Modified or Contingent Seniority

To illustrate:

In layoffs and recalls seniority shall control, provided the senior employee has the ability to do the available work.

In promotions, seniority shall govern, if the employee has the capability, physical fitness and experience for the job.

Seniority under this contract shall consist of (or be defined as or governed by) the following factors:

1. Length of service
2. Qualifications, ability, job performance, experience, and physical fitness.

Note that Type II expressly sets forth other qualifying factors such as ability, skills, experience, and job performance in addition to the length-of-service factor. Such ability factors modify that factor; that is, length-of-service preference is contingent upon the employee satisfying the ability factors at the time he claims his right of priority to the available job.

Under Type II, Mr. Foreman, before giving weight to length of service you first consider whether the senior employee meets the other qualifying factors of ability, skills and experience required for the job. If you decide he doesn't, you go to the next senior employee and use the same yardstick.

Type III—Relatively Equal in Ability Seniority

To illustrate:

Seniority shall consist of (or be governed by) the following factors:

1. Length of service
2. Qualifications, ability, skill, experience, physical fitness, and job performance
3. And if, as between two or more employees, their qualifications, ability . . . [factors in 2] are relatively equal, then length of service [factor 1—sometimes referred to as "seniority"] shall govern.

Now, note here that this Type III clause:

1. Sets forth, as other qualifying factors, ability, skill, qualifications, experience, and job performance in addition to the length-of-service factor and then further

13

2. Prescribes a relative evaluation between and among qualified employees as an additional qualifying factor that the supervisor considers and gives weight to before considering length of service.

Under the Type III clause, at the time he claims priority for the job, the senior employee must both:

1. Satisfy the expressed qualifying ability factors and
2. Be relatively equal or the best among the qualified employees at the time he claims his right of preference or priority to the available job.

To put that another way, before considering, that is, giving weight to length of service, you, Mr. Foreman, first determine which employee, if any, among the qualified employees who bid, best qualifies for the job. Under the Type III seniority clause the relatively better qualified employee gets the job. Only if two or more qualified employees stand relatively equal in ability and qualifications, then and only then length of service controls by breaking the deadlock, and the senior of those relatively equal employees gets the job.

Contrasting the Three Types of Seniority

What essentially distinguishes Type II from Type I?

Type I   being silent on the ability factors, emphasizes—implies— length of service as the sole factor.

Type II   expressly sets forth some ability factors as qualifying conditions before length of service applies.

Under Types I and II against what single standard does:

1. the supervisor judge qualifications and ability?
2. the arbitrator decide qualifications and ability?

The single standard: The duties, requirements and responsibilities of the available job, including job performance, attendance, safety and conduct records.

Under Types I and II what weight does the supervisor give to (1) length of service? (2) qualifications and ability?

Under Type I the supervisor apparently gives greater weight to length of service and often by past practice dilutes the requirements of ability and qualifications as qualifying factors. Under Type II the supervisor considers and gives weight to qualifications and ability as qualifying factors before considering length of service.

Now, what essentially distinguishes Type III from Type II?

Type II sets forth ability and qualifications as qualifying factors. Type III sets forth ability and qualifications as qualifying factors and further requires a relative evaluation among qualified employees as an additional qualifying condition.

Under Types I and II the supervisor and the arbitrator judge each employee's qualifications and ability by one standard, namely, whether each meets the duties, requirements, and responsibilities of the available job. Type III offers the supervisor and the arbitrator two standards to judge each employee's ability and qualifications.

The two standards: (1) Whether each employee meets the duties, requirements, and responsibilities of the available job, including job performance, attendance, safety and conduct records; and (2) Competitively, which employee best meets the duties, requirements, and responsibilities of the available job including job performance, attendance, safety and conduct records.

Note that under all types of seniority the supervisor or the arbitrator judges an employee's ability and qualifications against the duties, requirements, and responsibilities of the available job and no other job.

Even under Type III, the relatively equal in ability clause, the supervisor or the arbitrator determines the competitively best or better qualified employee for the available job and no other job.

THE AVAILABLE JOB, NOT POTENTIAL FOR ANY OTHER JOB

You see, Mr. Foreman, you cannot use an employee's potential qualifications or ability for any other job than the job in question. Under all three types of seniority you judge an employee's ability and qualifications for the available job and for no other job. Potential for

15

any other job, meaning the ability to advance in the future to another job, plays no part under any type of seniority. Unless your contract provides otherwise, claiming that an employee otherwise qualified for the job bid for lacks potential to advance to another job in the future knocks the bottom out of your evaluation; and that's a sure way to lose your case in arbitration!

Seniority Rules One to Seven

In administering your seniority clause—Type I, II or III—follow these rules:

Rule 1. Under any type of seniority judge the ability and qualifications of an employee against the proper yardstick, that is, the duties, responsibilities, and requirements of the job in question.

Rule 2. Interpret ability to cover total job performance, including attendance, safety, and conduct records.

Rule 3. Whether expressed or implied, ability and qualifications for the job constitute qualifying factors under every type of seniority.

Rule 4. In applying Type III—relatively equal in ability seniority—judge an employee's ability and qualifications for the job:

1. Against the duties, requirements and responsibilities of that job; and

2. Competitively against the ability and qualifications of other employees qualified for that job.

Rule 5. Potential—ability to perform or advance to any other job—plays no part under any type of seniority, unless your contract provides otherwise. Avoid the yardstick of potential and you will avoid losing your case.

Rule 6. If you pass over a senior employee under Types I or II, be prepared to justify your action on the ground that the

16

passed-over employee did not then have the ability and qualifications for that job.

Rule 7. Under Type III argue your case on the ground that the passed-over employee was not relatively equal in ability and qualifications as compared to the employee you selected for that job.

The Case of the "Relatively Equal in Ability" Claim

The company had posted a job opening for second-grade iron worker. After interviewing each employee who had bid for the job, the general maintenance foreman selected a junior-in-service employee on the basis that "he was better qualified than the other applicants in the skills required for the job."

The union filed a grievance claiming the company had violated Article VI, Section 3 of the contract, which provided:

The company will give careful consideration to applications received in relation to the following qualifications:

(a) seniority,
(b) requirements of the job,
(c) individual skill, efficient service and physical fitness.

Where qualifications (b) and (c) are relatively the same, seniority shall govern.

The company denied the grievance and the union appealed to arbitration.

At the hearing the union conceded that Section 3 sets up certain limitations on seniority but argued that the differences in the relative qualifications between the senior (the passed-over employee) and the junior employee did not warrant depriving the grievant of his seniority protection under the contract.

The proof showed that the junior employee had worked in the job of blacksmith for almost two years doing work comparable in major skills to those required in the second-grade iron worker's job. The union conceded that he possessed the qualifications for the job but claimed that the senior employee equally qualified. The evidence did not support this claim and even sharply conflicted as to whether the senior employee possessed the skills required for the job.

In my award denying the union's grievance I said:

> However, the material question at issue in this case—under Section 3 of the contract—concerns not only whether both of these employees possessed the skills and qualifications necessary to meet the requirements of the job at the time it opened up, but whether one of them qualified relatively better in individual skill to meet the requirements of the job than the other.
>
> Section 3 gives the company the right to initially determine and to select the relatively better qualified employee, from among a group of qualified employees; and under Section 3, seniority governs only when two or more of the employees who bid are relatively the same. Thus, under this type of seniority clause, even though a senior employee may have the basic qualifications to perform the requirements of the job, the contract does not obligate the company to select him because of his greater length of service if another applicant is relatively better qualified for the job.

Then, finding that under the contract seniority (the length-of-service factor) becomes operative only between two or more employees relatively equal in individual skills to meet the requirements of the job, I said:

> Under that type of clause, seniority, i.e. length of service, does not come into play in determining initially the qualifications and skills of the applicants to meet the requirements of the job. The seniority factor serves as a yardstick or guidepost to be applied in selecting, from among two or more applicants who have relatively the same qualifications, the particular one for the job. Here, seniority serves only as a final determinant to break a deadlock.
>
> Were the union's position to be sustained, there would be no need to judge the individual skill and qualifications of applicants, nor to deter-

18

mine if one or more were relatively better qualified than others. These latter factors and method of measurement would be rendered meaningless. In effect, the sole factor in promotion would be strict seniority—that is, length of service. However, that is not what Section 3 provides. That is not what the parties agreed to under the clear and unambiguous language used in Section 3.

I pointed out in my award:

This type of seniority clause, referred to as the relatively equal type, limits the arbitrator's authority essentially to decide whether the method followed by the company in arriving at its judgment that the employee whom it selected was the relatively better qualified one—in individual skill with reference to the requirements of the job—was fair and objective. This requires a showing:

1. That the company's supervisor, who made the selection, based his judgment upon valid and objective standards and criteria;
2. That these standards and criteria were fairly evaluated and equally applied in the case of each applicant; and
3. That the supervisor arrived at his judgment without bias, favoritism, prejudice or discrimination.

I found that in selecting the junior employee the supervisor

fairly considered the individual skills and qualifications of both employees after he had interviewed each applicant; that he based his judgment on valid and objective standards and criteria fairly evaluated and equally applied to each applicant in relation to the requirements of the job in question; and that he arrived at his judgment in good faith without bias, favoritism, prejudice or discrimination.

Then, I held:

In light of the proof offered in this case, the arbitrator finds no basis to disturb that judgment nor does the arbitrator have authority under the facts herein to substitute his judgment or the judgment of the union for the judgment made by the supervisor.

19

RELATIVELY EQUAL FOR THE JOB,
NOT POTENTIAL FOR A DIFFERENT JOB

In that case the union relied upon another arbitrator's award rendered in a prior arbitration case between the parties to support its position. The facts, however, showed that the way the company had attempted to apply Section 3 in the prior case materially differed from the way the company had applied Section 3 in the case before me. In the prior case, I found:

> The company sought to distinguish the relative qualifications between the two applicants upon such criteria as alertness, general intelligence, and educability which the company claimed affected the potential of the senior employee to advance to other jobs in the future. The arbitrator found, in effect, that both applicants possessed relatively the same qualifications for the job bid for and that the criteria relied upon by the company to distinguish between the relative qualifications of the applicants for further development—that is, potential—to fill more advanced jobs in the future, rested upon a misconstruction of the seniority provision.

In the prior case the arbitrator concluded his findings by stating:

> In that light the conclusion must be drawn that though undoubtedly O_____ is the better qualified for certain other posts, D_____ and O_____ are evenly qualified to be upstairs grindermen in terms of physical ability and health, willingness to work, steadiness, and probable capacity to master, remember, and dutifully observe the relatively simple routine prescribed by the company. This being so, it follows that seniority shall govern and that D_____ must be given the job he seeks.

Distinguishing that prior arbitration case from the one before me, I then said:

> In the instant case, the arbitrator finds that the supervisor evaluated these two applicants and based his judgment in selecting the junior man upon objective criteria directly related to the requirements of the

job of 2nd-grade iron worker and did not consider the potential qualifications of either of the two applicants to perform any other job.

How to Distinguish Among the
Three Types of Seniority

1. Type I, strict or straight seniority, implies ability and gives
   priority to the senior-in-length-of-service employee.

2. Type II, modified or contingent seniority, expresses ability and
   gives the priority to the senior-in-length-of-service qualified employee.

3. Type III, relatively equal in ability seniority, expresses ability
   and gives the priority to the better or best qualified employee.

Check the labor contract you're administering, Mr. Foreman, and
decide which of the three types of seniority it provides. Here's the
quick way you tell:

1. Type I, strict or straight seniority, uses only the word seniority
   or service.

2. Type II, modified or contingent seniority, uses the word seniority
   or service and then uses one or more words expressing the ability
   factors, such as ability, skills, experience, physical fitness, and
   so forth. The more words used to express the ability factors, the
   more criteria the clause gives you to evaluate each employee.

3. Type III, relatively equal in ability seniority, uses the word
   seniority or service; then uses one or more words expressing the
   ability factors; and then uses the phrase "relatively equal" or
   similar phrases such as "about the same," "equal," "reasonably
   equal," or some other words that express a relative evaluation.

Seniority Rules Eight to Eleven

As we proceed, keep in mind these additional rules negotiators
follow in drafting the seniority clause:

Rule 8. All seniority clauses fit into óne of three types defining seniority or into a combination of those three types:

Type I Strict or straight seniority

Type II Modified or contingent seniority

Type III Relatively equal in ability seniority

Rule 9. One type may be used for all seniority movements; or one type for layoffs, another type for recalls, another for promotions, and one of the three types for other employee movements or preferences under the same contract.

Rule 10. The type used for layoffs and recalls after layoffs should be written apart, in a separate clause, from the type used for promotions and upgradings even if the contract uses the same type for those seniority movements.

Rule 11. Unless your contract specifies different types for different employee movements or preferences, the one type used governs all seniority preferences under your labor contract.

Negotiating the Seniority Compromise

In drafting a seniority system that determines who's to be laid off or who's to get the job preference, the negotiators try to reconcile the parties' conflicting interests and the conflict among employees.

To reach an acceptable compromise the seniority system must satisfy the social rule of equality of treatment that motivated the workers to join the union and yet must take into account the new seniority problem that technological changes in production bring about. In talking about automation and the seniority problem the new type of member creates for the union, James Stern, assistant to Leonard Woodcock, vice president of the United Automobile Workers, said:

The traditional concept of seniority is one that is not shared generally by engineers. They may talk about service as a consideration in layoff [Type II] instead of strict seniority in layoffs [Type I]—but when you talk about promotion there are many of them who say, "This should be on the basis of ability" [Type III]. This raises a question regarding the solidarity of union membership. What substitute would we propose to a group of engineers who wanted a union but who didn't want seniority?

I think one substitute might be that the engineers themselves participate in the procedure of deciding who gets the promotion, that we take away from management the unilateral authority to decide who gets promoted. But this puts us into the area where for the last ten years we have been beaten back in one sense, bite by bite, in contract language—the management prerogative clause. I would say in terms of automation that this will be used against us in the next few years.

Now, what makes up those conflicting interests the seniority compromise tries to reconcile?

For the union, to:

1. Protect the workers' job security in layoffs and on recalls

2. Make available an equitable system for promotion from within

3. Protect its own union security in the bargaining unit that technological changes threaten.

For management, to:

1. Fully utilize the skills and abilities of its employees, and its available machines

2. Maintain efficiency in production with competent workers

3. Improve the quality of its work force in accommodating technological changes.

How do the negotiators resolve this conflict? By a compromise by which:

1. Management agrees to retain on the job or recall after layoff the senior qualified employee (Type II), thereby satisfying the union's objective to protect employee job security.

23

2. The union agrees to the promotion of the best or better among the qualified employees (Type III), thereby satisfying management's objective to improve the quality of its work force.

Yes, that's the compromise the union offers and most knowledgeable management negotiators accept. By that compromise management accords greater security to employees in their present jobs in the bargaining unit by agreeing not to improve the quality of its work force under the guise of a layoff; and the union accords management the opportunity to improve the quality of its work force by promoting the best qualified employee.

The Case of the Improper Layoff

The company had laid off the grievant, an employee with fifteen years seniority, on the ground of "lack of suitable work." The union protested, claiming that the company had violated the contract by not allowing the grievant to displace a junior employee in the same department on a job the grievant claimed he qualified for. The company denied the grievance, and the union appealed to arbitration.

The seniority clauses set up a series of consecutive steps for transfers to other jobs to protect the seniority rights of an employee laid off from his own job, provided he "possesses the basic qualifications" for the job transferred to. The contract defined the term basic qualifications as having "as determined by management the fundamental background, knowledge and ability to enable an individual to satisfactorily perform a job."

The consecutive steps of the layoff procedure first offered an employee with one or more years of service laid off from his own job the opportunity to transfer to an opening in the plant in the same classification or on a similar or related job. If no openings existed, the contract allowed him to displace a junior employee in his department in the same classification or on a similar or related job in the same labor grade or, successively, in lower labor grades.

For some time prior to his layoff the grievant had suffered from a heart ailment. The company's records listed him as having a "physical limitation against prolonged standing or walking; climbing high places or lifting heavy objects." At the time of his layoff from his own job an opening existed in a new job that the company had set up in another department; but because of his physical limitation the company judged the grievant unsuitable for the new job. The company then laid him off from work, claiming lack of suitable work, even though at the time other jobs existed in his department, held by junior employees, which the grievant qualified for, notwithstanding his physical limitation.

At the arbitration hearing the company claimed that since the grievant could not accept the opening in the new job because of his physical limitation, he had thereby exhausted his seniority rights; that even though he qualified for other jobs in his department, he did not have the right to displace a junior employee who did not suffer from any physical limitation; and that in the past the parties had applied the seniority provisions in that way in cases where the laid-off employee suffered a physical limitation.

The union claimed that the grievant did not forfeit his seniority rights to displace a junior employee in a job in his department he qualified for within his physical limitations and that neither the contract nor the past practice under it supported the company's position.

In my award sustaining the union's grievance I found that the past practice relied upon by the company failed to support its claim that the grievant, having exhausted his rights under step 2(a), had thereby forfeited his rights under step 2(b), stating:

> These past cases in no way establish that the parties intended that an employee who, because of his physical limitation, cannot be offered or transferred to an opening under Subdivision 2(a), thereby exhausts his rights under the layoff procedure of the Local Supplement. The arbitrator finds that an employee who, because of his physical limitation, cannot be transferred to an opening under Subdivision 2(a) has the right to pursue his seniority rights in the next step of the layoff procedure, Subdivision 2(b), to displace an employee in his department in the same grade on work for which he is qualified including his physical limitation.

25

Then, noting that the contract did not obligate the company to retain an employee who because of physical limitations could not meet the normal duties and requirements of the job but that removing him must be done "independently," and not under the guise of applying the layoff procedure, I said:

> Physical disability of employees creates a serious problem for the company in maintaining the quality of its work force. In the past, the company has tried to accommodate long-service employees, who become physically disabled, wherever possible, consonant with its operational needs. Neither the National Agreement nor the Local Supplement obligates the company to continue on a job an employee who, because of his physical limitation, is not competent to meet the normal duties and requirements of the job. The company may remove such an employee, irrespective of his seniority, as it has done in a number of cases in the past. Those agreements, however, do not give the company the right under the guise of a layoff to improve the quality of its work force by denying an employee his seniority rights to displace a junior employee in a job which he is qualified to perform, including his physical qualifications.
>
> Improving the quality of the work force, by removing an employee not competent to meet the normal duties of his job or who because of a physical disability becomes unable to continue to meet the normal duties of his job, can properly be pursued before or after—but independently of—applying the layoff procedure. Otherwise the very job security the parties intend to give employees under seniority and the agreed upon layoff procedure would be weakened, if not destroyed.

SENIORITY CREATES A RELATIVE STATUS,
NOT A PROPERTY RIGHT IN A JOB

In that case the union raised another issue, whether the contract gave employees the seniority right to trade jobs among themselves. Here's how that issue came up.

When the company refused to transfer the grievant to an opening in another department under Subdivision 2(a) because of his physical limitation, two union officers who had jobs in the same labor grade in the grievant's department offered to take a transfer to that opening to allow the grievant to take one of their jobs. The company refused to permit such a trading of jobs. I upheld the company's action, and in my award I said:

> Neither agreement gives employees nor union officers the right without the consent of the company to trade jobs under the layoff procedure or to swap jobs among and between themselves to accommodate one another. Seniority does not create a property right in a job nor does it create a proprietary interest on the part of an employee to a job. Seniority provisions establish a relative condition of employment that regulate the relationship status among and between employees to an available job.
>
> The seniority system that the collective bargaining agreements set up and the procedural steps that the parties have agreed to under their layoff procedure determine that relative status of employment and govern the conditional relationship between two or more employees to one available job. To allow employees to trade jobs because one or the other may be adversely affected by the layoff procedure could well lead to preferential treatment being accorded to some employees, as well as upsetting the very seniority system the parties had agreed to. The arbitrator finds the company properly exercised its rights under the agreements in refusing to consent to such trading of jobs.

Requisites One Through Three
for the Seniority Compromise

In bargaining out an acceptable seniority system, the negotiators try to reconcile the conflict between employee job security and improving the quality of the work force. The acceptable compromise that satisfies the interests of each side without detriment to the other will usually encompass the following requisites:

Requisite 1: Retaining on the job or recalling during periods of layoff the senior qualified worker (Type II), thereby avoiding any semblance of improving the quality of the work force under the guise of the layoff procedure.

Requisite 2: Promoting or upgrading the relatively better or best qualified worker (Type III), thereby improving the

27

quality of the work force without threatening the job security of senior employees.

Requisite 3: Removing from the job before or after layoff, but independently of the seniority procedures, an employee who fails to meet the normal duties, requirements, and responsibilities of his job, including attendance, job performance, safety, and personal conduct.

We now come to the next requisite in negotiating an acceptable seniority system—setting objective, demonstrable standards for governing the seniority preference for the available job. This calls for measurable criteria the parties can verify—prove and support—by objective facts.

Length of service satisfies this requisite because either party can readily measure and prove it by recorded facts. That's why it carries such a strong appeal as an objective standard in determining who's to be laid off, recalled, promoted, or get the shift preference.

But length of service alone does not create the qualifying factors of ability, competency, and fitness, including attendance, safety, and conduct records that apply to every job. Passage of time alone does not necessarily improve these qualifying factors. Therefore, an acceptable compromise must also provide for ability, competency, and fitness as factors governing the seniority preference. Do the parties have available recorded facts, as criteria, to support, prove and verify those factors? Yes! But first, let us consider the criteria for computing length of service.

THE LENGTH-OF-SERVICE STANDARD

The seniority preference extends only to those employees in the bargaining unit certified by law or otherwise agreed to by the parties and as set forth in the contract. Unless the contract provides otherwise, the seniority preference does not extend to employees or jobs outside the bargaining unit or to transfers out of or back to that bargaining unit.

Although recorded facts establish and prove an employee's length of service, legitimate grievances may still arise during the contract term over computing an employee's length of service. Generally, a newly hired employee does not acquire seniority, that is, length of service in the bargaining unit, until he has completed his probationary period. In the absence of a contractual guide, a question may arise over whether an employee's length of service commences on the date he completes his probationary period or goes back retroactively to his date of hiring.

When temporary, seasonal, or part-time employees come into the bargaining unit, a legitimate grievance may arise over whether such employees have seniority standing among themselves for available jobs.

Seniority movements to and from jobs within the bargaining unit—transfers, promotions, changed or consolidated jobs due to technological improvements—may affect an employee's length of service in his former job or in his new job and thereby give rise to legitimate grievances. Transfers from jobs in the bargaining unit to technical, administrative, or supervisory jobs outside the bargaining unit, unless otherwise provided for, likewise give rise to questions about whether the transferred employee loses, retains, or accumulates service while outside the bargaining unit.

Breaks in an employee's length of service may affect his seniority standing, such as those due to (1) voluntarily quitting, (2) discharge for just cause, (3) a layoff for a continuous period of time, as specified, (4) failing to report for work within a stipulated time after notice of recall, (5) being absent from work for a specified period of time without permission and without notifying the company, (6) accepting severance pay upon layoff, when his job fades out because of technological changes in production, or other expressed reasons that terminate seniority rights.

Leaves of absence for maternity, union business, or personal reasons sometimes raise legitimate grievances over whether an employee accumulates service during such nonworking periods.

Although questions may arise in all those kinds of cases, the parties have available recorded facts to prove an employee's length of service and support it as an objective factor in determining his seniority standing.

Do the parties have available recorded facts to prove an employee's ability and qualifications for a job, and support them as objective factors in determining his seniority priority? Yes! Well then, let's see what make up those recorded facts.

THE CASE OF PROVING ABILITY AND
QUALIFICATIONS BY RECORDED FACTS

The company had denied an employee's bid for a job in the lead-burner classification, an entry job in another promotional line, on the grounds that he had poor attendance and safety records. The union filed a grievance, claiming the seniority provisions did not permit the company to consider an employee's attendance, job performance, or prior disciplinary record in determining whether he had the qualifications and ability necessary to perform the job he bid for. After going through the steps of the grievance procedure, the union appealed to arbitration.

At the arbitration hearing the union claimed that the company had not in the past applied such criteria in determining an employee's qualifications and ability and that to allow the company to use an employee's prior disciplinary record to deny his bid for a job opening would constitute "double jeopardy" because that would result in the company punishing him twice for his prior offenses.

In support of its claim the union relied upon an earlier arbitration case between the parties involving the same issue, in which another arbitrator had denied the company's right to reject an employee's bid for a job because of his former disciplinary record. The union argued that that prior arbitration award, interpreting the seniority provisions of the contract, constituted a binding precedent in the present case.

In deciding the case, I held that neither the written conract nor any past practice under it precludes the company from using an employee's attendance, job performance, or prior disciplinary record to evaluate his qualifications and ability to perform the job under the seniority provisions of the contract, and in my award I said:

Section 1 of the seniority provision speaks of promotional opportunity for employees of necessary qualifications and ability. That section in

30

no way limits qualifications and ability solely to the technical or mechanical skills of an employee. An employee's ability to attend regularly and on time, to observe safety rules, and meet his responsibilities in personal conduct constitute proper evaluating factors in determining an employee's qualifications and ability for promotional opportunity. Section 4 of the seniority provision fortifies this finding and clearly shows that the parties intended such factors as attendance, job performance, and conduct would be considered in determining an employee's qualifications and ability.

Then, noting that Section 4 referred to an employee's ability and physical fitness as being "adequate to perform the work available in an efficient manner," I said:

Clearly, an employee's attendance, job performance, and conduct record provide the objective facts that determine whether an employee has the ability to adequately perform the work available in an efficient and safe manner. The arbitrator, therefore, finds that under the clear language of the seniority provisions, the parties intended that an employee's attendance and job performance records can properly be used to evaluate an employee's qualifications and ability in considering his bid for promotional opportunity.

However, to consider those factors in evaluating an employee's qualifications and ability, I said:

The employee's absences, latenesses, or failure to meet his job responsibilities must be unexcused, unauthorized, uncondoned and without reasonable cause; and must be shown—by corrective disciplinary action—to have been proven shop violations. If the absences, latenesses, or other misconduct had been excused or condoned because of bona fide illness or other justifiable cause—and consequently did not subject the employee to corrective disciplinary action—then such attendance or conduct record cannot properly be used in evaluating an employee's qualifications and ability under these seniority provisions so as to deny him promotional opportunity thereunder.

Finding that the company had improperly evaluated the grievant's attendance record because the recorded facts failed to prove that the grievant's absences and latenesses had violated his job duties, since his supervisor had not taken any corrective disciplinary action, I said:

> The grievant's attendance and job performance record shows that during his one year of active employment, he was absent or late on 39 full or partial days. But of those 39 days his supervisor had excused him or had condoned his absences on 37. Thus, the grievant was absent from work on 28 full days that included one continuous period of 17 days because of claimed sickness or injury. His supervisor apparently did not question those absences as being for valid reasons; and the company offered no proof to show that the claimed sickness was not bona fide. On 4 other days the grievant requested and had been granted permission to leave work early. Here again, apparently, the reasons the grievant gave were valid ones and had been accepted as valid by his supervisor. He cannot be disciplined for requesting and being granted permission to leave work early; and therefore such absences cannot properly be used to evaluate his ability and qualifications in his bid for the leadburner job. Likewise, on 3 other days that the grievant reported late for work, these cannot be used to show that he has a poor attendance record because, apparently, he gave reasonable or valid excuses that his supervisor had accepted; and on 2 other days, he was excused from work because of "personal reasons"—that the company does not question.

Since the recorded facts showed that the grievant had absented himself from work without leave on only two days during the period in question, one of which had occurred more than six months prior to the time the company turned down his bid and that ten months had elapsed since his supervisor had disciplined him by a warning letter for his failure to wear his safety helmet, I said:

> In evaluating an employee's prior disciplinary record, the nature of the offense or misconduct for which the employee had been disciplined— as well as the length of time that elapsed since the discipline taken —become material criteria to be considered in determining the weight to be given them. Here, 10 months or more had elapsed between the time the employee had been given the safety warning letter and the time the company turned his bid down. Of the 2 unexcused ab-

sences, for which he had been given written warnings, the first had occurred 6 months or more before the company turned his bid down; and the second one, a month or more before.

Considering the nature of the grievant's offenses and the length of time that had elapsed in 2 of the 3 instances, the arbitrator finds that his disciplinary record fails to support the company's evaluation that the grievant did not possess the necessary qualifications and ability to bid for the leadburner job. The arbitrator, therefore, finds that the company had improperly denied the grievant the opportunity to be tested for the leadburner job, and in this respect violated the seniority provisions of the contract between the parties.

WHEN PAST PRACTICES CONFLICT WITH THE WRITTEN PROVISIONS, WHAT CONTROLS?

In that case the union argued that in the past the company had never applied such evaluating factors of attendance and job performance. I found that that fact did not preclude the company from using those factors in the present case, and I said:

> Where one party refrains or neglects to enforce its rights under the written contract provisions, such withholding of action does not constitute a past practice whereby that party forfeits its rights under the written contract provisions. Likewise, the fact that one party may not have enforced its rights in the past, doesn't constitute a waiver of its rights under the written provisions for the future. Neither party relinquishes its contractual rights established by the written contract provisions by having refrained from enforcing its rights in the past.

Further noting that even an established past practice, "if it conflicts with the written provisions of a contract or contradicts what the parties clearly intended under those written provisions, would not result in either party forfeiting its rights under those written provisions in the future," I said:

> If in the past either party had condoned action that conflicted with the written provisions—or in the past had withheld enforcing its rights or the obligations of the other party under those written provisions—such

practice does not constitute a waiver of those rights; nor does it stop either party from enforcing its rights under the written provisions in the future for the balance of the contract term. An action that in the past had been permitted or condoned, though not void so as to be retroactively undone, may nonetheless be voidable by either party in enforcing its rights under the written provisions for the future of the contract term. Either party can insist that the written provisions be thenceforth complied with and have them enforced. In such case, the so-called past practice falls and gives way to the written provisions of the contract, that then govern the parties' relations for the future of the contract term.

That case presented another issue, raised by the union, of whether using an employee's prior job performance and disciplinary record to evaluate his qualifications under the seniority provisions would constitute double jeopardy by subjecting him to two punishments for the same misconduct. Before proceeding to that issue, let us sum up the additional requisites for negotiating an acceptable seniority compromise.

REQUISITES FOUR TO SIX FOR THE
SENIORITY COMPROMISE

Requisite 4: Objective standards to govern the seniority preference for the available job call for measurable criteria that recorded facts can support, prove, and verify.

Requisite 5: Length of service provides an objective measurable criterion that recorded facts can support, prove and verify.

Requisite 6: Ability and qualifications equally provide measurable criteria that recorded facts can support, prove and verify.

Now as to the plea of double jeopardy in using an employee's prior disciplinary record to evaluate his ability and qualifications under seniority to retain his job or to merit a promotion to another job.

THE PLEA OF DOUBLE JEOPARDY

Two years before the arbitration case referred to above arose, the parties had submitted the same issue to arbitration before a different arbitrator. In that prior arbitration case the company had also rejected an employee's bid for a job because of his poor performance and attendance record.

The union then filed a grievance challenging the company's right to consider an employee's attendance and job performance under the seniority provisions in determining whether he had the qualifications and ability to perform the job he bid for.

While that grievance awaited arbitration, the company discharged the employee because of his misconduct. The union filed another grievance protesting the discharge, and that case went to arbitration before the same arbitrator whom the parties had selected for the first case. The parties gave the discharge case priority over the job-bidding case. After hearing the discharge case, the arbitrator reduced the penalty of discharge to a "disciplinary penalty of 3 months" and reinstated the employee to his former job.

Then the arbitrator heard the job-bidding case and held that the company did not have the right to consider the employee's "past record of misconduct for which he has already been punished" in connection with his bid for the job. Finding in that situation that the employee had received appropriate punishment for his misconduct, the arbitrator held that to deny the employee's bid for a job because of his past conduct record would be punishing him twice for the "same offense or series of offenses" and would thus place him in double jeopardy.

Although the circumstances in the earlier case showed some factual basis for the arbitrator deciding the job-bidding case in the way he did, in the case before me I disagreed with the interpretation given to those seniority provisions; and I also disagreed with the reasoning expressed in that prior case, namely, that using an employee's prior disciplinary record of proven shop violations to evaluate his qualifications and ability for promotion under the seniority provisions would constitute double jeopardy or would result in punishing an employee twice for the same misconduct. In my award I said:

35

On the contrary, I hold that in using an employee's prior disciplinary record of proven improper conduct and violations of shop rules to evaluate his qualifications and ability for promotion under the seniority provisions does not constitute double jeopardy, as it does not mean that the employee is being punished twice for the same misconduct.

Noting that the seniority provisions did not limit qualifications and ability solely to an employee's technical or mechanical skills, I said:

Clearly then, an employee who bids for a promotion and whose past conduct, job performance, and attendance record shows that he does not possess the ability "adequate to perform the work available in an efficient and safe manner," does not satisfy those necessary qualifications and ability for the job. To ignore those expressed requirements of Section 4 and Section 5 would be to alter those provisions. While Article IX of the contract gives the arbitrator authority to interpret and apply the provisions of the agreement, it expressly provides that "he shall not have authority to alter or add to any of its provisions."

The Disciplinary Record Evaluates Ability and Qualifications

This oft-used plea of double jeopardy advanced against using an employee's prior disciplinary record to evaluate his ability and qualifications under seniority carries some appeal because it does seem as if the supervisor is punishing the employee twice for the same misconduct or breach of his job responsibilities. But in truth this plea of double jeopardy lacks merit and carries only a superficial ring of truth.

"Using an employee's prior disciplinary record," I said in my award, "to evaluate his ability and qualifications for promotion does not differ from using his record to determine whether he should be granted a merit increase within his rate range. In both cases, the employee's prior disciplinary record shows by objective facts that he doesn't merit the advancement, because he has failed to meet the duties and responsibilities required of him in the job." Then I went on to say:

In the first instance, when a supervisor disciplines an employee, he punishes him by either a written reprimand or a disciplinary suspension. In the second instance, the supervisor uses that employee's prior disciplinary record to evaluate him, by the objective facts that he and the union had been notified of and made aware of, to determine whether he meets the necessary qualifications and ability to be promoted or to merit the merit increase. In this latter case, the supervisor has not punished him again, even though that may seem superficially so. The supervisor uses the employee's prior disciplinary record not to punish him again but to evaluate his employment record to see if he meets the duties and responsibilities of attendance, job performance, safety and conduct that attach to every job so as to satisfy the necessary ability and qualifications required for the new job.

The Disciplinary Record Provides Recorded Facts

Precisely because the employee had been disciplined, can his disciplinary record be used to evaluate him for his bid for promotion. Because when the supervisor promotes an employee, after evaluating his prior disciplinary record, the supervisor thereby acknowledges that the employee has sufficiently corrected himself so that he now possesses the necessary ability and qualifications required to meet the duties and responsibilities in the job. And when the supervisor promotes that employee, he in effect washes out and eliminates that employee's prior disciplinary record as evaluating factors in the future.

Then I said:

Precisely because the employee had been disciplined for his past misconduct or offenses, can the supervisor properly use that prior disciplinary record to evaluate that employee's ability and qualifications under the seniority provisions. For if the supervisor had not taken disciplinary action because of the employee's absences, latenesses, misconduct, or failure to meet any of his other job responsibilities, then, in effect, the supervisor had excused or condoned such conduct. Where the supervisor does not take disciplinary action, he cannot use the absences or improper conduct of the employee because, in effect the employee has not done anything "wrong." It is precisely when the employee does something wrong, and only when he is disciplined for that wrong, does his discipline show that it was unexcused and not condoned.

37

The Horns of the Double Jeopardy Dilemma

The falsity of this plea of double jeopardy in seniority cases shows up clearly by the dilemma it would create if it had any merit. For as I noted in my award:

> On the one hand, if an employee's attendance, job performance, or conduct violates the responsibilities of his job, and the company disciplines him for such violations, then say the proponents of the double jeopardy plea, the company cannot use such discipline in the future to evaluate his ability and qualifications to continue on the job or to be promoted to a better or higher rated job because that would be punishing him twice for the same offense or misconduct.
>
> On the other hand, if the company withholds disciplining an employee for those same violations, the company cannot use such undisciplined conduct to evaluate his ability and qualifications to continue on the job or to be promoted because the company, not having disciplined him, had excused his violations or had accepted the employee's reason for his absences, latenesses, or misconduct, and thereby had acknowledged, by not having disciplined him, that he had done no wrong.

Then finding that the seniority provisions did not preclude the supervisor from using an employee's prior disciplinary record of proven shop violations to evaluate his qualifications and ability for promotional opportunity and that such evaluation would not constitute double jeopardy, I said:

> Just as a supervisor properly uses an employee's prior discipline within a reasonable period of time thereafter to determine the appropriate penalty in a future case where the employee, not having corrected himself, commits the same or comparable misconduct or breach of rule, so does a supervisor properly use an employee's prior disciplinary record to evaluate him for promotion or other job advancement under seniority, unless the labor agreement expressly provides otherwise.

DO PRIOR AWARDS CONSTITUTE BINDING PRECEDENTS?

In that case the union also claimed that the interpretation given in the earlier arbitration case constituted a binding precedent foreclosing an arbitrator in any subsequent case from interpreting in any other way the seniority provisions. I rejected that argument as being without substance or validity. Acknowledging the present situation "in which two arbitrators in different cases between the parties arrive at diametrically opposite interpretations of the same contract provisions," I said:

> A prior award between parties under the same contract may be considered as "persuasive argument" on a future dispute involving the same provisions, but it does not constitute a precedent binding upon or limiting another arbitrator's authority in future cases between the parties unless by their contract the parties agree that it does.

Holding that the legal doctrine of *stare decisis* (to stand settled), that is, judicial precedent, does not apply to the arbitration process, I said:

> That doctrine that prevails under our common law judicial system in effect cautions the courts against declaring wrongful that which custom and usage has sanctioned and which the weight of judicial authority has approved. Under that doctrine, legal principles of contract construction which have been distinctly enunciated have been given the force of law. Court decisions and judgments are thereby accorded authoritative weight as legal precedents in determining similar principles in future cases.
>
> Arbitrator's awards, however, do not have such corresponding authority or force. They are not accorded the weight of judicial authority or precedents in determining future disputes even between the same parties or over the same issues. They are not conclusive nor binding upon an arbitrator in subsequent cases. In arbitration, all questions of fact and law are deemed to be referred to the arbitrator selected for his decision. As long as the arbitrator keeps within his delegated authority, he can decide the issues submitted to him notwithstanding any prior awards between the parties, unless they have otherwise agreed.

Noting that a "prior award may be considered for its persuasive value in a subsequent case if in the arbitrator's judgment it accords with sound principles of contract construction and will help in deciding the case before him," I said:

A prior award, however, does not constitute a binding precedent that in any way limits an arbitrator's authority to interpret a contract provision in future cases, even though his interpretation may differ from or be opposite to another arbitrator's interpretation in a prior case on the same issue.

Seniority Rules Twelve to Twenty-Nine

In administering the seniority compromise, Mr. Foreman, and handling grievances under it during the contract term, follow these additional seniority rules:

Rule 12. An employee's ability to attend regularly and on time, to observe established plant rules of safety and personal conduct, and to meet the responsibilities of his job constitute measurable criteria by which to evaluate his ability and qualifications under seniority.

Rule 13. An employee's attendance, job performance and conduct records thereby provide objective criteria that can be verified, proved and supported by recorded facts, to assess his ability and qualifications under seniority either to retain his job or to merit promotion to another job.

Rule 14. In order to use an employee's attendance, job performance, and conduct records as objective criteria to evaluate his ability and qualifications to retain his job or to merit promotion to another job, his absences, latenesses, breaches of plant rules, misconduct, or failure to meet his job responsibilities must be verified by prior corrective disciplinary action to have been proven shop violations.

Rule 15. In evaluating an employee's prior job performance or disciplinary record, the nature of the offense and the seriousness of the misconduct, as well as the length of time that has elapsed since the discipline had been imposed must be considered in judging whether the employee has since corrected himself and in determining the weight to be given them in evaluating his ability and qualifications to retain his job or to merit promotion to another job.

Rule 16. Where one party refrains or neglects to enforce its rights under the written contract provisions, such withholding of action does not constitute a past practice whereby that party forfeits its rights under the written contract provisions.

Rule 17. The fact that one party may not have enforced its rights under the contract in the past does not constitute a waiver of its rights under the contract for the future.

Rule 18. An established past practice that conflicts with the written provisions of the contract or contradicts what the parties clearly intended under those written provisions does not constitute a forfeiture of a party's rights under the contract in the future.

Rule 19. If in the past either party had condoned an action that conflicts with its rights under the provisions of the written contract or in the past had not enforced its rights or the obligations of the other party under those written provisions, such past practice does not constitute a waiver of those rights; nor does it stop either party from enforcing its rights under the written provisions in the future for the balance of the contract term.

Rule 20. Such action that in the past had been permitted or condoned, though not void so as to be retroactively undone, may nonetheless be voidable by either party in enforcing its rights under the written provisions for the future of the contract term. In such case, the past practice falls and gives way to the written provisions of the contract that then govern the parties' relations for the future of the contract term.

Rule 21. Using an employee's prior disciplinary record of proven improper conduct or violation of shop rules to evaluate his qualifications and ability for promotion does not constitute double jeopardy because it does not result in punishing the employee twice for the same offense or misconduct.

Rule 22. The foreman properly uses an employee's prior discipline to evaluate his employment record to determine if he meets the duties and responsibilities of attendance, job performance, and safety and personal conduct that attach to every job to determine whether he has the ability and qualifications required to retain his present job or to be promoted to another job.

Rule 23. If the foreman refrains from disciplining—by corrective disciplinary action, with notice to the union—an employee because of his unexcused absences, latenesses, breach of plant rules, personal misconduct, or failure to meet any of his other job responsibilities, he has, in effect, condoned such failings or misconduct and cannot use them to evaluate that employee's ability and qualifications to retain his job or to be promoted to another one.

Rule 24. A foreman properly uses an employee's prior discipline record—within a reasonable period of time thereafter—to determine the appropriate penalty (but not to prove the offense or misconduct) in a future case where the employee, not having corrected himself, commits the same or comparable offense, or breach of plant rules.

Rule 25. The legal doctrine of judicial precedent *stare decisis* (to stand settled) does not apply to the arbitration process.

Rule 26. A prior award between parties under the same contract may be considered as persuasive argument on a future dispute involving the same provisions, but it does not constitute a precedent binding upon or limiting another arbitrator's authority in future cases between those parties unless by their contract the parties have otherwise agreed.

Rule 27. Prior awards between the same parties under the same contract or between other parties under different contracts do not have the weight of judicial authority or precedents in determining future disputes between the same parties or over the same issues. They are not conclusive or binding upon an arbitrator in subsequent cases.

Rule 28. A prior award does not constitute a binding precedent that in any way limits an arbitrator's authority to interpret a contract provision in future cases, even though his interpretation may differ from or be opposite to another arbitrator's interpretation in a prior case on the same issue.

Rule 29. In arbitration, all questions of fact and law are deemed to be referred to the arbitrator selected for his decision. As long as the arbitrator keeps within his delegated authority, he can decide the issues submitted to him notwithstanding any prior awards between the parties, unless they have otherwise agreed by their contract.

2

Five Ways to Improve the Quality of the Work Force

Recorded facts—of attendance, job performance, safety, and personal conduct—provide you with objective, demonstrable criteria to evaluate an employee's competency to retain his present job or to merit promotion to another job. But to use those recorded facts as proven shop violations, you must have made them known to the employee and his shop steward by written corrective action at the time each had occurred. Why? In order to inform the employee and the union of the employee's shortcomings, thereby giving him an opportunity to correct himself in the future. Otherwise, if you do not take corrective disciplinary action, you, in effect, condone his failure to meet fully his job responsibilities.

If the employee or his shop steward questions the propriety of your action, the grievance procedure provides an orderly way to air that challenge and through arbitration to have it finally settled. If your action goes unchallenged or has not been vacated by grievance settlement or arbitration, then your disciplinary action becomes a proven shop violation verified by the recorded facts. If within a reasonable period thereafter the employee fails to correct himself, he subjects himself to the consequences, namely, further disciplinary action, including discharge, because of his continued failure to meet his job responsibilities.

Applying corrective discipline because of an employee's personal misconduct constitutes, Mr. Foreman, the first effective way to improve the quality of your work force. If an employee's own fault subjects him to corrective disciplinary action, his seniority rights do not protect him in his present job or entitle him to promotion.

Similarly, when an employee through no fault of his own fails to meet the normal duties of his job, his seniority rights do not protect him in retaining that job. Seniority rights protect the job security of a qualified employee and only for as long as he continues qualified.

Thus, in the following three types of cases seniority does not protect an employee's right to retain his job even though the reason for losing his job comes about from no fault on his part.

1. Chronic absenteeism when, due to bona fide sickness or injury, an employee becomes unable to report regularly and on time.

2. Successive accidents occurring on the job that show that the employee no longer possesses the physical ability to meet the normal duties of his job or that those duties, through no fault of his own, expose him to the hazards of accidents.

3. Physical disability arising from causes beyond the employee's control that make him incompetent to continue to meet the normal work performance standards of his job.

In these three types of cases an employee's seniority does not protect his right to retain that job, and he can no longer claim a priority in that job because of his seniority.

The Case of the Chronic Absentee

Following a series of warnings to an employee about his poor attendance record, due to a chronic illness, the company placed him on a leave of absence for a period of six months. In its written letter informing the employee of the imposed leave of absence, of which the union had been given notice, the company set forth the employee's record of absences of the preceding year, a number of which had occurred on Mondays and Fridays, the first and last day of his regular scheduled work week.

Then, noting that following the prior warnings his "attendance record has become consistently worse," the company stated:

> Your physical inability to be available and report regularly for work has placed and continues to place an undue burden upon the Company in planning and scheduling its work and maintaining a regular operating staff in the department. This places an undue burden on other employees during these periods of absence from your department.
>
> It appears that your physical condition does not give assurance that you can be available to report to work on the regular basis as is required in your job. The Company finds it necessary to and does hereby place you on a leave of absence from work for a period of six (6) months commencing October 17 . . .
>
> If at the end of this period of leave of absence, April 17, . . . you are physically well and able to return to work and will be available to report regularly for the full normal hours as is required in your job, the Company will at that time reinstate you into your former job if then available, according to your present seniority standing in your job classification. Otherwise the Company will have to terminate your employment and discharge you as of this date.

The union filed a grievance protesting the company's action; and following the grievance steps under the contract, the parties submitted the following issue to arbitration:

> Was the company in violation of Article I, Section 6 of the Agreement, "Right to Manage Plant," when it placed the grievant on a prolonged leave of absence?

Section 6 of Article I of the agreement provided:

> The right to manage the plant and to direct the working forces and operations of the plant, subject to the provisions of this Agreement, is vested in, and retained by, the Company.

46

At the arbitration hearing the union did not question the grievant's excessive absences but tried to excuse them on the ground that the grievant suffered from a bona fide illness that necessitated constant medical care and that caused him to miss work.

The company did not dispute the grievant's claim that his chronic illness, supported by the doctor's certificates he had previously given the company, caused his absences; but the company argued that notwithstanding the reason, his inability to regularly attend his job interfered with the scheduling of its work, and his absences prevented the company from maintaining a regular operating staff in the grievant's department.

In my award I found that the company had just cause for placing the grievant on a leave of absence for six months, thereby affording him an uninterrupted period of time to receive medical care so as to enable him, if he overcame his disability by the end of that leave, to attend his job regularly and on time as required of all other employees. Accordingly, I found that the corrective action taken by the company did not violate the contract and I denied the union's grievance.

NO PREFERENTIAL TREATMENT FOR THE CHRONIC ABSENTEE

You see, Mr. Foreman, you do not punish by disciplinary action an employee who, because of illness or other justifiable reason beyond his control, fails to report regularly for his normal scheduled hours and days of work. Yet you cannot allow his sporadic attendance, which prevents appropriate staffing and interferes with the scheduling of work in your department, to continue uncorrected.

Of course, if an employee fails to attend regularly and on time because of fault on his part, he subjects himself to disciplinary action. Likewise, if you question the credibility of the oft-repeated excuses an employee gives you to explain his absences or latenesses, such as he overslept, missed the car pool, had to take care of a personal matter, or if you find his excuses not valid because he fails to corroborate them, you pursue corrective disciplinary action embodying the warning that unless he attends regularly and on time like all other employees, he faces further disciplinary action, including discharge.

47

In the case of an employee who because of bona fide illness fails to report regularly and on time, his absences or latenesses still place a burden not only upon you, Mr. Foreman, in manning your department and scheduling the work, but also upon his fellow workers. Although he substantiates the bona fides of his chronic sickness by doctors' certificates, he nonetheless fails to meet the job responsibilities required of him. On those days he is absent somebody has to take up the slack; and those in the group who attend regularly become the ones who often have to take on the extra burden of the absentee or latecomer.

Self-interest motivates each employee in the work unit, unionized or not unionized. That's the first social rule of the shop. To satisfy that self-interest, each employee wants his supervisor to treat him equally, both as to benefits received and responsibilities imposed. Equality of treatment—that's the second social rule of the shop. Equality of benefits and equality of responsibilities make up equality of treatment. No worker wants to see his foreman give preferential treatment to any other worker. That social rule of equality of treatment applies in the case of the chronic absentee, when the absence places an added burden of the job upon the other workers, who do not receive any added pay.

Workers resent most the casual chronic absentee, the one who remains away from work on Mondays and Fridays, the first and last days of the scheduled week; or the one who's out on the day before or after holidays, to make long weekends for himself. Workers know, or sense, that some of those chronic absentees malinger on the job. The malingerer feigns or exaggerates his illness and uses it as an excuse to work short weeks for his own convenience.

But here again, the third social rule of the shop comes into play. "Don't be an informer!" That's the unwritten code of the shop, and he who violates that unwritten code walks a lonely path. No worker dares inform on the malingerer. Yet those who respect their jobs and meet their responsibilities by attending regularly and on time don't want to see any other employee get away with it. They resent another employee who sets his own schedule of attendance to suit his convenience when they have to attend regularly and often have to do part of the job of the absentee without extra pay.

48

All the other workers who respect their jobs feel that it's up to you, Mr. Foreman, to make everyone toe the line and share the job burden equally, without preferentially treating anyone. They cannot take that responsibility unto themselves. That's your job.

Now, if the chronic absentee doesn't use his claimed sickness as a coverup for his intermittent absences but truly suffers from a bona fide illness that causes him to absent himself repeatedly, then, would it not be better, Mr. Foreman, to say to him something like this:

"Look, John, I know you're suffering from a serious ailment and receiving medical treatment; but your sporadic attendance makes it difficult for me and your fellow workers to do the job we're all being paid to do. Now, I don't want to discharge you, but I can't treat you differently from any of the other workers by allowing you to set your own working schedule even though I know your absences are not your fault.

"Therefore, unless you are physically well and able to attend regularly on your job equally with your fellow employees I'll have to put you on a six month's leave of absence. Take your absences all together during that six-month period and try to get well. I can no longer let you spread your absences over a year or two, as you have done in the past.

"Then, after that time if you've fully recovered so that you can return to work and thereafter report regularly and on time, the same as all your fellow workers, I'll put you back on the job."

You see, Mr. Foreman, you're not punishing the legitimate chronic absentee. You're not discharging him. You're providing a way for him to help himself without harming the self-interests of your other employees. Each of you has to meet the responsibilities connected with your respective jobs. Your job, Mr. Foreman, requires that you treat each of your employees without bias or favoritism and enforce equally, without preferential treatment, the job duties required of each employee. The chronic absentee's job requires that he attend regularly and on time. To allow him to use his illness as an excuse for not meeting his job responsibility to attend regularly his scheduled days of work accords him preferential treatment. Only by doing your job, Mr. Fore-

49

man, in the way that shows you respect the three social rules of the shop, will you earn the respect of all your employees.

Now, before you impose the leave of absence, you send the employee a letter setting forth his absences from work, full or partial days, during the preceding six-month or year period. Emphasize the days of the week his absences fell on, especially Mondays and Fridays (or the first and the last days in his scheduled work week) and the day before and after paid holidays.

In the letter advise him that you cannot accept his excuse of illness or physical disability, even though bona fide and supported by doctors' certificates, to relieve him from meeting his job duties of reporting regularly and working the full scheduled hours and days of his work week. And warn him in that letter that unless he's physically able to report for and work the regular scheduled hours and days of work in the future, as required of all other employees, you will have to take appropriate action to put a stop to his intermittent absences.

Here's a warning letter that may help you in handling the chronic absentee case.

LETTER OF WARNING

Chronic Absenteeism Due to Bona Fide
Sickness or Physical Disability

November 28, 19_____

Mr. Eugene Adler
(Home Address)

Dear Mr. Adler,

I am by this Letter of Warning notifying you about your absences from work during the past nine (9) months and your consequent inability to meet the duties required of you in your job with the Company.

Your attendance record shows that during the period from March 6, 19_____ to November 24, 19_____ you were absent from work a total of 40 days as follows:

50

March 6	Monday	July 5	Wednesday
March 10	Friday	July 17-18	Monday, Tuesday
March 21-24	Monday-	August 17-18	Thursday, Friday
	Friday	August 28-30	Monday, Tuesday,
March 31	Friday		Wednesday
April 17	Monday	September 18-22	Monday-Friday
April 28	Friday	October 2, 3, 4	Monday, Tuesday,
May 22-23	Monday,		Wednesday
	Tuesday	October 16-20	Monday-Friday
May 29	Monday	November 22-24	Wednesday-Friday
June 19-23	Monday-		
	Friday		

Of the total of 40 days, 20 days occurred on Mondays and Fridays and four days on the day before or the day after one of the holidays for which the Company pays you under the labor agreement with the Union. [Set forth any additional part-days of absences and any days of lateness and point out those that occurred on Mondays or Fridays, the day before or after a paid holiday, or after pay day.]

Each time upon your return to work from your absences, you told me that a chronic physical disability from which you suffer requires you to undergo medical treatment and causes your absences from work. And it appears from the doctor's certificates you gave me during this period that you do suffer from a chronic ailment.

As I pointed out to you after your return to work following your week's absence in October, your failure to attend regularly and on time, although due to a physical disability requiring medical treatment, prevents me from maintaining the necessary number of operating employees in your department, interferes with my scheduling of the work and in some instances places an added burden upon other employees in your department who attend regularly.

The labor agreement under which the Company and the Union operate, as well as the Company's established policies (and Plant Rules) require that all employees must be available for and qualified to perform work as regularly scheduled in their jobs (of eight hours per day and five days per week). Your record of absences during the past nine-month period shows that your physical ailment prevents you from meeting this requirement of your job.

51

The regularly scheduled hours of work in your department apply to all employees and I cannot accord you preferential treatment by allowing you to set your own schedule of working days, even though the cause, as you say, comes from a physical disability (or chronic illness) that you claim you suffer.

I hereby notify you by this Written Warning that unless in the future your physical condition allows you to be available regularly for work and report regularly and on time for the daily and weekly hours of work as scheduled in your job, I will have to take appropriate action in removing you from your job to prevent your absences from continuing to interfere with the necessary production schedules upon which the Company's production and the jobs of all the other employees depend.

Very truly yours,

_____

Foreman

cc: Mailed to the Union's place of business
cc: Given to the Union Shop Chairman

COMPULSORY LEAVE OF ABSENCE
FOR CHRONIC ABSENTEEISM

Now, Mr. Foreman, if during the next six or eight weeks following that written warning the employee continues his intermittent absences, claiming bona fide illness or physical disability, you impose a leave of absence, without pay, of three, six or more months not exceeding one year, depending upon the length of time you reasonably judge necessary for the employee to get well or overcome his physical ailment. You're not punishing the employee because you're satisfied that bona fide sickness or physical disability causes his absences. Yet you cannot let him set his own working schedule and interfere with your job in meeting your production needs and put an added burden at times upon the other employees.

Instead of allowing the employee to continue his intermittent absences, you give him a leave of absence of one continuous period of three months or more, during which he takes all his absences together; and you tell him that if he recovers sufficiently at the end of that leave to allow him to attend regularly in his job, meeting the normal days and hours of work the contract calls for, you will restore him to his job.

Here's a compulsory leave of absence letter for the chronic absentee.

COMPULSORY LEAVE OF ABSENCE LETTER

**Chronic Absenteeism Due to Bona Fide
Sickness or Physical Disability**

February 15, 19_____

Mr. Eugene Adler
(Home Address)

Dear Mr. Adler,

On November 28, 19_____ I sent you a Written Warning pointing out your failure to attend regularly (and on time) in your job and in that letter I set forth the days of your absences from work during the period from March 6, 19_____ to November 28, 19_____, totaling 40 days. I informed you in that letter that unless your health and physical condition allow you to attend regularly and undertake the duties required of you in your job equally with all other employees, I would have to take appropriate action to prevent your absences from continuing to interfere with the manning of jobs in your department.

Your record of attendance since November 28, 19_____ shows an additional nine (9) days of absence as follows:

December 11, 12	Monday, Tuesday
December 26, 27	Tuesday, Wednesday
January 15	Monday
January 25, 26	Thursday, Friday
February 9	Friday
February 13	Tuesday

As I had explained to you in that written warning of November 28th, your absences, though due to a physical ailment requiring medical attention, prevent you from being available for and reporting regularly for

53

work as required of you and all other employees; and your absences place an undue burden upon me in scheduling the work and maintaining a regular operating crew in your department, as well as placing an added burden at times upon your fellow employees during the times of your absences.

In view of the foregoing from which it appears that your physical condition does not give assurance that you can be available and report regularly for work as required of you in your job, the Company finds it necessary and does hereby place you on a Leave of Absence from work, without pay, for a period of six (6) months (or one (1) year) commencing February 19, 19____.

If following that period of leave of absence, to wit, August 18th, you have physically recovered and will then be able to undertake the duties of your job and thenceforth report regularly for work for the full, normal hours and days of work as scheduled and required of you in your job, the Company will at that time reinstate you into your former job, if then available, according to your present seniority standing in your classification (or department). Otherwise, the Company will have to discharge you and terminate your employment as of that day.

I have decided to pursue this method, which I feel appropriate to resolve for both yourself and the needs of the Company the problems caused by your present physical condition and your resulting absences from work, instead of terminating your employment and discharging you now. [State any benefits under the labor agreement or Company policies which may cease to accrue to said employee during said period of compulsory Leave of Absence.]

Very truly yours,

_____

Foreman

cc: Mailed to the Union's place of business
cc: Given to the Union Shop Chairman

The Case of the Accident Prone Worker

What has been said about the chronic absentee applies in great part to the employee who meets with accidents on the job through no fault of his own. In such case, you don't punish him, Mr. Foreman, but you

54

must take corrective action to remove him from the job for his own safety and for the safety of his fellow workers. The job may have become too much for him, exposing him to hazards he can no longer cope with; or the job may call for a degree of care or skill the employee doesn't have or has lost.

When an employee meets with accidents because of his own negligence, such as by failing to use his safety shoes, eyeglasses, gloves, or other protective devices or by not observing plant rules or commonly accepted safety practices, then his personal misconduct subjects him to corrective disciplinary action because he has done wrong.

But when you cannot trace the accidents he suffers to any wrongdoing on his part and yet he seems no longer qualified to avoid them, you say to him something like this:

"Look, John, you've been having a lot of accidents in the past year that are causing you to lose time from your job. Now, I can't say they have come about because of your carelessness but they're happening just the same. Maybe your eyesight's failing or you're getting on so that the hazards of the job have become too much for you. In any event, I can't allow you for your own safety to expose yourself to the possibility of further accidents and I must tell you that if another accident happens, I'll have to take you off the job—but of course for your own protection you understand and to protect your fellow workers coming to any harm."

Well, maybe he'll respond to that warning and eliminate the cause of further accidents or exercise more care in the future to avoid them recurring.

Of course, if he's playing a game with accidents to get time off or injury leave with pay or compensation settlements, then that warning should serve to make him decide whether he wants to retain his job or try to get a last claim.

Let's say you believe his accidents come about through no fault or game on his part. Then before you take him off that job, not as punishment but as a protective measure for his own welfare and that of his fellow workers, you send him the following type of warning letter and mail a copy to the union.

LETTER OF WARNING

Accidents or Injuries on the Job
Due to No Apparent Fault or Negligence

November 16, 19_____

Mr. Charles Gross
(Home Address)

Dear Mr. Gross,

On Monday, November 6, 19_____ you received medical treatment for an injury you claimed you sustained as a result of an accident on your job. The Company paid you for the balance of that day and you remained away from work on injury leave the balance of that week from November 7th to November 10th. When I spoke to you about the cause for the accident upon your return to work, you told me that you had observed all the safety practices and could not explain what had caused you to meet with that accident.

I have reviewed your record of accidents and injuries which you claimed you suffered during working hours (and compensation claims you filed and disability awards rendered to you by the Workmen's Compensation Board) during the past year and a half of your employment with the Company, which record shows the following:

[Set forth in chronological order:

1. The dates of accidents;
2. The treatment received;
3. The number of full or part days absent from work;
4. Brief summary of the findings and settlements, if any, of each compensation award; and
5. The accumulative total percentage, if any, of permanent or partial disabilities awarded.]

It appears from the number of accidents you have met with that your physical condition does not (or no longer) qualify you to meet the duties and responsibilities of your job (or the requirements of your job expose you to accidents which your physical condition prevents you from avoiding).

56

Accordingly, I hereby notify you that unless your conduct and physical condition from here on assure me that you possess the necessary ability and qualifications to continue in and meet the full duties and requirements of your job, for your own welfare and safety (as well as the safety of other employees who work in your department) and for the Company's needs to fill jobs with qualified and physically competent employees, I will have to remove you from your job (and terminate your employment with the Company).

Very truly yours,

_____

Foreman

cc: Mailed to the Union's place of business
cc: Given to the Shop Steward or Union Committee Chairman

The Case of Mixing Absenteeism with Abuse of Medical Leave with Pay

The company had discharged an employee for engaging in activities outside his employment while on medical leave with pay due to an injury he claimed he suffered on the job and, additionally, because of his past absenteeism record.

On Wednesday, about two hours after reporting late for work, the grievant claimed he suffered an injury to his back and right arm and couldn't continue to work. The company's doctor, after examining him, put him on sick leave. The doctor told him to "go home and take it easy" and to report on the following day for therapy treatment. In the afternoon of that day, Wednesday, a company representative saw the grievant working on his boat in the Anna Capri Boat Yard.

On the following day the grievant attended the company's medical department, received therapy treatment for his back and arm, and continued on sick leave for further treatment. On that day, Thursday, while on medical leave, for which he continued to receive sick pay, a company representative saw the grievant drive his automobile to a gasoline station, have two five-gallon cans filled, transport them in his

57

car to the boat yard, carry the two cans of gasoline aboard a boat, and hand them through the cabin window of that boat to another person on an adjacent boat. Shortly thereafter an explosion occurred on the latter boat, and, as reported by the newspapers, the grievant suffered burns and an ambulance took him to the hospital, where he remained for some time undergoing treatment.

The following Monday the company discharged him for engaging in activities while on medical leave with pay that showed him capable of performing his regular job for the company and, in addition, because of his past record of absences. The union protested the company's disciplinary action and, after following the steps of the grievance procedure of the contract, appealed to arbitration before a tripartite board of adjustment.

At the hearing the union claimed the grievant did not engage in any physical activities that the company's doctor had prohibited or that his injuries prevented him from doing. The union further claimed that bona fide sickness and injuries sustained on the job, and other legitimate reasons that the company's supervisors had not questioned, had caused the grievant's absences and latenesses and that therefore the company had no valid basis to use the grievant's past attendance record to support the disciplinary penalty of discharge.

The company claimed that the grievant's conduct while out on medical leave with pay for injuries he claimed he suffered on the job showed him capable of performing his regular job, that he abused his sick leave privileges under the agreement, and that his misconduct justified the company's action in discharging him.

The company further claimed that the grievant had an unsatisfactory attendance record over the past years; that his supervisor had warned him both orally and in writing on numerous times during those years to correct his attendance but he had failed to do so; and that his poor attendance record over the years, together with his improper conduct while out on sick leave with pay, fully warranted the disciplinary penalty of discharge.

The board of adjustment, consisting of a company's representative, a union's representative, and myself as chairman, unanimously found that the grievant had abused his sick leave privileges under the agreement by engaging in activities while out on sick leave with pay and that his misconduct fully warranted disciplinary action.

However, the board held that it could not properly consider the grievant's past absentee record as material evidence to support either the discipline for misconduct in the present case based upon his abuse of sick leave privileges or the penalty of discharge. Accordingly, the board reduced the penalty of discharge to a disciplinary suspension of three months without back pay, which the board found appropriate.

In the decision written by me as chairman of the board I rejected the company's argument that the grievant's past attendance record supported the disciplinary penalty of discharge for personal misconduct.

The proof does establish that during the past four years, the grievant's absences from work prevented him from meeting the normal duties and requirements of his job and had interfered with the company maintaining its regular production schedules. Yet, the evidence shows that practically all his absences from work, either for full or partial days, were due to illness or injuries sustained on the job, the validity of which the company did not and does not question . . .

As to absences for excusable reasons, the chairman finds that the agreement does not obligate the company to continue in its employ an employee who cannot normally be available for and meet his responsibilities of attending regularly and on time, even though his inability to do so arises from illness or injuries. Yet, in such cases, the company must pursue corrective action independently of a disciplinary proceeding for personal misconduct, arising from abuse of sick leave privileges, from which the company's disciplinary action in this case stems.

Further, unexcused or unauthorized absences or latenesses for which prior corrective disciplinary action had been taken, may also properly subject an employee to a disciplinary penalty of discharge if he fails to correct his attendance. But here, the company offered no proof to support a finding that the grievant's absences or latenesses over the years were unexcused or unauthorized. Apparently, the grievant's supervisors accepted the fact that his absences were caused by bona fide illness or injuries; and apparently, his supervisors over the years accepted without question or inquiry whatever the excuses the grievant offered for his latenesses.

59

As to the company's claim that "irrespective of the reasons for his absences or latenesses, the grievant's poor attendance record over the years supports and warrants the disciplinary penalty of discharge," I said:

> The chairman finds that the grievant's record of absences and late-nesses during all the past years is not material to and cannot properly be asserted as additional grounds to support the disciplinary penalty of discharge in the present case. The agreement and the established employee rules provide sufficient grounds upon which the company can terminate an employee's employment in his job if sickness or injuries received on the job cause him to be absent and thereby unable to meet the normal responsibilities of his job.
>
> The company's rules provide: "Because of the loss of production, disorganization and increase in the cost of operations resulting from absenteeism and tardiness, punctuality and regularity of attendance are required of each employee. Absenteeism and tardiness are causes for dismissal."

Then, noting that chronic absenteeism even if due to bona fide illness or because of injuries suffered by on-the-job accidents, even though due to no fault on the employee's part, do not relieve an employee from his job responsibility to report for and work the regularly scheduled days and hours of work in his job, I said:

> Chronic absenteeism even if due to bona fide sickness does not excuse an employee from meeting the normal responsibilities of attending regularly and on time equally, as required of the other employees. The contract between the parties does not require the company to give preferential treatment to any employee, allowing him to set his own schedule of work even if his absences are due to bona fide illnesses that prevent him from being available for the normal days and hours of work as required under the contract.
>
> Further, the grievant's record of injuries that he claims he suffered on his present job over the years, causing him to lose time from work, shows that he either does not possess the physical abilities to perform his present job in a safe and healthful manner; or else the nature of his work in his present job is such that it threatens his health and safety.

60

In such cases, to protect the employee's own health and safety and the health and safety of other employees working in his department, should the conditions in his present job continue to cause him to suffer injuries, the company can, under the agreement, remove him from his job. In either case, where sickness causes an employee to be chronically absent or injuries sustained on the job result in loss of time, the agreement does not obligate the company to continue that employee on his job.

Noting that the plant rules subjected an employee to disciplinary action in cases of "failure to maintain a satisfactory attendance record" and for "unauthorized absence," I said:

> Under the agreement, the company's supervisors have the right to require an employee to give supporting proof of claims for sick leave when doubt exists as to whether the sick claim is bona fide or not. Likewise, the supervisor has the right to inquire of an employee the reasons for being absent or reporting late for work; and if the employee fails to give a satisfactory reason that the supervisor can accept to excuse him, then the supervisor can take corrective disciplinary action.
>
> The evidence in this case fails to show that the grievant's supervisors questioned the bona fides of his claimed sickness or that his absences or latenesses were unauthorized.

Pointing out that the board of adjustment "in reducing the penalty of discharge to a disciplinary suspension, without any back pay or active service credits for the time during the period of suspension, based its award solely on the personal misconduct of the grievant on November 4th and 5th—and in no wise absolves the absences or latenesses of the grievant as shown by his attendance record," I said:

> As pointed out above, if the present job of the grievant continues to threaten his bodily health and safety, by exposing him to injuries and causing him to lose time from his job, the agreement between the parties provides ample means to remove him from his job. Likewise, if illness or physical disabilities from which the grievant may be suffering cause him to be chronically absent, and prevent him from being available for and reporting regularly and on time in his job, equally as

61

required of all other employees, the agreement and the rules provide remedial measures that the company can undertake to terminate the grievant's employment in his present job.

Handling the Incompetency Case

Seniority rights protect the job security of a qualified employee only for so long as he continues qualified for his job. When an employee, through no fault of his own, such as failing eyesight, physical incapacity, or other shortcomings, becomes incapable of meeting the normal duties of his job, his seniority rights do not protect him in retaining that job.

Here again, Mr. Foreman, when you remove an employee from his job because of incompetency, you do not punish him; and consequently, you must act independently of disciplinary action.

Likewise, you don't wait for a layoff to remove him from his job, for then you'd be trying to improve the quality of your work force under the guise of a layoff. You must act before or after, but independently of, a layoff to remove an employee because of his incompetency to meet his job duties.

Now, how do you prove that an employee has become incompetent, unable any longer to meet his job duties? Here again, by objective, demonstrable, sensory facts that make clear to him his shortcomings and warn him that he must correct them if he wants to retain his job.

Now, what make up those objective, demonstrable, sensory facts?

OBJECTIVE, DEMONSTRABLE, SENSORY FACTS
SPEAK FOR THEMSELVES

1. Spoilage—rejects, reworks, waste, breakage, mix-up of orders, inability to follow instructions. In essence, any failings in his work not due to negligence or personal misconduct on his part that causes him to muff his job.

What you see, touch, taste, smell, or hear constitutes objective, demonstrable facts. A worker's incompetency shows up when he makes mistakes in performing his job or in applying the skills his job calls for.

2. Time taken—to perform his required tasks as compared to the established normal or average time for those tasks. The tell-tale of incompetency, if in fact the employee is incompetent, usually reveals itself in the time he takes to meet the production standards of quantity and quality established for his job.

You judge a worker's time in doing a job against the time norm set for that job, not against the time taken by other employees doing the same work. You may have determined the normal time for the job from the average of times other qualified employees had taken in the past to do the job. But you cannot compete the time taken by one worker against the time taken by any other worker by saying, "He's slower than everybody else in the group." You judge him against the norm set for the job, not competitively against the time taken by any other worker.

3. Supervision or help required—in performing the normal tasks a qualified worker should have the ability to do without extra help or supervision. The incompetent usually requires more help from you, his foreman, as well as from his fellow workers, who often have to help him out, thereby burdening themselves with additional work for which the company does not pay them.

As in the case of the chronic absentee, the three social rules of the plant come into play here:

1. Self-interest, which motivates each worker to do the job he's being paid for and not an added part of someone else's job.

2. Equality of treatment, which requires each worker to hold up his own end of the fence and share equally in the responsibilities of the job as well as its benefits.

3. The unwritten code of the shop, which restrains workers from informing on a fellow worker's shortcomings and at times compels them to cover up for him.

THE WARNING LETTER FOR INCOMPETENCY

To use those objective, demonstrable, sensory facts—(1) spoilage, (2) time taken, or (3) help required to do the job the employee should be qualified for and for which the company pays him to do—you must first make known to him his shortcomings. You do this by sending him a letter, mailing a copy to the union, telling him of his failings and warning him that unless he corrects himself and meets his job duties, you will have to remove him from his job.

Note, Mr. Foreman, that when you remove an incompetent from his job, you do not necessarily terminate his employment with the company. Though no longer competent to do his present job, he may qualify for another job in the bargaining unit provided an opening at that time exists.

Unless your labor contract provides otherwise, removing an employee from his job because of incompetency does not constitute a layoff. Consequently, that employee's seniority rights do not give him a priority to any other job then being filled by another employee with less seniority. His seniority does not give him the right to displace a junior employee filling another job even though he may qualify for that job. If an open job exists, he may, if qualified, bid for it according to his seniority rights.

Removing an employee because he no longer qualifies for his job, does not give him any bumping rights. Only when his removal comes about through no fault of his own does his seniority standing give him the right to displace a junior employee in an equally or lower-rated job for which he qualifies. His seniority rights of displacement come into play upon a layoff, because of lack of work. When an employee's inability to perform the normal duties of his job necessitate his removal, his seniority rights don't give him any preference over any other employee then filling any other job. But before you remove an employee from his job because of incompetency, you must notify him and his union representatives, in writing, of the facts upon which you evaluated his performance and found him lacking.

Here's the type of warning letter that may help you in handling the case of the incompetent.

LETTER OF WARNING

Incompetency: Inability to Meet Requirements of the Job, Not Due to Fault or Negligence

---

October 5, 19_____

Mr. Charles Lange
(Home Address)

Dear Mr. Lange,

I am giving you this Written Warning because of your failure during the past three months to satisfactorily perform the work assigned to you and to meet the requirements of your job as a Machinist Class B.

On September 26, 19_____, I assigned you the following work: Machine Shop Order No. Y312-SO. Six cast iron levers for a screw cap assembler per drawings Nos. 2564J, 1-6. You ground the point of the cutting edge to a coarse and rough finish. You failed to follow the specifications and exceeded the permissible tolerances specified in the drawings. As a result, you spoiled three out of the six levers, which cannot be used.

Furthermore, although the normal time for this job is 25 hours, you took 76 hours to do it and failed to do it properly.

On September 4, 19_____, I assigned you the following work: Machine Shop Order No. Y321-M. Machine two bronze slide castings per drawing No. AR4037. You exceeded the permissible tolerances specified in the drawing. You followed such improper machining practice that you left thread marks from a tap in a reamed hole. You spoiled the castings and they cannot be used.

In addition, though the normal time for this job is 24 hours, you took 41 hours to do it and failed to do it properly.

Furthermore, during the time you worked on this job, you kept asking help of other employees in your section. You thereby interfered with their regular work assigned to them and for which they were responsible. This increased the time spent by you on this job which presumably you should be qualified to do without such help, since the skills required are part of the normal duties of your job classification.

On August 14, 19____, I assigned you the following work: Machine Shop Order No. Y1437-MS. Oscillating liner punch for a screw cap assembler per drawing No. PB460. You made four errors in doing this job. You exceeded the permissible tolerances specified in the drawing. To correct this poor workmanship, I instructed you to remove ⅛" off the face of the punch. This resulted in reducing the life of the punch by one half.

In addition, though the normal time for this job is 15 hours, you took 27 hours to do it and failed to do it properly.

On July 9, 19____, I assigned you the following work: Machine Shop Order No. Y1471-CM. Machining rollers out of brass per drawing No. BP614. These were to be used as chlorothene applicators. The O.D.s of the rollers had to be concentric to the I.D. holes. You exceeded the permissible tolerances specified in the drawing. You were $\frac{1}{16}$" out of concentricity; the knurled O.D.s were uneven and no two knurls were alike. You spoiled the part and the work had to be done over by another man.

Though the normal time for this job is 10 hours, you took 17 hours to do it and failed to do it properly.

Furthermore, during the time you worked on this job, you found it necessary to leave your work (or called me over to your work bench) three times to have me help you on this job. As you know, the skills and responsibilities involved in this job are the normal requirements of your present job classification, and you should be qualified to do this work without close supervision. The time which you required me to spend in helping you with the job, which you should be qualified to do, interfered with my regular supervisory duties in the department and with meeting the normal production of our department, upon which your job and the jobs of the other employees depend.

Further, during the past six-month period, I had on two other occasions (give dates) orally warned you with respect to properly performing the work assigned to you in accordance with the requirements of your job and had pointed out to you the errors in your work which you had made; and I had cautioned you that unless you improved the quality of your work and observed the normal time requirements for doing such work, I would have to remove you from your job.

In view of the foregoing, showing that you fail to satisfactorily perform and meet the requirements of your job of Machinist Class B, I am giving you this Written Warning as a final notice and opportunity to correct your work performance in the future. Unless you correct your failings, improve the quality of your work, and meet fully the requirements of your job, I will have to terminate your employment in your present job.

Very truly yours,

_____

Foreman

cc: Mailed to the Union's place of business
cc: Given to the Union Shop Chairman

Summing Up the Rules for Improving the Quality of the Work Force

Rule 1. Seniority rights protect the job security of a qualified employee only as long as he continues qualified and able to meet the duties and responsibilities of his job.

Rule 2. Corrective disciplinary action for personal misconduct or violation of plant rules or safety practices provides the first effective way to improve the quality of your work force.

Rule 3. The seniority rights of an employee disciplined because of his own fault or neglect do not protect him in retaining his job.

Rule 4. When an employee becomes incapable of meeting the normal duties and responsibilities of his job through no fault of his own, his seniority rights do not protect him in retaining that job.

Rule 5. Corrective written warning, for chronic absenteeism due to bona fide sickness or injury that prevents an employee from reporting regularly and on time, provides the second effective way to improve the quality of your work force.

Rule 6. The seniority rights of a chronic absentee, after opportunity given by written warning has failed to help him correct his attendance, do not protect him in retaining his job.

Rule 7. Corrective written warning for successive accidents occurring on the job that show that the employee no longer possesses the physical ability to meet the normal duties of his job or show that those duties, through no fault of his own, expose him to the hazards of accidents provides the third effective way to improve the quality of your work force.

Rule 8. The seniority rights of an accident-prone employee, after opportunity given by written warning has failed to help him correct his shortcomings, do not protect him in retaining his job.

Rule 9. Corrective written warning for physical disability arising from causes beyond the employee's control that makes him incompetent to meet the normal work performance standards of his job provides the fourth effective way to improve the quality of your work force.

Rule 10. The seniority rights of an incompetent employee, after opportunity given by written warning has failed to help him correct his shortcomings, do not protect him in retaining his job.

Rule 11. Recorded facts of personal misconduct, attendance, safety, and job performance provide objective, demonstrable criteria against which to evaluate an employee's ability, qualifications, or competency to retain his present job.

Rule 12. To use those facts to evaluate an employee's ability, qualifications, or competency, you must have made them known to the employee and the union at the time each occurred by written corrective action.

Rule 13. If you withhold taking corrective action, you in effect condone the employee's misconduct or shortcomings in meeting fully his job duties and responsibilities.

Rule 14. If the employee or his shop steward questions the propriety of your corrective action, the grievance procedure provides an orderly way to handle that challenge and through arbitration to have it finally settled.

Rule 15. If your corrective action goes unchallenged or has not been vacated by grievance settlement or arbitration, then your action becomes proven fact, verified by the record.

Rule 16. If within a reasonable period thereafter the employee fails to correct himself, he subjects himself to the consequences, namely:

> Further disciplinary action including discharge in cases of personal misconduct, or removal from the job in cases of chronic absenteeism, accident proneness, or incompetency.

You see, Mr. Foreman, you have wide latitude to improve the quality of your work force and manage along lines of excellence regardless of the seniority system your contract sets up. So don't put the blame on your employees, on the shop steward or the union if you fail to follow the rules and play the game of labor relations as a professional.

The shop steward can't and won't do your job for you. As the United Glass and Ceramics Workers manual advises its shop stewards:

> The problems of management are not your problems. It is not up to you, to make the workers toe the line or to increase efficiency. That's the employer's worry. Your job is to protect the workers and to get their grievances settled quickly and satisfactorily.

Yes, you're the employer of the employees you supervise in your bailiwick, and it's up to you to make the workers toe the line and to increase efficiency without preferentially treating any one over the others.

And don't blame your boss or the contract for your own short-comings. You're the boss in your department, and you should have the authority to manage your employees along lines of excellence within the framework of the contract you're administering.

Now, let's see how seniority may provide you with a fifth way to improve the quality of your work force, if you have the "relatively equal in ability" (Type III) clause and you follow the rules in determining the relatively better qualified employee.

3

Administering the Relatively Equal in Ability Clause: Type III

How do you, Mr. Foreman, competitively judge ability and qualifications between two or more employees who bid for an open job in order to determine the better qualified one? Well, you make a qualitative judgment, or you may call it an opinion. Upon what facts do you base your opinion—your qualitative judgment?

Here again, on the same objective, sensory, demonstrable facts, verified by the written record, that you use to evaluate an employee's competency to determine whether he meets the responsibilities of his job, including attendance, quality of work, personal conduct, and safety practices. Otherwise, you begin to rely on your personal feelings, your likes and dislikes, and that may imply, when unsupported by recorded facts, bias, favoritism, or prejudice on your part in arriving at your judgment.

Let's assume your contract contains the relatively equal in ability clause, Type III. An opening has occurred in the machinist A classification. Sam Slade, who has six years seniority, and Jim Jordan, who has four years seniority as machinist B, both bid for the job. You decide to

71

promote Jim Jordan because you believe him better qualified for the A job than Sam Slade. Your boss, the plant manager, calls you in to find out why you passed over Sam Slade, and the following dialogue takes place:

Manager: I hear you picked Jim Jordan for promotion over Sam Slade. Any particular reason?

Foreman: Well, Jim has been working very hard and he's been doing a far better job than Sam.

Manager: In what way? You know the shop committee will, as usual, file a grievance, and you'll have to be ready to justify your choice. So, you may as well be prepared.

Foreman: Oh, I'll handle that when it comes up. Everybody knows that Jim's a far better worker. He's got a good attitude toward his job, and he's always ready to cooperate.

Manager: In what specific way has Sam not shown a good attitude? Or how has he refused to cooperate?

Foreman: Well, Jim's never refused to work overtime, when we needed it. Sam's always got some excuse to get out of it, and when I try to pin him down, he just shrugs his shoulders. Seems he's got a truck that he does some outside work with and doesn't want the overtime.

Manager: What did you do about it? Did you tell him that every machinist must be ready to take on some overtime work when production difficulties require it and that you can't treat him differently from the others?

Foreman: Sure I did. About three weeks ago when we had to have the whole group work overtime, he alone refused. I told him then I wasn't going to excuse him any longer and only on Wednesday of last week he again refused to do an hour's overtime work that we needed, and he left at the end of his shift.

Manager: Well, did you give him a written reprimand and send a copy to the union?

Foreman: No, I asked Jim and he put the extra hour in.

Manager: Well, it seems to me you're not going to get far with the committee with that. Anything else about his work?

Foreman: Sure, Jim's always been on time, and he hasn't missed a day in the past year. Sam, on the other hand, has been late

	six times in the last two months and has been absent on four days.
Manager:	Did you ask him why? And what excuses did he give you?
Foreman:	Oh, he always has some reason—tie-up of traffic, car broke down, or some other personal excuse. He's always handy with one.
Manager:	Don't you think you should have given him a written warning when you felt his excuses were not acceptable and put him and the union on notice that he wasn't meeting his job responsibilities of attending regularly and on time?
Foreman:	Well, about two years ago I did give him a written reprimand and he was okay for a while, but in the last six months he got back to his old habits again.
Manager:	It seems to me you won't get far in justifying your choice by going back two years, especially since he did correct himself after that. But why didn't you take action when he started all over again? You know, John, that's what the committee will want to know, because by not taking action you've really accepted whatever excuses he gave at the time. And if they take you to arbitration—well, that's how the arbitrator will feel.

Yes, Mr. Foreman, that's how the shop steward will question you at the grievance meetings; and that's very likely how the arbitrator will feel at the arbitration hearing.

You see, the same reasoning applies to any complaints you may have about the shortcomings of any worker in not meeting fully the responsibilities of his job. Unless you can support your qualitative judgment that the junior-in-service employee qualifies better than the senior one by the written record, your opinion as to who's better qualified won't carry much weight with the shop steward or an arbitrator. Yes, you must have taken corrective action, in writing, warning the employee of his failings with notice to the union. Then, if your corrective action has not been challenged or, if protested, it stands, you have recorded facts verified by the written record to support your qualitative judgment.

You see, Mr. Foreman, in the absence of factual data of an employee's skills on or related to the new job to justify your opinion that a junior employee qualifies better than a senior one, you must prove that the senior employee has done some "wrong" in meeting his job duties and responsibilities. Otherwise, your qualitative judgment lacks substance, especially when you try to rely on such generalities as poor attitude, not cooperative, lacks initiative, undependable, or hasn't the aptitude. Avoid such general conclusions like the plague! Unless you give facts showing how the passed-over employee failed to meet his job responsibilities, such conclusory words will wholly fail to support your opinion.

You have the right, Mr. Foreman, in administering the relatively equal in ability clause (Type III) to improve the quality of your work force by promoting the better-qualified employee. But you must prepare yourself to justify your action by facts recorded and verified by the written record.

Now, if no record exists showing that a passed-over senior employee has, within a reasonable period prior to the promotion, done something wrong in failing to meet his job responsibilities, how do you secure demonstrable facts to judge the relative ability between two employees for the new job? In such cases, you should consider using tests—manual, oral, or written—or provide each qualified bidder with a demonstrable trial period of up to three or five working days, depending on the skills needed, to determine the better-qualified employee under Type III. Then your record of the tests or the results of the trial period will provide objective facts you can offer to support your judgment in selecting the one you did as the better qualified for that job.

A word of caution: only if the seniority system of your contract provides Type III, the relatively equal in ability clause, can you select the better-qualified one irrespective of his length of service. The other types of seniority (Type I—strict or straight, Type II—modified or contingent) require you to select the senior qualified employee. Under those types (Type I or Type II), if you pass over a senior in length of service employee, base your action on the sole ground that he did not then, at the time, possess the ability and qualifications required for the new job.

Further, as you will recall, in judging between two or more employees as to which one qualifies relatively better under Type III, you must judge them against the requirements of the job in question and not on their potential ability for any other job in the future, unless your contract allows you to consider potential as a factor under your seniority system.

Now, a case may arise where the requirements of a job do not fully allow you to judge relative qualifications solely by objective criteria and where, to some extent, subjective elements may come into play. That's the really tough case for you and the arbitrator.

The Case of Promotion to Assistant Foreman

The company had promoted two employees to fill two vacancies in the job of assistant foreman in the bichromate plant. The contract covered these jobs and made them subject to bidding by the employees in the bargaining unit. The job description of bichromate assistant foreman provided:

> Under foreman's direction, supervises and works with men. Makes out production reports and substitutes for absentees.

The union filed a grievance protesting the company's selections, claiming that the supervisors had violated the promotion clause by passing over five other employees, each of whom had greater seniority and qualified as well as or better than the two men selected. The company denied the grievance and the union appealed to arbitration.

The promotion clause provided:

> (9) (a) It will be the policy of the Company to fill permanent jobs in the higher classifications, under this agreement, by transfer from lower classifications wherever possible. When other than temporary vacancies in such jobs are to be filled, they will be posted on the plant bulletin boards. Employees wishing to be considered for permanent transfer to such jobs may make application within one (1) week thereafter. The Company will select the best man qualified to fill the job; however, where ability and other qualifications are relatively equal, company seniority shall govern.

75

At the arbitration hearing the union claimed the company's supervisors had relied upon intangible qualifications of the two employees selected and did not use objective standards in evaluating the relative ability and qualifications of the other applicants who had bid for the job.

The company claimed that six of its supervisors who personally knew the bidders and the supervisory duties of the assistant foreman's job had considered the ability and qualifications of all the applicants in relation to the job requirements; and each supervisor, except one, had independently recommended the two men who had been promoted (only one supervisor having recommended another one of the applicants).

As to one of the two selected, I found no room for doubt. Although there had been a break in his seniority, he had previously served as an assistant foreman in the bichromate plant, the very job in question, for over two years. I found present in his case sufficient objective factors to warrant the company's supervisors judging him the best qualified for the job. Then, noting in my award that the promotion clause allowed the company to select the best qualified man for the job, I said:

> Under this clause, the seniority factor becomes operative after the ability and other qualifications of the applicants are considered and a judgment thereon is made. Seniority comes into play only when it is found that two or more applicants are relatively equal in ability and other qualifications for the job. Under this clause, seniority is not a factor to be considered in determining the ability and qualifications of applicants. It is a guidepost or yardstick to follow in choosing, from among several applicants relatively equal, the particular one for the job. It serves as a final determinant to break a deadlock. It removes from the company's or the union's discretion the right to choose the one who, among relatively equal employees, shall get the job. In such cases, seniority provides an objective standard which effectively avoids bias or favoritism. In such cases, it only governs the selection from among a group of employees who are found to be equally qualified.
>
> Were the union's position under the promotion clause in this case to be sustained, there would be no need to judge ability or qualifications.

They would be meaningless words. In effect, the sole factor or criterion in promotions would then be strict seniority. This is not what the promotion clause says. This is not what the parties agreed to.

In the case of the second employee selected, I found room for doubt as to the basis for the company's supervisors' judgment that he qualified better than the other applicants who had greater seniority. Referring to the fact that the prime duties of assistant foreman entailed "leading and supervising production workers," I said:

The proof establishes that the ability and qualifications of all the applicants for the job in question were fairly considered by six men on the company's supervisory staff, who had knowledge of the facts. They were the superintendent of operations and five foremen in the bichromate plant. Some of them had previously been employed as assistant foremen. All were familiar with the nature and duties of the job of assistant foreman. They personally knew the applicants and in many cases worked with them and supervised them in their production jobs. Some were personal friends of several of the aggrieved applicants . . .

The factors and standards each used in evaluating the applicants for the assistant foreman's job were inquired into. They included experience on the various jobs, knowledge of the work and requirements of the jobs to be supervised, ability to learn new jobs or difficult operations, ability to supervise and get along with men, exercise independent judgment, and respond to emergencies, reaction to difficulties in operating processes, attendance record, and others. They brought to bear in their judgments the personal experience gained over the years working with the applicants and on the job.

It is true that many of the standards used were subjective in nature, and in some instances, positive facts were lacking to support some of the conclusions reached by the supervisors. Yet, the very nature of the job of assistant foreman, entailing supervisory duties, compels the use of such subjective factors. These factors do not lend themselves to an exacting degree of proof. They are nonetheless valid factors to be considered in such cases. The sum total of the proof convinces the arbitrator that the independent judgment of these six men was based upon a fair appraisal of the relative ability and qualifications of all the applicants for the job of assistant foreman.

Then, finding that each supervisor had arrived at his judgment objectively and without bias, prejudice, or favoritism, I found no basis to disturb their judgment and said:

> Even were the arbitrator to judge the relative ability of the applicants and come to a contrary judgment, it would not be sufficient to set aside the almost unanimous judgment of these men. Judging the relative ability of men for a job, such as this one, is a difficult task. There is room for reasonable men to disagree and to come to opposite conclusions on the same set of facts. The arbitrator cannot say that the union's disagreement with the judgment of these supervisors . . . is without foundation. The arbitrator also has doubts. But disagreement in judgment alone is not sufficient to find error in fact.
>
> The arbitrator finds that the method used by the company in arriving at its judgment in this case was fair; that it was based upon valid standards and criteria applicable to the job in question; that these standards were fairly considered and equally applied in the case of each applicant; and that the judgment was arrived at in good faith and without prejudice, bias or discrimination.
>
> Where these facts appear, as the arbitrator finds they do in this case, the arbitrator is constrained not to substitute his judgment for that of the company. Nor has the arbitrator, under these findings, the authority to substitute the union's judgment for that of the company. Therefore, in light of the proof in this case, the arbitrator is constrained not to disturb the company's selection . . . for the job of assistant foreman.

How "Bumping" Operates Under Seniority

Seniority establishes the priority of a qualified employee to an available job over other employees who have less seniority. When layoffs occur in the work unit within which the affected employee's seniority rights operate, the senior qualified employee has priority to the remaining jobs under Type I (strict or straight seniority), under Type II (modified or contingent seniority), and with limited exceptions, even under Type III (relatively equal in ability seniority).

The fact, Mr. Foreman, that you have allowed a senior employee to continue in his classified job before layoffs take place shows that you still regard him as qualified, even though you may have previously given him a written corrective warning or imposed corrective disciplinary action. In such cases, were you to lay him off, you would be either:

1. Denying him the opportunity to correct his shortcomings that you intended by your corrective action, by not allowing him to continue on his job, or
2. Trying to improve the quality of your work force under the guise of a layoff.

Yes, in most cases, either of the above would follow even if your contract provides Type III to govern layoffs and recalls. Only in a limited number of cases, where special circumstances prevail, could one reasonably conclude that the negotiators intended the relatively equal in ability standard under Type III to apply to layoff and recall.

Thus, in a case where the senior employee in the classified job does not possess at the time of layoff the technical skills required to perform the remaining available work, due to no fault or neglect on your part, he may be subject to layoff because he is not then qualified. By "no fault or neglect on your part" I mean a case in which in the past the senior employee operated a single machine or performed only one type of work in his classification, for his own convenience or because that's what he wanted to do; or one in which you had in the past offered him an opportunity to acquire the technical skills necessary to perform other jobs in the work unit within which his seniority rights operated but he showed then he did not possess the necessary skills to do the other jobs. If the facts show that the senior employee does not qualify at the time of layoff to do the remaining work available, one could not reasonably charge you with retaining without cause the junior, better-qualified employee. Rather, you laid off the senior employee because he did not then qualify for the remaining work. Consequently, in such cases, one could not reasonably conclude that you tried to improve the quality of your work force under the guise of a layoff.

Likewise, when technological changes, improved methods of production, or new facilities reduce the number of available jobs in the work unit in which the senior employee's seniority rights operate and layoffs have to take place, the senior employee may not possess the new technical skills required to do the changed jobs under Type I or Type II; or under Type III the technical skills of the junior employee may qualify him relatively better than the senior employee. In such cases you lay off the senior employee either because he does not qualify at the time under seniority Types I or II or because the junior employee demonstrates that he qualifies relatively better to perform the changed job. Here again, in laying off the senior employee under such circumstances, one could not reasonably conclude that you tried to improve the quality of your work force under the guise of a layoff.

BUMPING IN LIEU OF LAYOFF

Bumping applies wherever seniority operates. Bumping does not add any other rights, such as trial, training, or learning periods, to a seniority system. Bumping only fulfills an employee's seniority right to an available job that at the time another employee with less seniority occupies.

Bumping means the right of a senior qualified employee to displace a junior employee who has less seniority in the work unit within which the seniority rights of both employees prevail. Bumping serves only a procedural function that effectuates, satisfies, the priority to an available job even though another employee may occupy that job at the time.

Your contract, Mr. Foreman, may not use the word "bumping." Nonetheless, the procedure of bumping applies whenever one employee exercises his seniority right to an available job against another employee.

THE CASE OF BUMPING-UP ON A LAYOFF

The available work in the millwright department having decreased, the company had to eliminate certain jobs, among them that of maintenance repairman, labor grade 5, on the first shift. The grievant, a shop steward in the department, held that job.

The company retained another employee in his classified job of maintenance repairman, labor grade 4, a higher-rated job. The established job descriptions called for a higher degree of experience and responsibility in the labor grade 4 job than in the lower labor grade 5 job. The grievant had greater seniority in the department, the work unit within which seniority operated, than the retained labor grade 4 employee but as a labor grade 5 employee.

The seniority clause provided:

> In the event of a permanent layoff that involves regular employees in a department, regular employees having least seniority will be laid off first provided that employees with greater seniority have ability, and provided the senior employee accepts the job.

The contract gave top seniority to departmental shop stewards and provided: "Top seniority can be used only against transfer from shift or layoff from department."

To accommodate the grievant's top seniority as shop steward from layoff on his shift, when the company eliminated his labor grade 5 job, his foreman transferred him to the next available job, in labor grade 6, thereby allowing him to bump out of that job another employee, whom the foreman then transferred to the same job on the second shift. The downgrading of the grievant from a labor grade 5 to a labor grade 6 job in lieu of laying him off from his first shift to satisfy his top seniority in the department, resulted in reducing his wages.

The union filed a grievance, claiming the grievant had the ability to perform the work in the higher labor grade 4 job and that the company had violated the contract by retaining in the labor grade 4 job an employee who had less departmental seniority than the grievant. The company denied the grievance, and the union appealed to arbitration.

At the arbitration hearing the union argued that regardless of the grievant's top seniority as shop steward in the department, he had greater departmental seniority than the employee retained in the labor grade 4 job, that the work of both labor grades 4 and 5 jobs involved interchangeable skills and constituted an occupational group within which the company had in the past distributed the maintenance repair work, and that since the grievant had from time to time performed the work in the higher labor grade 4 job, the company should not have downgraded him to a labor grade 6 job.

The company claimed that the higher classified labor grade 4 job differed materially in duties and responsibilities and carried a higher rate of pay than that of the lower labor grade 5 job and that the grievant had never occupied the higher labor grade 4 job and did not possess the skill and experience required to perform the higher-rated job.

The company also claimed that the contract did not require it to advance an employee laid off from his own job to a higher-rated job he had never filled because that, in effect, would constitute a promotion and further that the arbitrator did not have the authority to merge the established jobs or labor grades of existing classified jobs the parties themselves had set up under the contract.

In my award denying the union's grievance I found that the higher labor grade 4 job differed materially in skills and experience required from the labor grade 5 job and that even though the grievant may have in the past, as the union claimed, performed some of the repair work covered by both labor grade jobs, I held that the contract did not require the company to promote an employee laid off from his job to a higher rated job in his department.

> The contract does not obligate the company to advance [the grievant] to a higher labor grade job, which he had never performed and had never been classified in, upon his layoff from his labor grade 5 job. Nor does the contract obligate the company to retain in an occupational group an employee classified in a lower labor grade in place of an employee classified in a higher labor grade in that group, when the available work required the skills and experience of the higher labor grade man.

Holding that the "arbitrator does not have the authority under the guise of interpreting clear contract language to ignore the very evaluating factors the parties themselves agreed to, which distinguish the labor grade 4 maintenance repair job from that of labor grade 5, and upon which the parties have based their wage structure," I said:

82

Although the grievant had never held a higher rated job than labor grade 5—the union's position, if sustained, would result in either of the following: Either the grievant while being retained in the occupational group and required to do . . . labor grade 4 work would continue to be classified and receive the pay of a labor grade 5 man; or the grievant would displace the employee in labor grade 4 and be upgraded upon a layoff to a higher rated job in the occupational group, which job he had never been classified in. The arbitrator finds no evidence, under the contract nor under the past practice of the parties, to support either of such results.

Training Periods Under Types I, II or III

Seniority rights extend the preference or priority to an available job to a qualified employee. Therefore, the employee who claims priority to a job must qualify for that job at the time he asserts his seniority rights.

Unless the contract or an established practice provides otherwise, you need not, Mr. Foreman, provide a training period under seniority Types I, II or III for an employee to learn the new job or to acquire the ability for another job upon bumping or upon a lateral transfer or downgrading in lieu of being laid off from work or on promotion to a higher rated job.

THE CASE OF A TRIAL-TRAINING PERIOD FOR PROMOTION

The company had posted an opening in the job of production clerk, labor grade 7. The job called for, among other clerical duties, preparing shop orders and material requisitions for repair and stock parts, which required a familiarity with the processing of blueprints in order to know the size and shapes of materials to use and the tolerances permitted in cutting materials.

Three employees bid for the job. To test their ability the company gave each of them an opportunity to read some blueprints, but none of them passed the test. Two admitted they knew nothing about blueprints and couldn't read them. The third employee, who had the least seniority of the three, had some familiarity with blueprints gained from his experience in his job of production inventory control in judging the standard sizes of steel and the different types and shapes of materials to use. The company found that none of the employees had the ability to perform the job and denied their bids. The three employees then filed grievances, claiming the company had violated their respective seniority rights by turning them down without affording them a trial period. The company denied the grievances.

About a month later the company decided to train the employee who had the least seniority of the three for the higher rated job because he had some familiarity with blueprints and with machine-shop methods gained from his work in the production inventory control job. The company trained the junior employee for the substantial part of the first three months he worked on the new job. The union then appealed to arbitration the grievances of the two senior employees.

At the arbitration hearing the union claimed the company violated the contract by passing over the two employees who had greater seniority, had the ability for training and further, that the company had failed to give the two senior employees a trial period. The union demanded that the arbitrator direct the company to promote and train the senior employee to the job of production clerk.

The company claimed that none of the three employees possessed the necessary ability to perform the requirements of the job without additional training as stipulated under Article X of the contract; that the contract did not obligate the company to provide a trial period for training; and therefore the company did not violate the contract in denying promotion to the senior employee among those who had bid for the job.

The company further argued that it chose to train the junior employee, although the contract did not obligate the company to do so, because his former job experience would allow for a shorter period of training than that of the other two employees.

Article X of the contract, dealing with promotions, provided:

Section 2. Promotions shall be made on the basis of office-wide seniority provided the ability of the senior employee meets the job requirements.

For the purpose of this agreement, ability shall be construed to mean the employee involved can fulfill and perform the requirements of the job without additional training.

Section 3. Employees promoted to a higher office grade shall be on a trial basis of one (1) to four (4) weeks on the job after the date of promotion. If during the trial period, the employee is not able to satisfactorily perform the job as required, such employee shall be returned to the former job and former rate of pay.

Finding that none of the grievants possessed the ability to meet the job requirements at the time they bid for the job, I denied the union's grievance, and in my award I said:

The proof further establishes and the arbitrator finds that the contract does not obligate the company to train an employee for a job for which he bid; nor does the contract obligate the company to provide the senior employee with a trial period to acquire the necessary qualifications for the job.

Then, finding that none of the grievants had the ability to fulfill the requirements of the job without additional training at the time they bid, I said:

Section 3 does not obligate the company to provide a trial period to train an employee to meet the requirements of the job. Section 3, by its very language, provides a trial period only for an employee promoted to a higher office grade so as to protect the seniority rights of that employee to return to his former job and former rate of pay should he demonstrate during the trial period, after he had been promoted, that he was not able to satisfactorily perform the job as required.

Noting that the junior employee "whom the company chose to train for the job, though the contract did not obligate the company to do so, had more familiarity with the processing of blueprints and the necessary machine shop methods which reasonably would require a lesser period of training than would be required by the other two grievants," I said:

The arbitrator therefore finds that the company did not violate the contract by originally denying promotion to the three grievants for the job of production clerk; and the company did not violate the contract by subsequently selecting the [junior] employee to train him for the job so that he could acquire the necessary ability to perform the job.

THE CASE OF TRAINING FOR ANOTHER JOB
IN LIEU OF LAYOFF

The company established a new job of sprayer in the relay department. The foreman canvassed the employees in the department according to their seniority standing, as the contract provided, and asked each whether he wanted to undertake training for the new job, since none of them had the experience needed for the job.

At that time the company had not yet set the job description or labor grade for the new job; but since it required a period of training, the foreman told the men the company would slot the job when filled in a higher labor grade than the jobs of the employees canvassed.

None of the employees, including the grievant, who held a labor grade 10 job, wanted the job. Each refused the training offer and, in accordance with the contract, the foreman assigned the new job to the employee with the lowest seniority in the department, who also held a labor grade 10 job. Later the company set up the description for the new job, which called for a "training period of 9 to 12 months in order to acquire the spraying technique," and slotted it in the higher labor grade 7.

About two months after the foreman had assigned the junior employee and had trained him in the basic skills needed, layoffs occurred in the department. Upon his layoff from his labor grade 10 job, the grievant claimed he had the right to displace the junior employee in the labor grade 7 job because he had greater departmental seniority and the junior employee had not yet completed his training period. The company denied the grievance, and the union appealed to arbitration.

At the arbitration hearing the union argued that the grievant could acquire the necessary skills within a reasonable training period and since the junior employee had not "reached the fully qualified stage in his training period," the grievant's departmental seniority gave him the right to displace the junior employee in training for the sprayer's job.

The company claimed that the contract did not obligate it to train an employee for any job and argued that the company had promoted the junior employee to the sprayer job because none of the other employees in the department, including the grievant, wanted to take the job.

In my award denying the union's grievance I found that the grievant did not possess the ability required to perform the sprayer job at the time the company laid him off from his own job; and even though the junior employee had not completed his training period, I held that the grievant did not have the right under the contract to displace the junior employee and have the company begin a new training period. I said:

> The contract does not obligate the company to train an employee for a job; nor does the contract grant an employee, who may have greater seniority, the right to displace another employee with lesser seniority unless the senior employee possessed at the time the ability, skill and experience necessary to perform the job.

The fact that the junior employee had not completed the full training period called for by the sprayer's job description at the time layoffs took place in the department did not give the grievant, I held, "greater seniority rights to that job nor does that fact obligate the company to begin all over to start training another employee for that job."

Then, finding that to sustain the union's position "would require the arbitrator to ignore or change the very standards the parties themselves set up to determine the relative seniority status of employees in the bargaining unit," I said:

> The company had trained [the junior employee] for a little over two months on the sprayer job. He had, by the time the layoff took place, acquired the experience and ability to perform the normal duties of the job. To require the company to lay him off and begin training [the grievant] would be contrary to and violate the clear language of the contract . . . The agreed-upon provisions of the contract determine the seniority rights among and between employees to available jobs; and those contract provisions constrain the arbitrator to apply them in the way that the parties intended and not to enlarge or restrict any individual employee's seniority rights under them.

87

TRIAL PERIOD TO DEMONSTRATE ABILITY

Giving an employee a trial period to demonstrate that he possesses the technical skills to do a job differs widely from a training period to learn those skills.

Tests—manual, oral, or written—or a demonstrable trial period up to three or five working days, depending on the skills needed, provide objective facts that you can offer, Mr. Foreman, to support your judgment that the employee you laid off or passed over did not at the time he asserted his seniority rights possess the ability to perform the available job.

The Case of Laying Off the Senior Worker on Conjecture

The company laid off a senior employee who operated a semi-automatic butt machine while retaining a junior employee who operated a fully automatic bacon-packing machine. The seniority unit, plant wide, within which both employees' seniority rights operated, covered both jobs. The senior employee's job carried a higher rate than that of the junior employee's job.

The union filed a grievance claiming that the senior employee had the ability to operate the bacon-packing machine and that since he had greater seniority in the work unit, the company should have allowed him to bump the junior employee in his job. During the grievance steps the union had requested the company to try out the senior employee on the job to show that he could operate it without any training. The company refused to give the trial period and denied the grievance, claiming that the senior employee did not have the necessary ability for the lower-rated job. The union then appealed to arbitration.

The seniority clause provided:

Branch wide seniority shall be in effect in the Company's branch. In all cases of increase or decrease of work force and in all cases of promotions and demotions, length of continuous service shall be the determining factor, provided the necessary ability is present.

At the arbitration hearing the union acknowledged that the contract did not obligate the company to train a senior employee who exercises his seniority rights to a lower-rated job in lieu of being laid off but claimed that the contract did obligate the company "to give the employee a chance—an opportunity—to show that he had the necessary ability."

The company claimed that "in its opinion" the senior employee did not have the ability to operate the bacon-packing machine; and to allow him a trial period, the company would suffer loss in production.

I sustained the union's grievance. I found that the company's supervisors had based their opinion as to the senior employee's ability solely on conjecture without showing any objective facts to support their opinion. In my award I said:

> The company's opinion or judgment must be more than a feeling or a belief; it must be arrived at by demonstrable facts, which can be subjected to examination and verification. Under this type of seniority clause, a trial period for the employee to show that he has the necessary ability, as he claims, is perhaps the best way to demonstrate those facts. But it is not the only way. Demonstrable facts can be gotten in other ways—from records showing the employee's past experience, his performance on his former and other jobs, personal observations of his supervisors and other comparable factual sources of material information and data.

Then, finding that the company's supervisors had arrived at their judgment "purely subjectively, without any objective criteria, without offering the union or the employee or the arbitrator any objective facts upon which its judgment was predicated and from which a judgment could reasonably be arrived at," I said:

> The reason the arbitrator finds the company violated the seniority clause in this case, therefore, is not that the company failed or refused to give [the grievant] a trial period or an opportunity to demonstrate he had the necessary ability present at the time as he then claimed; it is that the company failed to show or offer to the arbitrator objective or demonstrable facts to support its opinion that the grievant did not have the necessary ability.

Noting that no one on behalf of the company testified with any reasonable degree of certainty as to the grievant's ability and that the company's supervisors had based their appraisal of the employee's ability to operate the bacon-packing machine on his "aptitude," I said:

> Where, under the contract, management has the right to exercise administrative initiative, i.e., has the right, initially, to say who should be laid off and who should be retained, and the union has the right to protest and appeal that action, if it feels aggrieved, management must exercise the co-relative responsibility to support that action by facts— facts which demonstrate a reasonable basis for the opinion or judgment arrived at. The judgment arrived at does not have to coincide with the union's judgment, or necessarily with the arbitrator's judgment. Reasonable men can arrive at contrary judgments on the same set of facts. But the irreducible minimum to sustain a judgment is a showing that it was based upon objective facts and criteria.
>
> Here, in the instant case, the company did not offer any material facts which reasonably could be held to support its "opinion" that [the grievant] could not perform, without additional training, the lower rated job at the time he asserted his seniority right of preference.

Rules for Administering the Relatively Equal in Ability Clause—and Trial Periods

Summing up the rules for improving the quality of the work force under the relatively equal in ability clause (Type III) and the rules of bumping, trial, training, and learning periods under seniority.

Rule 1. In judging competitively the ability and qualifications of two or more employees, base your qualitative judgment— your opinion—on objective, demonstrable facts, not conjecture, not surmise, not feelings.

Rule 2. In the absence of factual data about an employee's experiences and skills on or related to the new job to justify your opinion that a junior employee better qualifies than a senior employee, you must prove that the senior employee has done some "wrong" in meeting the duties and responsibilities that apply to every job.

Rule 3. The written record showing that you have taken corrective action against an employee because of his failings or shortcomings provides you with objective, demonstrable facts to support your qualitative judgment of the relative abilities of employees.

Rule 4. In the absence of any written record showing that the passed-over employee has done something "wrong" in failing to meet his job duties and responsibilities, you secure demonstrable facts by:
1. Tests—manual, oral or written; or
2. Providing each qualified bidder with a demonstrable trial period—up to three or five working days depending on the skills and experience needed—to determine an employee's ability under Types I and II or to determine the better qualified employee under Type III.

Rule 5. Your written record of tests or the results of the demonstrable trial period provide the objective facts to support your opinion or qualitative judgment.

Rule 6. In evaluating the ability and qualifications of an employee under Types I, II or III, avoid such generalities as poor attitude, not cooperative, lacks initiative, undependable, hasn't the aptitude. Give the facts to support such conclusions. Facts speak for themselves, and only facts will lend support to your judgment or opinion.

Rule 7. Administering the relatively equal in ability clause (Type III) according to the rules of seniority provides you with the fifth way to improve the quality of your work force.

Rule 8. When layoffs occur in the work unit within which the affected employees' seniority rights operate, the senior qualified employee has priority to the remaining jobs under Type I (strict or straight seniority), under Type II (modified or contingent seniority), and, with limited exceptions, even under Type III (relatively equal in ability seniority).

Rule 9. Under Type III, when due to no fault on your part the senior employee does not possess at the time of layoff the technical skills required for the remaining jobs in the work unit where his seniority rights prevail, his seniority rights do not protect him from layoff.

Rule 10. Under Type III, on layoff or recall after layoff, when the skills required for the remaining available jobs have materially changed due to changes in means, methods, or processes of production and the senior employee does not possess at the time the new skills required to do the changed job (under Type I or Type II); or when under Type III the junior employee possesses relatively better skills for the changed job, the seniority rights of the senior employee do not protect him from layoff or give him priority for recall.

Rule 11. "Bumping" means the right of a senior qualified employee to displace from a job another employee who has less seniority in the work unit within which the seniority rights of both employees prevail. Bumping applies wherever seniority operates.

Rule 12. Bumping does not add any other rights, such as trial, training, or learning periods, under a seniority system. Bumping serves a procedural function that satisfies the senior employee's priority right to an available job even though another employee fills that job at the time.

Rule 13. Unless the contract provides otherwise, seniority rights do not give an employee laid off from his job the right to bump up and displace an employee in a higher-rated job.

Rule 14. Bumping doesn't extend an employee's seniority rights to advance or be promoted to a higher-rated job upon layoff from his own job. If an opening or vacancy in any other job, including a higher-rated one, exists at the time of layoff, the employee laid off from his own job may bid for the opening according to the procedures that the contract sets up to fill such vacancy.

Rule 15. An employee who asserts priority to a job must be qualified at the time he exercises his seniority rights. Unless the contract or an established practice provides otherwise, seniority does not obligate you to provide a training period under any type of seniority—I, II or III—for an employee to learn the new job or to acquire the ability and qualifications for another job upon bumping, or upon a lateral transfer or downgrading to another job in lieu of being laid off from work, or on promotion to a higher-rated job.

Seniority Rules to Control Chain Bumpings and Extended Benefits

Rule 16. When a layoff becomes necessary in a work unit within which seniority operates, you first decide whether the senior employee, at the time he asserts his priority to another job, possesses the skills and ability required for that job.

Rule 17. You avoid initiating training or learning periods that may start a practice that will bind you and the other foremen in their departments who administer the same seniority provisions.

Rule 18. In administering transfers and bumpings in lieu of layoff from work you construe the seniority provisions to permit one displacement—of the least senior employee in the job classification, shift, or operating group.

Rule 19. Distinguish between temporary and permanent transfers under seniority; and retain—or regain—flexibility in assigning qualified workers to and among available jobs, tasks, or machines.

Rule 20. Control shift transfers under seniority to maintain balanced qualified crews on each shift.

Rule 21. Limit, control or eliminate extending seniority rights to other job benefits that may from time to time attach to a job, such as choice of machine, work location, incentive work, overtime opportunity, or other pay, meal, or benefit allowances.

Avoid beginning a practice that may extend seniority rights to such additional areas. Remember: twenty-seven foremen administering one contract don't make twenty-seven separate contracts!

We now come to the work unit, the second part of the seniority system, within which the three types of seniority operate.

4

The Work Unit Within Which
Seniority Operates

You can set up the work unit within which one or another of the three types of seniority operates (Type I, strict or straight seniority; Type II, modified or contingent seniority; Type III, relatively equal in ability seniority) in only two ways:

1. *Geography or area,* such as plant-wide, department, company-wide, multiple plants, yard, floor, or other area.
2. *Job or craft,* such as classification, occupation, operating group, family of jobs, grouping or bailiwick of related jobs, skills or crafts.

Of course, the negotiators can combine area with job classifications to serve operational needs or to fortify the job security of long-service employees. Essentially, however, seniority rights operate in either a geographic work unit or an occupational work unit. The geographic work unit usually encompasses a variety of unrelated jobs and job skills; the occupational work unit, of related jobs or job skills.

The Function of the Work Unit

The broader the area or the greater the grouping of jobs:

1. For employees—the greater the opportunities to exercise seniority rights.
2. For the foreman—the greater the flexibility to utilize available employees' skills and to assign work.

Conversely, the narrower the area or the more limited the grouping of jobs:

1. For employees—the less opportunity to exercise seniority rights.
2. For the foreman—the less the flexibility to utilize available employees' skills and to assign work.

You see, Mr. Foreman, a direct ratio exists between an employee's seniority right to an available job and your right to assign him to an available job when production needs require. To the extent that upon layoff from his own job an employee may have priority to another available job that he then qualifies for, you have the correlative right, Mr. Foreman, to assign that employee to an available job for which he's qualified.

The Case of the Temporary Promotion
to Another Job

Just before the noon break one of the regularly assigned set-up men in the department asked his foreman to excuse him for the rest of the day. His foreman agreed. To fill the vacancy the foreman assigned the most senior operator in the department, following the seniority provisions of the contract. The operator qualified for the job and had in the past performed it. The set-up job carried a 21-cents-an-hour increase over the operator's job.

The operator told the foreman he preferred to remain on his own job because he had just finished setting up the machines in his battery, and he felt he could earn more through bonus earnings on his own job. The foreman ordered him to undertake the temporary assignment. The operator complied and then filed a grievance protesting the foreman's action. The company denied the grievance, and the union appealed to arbitration.

The contract provided:

> An employee who is temporarily transferred from his regular job classification to another job classification shall continue to accrue seniority in his regular job classification. The Company shall notify the Union whenever an employee has been temporarily transferred for a period of thirty (30) consecutive calendar days. The period of a temporary transfer shall not exceed thirty (30) days without the consent of the employee and the Union. Seniority shall prevail in all transfers so far as practicable.

At the arbitration hearing the union claimed that "an employee has the right under the contract to decline a promotion on a temporary basis if he feels it is more practicable for him to do so" and that the foreman did not have the right to direct an employee to take a temporary promotion.

The company claimed that an employee did not have the right under the contract to refuse a temporary transfer made in accordance with the seniority provisions; and since the grievant had greater seniority than other operators and qualified for the vacancy, the foreman had acted properly in temporarily transferring him to that vacancy.

Finding that under the contract an employee had the right to refuse promotion to a permanent vacancy, I held that he did not have the right under the seniority section to refuse a temporary transfer not exceeding thirty days, saying:

> That section only requires the company to notify the union where the employee has been temporarily transferred for a period of thirty (30) consecutive calendar days. It expressly provides that the temporary transfer shall not exceed thirty days without the consent of the em-

ployee and the union. Clearly, therefore, in a temporary transfer of less than thirty days, the company does not have to get the consent of the employee or the union.

Referring to the last sentence of that section, which provided: "Seniority shall prevail in all transfers so far as practicable," the union argued that the word "practicable" gave the employee the right to decline a temporary transfer to another job, "if in his judgment he finds the transfer is not practicable." I rejected that argument and said:

> The arbitrator finds this argument without substance or merit. The proof shows that the parties intended the sentence "Seniority shall prevail in all transfers so far as practicable," to limit the company's rights in making temporary transfers. It obligates the company to follow seniority in all cases so far as practicable. That's just what the foreman did in this case. He assigned the employee who qualified and who had the greater seniority in the department. That, in the past, [the foreman] or other foremen in other departments have not insisted that the senior qualified employee undertake the assignment and allowed an employee next below in seniority fill it, does not detract from the contractual right of the foreman in this case . . . to make the assignment in accordance with the seniority provisions of the contract, as agreed upon by the parties.
>
> The expressed language of the contract does not give an employee an option to accept or decline a temporary transfer to a job which he is qualified to fill and which is made in accordance with his seniority under the seniority provisions of the contract. No such option can be implied. The fact that in accepting the transfer, [the grievant] would have suffered some loss in earnings does not give him the individual right to accept or decline the temporary transfer.

As to the union's claim that in accepting the transfer the grievant suffered a loss in earnings, I said:

> The parties have agreed that in making transfers, seniority shall be followed by the company as far as practicable. This is the cardinal standard which the parties have agreed to. Any resulting loss of earnings or other effects upon an individual employee cannot be asserted

to negate that cardinal standard. In complying with that standard the company also, at times, suffers loss in efficiency and "earnings" which it perhaps could avoid if it did not follow seniority. These are the detriments which of necessity result to an individual employee and the company in applying the standards which the parties have agreed upon.

In my award I pointed out that other clauses of the contract intended to lessen the detriment that an employee may suffer from the application of that seniority standard, namely, that on a temporary transfer he continues to accrue seniority in his regular job classification; when temporarily transferred to a lower-rated classification, he retains his own rate; and when temporarily transferred to a higher-rated classification, he receives the higher rate and participates in the overtime and the overall bonus in the department to which he's transferred.

Finding that the foreman's action did not violate the contract and that the grievant did not have the right to refuse to undertake the temporary transfer, I said:

> Section 17 of the contract expressly reserves to the company the "Direction of working operations . . . " The need of the company to make temporary transfers to higher or lower rated jobs has been expressly recognized by the parties. These needs stem from such cases as absenteeism, illness, temporary increase in the work-load, decrease in the work-load, breakdowns, accommodating an employee by transferring him to work in other departments where work is available rather than lay him off, and so forth. The contract recognizes the company's right to make temporary transfers when such need arises, without the consent of the employee or the union as long as the temporary transfer doesn't exceed a thirty day time limit.

The Case of Operating Section vs. Job Classification

The company had set up a new job of group leader in the experimental tool room section and had promoted an employee classified as die worker who worked in that section to the job. The union filed a grievance claiming that two other die makers, though assigned to another section called the tool room, had greater seniority; and since they both qualified for the new job, the company should have promoted either one of them in place of the junior employee.

The company denied the grievance, claiming that the promoted die worker "was the senior employee in the experimental tool room section —as distinct from the tool room section" and that the seniority provisions and past practice under them justified the company's action. The union then appealed to arbitration.

At the arbitration hearing the company did not question the ability and qualifications of either of the grievants to perform the job of group leader but defended its action on the ground that the employee promoted "was more familiar with the work in his section."

The union claimed that under the seniority provisions the classification of employees governs their promotional rights and not the operating groups or sections set up by the company for its convenience in which an employee may be working at any time.

I sustained the union's grievance, and in my award I held that "under the seniority provisions of the contract, seniority in the job classification of die maker governs promotion to the job of group leader . . . and not seniority in the section to which a die maker may be assigned or working in at any particular time." I said:

> Though the company has set up two operating sections in which die makers work or are assigned to and from and between which die makers are promoted or laid off according to their seniority standing in their job classification, that fact does not warrant the company from failing to apply the seniority provisions, agreed upon by the parties in filling a group leader's job in either section.
>
> The fact that a group leader job is involved, does not, by itself, remove it from the coverage of the seniority provisions. Since the contract covers group leader jobs which the company fills by employees in the bargaining unit, in the absence of any expressed exception, the agreed upon seniority standards set forth in the contract determine the promotional rights of employees to that job.

Finding no basis, either in the past practice or for the "practical reasons" advanced by the company for promoting the junior employee, I said:

The language of group A classifications is clear and unambiguous. The arbitrator has no authority under the guise of interpreting clear and unambiguous language to find that the parties intended something else or something different than that which the language itself speaks of . . .

The "practical" reasons advanced by the company for selecting the junior employee to fill the group leader job—in preference to either of the other two die makers who had greater seniority and whose ability and qualifications have not been put in issue—do not warrant either the company or the arbitrator substituting those practical reasons in place of the seniority standards the parties agreed upon.

The Seniority Conflict Between Job Security and Operational Efficiency

As pointed out earlier:

1. A broad seniority unit—area or jobs—apparently offers greater opportunities for an employee to exercise his seniority rights to available jobs to avoid layoff from work and, correspondingly, apparently also affords greater flexibility to the foreman in assigning available work among qualified employees.
2. A narrow seniority unit—area or jobs—apparently limits an employee's opportunities to avoid layoff from work and, correspondingly, apparently also restricts the foreman's latitude in assigning work among qualified employees.

Conversely, however, the broad seniority unit—area or jobs—brings about:

1. For employees—increased competition for an available job, thereby limiting an employee's job security and increasing the likelihood of layoff.
2. For the foreman—increased chain bumpings and multiple transfers among employees for available jobs, thereby leading to more training periods and more inefficient practices.

101

On the other hand, the narrow seniority unit—area or jobs—offers:

3. For employees—reduced competition among employees for an available job, thereby increasing job security and decreasing the likelihood of layoff.
4. For the foreman—reduced chain bumpings and multiple transfers among employees for available jobs, thereby eliminating the need for training or learning periods and avoiding inefficient or costly practices.

You see, Mr. Foreman, here again a direct ratio exists between an employee's opportunities for job security and the company's need for operating efficiency in meeting its production needs. A broad work unit only superficially gives an employee greater latitude in exercising seniority rights because more employees compete in that broader unit. Likewise, a broad work unit only superficially gives you greater flexibility in filling available jobs because chain bumpings and multiple transfers result from employees competing for the available jobs.

Can the negotiators set up a work unit within which your type of seniority operates that will lessen the disadvantages of too broad or too narrow a work unit and resolve to a greater extent the conflict between job security and operational efficiency? Yes, by setting up a work unit based on groupings of jobs and job skills, that is, a work unit composed of related jobs and interchangeable job skills. A work unit of a family of related or interchangeable jobs!

HOMOGENEITY OF JOBS AND JOB SKILLS

Yes, that's the key to operating efficiency as well as to increased job security. A work unit composed of homogeneous jobs and job skills best accommodates the technological changes that constantly take place in production and satisfies to a greater extent the individual employee's gnawing worry over job security.

Not geography but a series of work units each of which consists of jobs with related skills or readily interchangeable jobs. Not company-wide, plant-wide, floor, yard, or other area, because in such areas employees may exercise their seniority rights to remotely related or noninterchangeable jobs. Family, bailiwick, or groups of related or interchangeable jobs, job skills, or crafts provide:

For employees:

1. Increased job security by giving employees priority to jobs with related skills within their own work unit within which their seniority rights operate, thereby limiting other employees in other work units from competing for those jobs.
2. Increased opportunity to exercise their seniority rights for promotion when vacancies occur in higher skilled jobs along lines of progression—up or down—within their family of related or interchangeable jobs.
3. Increased economic benefits in wage rates and earnings by advancing to higher paid jobs within their family of related or interchangeable jobs.

For the union:

1. Increased union security as the exclusive representative of employees in the bargaining unit by removing the threat of competing unions to fractionalize the bargaining unit into separate skilled units and lessening the possibility of eliminating parts of the bargaining unit through the subcontracting of production or maintenance work.
2. Fortifying the union's security in the bargaining unit by providing the means for the union to better satisfy the legitimate reasons that motivated the workers in joining that union, namely, job security, opportunity to advance in jobs and job skills, and increased earnings.

For the foreman:

1. Increased flexibility in assigning available work and jobs among qualified employees.
2. Increased control over chain bumpings and excessive multiple transfers among employees competing for available jobs.

3. Reduced need for training or learning periods among employees who possess related or interchangeable skills.

4. Greater utilization of available employees' skills and equipment.

5. Increased control over inefficient or costly practices.

6. Increased opportunity to improve the quality of the work force.

7. Accommodation of future production and personnel needs in an expanding or contracting bargaining unit.

You see, Mr. Foreman, a work unit based on geography or area within which employees may exercise seniority rights to remotely related or noninterchangeable jobs:

1. Reduces job security by increasing competition from other employees.

2. Limits employees' opportunities to advance to more skilled and higher paying jobs.

3. Limits the objective means for the foreman to determine ability and qualifications under seniority Types I, II, and III.

4. Limits the foreman's opportunity to improve the quality of his work force.

5. Satisfies to a much lower degree employee job security, union security, and your management's security of enterprise.

Note: Sometimes a work unit may be designated as an "area" such as Inspection Department, Experimental Section, or Machine Shop when in fact related or interchangeable jobs or job skills make up that department, section, or shop. In such cases, of course, those areas satisfy the key that reconciles the conflict between job security and operating efficiency, namely, a work unit composed of homogeneous jobs or crafts of related or interchangeable jobs and job skills.

A work unit made up of families of related or interchangeable jobs or crafts with agreed-upon lines of progression—up or down—more readily accommodates an expanding or contracting work force that business cycles or technological changes in production may bring about. Thus, a family of related or interchangeable jobs or crafts accommodates a work force that expands from forty to four thousand employees or one that contracts to four hundred.

Now let's see what happens when the seniority provisions of a contract mix up an area work unit with a job work unit.

THE CASE OF COMPANY-WIDE VS.
JOB CLASSIFICATION SENIORITY

The union filed a grievance claiming that the company had violated the contract by denying an employee who had eleven years company-wide seniority, including three years seniority in the job classification of group leader, the right to bump an employee who had only eight years company-wide seniority including seven and a half years seniority in the group leader's job classification.

The company denied the grievance, claiming that it had properly applied the seniority rights of both employees under the contract. The union then appealed to arbitration.

The seniority provisions provided:

48. At time of layoff, employees may exercise seniority in any job classification provided they have a minimum of four (4) months seniority gained with the Company in the job classification and provided further that whenever the order of layoff is based on a greater period of seniority gained in the job classification, the employee shall have the minimum seniority gained in the job classification, as set forth in the Seniority Schedules, in order to exercise seniority over an employee who does have the minimum seniority in that job classification.

The seniority schedules referred to in the foregoing section set forth the "minimum seniority gained in the job classification" of group leader as follows:

Group Leaders . . . having less than five (5) years seniority gained in their job classifications shall be laid off first within their own section of a department.

At the arbitration hearing the union claimed that the grievant met the "minimum of four (4) months" seniority in the group leader

105

classification as provided for by the first part of Section 48; and since he had greater company-wide seniority, he had the right upon his layoff from the job of expediter to bump a group leader who had less company-wide seniority.

The company claimed that the grievant, not having gained the minimum of five years seniority in the group leader job classification as prescribed in the seniority schedules and expressly referred to in the second half of Section 48, did not have the right to displace an employee who had over five years seniority in the job classification even though the grievant had greater company-wide seniority.

In support of its position the company argued that the "history of negotiations, whereby the parties prescribed minimum standards of job seniority . . . to govern bumping rights among employees, shows the parties intended to give a greater degree of job security to employees in certain job classifications, who had gained the minimum job seniority, as against other employees in the bargaining unit who may have acquired greater company seniority."

In my award denying the union's grievance I found that the parties had set up two qualifying requirements to govern the seniority rights of an employee to displace another in the group leader job classification. I held:

> The proof establishes that [the grievant] did not meet the minimum requirements of 5 years seniority gained in the job classification of group leader—as expressly required in Section 48—entitling him to displace [another employee] from the group leader job . . . who had gained over 5 years seniority. The history of Section 48, in the progressive contracts which the parties negotiated . . . satisfies the arbitrator that the parties intended under that section that as to certain specified jobs—including the group leader job—an employee who had gained a minimum of four months seniority in these jobs could exercise his company-wide seniority to displace another employee with less company-wide seniority only if he further satisfied the requirement of the "minimum seniority gained in the job classification"—as set forth in the seniority schedules. In this case, the seniority schedules require the minimum of 5 years gained in the job classification of group leader. The grievant had gained only about 3 years. The other employee had gained over 7½

years. Under Section 48, therefore, the grievant did not have the right at any time to displace the other employee in the job classification of group leader—or bump [him] from his job.

Noting that the "dispute in this case involves seniority rights between two employees to one available job," I said:

The parties negotiated and agreed upon certain seniority standards which would govern the seniority rights of employees upon layoff. 'Of necessity, when only one available job exists, the agreed-upon seniority standards operate to give preference to one employee over the other. Neither party can unilaterally change those seniority standards during the contract term, so as to prefer one employee for any particular job to the detriment of another employee's rights under those seniority standards.

Finding that the seniority provisions did not give the grievant the right to exercise his greater company-wide seniority to displace an employee who had less company-wide but greater job classification seniority, I said:

Since no vacancy in fact existed in the group leader classification at the time of his layoff, the grievant could only acquire a group leader job by displacing one of the two employees who were then filling the only two available group leader jobs. Both employees in the group leader job had gained the minimum of 5 years or more seniority in the group leader job as required under Section 48 and therefore he did not have the right to displace either one of the other group leaders.

During the arbitration hearing in that case the union's international representative, in presenting his side of the case, swung from one position to another. At times he seemed to argue for company-wide seniority and at other times for job classification. Twice during the hearing he requested a recess in order to consult with the seven members of the shop committee who were present.

When they returned after the second recess, I asked the international representative to plainly state what position he was arguing—company-wide or job classification. Looking me straight in the eye, he

107

said: "Look, Mr. Arbitrator, you see the trouble I'm having. These members of the committee," pointing to the four men on his right, "insist that company-wide seniority controls; and these," pointing to the three members on his left, "insist upon job classification seniority. I've done the best I can. You're the arbitrator—you decide what controls under the contract!"

THE CASE OF CLAIMED SENIORITY RIGHTS TO
WORK LOCATION WITHIN A JOB CLASSIFICATION

For operating efficiency the company maintained four work locations, referred to as operating sections, within the single job classification of stock clerk. When the company promoted an employee into the stock clerk classification, the company assigned him to one of those four operating sections, namely, finished stock, warehouse, receiving, or fiber crib.

Under the seniority provisions an employee assigned to the finished stock section had the right to exercise his seniority to advance to five other jobs in that section when an opening occurred; and when laid off from one of those five jobs in that operating section, he could exercise his seniority rights in reverse order. One of those five jobs carried a rate five cents higher than the rate of the stock clerk classification.

When the company promoted an employee into the stock clerk classification, the contract did not give him seniority rights for assignment to any one of the four work locations or operating sections. However, an employee had the right under the contract to accept or reject promotion into the classification. Consequently, employees would bid or refrain from bidding for the promotion depending upon the operating section in which the opening existed.

Employees regarded the fiber crib section as the least desirable one and usually avoided promotion to the stock clerk classification when an opening occurred in that operating section. They called the fiber crib "Siberia," because once you got into the section, you had no opportunity to advance to a better-paying job or to participate in overtime work that the other operating sections offered.

Due to a cutback in the stock clerk classification, the company laid off the employee in the fiber crib section who had the least seniority in the classification and then transferred the grievant from his job in the finished stock section to the vacancy in the fiber crib job while retaining in the finished stock section another employee who had less classification seniority than the grievant.

The union filed a grievance claiming that the company had violated the seniority provisions of the contract by transferring the grievant from his job in the finished stock section to the fiber crib section while leaving an employee with less classification seniority in the finished stock section.

The union further claimed that by such transfer the grievant had been "deprived of the opportunity of working Saturdays and daily overtime which accrued to employees in the finished stock section," and demanded that the company retroactively pay him for such loss.

The company denied the grievance, claiming that it had laid off the least senior employee in the stock clerk classification, who happened to work in the fiber crib section, as required by the seniority provisions of the contract and had then assigned the grievant to the fiber crib section "because he had previously worked in the fiber crib section —and in the interest of efficient operation, the company decided to use his experience and avoid the necessity of training a new employee."

The company further claimed that even though the grievant had greater classification seniority than the employee retained in the finished stock section, it "had the right to assign him or any other employees classified as stock clerks to any of the other operating groups or sections within the stock clerk classification" according to its operational needs and that "overtime opportunities go, as the other contract provisions provide, with the section in which the employee may be assigned or transferred to."

The union having appealed to arbitration, I found that the case presented two issues:

1. The grievant's seniority right to advance in jobs within his classification.

2. His loss of overtime opportunity upon transfer to the fiber crib section.

109

I sustained the union's grievance on the first issue and upheld the company's claim on the second issue.

On the first issue, I found that the company's action in transferring the grievant from the finished stock section to the fiber crib section adversely affected his "promotional opportunities" within his classification, which the seniority provisions of the contract expressly protected. Though the contract provided that employees with the least seniority in the classification be laid off first, other parts of the seniority provisions detailed the seniority rights of employees to jobs within the section of their classification. As to jobs in the stock clerk classification, the seniority provisions provided:

> At time of layoff employees in this class may exercise seniority within their own job classifications within their own section of a department and also in the reverse order in which they may be promoted.

I held that that provision protected the grievant's seniority rights to promotional opportunities to jobs within his own section and the company did not have the right to deprive him of those promotional opportunities when the company assigned him to other jobs within his classification.

Finding, however, that the contract did not restrict the company "in assigning or reassigning employees from one section to another section in the stock clerk classification, where production needs or operating efficiency require such assignment or reassignment—provided that the reassignment does not take away any seniority rights granted the employee under the contract," I said in my award:

> The fact that the seniority provision grants certain preferences or opportunities to employees assigned to one section in a classification—as against employees assigned to another section of that same classification —does not, in the absence of any contrary expressed contract provision, give the employee any prescriptive right to work in or be assigned to any particular section of that classification—nor does it restrict the company from reassigning employees within the same classification from one section to another, depending on the company's needs and consonant with the seniority rights expressly granted by the contract.

Although I sustained the union's claim of contract violation on this issue, the proof showed that during the period of about four weeks the grievant had worked in the fiber crib section—after which the company had reassigned him back to his former section—"no promotional opportunities had arisen to which he could have exercised his seniority rights—and consequently, [he] did not suffer any loss of seniority benefits, entitling him to any damages."

As to the second issue, the union claimed that the company should pay the grievant for the overtime opportunities he lost during the four-week period he spent out of the finished stock section. Finding that the contract required the company to equalize "extra work and overtime . . . among the group engaged in similar work in a department so far as practicable," I denied that claim and in my award I said:

> The contract protects the seniority rights of the employees within a given classification—it does not guarantee that overtime work will be available in any particular section of the classification—or that an employee has a proprietary right to overtime work in any particular section . . .
>
> In fact, were the arbitrator to uphold the union's claim for damages for [the grievant's] loss of extra work or overtime during the period he was in the fiber crib section, the arbitrator would, of necessity, have to find that once an employee is assigned to a particular section within a classification, the company cannot assign him to another section in that classification. The effect would be to "alter, add to or supplement" the contract provisions which Section 27 of the contract expressly states the arbitrator has no authority to do. The contract insofar as it relates to this case protects the grievant's seniority rights accruing from the seniority he had gained in the stock clerk section. It does not restrict the company from assigning him to other sections in his classification, as long as his seniority rights are protected—and it does not entitle him to overtime work that may arise in any other section of his classification in which he is not working.

The Case of the Retired First Grade Welder

For some time prior to the dispute in this case the company had employed in the occupational group of welders six first grade and one

111

second grade welder. Then the company added another second grade welder, making the ratio six first grade to two second grade welders.

Shortly thereafter a first grade welder retired. The company did not post a vacancy or fill his job.

The union filed a grievance claiming that the retirement of the first grade welder created a vacancy in that job and that the company had violated the wage structure of the contract by failing to post such vacancy.

The company denied the grievance on the ground that it had no available work for another first grade welder and therefore no vacancy in fact existed.

At the arbitration hearing the union argued that the company's refusal to fill the job left by the retired employee "constituted, in effect, a wage cut by depressing the ratio between first and second grade welders theretofore existing."

The company argued that the contract did not obligate it "to maintain any fixed number of employees in any job or occupational group"; and since no second grade welder performed first grade work, the company had not violated the wage scale of the contract.

I denied the union's grievance, finding that the retirement of the former employee did not create a vacancy in the job of first grade welder; and since the second grade welders performed only the work called for by their job classification, the company had not violated the wage scale under the contract. In my award I said:

> The contract does not obligate the company to post a vacancy for a non-existent job—nor to fill a job where there is no available work. Section 3, Article VI, relied upon by the union, obligates the company to post a vacancy, which in fact exists, and which it intends to fill. That section does not obligate the company to create more jobs than it has available work for—nor to post jobs for which no vacancy in fact exists. Nor does Section 3 of Article VI obligate the company to maintain any fixed number of employees in any job—or any ratio between the number of first grade welders and second grade welders in any occupation.
>
> If, in fact, as the company correctly points out, any employee in the job of second grade welder is actually performing the work of first

grade welder, then that employee may have redress under Section 2 of Article XI—which requires that " . . . an employee . . . assigned to work on a higher paid job . . . shall receive the established rate of the higher paid job . . . " No such facts are presented in this case.

Now, what makes up a "job" when a vacancy occurs in the work unit? Does the shift constitute an integral part of the job? Do the seniority rights of employees in the work unit extend to the shift in which the vacancy occurs? Those questions arose in another dispute between the parties in the foregoing case under the seniority provisions of the same contract.

The Case of the Wrong Turn in the Posted Job

The company had promoted the head repairman working on the day shift—8:00 A.M. to 4:30 P.M.—to assistant foreman, a job outside the bargaining unit. The contract referred to the day shift as turn 2 and the shift from 4:00 P.M. to 12 midnight as turn 3.

The company then transferred the head repairman working on turn 3 to the opening in turn 2 and posted the resulting turn 3 job as the open one. The seniority provision, Article VI, Section 3, of the contract, provided:

Section 3. All employee vacancies and new jobs created shall be posted for five (5) days to allow employees to make application in writing for such jobs. The company will give careful consideration to applications received in relation to the following qualifications: (a) seniority, (b) requirements of the job, (c) individual skill, efficient service and physical fitness. Where qualifications (b) and (c) are relatively the same, seniority shall govern.

The union filed a grievance claiming that the company had violated that section by unilaterally transferring a junior employee from turn 3 to the vacancy on turn 2, "thereby preventing other employees of greater seniority and equal or greater experience" from bidding for the job on turn 2.

The company denied the union's grievance, claiming that the "turn of a job is not an integral part of a job and that Section 3 does not ex-

pressly require that in posting a vacancy, the turn has to be included."
The union then appealed to arbitration.

At the arbitration hearing the union argued that the "turn of a new
job or vacancy is a material part of the job—necessary to allow the
employee to determine whether or not he wished to bid for it" and
that the company had applied Section 3 that way in the past. The union
demanded that the company declare the turn 2 job open and post and
accept bids for it in accordance with Section 3 of the contract.

The company did not dispute the fact that "over the years in the
past, it generally posted the turn on any vacancy or new job that
occurred—and opened it for bidding." The company argued, however,
that it had done so only for the convenience of or as a courtesy to the
employees and that its "past actions cannot be construed so as to
change or enlarge upon the company's contractual obligations, as
expressed by the language of Section 3."

I sustained the union's grievance, finding that the company had in
the past "uniformly posted the turn of a vacancy or new job—so that
the employee knew which turn was opened for bidding on the posted
job." I rejected the company's argument as to why it had posted the
turn in the past and in my award I held:

> The proof fails to support the company's claim that its action, in posting
> the turn of a vacancy or new job, was solely a courtesy or convenience
> for the employees. On the contrary, the arbitrator finds the parties in-
> tended that the turn of a job was an integral part of the job—and that
> it was a material fact to be made known to and considered by an em-
> ployee to help him decide whether or not he wished to bid for the
> vacancy or the new job.

Finding that the company's own explanation of why it made clear
the turn when it posted vacancies or new jobs over the years in the
past supported the union's claim, I said:

> The company candidly states it posted the turn of the vacancy or new
> job to save the company's and the employees' time and avoid the re-
> sulting inefficiency in the event an employee bid for the job and then
> found out he didn't want to work the particular turn available. The

turn of a job thus constituted a material and integral part of a job—and the way the parties applied said Section 3 in posting a vacancy or new job confirms these facts.

Then, noting that Section 3 said nothing about what the posting should contain, I said:

> The way the parties applied that section in the past removes any ambiguity and shows what the posted notice was to contain. With the two exceptions, referred to below, the proof shows . . . the company consistently posted all vacancies in new jobs and always indicated, in one way or another, the turn of the job—to allow the employee to decide whether he wanted to bid for that job on that particular turn. This uniform past practice resolves any ambiguity as to what the parties intended to be included in the posting under Section 3—and fully supports the claim of the union in this case.

Finding that the promotion of the former head repairman created a vacancy on turn 2 and that Section 3 obligated the company to post that vacancy, I held:

> Section 3 does not give nor can it be reasonably construed to give the company the right to unilaterally transfer another employee to that vacancy and only post the resulting second vacancy. Were the company's action . . . upheld, it would, in effect, negate the very purposes intended by the parties under Section 3, as expressed and applied over the years.

Accordingly, I directed the company to declare the turn 2 job vacant and post such vacancy for bidding in accordance with Section 3 as applied by the parties in the past.

DO EXCEPTIONS NEGATE AN ESTABLISHED PAST PRACTICE?

In that case the company claimed that on two occasions in the past it had "similarly transferred an employee from one turn to another turn in the same job category and that the union did not then complain." The union did not dispute those two exceptions in the past but argued

115

that in neither of those two cases "did any employee file a grievance and, therefore, the union was not in a position to protest the company's action, and that in one of the cases no employee wanted the turn of the job which the company had unilaterally filled."

Finding that two instances varying an otherwise uniformly established practice existing over many years did not negate that practice, I said:

> The arbitrator finds that the union's action in those two instances, under those facts out of an otherwise uniform practice . . . did not constitute a waiver of the union's rights under Section 3, as expressed by the clear language of that section and as applied by the parties themselves over the years.

The Case of the Down-Graded Group Leader

The company had down-graded a group leader to his former job of inspector D and then reduced his rate by fifteen cents per hour, the differential provided by the wage schedule for the leadman's job. The contract covered both jobs in the bargaining unit.

The union protested, claiming that the company did not have just cause for demoting the grievant from leadman to inspector. The company denied the grievance on the ground that it no longer needed a leadman for day shift inspection. The union then appealed to arbitration.

In addition to performing regular production work of inspector, the group leader's job required him "to perform some of the routine supervisory functions of a foreman, as distributing work under the direction of the chief inspector to employees in the group, in accordance with production schedules; checking work of other inspectors; instructing other employees in the group in their jobs; and forwarding production information to other departments."

Prior to the time the company had promoted the grievant to the group leader job and during the period he served in that job the company did not employ a foreman in the inspection department on the day shift.

Then, in order to improve its supervision in the inspection department on the day shift, the company employed a foreman for that shift and assigned to him, as part of his supervisory duties, those routine group leader duties theretofore performed by the grievant. Since the need for a group leader for inspectors on the day shift no longer existed, the company transferred him back to his former job of inspector, in lieu of laying him off, at the maximum rate for that grade, as provided for by the contract.

The seniority provisions provided, in that part material to the dispute:

> Seniority shall be based upon length of service from the date of hiring in the plant. In all cases of layoffs, rehiring and transfers, length of service within the plant shall govern within each of the occupations listed in Schedule A attached hereto. In the event a layoff is required, then the employee in that occupation who has the shortest seniority in the plant, rather than in that occupation, shall be the first to be laid off. Rehiring within any occupation shall be in the reverse order to that in which the employees were laid off.
>
> So far as is reasonably practical, the Employer will transfer employees (by virtue of their plant-wide seniority and who would otherwise be laid off) to work in another group or department, provided that they are qualified and competent to do the job to which they are transferred. An employee accepting another job in lieu of layoff shall be entitled to the job from which he was laid off when it becomes active.

During the processing of the grievance the union had claimed that the company should have offered the leadman's job on the night shift to the grievant because he had greater seniority than the employee then filling it. At the third step of the grievance procedure the company conceded that the grievant had seniority under the contract to bump the leadman on the night shift; but the grievant refused to accept transfer to the night shift and refrained from exercising his seniority rights to that job.

At the arbitration hearing the union claimed that the company did not have the right to demote the grievant from the leadman's job on the day shift.

117

The company claimed:

Operational and production needs to improve its supervisory functions in inspection on the day shift necessitated the hiring of a foreman on that shift; that upon transferring the routine supervisory duties theretofore performed by [the grievant] . . . to the foreman, the need for a group leader in inspection on the day shift no longer existed; and that the group leader's job on that shift, having been eliminated, the company demoted the grievant to his regular production job of inspector D in lieu of laying him off in accordance with his seniority rights and at the proper rate of pay for his production job, as called for by the contract.

Finding that the company had not violated the contract when it eliminated the group leader job on the day shift and demoted the grievant to his former production job of inspector, I denied the union's grievance. In my award I said:

The proof establishes that the need for a group leader in inspection on the day shift no longer existed, when the company employed a foreman and transferred to him the limited supervisory duties which had theretofore been performed by the group leader. In the exercise of its management's rights to determine the composition and duties of its supervisory staff, which the collective bargaining contract does not circumscribe, the company sought to better its supervision and improve its production efficiency among the inspectors. The proof establishes and the arbitrator finds that the company predicated its action in eliminating the group leader in inspection upon business and operational needs—and that its action did not violate the rights of the employees in the bargaining unit covered by the contract.

Then, finding that the contract "does not restrict the company from eliminating a job filled by an employee in the bargaining unit—when the need for that job no longer exists—and laying off an employee who theretofore had filled that job, in accordance with his seniority rights under the contract," I said:

When the company employed a foreman on the day shift and transferred to him those limited supervisory duties theretofore performed

118

by the group leader, its action constituted a material change in means, methods and procedures of production which the contract does not restrict the company from undertaking. The group leader job, having been eliminated, the company demoted the grievant to his regular production job of inspection D at the maximum rate of his classification, as called for by the contract. Though the grievant did have the right to displace the group leader inspector D on the night shift over whom he had seniority, it appears he did not choose to exercise such seniority right, though the company had offered him that opportunity during the processing of the grievance.

The Case of Superseniority for Union Officers

During a slack period in production layoffs occurred in several departments of the plant. To provide work for some of the retained employees, the company assigned them to what the parties called miscellaneous "fill-in" work available in some of the departments.

Such fill-in work did not constitute classified jobs and only indirectly related to the regular production jobs of employees in those departments. The company paid an employee assigned to such fill-in work, in lieu of laying him off, an hourly rate equal to his average earnings.

At the time the layoffs occurred the union requested the company to allow several union officers from other departments affected by the layoff to perform the fill-in work exclusively as a regular job. The seniority provisions of the contract provided:

> Seniority lay-offs and recalls shall be by categories, departments and operations, not plant-wide, both as to existing and new departments and operations . . .
>
> In any event, the Union trustees, sergeants at arms, Shop Stewards and Executive Board, not exceeding respectively three (3), two (2), three (3) and nine (9) in number, the President, Vice-President, Financial Secretary and Recording Secretary of the Union, shall, during their respective terms of office, have plant-wide seniority on lay-offs and recalls, provided such official can satisfactorily perform the operation affected.

Under that latter provision those union officials had the right to exercise their plant-wide seniority to displace retained permanent

119

employees in other departments. But some of the union officials didn't want to exercise their preferential seniority because it would cause the layoff of an equivalent number of retained permanent employees in other departments. Instead, the union requested the company to allow those union officials to perform the miscellaneous fill-in work in other departments in lieu of accepting layoff.

The company refused on the grounds that the fill-in work did not constitute regular production work or separate job categories; and in conformity with its long-standing practice the company had kept such miscellaneous work in reserve as fill-in work for employees working regularly in those departments.

The company did not object to the affected union officials exercising their plant-wide superseniority to replace a retained permanent employee. The officials affected, however, declined to do so and instead accepted layoff. The union then appealed to arbitration.

At the arbitration hearing the union claimed that the company "should have acceded to its request, and should have provided these union officials with such miscellaneous fill-in work, wherever it was available, thus avoiding their making a choice of displacing regular production workers or accepting a layoff."

The company claimed that the "contract establishes the scope and manner of exercising preferential seniority rights of union officials, which the union voluntarily refused to follow in this instance," and that to grant the union's request would conflict with the seniority provision and the past practice under it.

I denied the union's grievance, finding that the union sought a "right" for its officials the contract did not give. In my award I said:

> It is conceded that the layoffs took place in conformity with the above-quoted article. The union officials involved were not denied their right to exercise plant-wide seniority under the contract. The purposes for which union officials are granted preferential seniority rights during their respective terms of office are to retain in the plant, during periods of layoff, experienced union officials and shop stewards to handle the day-to-day problems that may arise, and to aid in the observance of the contract provisions. By exercising their right of plant-wide seniority, the affected union officials could have satisfied these purposes. They,

however, voluntarily chose not to do so, and, instead, voluntarily accepted a layoff. In so doing, the union cannot now validly claim a breach of the contract by the company.

Noting that the union sought, in effect, "another or supplementary method of preferential seniority for union officials than that set forth and agreed to by the parties in their contract," I said:

> In the absence of a modification of the contract by mutual agreement of the parties, the present contractual provisions are binding upon the arbitrator, as well as upon the parties. Subdivision J of Article 24 of the contract, which confirms this conclusion, provides, in part, as follows: "This Agreement contains the entire understanding between the Parties, and shall not be waived or in any respect changed, except in a writing signed by both Parties."
>
> That the union's proposal may have been a salutary expedient under the circumstances facing it is not material nor controlling. The language and intent of the parties under the above-quoted seniority provision is clear and unambiguous. It must be applied by the arbitrator to the facts of this case.

Then, finding that the company had assigned the fill-in work in the way it had assigned it in the past, I said:

> In the absence of any contractual right of the union to exclusive performance by union officials of this miscellaneous work, no right thereto can be held to exist. The company is not obligated to change its normal method and procedure of production for the convenience of union officials, who for their own reasons, prefer to waive their right of preferential seniority given them under the contract. In fact, had it done so in the instances complained of, a number of the retained permanent employees in some of the departments would not have had . . . work and some of them would probably have been laid off. The very result the union sought to accomplish by waiving its right of preferential seniority under the contract would have been defeated. No basis exists under the contract to substantiate the union's claim for a substituted or supplementary method of preferential seniority for union officials. The arbitrator has no authority to uphold such claim.

121

Acquiring, Retaining, Accumulating, and Losing Seniority Rights

The contract between the parties creates and governs the seniority rights of employees covered by that contract. No other contract, nor any past practice under any other contract, determines the seniority rights of those employees.

Most contracts provide a trial or probationary period for a newly hired employee before he attains any seniority. Usually the company retains the right to discharge an employee during his probationary period with or without cause and without recourse to the grievance or arbitration procedures. In such cases the law prohibits a company from discriminating against any employee because of his union membership or activity or because of race, creed, color, national origin, age, or sex; and the law protects an employee's seniority rights, to the extent prescribed, during the period of his military service.

Many contracts provide that if the company continues in its employ an employee who completes his probationary period, his seniority dates back to his original date of hiring. Other contracts may grant limited seniority rights to part-time or seasonal employees, among themselves, depending upon what the parties to that contract agreed to.

Essentially then, the contract creates and governs the seniority rights of employees it covers. Usually the contract allows an employee to retain or accumulate seniority upon temporary transfers or promotion to another job or to consolidated jobs resulting from changes in production methods and upon temporary layoffs and during periods of excused leaves of absence, such as for sickness or injury, maternity, personal reasons, or union office or activities.

Contracts usually set forth certain reasons that will break or terminate an employee's seniority rights, such as:

1. Voluntary resignation from employment.
2. Discharge for cause.
3. Layoff extending for an uninterrupted specified period of time.
4. Failure to report for work or to respond while on layoff within a specified period after written notice of recall.

5. Absence from work for a specified number of days without permission and without a reasonable excuse.

6. Permanent shutting down of plant or departments or removal of operations to a new location.

7. Acceptance of severance pay, if provided for, that terminates employment.

8. Transfer or promotion to a job outside of the bargaining unit, such as to a supervisory, technical or salaried job:

    1. in excess of a specified period of time; or

    2. retaining the seniority gained while in a job in the bargaining unit, but not accumulating seniority rights while outside the bargaining unit.

Unless by their contract the parties agree otherwise, seniority rights apply only to employees within the bargaining unit. Seniority rights do not extend to employees filling jobs outside of the unit, nor upon transfers out of or back to the bargaining unit unless the contract covers the seniority rights of such employees.

THE CASE OF THE TRANSFER BACK
TO A BARGAINING UNIT JOB

The company had promoted an employee from his bargaining unit job of milling machine operator to dispatch planner, a job outside the bargaining unit. He had acquired a little over eight years seniority in his bargaining-unit job and had worked in his job outside the bargaining unit for two and a half years.

Then, due to a change in production needs, the company transferred him back to his former operator's job in the bargaining unit, leaving on layoff other operators all of whom had less than eight years seniority.

The union filed a grievance claiming that the company had violated the contract by failing to recall one of the laid-off operators in preference to the former operator the company had transferred back to the bargaining unit.

123

The company denied the grievance on the ground that the employee it had transferred back to the bargaining unit had retained, under the contract, the seniority he had acquired while in the bargaining unit; and since he had greater seniority than any of the operators on layoff, he had priority to the job. The union then appealed to arbitration.

At the arbitration hearing the union argued that "employees have seniority rights to jobs in the bargaining unit only so long as they continue in the bargaining unit" and that "once an employee leaves the bargaining unit, to accept a promotion or transfer to a job outside the unit, he loses all rights he had acquired while in the unit." In support of its position the union relied upon the recognition clause, which provided:

> This Agreement applies only to the hourly paid production, maintenance, receiving and shipping department employees, including store clerks and inspectors having no supervisory duties over other inspectors, employed at the Employer's factory . . . and shall not apply to executives, foremen, assistant foremen, clerical workers, timekeepers, engineering department employees (including technicians, engineers and draftsmen), salaried employees, rest-room matrons, guards, watchmen, professional employees and supervisors as defined in the Act.

The company argued that "an employee transferred to a job outside the bargaining unit does not forfeit the seniority he has gained while working in the bargaining unit so long as he continues to be employed by the Employer" and that the contract "specifies only five reasons for which length of continuous service of an employee shall be deemed broken," none of which had occurred to break the transferred employee's seniority rights gained during the time he worked in the bargaining unit job.

In support of its position the company relied upon the seniority provisions which provided:

> The length of continuous service of an employee shall be deemed broken for any of the following reasons:
>
> 1. If the employee voluntarily terminates employment.
> 2. If the employee is discharged.

3. If the employee, within ninety-six (96) hours after date of mailing notice of recall by registered mail . . . does not notify the Employer that he will return to work immediately.
4. If the employee is absent for forty-eight (48) or more consecutive hours . . .
5. If the employee has not been reemployed by the Employer within twelve (12) months from the date of the employee's last layoff.

In further support of its position the company argued that the union had raised this "very issue" during the negotiations for the present contract by its demand to add to seniority the following clause:

K All employees leaving the established bargaining unit shall relinquish all seniority rights within the scope of this Agreement.

The company claimed that it had then asserted its present position, and the union had withdrawn its demand for the "forfeiture clause" in the renewal contract, and therefore the arbitrator "has no authority to grant indirectly, such a clause" which the parties themselves had washed out during negotiations.

I denied the union's grievance solely on the ground that since the union had raised during negotiations the very question submitted in this arbitration case, the arbitrator did not have authority to bargain in what the parties themselves had bargained out at the negotiations. In my award I said:

The existing contract is silent on the question involved in this case. It contains no direct reference or clause as to what is to happen to an employee's accrued seniority rights, when he is transferred to a position outside the bargaining unit. The reason for its omission has been established by the proof. The union raised the question during the negotiations leading to the present contract. It was then bargained out. It cannot be bargained in by way of an arbitration, under the guise of interpreting or construing other contract clauses, however related.

Then, noting that the arbitration clause limited the arbitrator's authority to a "question of construction or interpretation or application of the provisions of this Agreement" and further provided that he shall "not add to or subtract from" the agreed upon clauses, I said:

125

From the clauses relied upon by the union, under the facts in this case, the arbitrator cannot find that the parties intended that an employee forfeits his accrued seniority when he takes a job outside the bargaining unit. The facts clearly establish that the parties did not intend to include such a forfeiture clause. They bargained it out during contract negotiations. A forfeiture of an employee's accrued seniority rights cannot be implied or construed from other unambiguous contract clauses. To do so, under the facts in this case, would be stretching accepted rules of contract construction beyond reason. It would result in the arbitrator adding to the contract the very clause that the parties agreed would not be in their contract . . .

To imply the presence or effect of a clause that the parties discussed but did not put into their contract, is clearly beyond the arbitrator's jurisdiction and authority.

Finding that the issue in dispute did not concern "jobs that may or may not be covered by the contract" but essentially "with the contractual rights, as between two or more employees to one available job" and that the negotiating history showed the parties themselves had not incorporated the forfeiture clause the union had demanded, I said:

The union sought to have this added during negotiations. It was not. It cannot now be added by the arbitrator under the cloak of interpreting other unambiguous contract clauses. That is a matter for collective bargaining. It must be left to the parties themselves to work out in future negotiations.

THE CASE OF CHANGING SENIORITY RIGHTS
DURING THE CONTRACT TERM

The company began laying off its employees preparatory to shutting down operations in all its branches. Then, following discussions with the union, the company agreed to consider maintaining operations in the bacon slicing and packing department and the shipping and warehouse department in one of its branches provided it could retain the "most experienced operators in each irrespective of the seniority provisions of the contract." This would save the jobs of about 20 percent of the employees in that branch.

126

The union agreed to allow the company to retain or recall from layoff the most experienced operators regardless of their seniority standing provided the company agreed to retain or recall from layoff three other employees, also out of seniority, to represent the union's interest in the reduced work force. The company agreed to the union's request, and the parties made the bargain on that basis.

The company then recalled those employees whom it considered most experienced as well as the three employees the union had requested, leaving on layoff other qualified employees who had greater seniority.

The seniority provision of the contract provided:

33.   Branch-wide seniority shall be in effect in the Company's branch. In all cases of increase or decrease of work force and in all cases of promotions and demotions, length of continuous service shall be the determining factor, provided the necessary ability is present.

Shortly thereafter the union filed a grievance claiming that "it had not intended that the company could retain employees with less seniority, as long as there were employees on layoff with greater length of service who had the necessary ability . . . to do the work, as provided for by the contract."

The company denied the grievance, claiming "that was the very basis upon which the company had decided to continue operations in the two departments and upon which it had gone along with the union in agreeing to retain or recall three employees, proposed by the union, out of seniority standing." The union then appealed to arbitration.

At the arbitration hearing the union argued that it had not "intended during the discussion . . . that the company could determine in its own discretion who, among the employees, had the necessary ability to do the available work; or that the company could select those from among the qualified employees whom it wanted."

The company argued that the "union had agreed to allow the company to determine who, among the men employees in the shipping and warehouse department, it thought had the necessary ability to do the available work, irrespective of the seniority provisions—just as the union had, concededly, agreed with respect to the women operators in the bacon department"; and the "fact that the union, during those discussions, requested the company to retain or recall three employees out of seniority, shows the bargain the parties had made to resolve the problem that faced them and to accommodate the needs of each under the special circumstances then prevailing."

I denied the union's grievance, finding the evidence established that the "parties agreed and intended to suspend the operation of the seniority provisions of the contract, in staffing both departments which the company sought to continue." In my award I said:

> The company agreed to recall, outside of the seniority provisions, three employees whom the union wanted to have retained among the remaining employees—and the union agreed that the company could select those remaining employees, whom it considered had the necessary ability to do the available work, irrespective of their seniority standing. That was the "bargain" that the parties made. Any contrary finding would do violence to the whole solution of the unusual problem which faced the parties at that time.

Noting that the present dispute stemmed from a misunderstanding as to what each party had agreed to in their discussions, I said:

> The requests and counter-requests of the parties and their subsequent actions satisfy the arbitrator that the parties made a bargain for staffing both departments on the basis of disregarding the seniority provisions of the contract. The company fulfilled its part of that bargain by retaining three employees, outside of their seniority standing, selected by the union . . . If the other half of the bargain had not been as the company's representatives testified to, namely, that the company could select the remaining employees it determined had the necessary ability to do the available work, there would have been no justification for the union to have made its request or for the company to have agreed to it.

Then, finding that the parties had "the power . . . to change or suspend by mutual agreement, during the contract term, the operation of the seniority clause," I said:

128

Seniority under a collective bargaining contract establishes only employee contractual rights of preference or priority—not proprietary rights to a job. The contract grants the priority to a qualified employee, as between two or more employees, within the bargaining unit or covered by the contract.

The priority extends only to an available job, within the agreed-upon work unit, and is conditioned by the objective factors by which the parties define seniority under their contract.

Section 33 of the contract established a geographical work unit—"branchwide"—and defines seniority by two objective factors, "continuous service" and "necessary ability . . . present" at the time the employee seeks to exercise his priority.

The parties having the power and authority in the first instant to contract for the type of seniority system they want, have the power and authority to change, alter or modify it, by mutual agreement at any time during or after the contract term and to contract for a different system.

Finding that the parties had "agreed and intended to change their seniority system to meet the change in circumstances and to satisfy the needs of each," and that the company's action did not violate the new agreement, I said:

> It was upon that new contractual agreement that the company and the union agreed to staff the complement of employees in the two remaining departments. The parties having mutually agreed to such change, their new contractual agreement binds the arbitrator, as it does both parties. The arbitrator has no authority under the guise of an arbitration, to change a clear and unambiguous agreement.

Rules Governing the Work Unit, Transfers, Retention and Loss of Seniority Rights

Summing up the seniority rules for administering the work unit and the seniority rules governing transfers, vacancies, posting openings, superseniority, and acquiring, retaining, and losing seniority rights during the contract term:

129

Rule 1. The negotiators can establish the work unit within which seniority operates—Types I, II or III—in two ways:

1. Geography or area;
2. Jobs or crafts.

Rule 2. A broad work unit—area or jobs:

1. Increases competition among employees for available jobs, which offsets the apparent increase in opportunities for an employee to protect his job security and to avoid layoff.
2. Increases chain bumpings, multiple transfers, training or learning periods and inefficient or costly practices among employees for available jobs, thus offsetting the foreman's apparent flexibility in utilizing available employees' skills and assigning work.

Rule 3. A narrow work unit—area or jobs:

1. Reduces competition among employees for available jobs, thus offsetting the apparent decrease in opportunities for an employee to protect his job security from layoff from work.
2. Reduces chain bumpings, multiple transfers, training or learning periods, and inefficient or costly practices, thus offsetting the foreman's apparent restriction in utilizing available employees' skills and assigning work.

Rule 4. Homogeneity of jobs and job skills is the key to operating efficiency and job security. A work unit composed of homogeneous jobs and job skills best accommodates technological changes in production and best satisfies employees' job security.

Rule 5. A family or group of related or interchangeable jobs, job skills, or crafts with lines of progression up or down:

Fortifies union security by removing the threats of competing unions to fractionalize the bargaining unit into separate skilled units or the possibility of contracting out work.

Fortifies employees' job security by reducing competition for available jobs and by offering opportunities to advance in jobs, job skills and earnings.

Fortifies the foreman's supervisory job by providing flexibility in assigning available work and jobs among qualified employees; by allowing employees' skills and operating equipment to be fully utilized; by affording greater opportunities to improve the quality of the work force and accommodate future production and personnel needs in an expanding—or contracting—bargaining unit; and by protecting his management's security of enterprise in a competitive market.

Rule 6. Unless the contract provides otherwise, the foreman retains the right to transfer qualified employees to and among jobs or operating sections in the work unit when necessitated by lateness, absenteeism, temporary increase or decrease in workloads, changes in production methods, machine breakdowns, or other operating, production, or personnel difficulties.

Rule 7. Seniority rights apply only to an available job. Seniority does not create jobs or work. A job or work must be available at the time an employee asserts or exercises his seniority rights.

Rule 8. Unless the contract provides otherwise, the shift of a job constitutes an integral part of that job to which an employee's seniority rights in the work unit apply.

Rule 9. Superseniority of authorized shop stewards or union officers, if agreed upon, applies only to layoffs and recalls after layoffs if qualified for the available work and does not extend seniority rights to other job preferences or benefits unless the contract provides differently.

Rule 10. Unless the applicable law provides otherwise, the contract creates and governs seniority rights of employees covered by that contract. No other contract—nor any past practice under any other contract—determines the seniority rights of those employees.

Rule 11. Seniority rights apply only to employees within the bargaining unit or otherwise covered by the contract. Seniority rights do not extend to jobs or employees outside the bargaining unit or upon transfers out of or back to the bargaining unit unless the contract covers the seniority rights of such employees to such jobs.

Rule 12. The parties to the contract retain the legislative power, as distinguished from the delegated authority of an arbitrator as the parties' mutual agent, to change, modify, or suspend during the contract term, by mutual agreement, the seniority system set up under that contract, and to set up, by mutual agreement, a new or different seniority system before, during, or after the contract term.

SECTION TWO

The Rules of Past Practice

5

What Makes a Past Practice?

To begin with, an established past practice shows:

1. What the parties meant or intended by a word, phrase, or clause in the written contract by the way they themselves interpreted, construed or applied that word, phrase or clause in the past; or

2. A benefit or working condition not set forth in the written contract that the company, through its supervisors, granted or allowed the employees to enjoy in the past.

You see, Mr. Foreman, your management has been a party to every past practice! You, or other supervisory personnel administering the written contract, initiated or acquiesced in every past practice under it. No employee, no shop steward, and no arbitrator created a past practice that you or your predecessor started or allowed to come into being. You and your fellow foremen alone created every past practice!

Of course, in deciding a dispute over the meaning of a clause or a working condition under the contract, the arbitrator's award constitutes a contract of settlement, and his decision may eliminate a past practice or start a new practice under it. But as to the past practices you or your predecessor started or allowed, the arbitrator takes them as he finds them to help him resolve an ambiguity in the written contract. As the United Rubber Worker's manual tells shop stewards:

> You'll understand the contract better if you know about actual grievance settlements in other departments. Sometimes the union and the employer have agreed on interpretations that aren't written into the contract.

Maybe you, Mr. Foreman, started a past practice in your department by paying employees for overtime hours missed because you passed them over in the overtime roster by mistake even though the written terms of the contract didn't obligate you to make such payments.

Suppose the contract requires you to "equally distribute" overtime among the employees in your department. By error you passed over an employee whose turn came up for the overtime. Does the contract require you to pay for the overtime hours the employee missed? Does it require you to distribute equally available overtime every day? Every week? Every month? Your contract may say nothing on that point because the negotiators just didn't consider over what period you had to equally distribute overtime. Then why not interpret the clause to require you to equalize overtime over a reasonable period, say, six months or a year, depending upon the amount of overtime that usually becomes available in your department?

Instead of correcting your error in the overtime roster by assigning the next opportunity for overtime to the passed-over employee, you begin a practice of paying twice for work done once. But the written provision didn't obligate you to equalize overtime that way; and the negotiators may never have intended that when they bargained out the clause.

But the practice you started doesn't stop there. The union, through its monolithic shop steward system in the plant, confronts your fellow foremen in their departments with your practice. If you do it, why shouldn't they? And for a very good reason: to satisfy the social rule of equality of treatment in administering the single written contract. If your fellow foremen in other departments follow suit, you have the beginnings of a past practice that may bind you and them in the future.

On the other hand, perhaps you've started a practice under another clause that serves your management's interests. Thus, you may have interpreted the language of the grievance provision so as to limit the shop steward's activities in your department to handling pending grievances according to the time limits and steps set forth in the grievance procedure. In that way you've started a practice that restrains the shop steward from engaging in other activities during working hours, such as looking into complaints, consulting with shop stewards in other departments, or carrying on union business that interrupts his and other of your employees' production time—activities he could reasonably do outside of working hours.

You see, Mr. Foreman, past practices necessarily arise when you exercise your right of administrative initiative by initially interpreting each written contract provision and initially applying every benefit and working condition under the written contract. In doing your job of managing you will of necessity create past practices in administering the written contract clauses. You can't avoid starting them; but you can avoid inefficient or costly ones.

How Past Practices Arise

The collective bargaining agreement states the rights and duties of the parties. It is more than a contract; it is a generalized code to govern a myriad of cases which the draftsmen cannot wholly anticipate . . . Gaps may be left to be filled in by reference to the practices of the particular industry and of the various shops covered by the agreement. Many of the specific practices which underlie the agreement may be unknown, except in hazy form, even to the negotiators.

That's how the United States Supreme Court described the labor contract in the case between the Warrior and Gulf Navigation Company and the United Steelworkers of America. In administering that generalized code, Mr. Foreman, you try to determine what the negotiators intended under the language used. The seniority provision may speak of "ability" without defining what the word covers.

Did the negotiators intend you to limit the standard of ability solely to the technical skills required for the job? Or did they intend to cover equally the normal responsibilities that attach to every job, including attendance, personal conduct, and observance of plant rules and safety practices?

Similarly, if the contract provides for a trial period upon promotion, did they intend you to allow the promoted employee an opportunity to demonstrate that he qualifies for the new job? Or to provide a training period to learn the new job? In computing vacation pay, did the negotiators intend you to count only time worked? Or to give you latitude to include such nonworking periods as absences during personal leaves or on layoff?

How you initially interpret the generalized code the contract sets up and how you fill in the gaps the negotiators didn't anticipate determine whether the practices you start will serve your operating needs or end up as costly ones. Therefore, when you initially interpret the contract language or initially apply the contract benefits, consider the future operating needs in your department as well as the operating needs of your fellow foremen in their departments, who administer the one contract. Retain flexibility in applying contract terms, avoid interpreting language that may restrict you in the future, and construe contract benefits so as to prevent abuse from arising under them later on.

THE FOREMAN'S AREA OF DECISION MAKING

Rumors sometimes start a past practice. What one shop steward suggested at a union stewards' meeting: "It's about time we got a paid meal after two hours overtime," became an accomplished fact, as retold by another shop steward to his foreman. Investigate the facts before you carry over, Mr. Foreman, a claimed practice from another department that the contract doesn't provide for.

Circumstances may arise in your department warranting an additional five-minute wash-up time on some days at the end of the shift; or production difficulties may necessitate giving the maintenance crew a twenty-minute paid lunch to get the machines going. Although the written contract may not provide for such benefits, the occasional granting of them, supported by the operational needs out of which they arose, does not create a practice that binds you or other foremen in the future. But when the production difficulty or operating need ends and you allow that extra benefit to continue uninterruptedly in the future, you may have a past practice that added itself to the written contract.

"There is a small area of decision that the foreman does make interpreting policy," the UAW *Steward's Guide* tells its shop stewards, "and it is in this area that the union can gain by establishing a cooperative relationship."

Correct, but if that "cooperative relationship" starts whittling away your management's rights your negotiators fought so hard to preserve at the bargaining table, Mr. Foreman, you may find yourself strait-jacketed in the future by practices you had no idea would come to pass. The contract may require you to pay average earnings for non-working time caused by lack of materials or breakdown of machines due to no fault on the employee's part; but if you begin paying average earnings for reworking improperly machined parts, you've begun a practice that may bind you and your fellow foremen in the future. Likewise, if you begin pyramiding shift differentials and overtime with other types of premium pay instead of paying the single highest premium rate, you've initiated a practice that may end up adding itself to the written contract.

How do you distinguish between an occasional practice and an established practice? How do you tell, Mr. Foreman, whether a practice you started or acquiesced in adds to the written contract that binds your management and the union?

THE CASE OF COMPUTING PAY FOR SPLIT VACATIONS

The union filed a grievance claiming that the company had improperly computed the increased vacation benefits granted certain employees by the renewal contract.

Under the renewal contract, which became effective August 1st, the parties increased vacation benefits and agreed to apply them retroactively to those employees who had already received their vacations before August 1st, under the prior contract.

The renewal contract continued unchanged Section 4 of the prior contract, which set forth the method for computing vacation pay. It provided:

4. For the purpose of vacation pay the straight time weekly pay of an employee shall be equal to his average straight time earnings received by him during the ten (10) week period immediately preceding such vacation.

The renewal contract granted the grievant, whose case the union submitted as representative of other employees similarly affected, four additional days vacation. He had already received his vacation pay in June based on the five-day work week he had worked during the preceding ten-week period. The company paid him his extra four days vacation pay computed on the basis of the vacation pay he had received in June. However, he and the other employees similarly affected had worked a six-day work week for an extended period after they returned from vacation. The company denied the grievance and the union appealed to arbitration.

At the arbitration hearing the union claimed that under Section 4 the "company should have computed [the grievant's] vacation pay—as well as the additional vacation pay of all other employees similarly situated, who had received increased vacation benefits under the renewal contract—on the employee's average earnings during the ten week period immediately preceding the taking of the additional vacation benefits."

The company claimed that the grievant "had been properly paid his additional vacation benefits; and the company's method of computing the additional vacation benefits, on the basis of the employee's original vacation pay, was a fair method and equalized the vacation benefits for all employees."

I sustained the union's grievance, finding that the parties had agreed "to apply the increased vacation benefits retroactively to all employees, including those who had, prior to August 1st, received their vacation under the schedule of the then existing contract." In my award I said:

During the negotiations of the renewal contract, neither party raised the method to be used in computing the additional days of vacation to be granted retroactively. The parties frankly stated at the oral hearing in this case that they did not discuss this subject during negotiations. They did, however, continue unchanged Section 4 of the contract, which provided that vacation pay shall be equal to average straight time earnings . . . during the ten (10) week period immediately preceding such vacation.

Then, finding that the "way in which the parties themselves applied this section in the past, in situations comparable to the present one, removes any ambiguity as to what the parties intended by the phrase 'such vacation' in that section," I said:

> The proof establishes that during [the two prior years], employees who had taken split vacations under the vacation article had received vacation pay computed on their average earnings during each separate ten week period, immediately preceding each part of the split vacation. Thus, the parties themselves applied this section in the past in the very way the union contends it should be applied in the present case.
>
> The way the parties themselves applied an ambiguous clause in the past provides material facts for the arbitrator to determine what the parties meant by that clause, and how they intended it should be applied. The past actions of the parties under Section 4 satisfies the standards which the arbitrator finds necessary to support such a past practice, namely: (1) an unequivocal practice (2) that has been clearly enunciated and is readily ascertainable over a reasonably long period of time, and (3) that has been acted upon and accepted by the parties themselves as a fixed and established method to be applied under Section 4 of the contract.

Accordingly, and based upon that established practice, I awarded that "pay for the additional vacation benefits granted to employees under the renewal contract, effective August 1st, shall be computed upon the employee's average straight time earnings during the ten-week period immediately preceding the time he received his additional vacation benefits."

The Three Standards to Determine a Binding Past Practice

When the language of a written provision clearly shows what the parties had agreed to or how they intended to apply it, then the written provision controls, and a contrary past practice that has misinterpreted or misapplied that written provision gives way and falls.

When, however, the language of a written provision does not, on its face, clearly show what the parties had agreed to or how they intended to apply it, then the way the parties themselves, through their authorized representatives, foremen and shop stewards, interpreted or applied that ambiguous written provision in the past provides material facts in determining what they had agreed to or intended thereunder.

To find an established past practice that binds both parties, those material facts must satisfy the following three standards that show that the past practice has been:

1. *Unequivocal*—granted, allowed, interpreted, or applied consistently, regularly, uniformly, and without break

2. *Clearly enunciated*—freely and openly allowed or acquiesced in, and readily ascertainable as existing over a reasonably long period of time

3. *Accepted and acted upon*—by the parties themselves through their authorized agents in administering the written contract and settling grievances under it during the contract term.

Unless the written contract provides otherwise, a practice that satisfies those three standards becomes a fixed and established past practice that supplements—adds to or modifies—the written contract.

THE CASE OF THE EQUIVOCAL AND
UNEQUIVOCAL PAST PRACTICE

On February 16th the company temporarily shut down operations in its plant and laid off all its employees. The layoff continued until about the middle of March.

The holiday clause included Washington's Birthday, February 22nd, as one of the paid holidays. The company did not pay any employees for that holiday on the ground that it fell during the period of layoff.

Prior to February 16th the grievant and some other employees had taken their regular vacations, which ended during the plant shutdown period. The company did not recall them after their vacation period ended because of the plant shutdown until about the middle of March, when the company recalled the other employees on layoff.

The union filed a grievance claiming that the contract entitled the grievant, as well as other employees similarly affected, to holiday pay for Washington's Birthday. The company denied the grievance, claiming that the grievant and the other employees did not qualify for that paid holiday. The union then appealed to arbitration.

Article IX of the contract provided:

Section 1. The following days will be considered holidays for the purpose of this article: . . . Washington's Birthday . . .

Section 2 . . . In order to qualify for holiday pay under this section, an employee must meet all of the following conditions:

(a) The employee shall have sixty (60) days or more of continuous service with the Company immediately prior to the holiday.

(b) The employee performs his scheduled hours of work on his last scheduled work day preceding the holiday and also on his first scheduled work day following the holiday.

Employees scheduled to work on a holiday but failing to report for and perform such work shall not be entitled to any holiday pay.

At the arbitration hearing the parties stipulated the following issue:

Did the corporation violate the contract and/or past practice in failing to grant holiday pay . . . for February 22nd?

The union claimed that the grievant "fulfilled the eligibility requirements of Section 2(b) in that he performed his scheduled hours of work on his last scheduled work day preceding the holiday . . . the work day before he left on his vacation; and his first scheduled work day following the holiday . . . the first day the company scheduled him to return to work following his vacation period and the re-opening of the plant after the shutdown."

In support of its claim the union argued that "the language of Section 2(b) is clear and unambiguous and the parties' submission agreement constrains the arbitrator to apply that Section literally, as the parties agreed to under the contract language."

143

The company claimed that "though the language of Section 2(b), relied upon by the union, speaks of his first scheduled work day following the holiday, the parties had applied said Section 2(b) in the past to mean that the employee must perform work in the week immediately following his vacation, in accordance with the procedure of administration which the company had established . . . and which the company claims, the union had accepted without question" during all the prior years.

In support of its claim the company relied upon the history of negotiations of prior contracts as well as the present one during which the union had demanded changing the "strict, literal requirements" of Section 2(b) to provide for holiday pay to employees excused from meeting those eligibility requirements because of acceptable personal reasons. The company refused to change the language of Section 2(b) on the ground that the procedure of administration it had set up and which the union had gone along with in the past years satisfied the changes the union sought.

The procedure that the company relied upon in applying Section 2(b) provided:

1. Procedure of Administration Covering Holidays Other Than During Vacation Period:

Contract provides that in order to qualify for holiday pay an employee must perform his scheduled hours of work on his last scheduled work day preceding the holiday and also on his first scheduled work day following the holiday. Under our administration we have not required that a man work either of those days, so long as he has an acceptable reason for missing them, but in any event he must perform work in the week in which the holiday falls. This is a "must" requirement, and, unless complied with, no further consideration is given. One day of work in such holiday week will satisfy this requirement. There is only one exception to this otherwise inflexible standard of having to perform one day of work in the holiday week, and that is, when vacation prevents a man from actually working in the holiday week.

2. Procedure of Administration Covering a Holiday Falling During Vacation Period:

There is nothing in the contract which says a man is entitled to pay for a holiday falling during a vacation period; however, our past practice has been to grant same, but, here again it was necessary to provide certain standards. We have not required that a man work his last scheduled shift prior to his vacation nor his first scheduled shift following his vacation, if his excuse for missing either shift is acceptable, but in any event he must perform work in the week immediately preceding his vacation and in the week immediately following his vacation. This is a "must" requirement, and, unless complied with, no further consideration is given. One day of work in each of these weeks satisfies this requirement.

The parties executed their renewal contracts, including the one under which the present dispute arose, without changing the language of Section 2(b) and without reference to the company's procedure of administration.

As to the first part of the company's procedure of administration, relating to employees not on vacation, the proof showed that for the past five years the company had waived the literal language of Section 2(b) that required an employee to perform work on his scheduled work day before and after the holiday in order to make him eligible for holiday pay and that the company had paid holiday pay consistently, regularly, and without break to employees who worked at least one day in the week in which the holiday fell. The proof also showed that the union did not question the company's procedure of administration as it had applied it to employees other than those on vacation during the period of layoff; and the union had acquiesced in that past practice of applying more liberally the holiday provision than the literal language called for. Finding that employees not on vacation had, during all those past years, accepted the benefits under that past practice, I said in my award:

The evidence establishes and the arbitrator finds that the procedure of administration set up by the company . . . had, insofar as the company had applied it in the past, been accepted and acquiesced in by the union; and the union and the affected employees had accepted the

145

benefits allowed under the more liberal application of Section 2(b) than the literal language of Section 2(b) required. To the extent that the company's procedure established a past practice in construing and applying Section 2(b) that is unequivocal, clearly enunciated, accepted and acted upon by the parties and existed . . . over a reasonably long period of time, such past practice binds the company and the union as well as the arbitrator.

Then, finding that the parties had accepted by their past practice the first part of the company's procedure, I said:

Thus, those employees who were not on vacation during the week in which the holiday, February 22nd, fell and who did not perform work in the week in which the holiday fell, because they had been laid off, were not entitled to holiday pay.

The Exception to the Past Practice Rule

Here the union, having acquiesced in the increased benefits under the more liberal past practice, did not dispute that the parties had made an agreement to substitute the first part of the company's procedure of administration for the language of Section 2(b).

This illustrates the single exception to the rule that if a past practice conflicts with, or contradicts, a clear written provision, the written provision controls for the future of the contract term.

If one party accepts and retains benefits under an established past practice that more liberally construes a written clause, that party cannot complain that the other has not followed the literal language of the written clause. In such case, the past practice constitutes an agreement that modifies the written provision.

Since arbitration functions as a quasijudicial system, the rules of equity apply, just as in any other system that dispenses justice. In seeking equity, both parties must come in with "clean hands." Equity does not countenance one party being unjustly enriched by its own action.

To allow one party to accept and retain the greater benefits under a more liberal past practice would result in that party becoming unjustly enriched by his own conduct. Having voluntarily accepted the con-

146

sideration given under the past practice, it would be inequitable to allow that party to go back to the literal language of the written provision in the future when it serves its convenience in order to obtain additional benefits.

The parties having executed a new agreement for value received, that new agreement represented by the past practice substitutes for the literal language of the written clause and binds both parties for the remainder of the contract term.

Contract Language Prevails over an Unexecuted Agreement

As to the second part of the company's procedure of administration, relating to employees on vacation during the week of the holiday, the proof showed that the company had not in the past applied that part to any employee not recalled to work after his vacation; and since no past practice existed, the union had not in fact accepted or acquiesced in that part of the procedure. In my award I said:

> The evidence, however, fails to establish and the arbitrator does not find that a past practice existed showing that the company had applied its procedure in the past so as to disallow holiday pay to an employee who was on vacation during the week in which the holiday fell; and who, though available, had been prevented from reporting for work in the week immediately following the holiday because he was laid off due to a plant shutdown.

Then, noting that the company relied on its procedure of administration even though it had never applied that part in the past, because no plant shutdown had occurred, and the union relied on the literal language of Section 2(b), which required an employee to work on his last scheduled work day preceding and on his first scheduled work day following the holiday, I held that the language of Section 2(b) prevailed over that part of the company's procedure, which it had never applied in the past. In my award sustaining the union's grievance I said:

147

The evidence offered in this case establishes . . . that the company had not in the past applied this procedure to an employee who was on vacation during the week in which the holiday fell and who, though available, could not work in the week immediately following because he had been laid off. To that extent, the arbitrator finds that no established past practice exists under the company's procedure so as to modify or supersede under the facts in this case the clear language of Section 2(b)—and to that extent the arbitrator sustains the union's grievance and finds that the company violated the contract in failing to grant holiday pay to the grievant . . . for February 22nd . . . [and the other employees similarly affected who would have returned to work after their vacation period ended but for the plant shutdown].

WHAT CONSTITUTES A REASONABLY LONG PERIOD OF TIME?

That depends on how frequently the parties have interpreted a clause in the past or how frequently the company has granted or allowed the benefit or working condition. The type of practice determines its frequency. To put that another way, an inverse ratio between the repetitiveness of the practice and the length of time it existed determines what makes up a reasonably long period of time.

Thus, a period of six to nine months would suffice if the practice occurred every day, such as a ten-minute wash-up on the first shift or a twenty-minute paid lunch period for the third shift. On the other hand, for a Christmas or year-end bonus to become an integral part of the wage structure, the company would have to pay it for, say, three to five years to satisfy that standard since that kind of benefit occurs only once a year.

Likewise, the number and frequency of the times, Mr. Foreman, you interpret the thirty-day trial period for newly hired employees to mean thirty working days and not thirty calendar days, or conversely, would determine the length of time required to satisfy the standard of a reasonably long period of time.

Keep in mind that if the language of a written provision clearly shows what the parties agreed to or how they intended to apply it, then the written provision controls, and a contrary past practice that conflicts with the language or contradicts what the parties reasonably intended under that language falls.

The Umbrella Effect of the Renewal Contract

Suppose a practice meets the three standards to make it a fixed and established practice:

1. Unequivocally granted, interpreted or applied, consistently, uniformly, and without break;
2. Clearly enunciated and freely and openly allowed or acquiesced in (not one that's *sub rosa,* that is, indulged in when the foreman's not around) over a reasonably long period of time; and
3. Accepted and acted upon in administering the written contract and settling grievances during the contract term.

Then negotiations for the renewal contract come around, and neither party says anything about that practice during bargaining. Does the renewal contract carry over and, like an umbrella, bring that past practice into the succeeding contract term? Yes, because by keeping silent about that past practice, an arbitrator could reasonably construe the negotiators' silence to mean that they intended to carry it over into the next contract. Why? Because both parties knew or reasonably should have known that that practice existed unequivocally, clearly enunciated and mutually accepted and acted upon over a reasonably long period of time.

If during the negotiation of the renewal contract one party demands to eliminate an established practice and the negotiators wash out or forget about that demand during bargaining and the renewal contract says nothing about it, then an arbitrator could reasonably find that the negotiators intended the past practice to continue.

In such cases, the past practice forms part of the backdrop of the negotiations and shows the conditions under which the bargain took place. As Arthur J. Goldberg said in his paper "Management's Reserved Rights: A Labor View", delivered at an Annual Conference of the National Academy of Arbitrators:

> In examining the meaning of an agreement, it is proper to inquire about the conditions under which the bargain took place with a presumption that the normal practices which did exist are expected to continue

except as the agreement would require or justify alteration and except as conditions make such past circumstances no longer feasible or appropriate.

As we proceed, keep those two exceptions in mind: (1) "except as the agreement would require or justify alteration"; and (2) "except as conditions make such past circumstances no longer feasible or appropriate."

The Case of the Inequitable Past Practice

For upwards of twenty years the manager of the company's warehouse permitted Jewish employees to take time off from work without loss of pay at certain times of the year to attend religious services. When the practice started, those employees attended services during their regular lunch period and sometimes beyond it. Then, as the years went by, the extra time taken amounted to about two hours on each of those days, and the practice had extended to some of the office personnel.

After relocating its warehouse the company reorganized its operations and made changes in its supervisory personnel. Shortly thereafter the company informed all employees and the union that it would not pay employees who took time off for memorial services for such time.

On the following October 1st, ten employees took time off to attend memorial services, and the company refused to pay them for the time lost from work. The union filed a grievance on their behalf. The company denied it, and the union appealed to arbitration.

At the arbitration hearing the union claimed that the "practice of allowing employees time off to attend memorial services without loss of pay is one of long standing in the plant; that the company knew of this practice, has acquiesced in it, and is therefore bound by it; and the company has no right to discontinue this practice nor to refuse to pay the employees involved for the time lost on October 1."

The company claimed the contract did not obligate it to "pay for time voluntarily taken off from work by any of the employees; that the holiday clause of the contract provides for the observance of certain enumerated religious holidays with pay, and does not include pay for

150

time spent in observing the memorial services; and the company is not obligated under the contract to continue this practice."

I denied the union's grievance, and in my award I said:

> The contract sets forth the rights and obligations of the parties, covering the wages, hours and working conditions of the employees in the bargaining unit, as agreed to by the parties. The holiday clause provides for 11½ holidays with pay. Included are three religious Jewish holidays. Three equivalent days off with pay are provided for non-Jewish employees. The contract does not require the company to pay for time voluntarily taken off by the employees for religious purposes, other than those holidays enumerated.

Noting that the "practice of allowing time off to attend memorial services has materially changed over the years; that what formerly was a short extension of the lunch period for the convenience of those employees desiring to attend such services, has now extended so as to constitute a substantial portion of a work day," I said:

> The contract does not incorporate, by reference, this past practice; nor can it be reasonably inferred, under any of the provisions of the contract, that the parties intended such practice, in light of its history and the fact that it has changed materially, to become a contractual part of their agreement, obligating the company to continue it.

Finding the practice created "an intraplant inequality," I said:

> Workers of other than the Jewish faith in the bargaining unit, who have taken time off to observe their own religious services, have not been and are not being paid for such time off. In light of the history of this past practice and its material extension, the arbitrator cannot reasonably conclude the parties intended to create or to continue such an intraplant inequality.

Must the Contract or Past Practice Be in Writing?

No. The Labor Management Relations Act (Taft-Hartley Law) covering collective bargaining affecting interstate commerce does not require the parties to execute a written contract.

151

The Act, in defining the duty to bargain collectively, requires the parties to:

1. meet at reasonable times,
2. confer in good faith with respect to wages, hours, and other terms and conditions of employment, or the
3. negotiation of an agreement, or
4. any question arising thereunder, and
5. the execution of a written contract incorporating any agreement reached if requested by either party.

The law does not require the parties to set forth in a written document its collective bargaining agreement or any collateral agreements or fixed past practices the parties may have entered into before or after negotiations. The parties need not reduce to writing, if neither one wishes, past grievance settlements, understandings, customary benefits, or precedents that have become fixed as established practices. Where no writing exists to support a past practice, the claiming party may resort to testimony of witnesses. When proved by material facts, oral or in writing, that satisfy the three standards of an unequivocal practice, clearly enunciated and mutually accepted and acted upon over a reasonably long period of time, that practice binds both parties.

You see, Mr. Foreman, the collective bargaining contract, usually in writing, determines the relations of the parties during its term. A fixed past practice adds to or supplements the written contract unless the past practice contradicts a clear contract provision. In handling a grievance in the grievance steps or in arbitration based on a past practice, you frame, submit, and argue—and the arbitration tribunal decides—the same material issue as in any other case: Did the company violate the contract as modified or supplemented by the past practice?

The way you and your fellow foremen administer the contract establishes the custom and usage under that contract; and in the absence of any conflict a fixed past practice shows how the parties intend to interpret the contract clauses, and apply the working conditions.

"A good contract is worth nothing," the UAW *Steward's Guide* tells its committeemen, "unless there is an active and militant group of committeemen who are ready and able to put the contract into effect and make certain that neither the spirit nor the intent of the contract is violated by management."

Proving a Past Practice by the Grievance Record

The United Papermakers and Paperworkers manual tells its shop stewards:

> Your most important tool is the *CONTRACT!* Another important tool is the *RECORD*. An efficient Steward
>
> ✔ Keeps a written record of every grievance—even those not submitted in writing.
> ✔ Keeps file copies of every written grievance, plus a record of the results.
> ✔ Keeps a written record of company practice on working conditions not covered in the contract.
>
> When taking over the job of Steward, ask your predecessor for his records.
>
> When leaving the job of Steward, pass your records along to your successor.

THE WRITTEN GRIEVANCE

> Keep a Record. Written grievances form an important record. They can be used to check on whether the company has lived up to the settlement. Records of past settlements may guide the handling of similar future grievances. Thus, they build up a valuable addition to the original contract, plus providing useful information for next year's bargaining. For the record shows which types of grievances are usually won and which lost. This helps fill in loopholes when a new contract is drafted.

That's what the Communications Workers of America *Steward's Manual* says. "Keep Records of all Grievances," says the UAW *Steward's Guide*. "The written grievance is a valuable record for the union. This record can be used to check on whether the company has followed through on a settlement. This is a way to build up a valuable addition to the general contract. The record of past grievances settled favorably serves in getting good settlements in the future."

"A written record of grievances—especially those you lose—is good

153

to have when the contract comes up for negotiation," says the International Chemical Workers *Handbook For Stewards.* "The record will remind you of your trouble spots, and indicate where changes in the contract should be made to avoid losing some of the grievances in the future."

THE FOREMAN'S WRITTEN ANSWER

"The Foreman may have information about a grievance that you don't have, no matter how carefully you collected the facts," says the United Brewery, Flour, Cereal, Soft Drink and Distillery Workers *Steward's Manual.* "Whenever there's a doubt in your mind, take the complaint up with the foreman. Sometimes you won't know whether it's a grievance until you have gotten further facts from him."

"Once a decision is made, and you not only have the facts written but the decision as well," the Chemical Workers *Handbook* tells its stewards, "you have a written record of the grievance. You may be able to use this later as a precedent in settling another grievance."

SETTLEMENT OF GRIEVANCES

"Often there are grievances which the Foreman can settle in your favor if he feels like it," says the AFL–CIO Shop Steward's manual. The Aluminum Workers International Union *Shop Steward's Manual* tells its shop stewards, "Once the decision is made you have a written record which can be used as a precedent when similar grievances arise at a later date."

The UAW *Steward's Guide* frankly tells its shop stewards: "The grievance procedure is machinery set up in our Contracts so that supplementary agreements can be made as well as establishing precedents and new policies."

The United Glass & Ceramic Workers Union manual *So You're A Grievanceman!* tells its shop stewards:

For the Record
  If a certain grievance is favorably settled once, keep a record of it.
  When a similar case arises again, demand the same result. In court,

cases are frequently decided by rulings handed down in the past. This is called a precedent, and it should be made use of whenever possible.

Yes, that's how the professional administrator plays the game of labor relations; and as professionals you and your fellow foremen should follow the same rules in administering the contract and in handling grievances under it.

KEEP A WRITTEN RECORD IN YOUR DEPARTMENT! ASK YOUR PREDECESSOR FOR HIS WRITTEN RECORD. PASS YOUR RECORD ALONG TO YOUR SUCCESSOR.

When a Past Practice Conflicts with a Written Clause, What Controls?

The written clause! Why? Because the words used in the written clause embody the bargain the negotiators made.

When the language of the clause shows on its face what the parties agreed to, the words used suffice. You need nothing more to interpret those words, for the language itself says what the parties intended and agreed to.

When, however, the negotiators use ambiguous or compromise language to express their bargain, or when you cannot clearly gather from the words used what they intended, then the way foremen and shop stewards interpreted those words or applied the benefits under them in administering the written clause shows what the negotiators meant by the language used to express their intent. A fixed practice then attaches itself to and becomes part of the written clause and, in that sense, supplements the written clause.

The rules of contract construction, to determine what the parties intended by their written agreement, apply to a collective bargaining contract just as to any other contract. Consequently, when a foreman or shop steward relies on an established past practice to support his position in processing a grievance or arbitrating a case, the single standard still applies: Has the foreman's action violated the contract! Not has the foreman violated the past practice, but has the foreman violated the contract as supplemented by the past practice.

155

PAST PRACTICES SUPPLEMENT THE WRITTEN LANGUAGE

The International Chemical Workers *Handbook For Stewards* tells its shop stewards:

> Borderline cases may be harder to win because the contract language may be vague—or there may not be any language at all—or maybe there's a loophole. For example, if the contract says that the workers must work a "reasonable" amount of overtime and the men in your department don't want to work, the settlement of the grievance depends on just what the word "reasonable" means in this situation.

In distributing overtime a past practice may show over what period of time the negotiators intended to equalize the distribution of available overtime. In computing vacation pay an established practice may show what absences from work the parties intended to count or exclude as time worked during the year preceding vacation time. When the holiday clause relieves an employee from meeting the eligibility requirement of working the day before and the day after the paid holiday if he has an "acceptable reason," an established practice may show what the parties meant by an acceptable reason.

The United Steelworkers of America manual *Job of the Steward* advises its shop stewards to look for "interpretations which aren't written into the contract" in this way:

> A contract is like an iceberg—there's a lot below the surface. Sometimes the Union and the employer have agreed on interpretations which aren't written into the contract. To know if the company and the Union are living up to their agreement, you must know what's in it—AND how to interpret it . . . You'll understand the contract better if you know how actual grievances were settled in other departments. Watch for new interpretations of the different clauses and keep up to date with arbitration decisions.

A PAST PRACTICE DOES NOT FORFEIT RIGHTS
UNDER THE WRITTEN CONTRACT

"Your job," the IUE *Leadership Manual* tells its shop stewards, "is to see that the company lives up to the contract every day in every case.

If the employer violates the contract—and gets away with it—on one occasion, he will try it again some other time."

A practice that conflicts with a written clause in effect violates that clause. And a practice, even an established one, that violates a written clause does not supersede the written clause.

Thus, suppose the contract says that foremen shall not do production work except to overcome production difficulties in line with their supervisory duties. If a foreman engages in regular production work that clearly exceeds his supervisory duties and the union hasn't protested for ten years, would that constitute a past practice that binds the union in the future? No, because neither party waives its right for the future to enforce the contractual obligations of the other that the written contract stipulates.

Likewise, if the contract requires employees to work a reasonable amount of overtime and in the past foremen had excused employees from working overtime without asking for a reason, would that past practice make working overtime voluntary on the part of each employee? Or if in the past foremen had not equalized available overtime, as the contract called for, would that past practice leave it up to each foreman to distribute the overtime any way he saw fit? You can see, Mr. Foreman, that those questions implicitly give the answer—No!

Similarly, if one party or the other saw fit in the past not to enforce its rights under the contract, its failure to act would not create a practice whereby it forfeits its rights for the future. Thus, if the union refrains from protesting a foreman's action in assigning work out of classification, that would not create a practice foreclosing the union from protesting similar violations in the future. If the written contract does not prevent the company from subcontracting production or maintenance work, the fact that the company had never in the past subcontracted would not create a practice prohibiting the company from subcontracting in the future.

So too, with enforcing plant rules. If you, Mr. Foreman, in the past did not enforce rules prohibiting smoking, gambling, horseplay, or other personal misconduct, that past practice would not prevent you from starting to enforce those plant rules in the future—after reasonable advance notice of your intended action to the employees and the shop steward.

A past practice that conflicts with a written clause does not constitute an agreement to change that written clause. Neither party waives its contractual rights under the written agreement by any practice that violates its rights under that agreement.

Likewise, neither party relinquishes its rights under the written agreement by failing to enforce those rights in the past. When the language of a clause shows on its face what the parties intended, the language controls and any past practice that misinterpreted the language falls. The written contract determines the wages, hours, and working conditions that govern during the contract term.

You, Mr. Foreman, cannot give more, nor the shop steward accept less, than the written contract calls for. If in the past you or the shop steward had misinterpreted a written clause by giving more or accepting less, neither of you may undo the violation retroactively. However, neither of you forfeit your right to properly interpret and apply the written provision in the future.

"If a practice violates the contract, either side can demand that the agreement be enforced"—says the AFL–CIO *Manual For Shop Stewards*. The manual states the rules of past practice in this way:

> A past practice can be the basis for a grievance, particularly in areas where the contract is silent or unclear. However, grievances in this area can be quite complicated and are governed by some of the following rules: 1) A practice, in order to be considered valid, must be repeated over an extended time period. 2) A practice must be accepted explicitly or implicitly by both parties. In the first case, the union and management have formally agreed to the procedure either orally or in writing. Implicit acceptance exists if neither party formally objected to the procedure over a period of time. 3) If a practice violates the contract, either side can demand that the agreement be enforced. 4) If a practice is bad or unsafe, an arbitrator may throw it out on the grounds that it should never have been established in the first place. 5) Past practice grievances arise out of problems such as subcontracting, job descriptions, and work practices like "wash-up time."

THE CASE OF THE WRITTEN PROVISION VS. PAST PRACTICE

Section C 2 of Article IX of the written collective bargaining contract provided:

158

2. Death Leave—An employee will be assured against loss of pay for absence due to death in immediate family . . . up to three (3) days. Normally this assurance is only to apply up to and including the day of the funeral; however, in cases where extended travel is involved to attend the funeral, the following day will also be included.

The company paid an employee who had traveled to Florida to attend his father's funeral three days pay under that section. The union filed a grievance claiming that the company should have paid him four days pay because of "extended travel." The company denied the grievance, and the union appealed to arbitration.

At the arbitration hearing the union argued that "in all prior cases where an employee had extended travel to attend a funeral, the company's foremen had interpreted the provision as providing 4 days pay and had paid such employees 4 days pay; that the consistent past practice shows the parties had intended Section C 2 to be applied that way; and that such past practice should control in resolving any ambiguity in the language of that section."

The company argued that Section C 2 limited pay in all cases "up to three (3) days; that at no time during negotiations of the present contract nor of any prior contracts covering this benefit did the union demand nor did the company agree to more than 3 days pay in any case; and that any contrary practice by its foremen in granting in the past to some employees more than 3 days leave does not foreclose the company from properly interpreting Section C 2 in the way the parties had expressly agreed to under the explicit language used."

Finding that the parties had agreed by the written provision "to limit the company's obligation, to assure an employee against such loss of pay, for a period up to three (3) days," I denied the union's grievance and in my award I said:

The clear language of Section C 2 as well as the negotiating history support these findings . . .

Under all the contracts including the present one not all employees who suffered death in the family, as defined, received pay for 3 days. In cases where an employee's absence occurred on, say, a Saturday or Sunday—a day outside of his regularly scheduled work week—he did not receive pay for those days. Only where his absence occurs on one or more of his regularly scheduled work days is he assured against loss of pay for such days up to a total of 3 days.

To clarify how the "up to 3 days" should be counted—since some foremen had automatically granted some employees 3 days even though one or more of those days fell outside of an employee's scheduled work week; and other foremen in some cases had failed to include in the 3 days an employee's work day following the day of the funeral, where the employee had to travel a long distance to attend the funeral —the company proposed and the union accepted the second sentence of Section C 2 that states:

"Normally this assurance is only to apply up to and including the day of the funeral; however, in cases where extended travel is involved to attend the funeral, the following day will also be included."

Then, finding that at "no time during any of the contract negotiations did the union demand nor did the company suggest that that sentence added another day to the up to 3 days total explicitly limited in that section," I said:

The evidence establishes and the arbitrator therefore finds that the parties did not intend to add another day to the total 3 days assured under Section C 2—but only to clarify the method in figuring what days were to be included in the 3 days limit the parties had agreed to. The arbitrator finds that the clear language and the negotiating history show the parties agreed to and intended only to provide "up to three (3) days" against loss of pay; and that in counting the days to be included, the day following the funeral, in cases of extended travel, would also be included in the counting. The arbitrator finds Section C 2 clear and unambiguous. The first sentence sets the limit of 3 days; the second sentence explains the method to be followed in figuring those 3 days in cases of extended travel.

As to the union's claim "that in the past foremen had consistently granted employees who had extended travel, 4 days pay; and such past practice shows the parties intended to provide an additional day's pay in such cases," I said:

The evidence does show that in the past foremen had interpreted Section C 2 that way—one former foreman frankly stating that the

160

shop steward in his department had told him that was the way it should be interpreted and had paid some employees 4 days pay. The fact that foremen in those cases—about 6 out of 200 "death leave" cases over the years—had misinterpreted Section C 2, does not constitute an agreement of the parties to change the written terms of that section. Nor does such action of foremen in misinterpreting the clear language of a written provision constitute a past practice that forecloses the parties from applying in the future the written provision according to its terms.

Then, noting that where "the language of a written provision is ambiguous and what the parties intended under it cannot be clearly gathered from the words used, the way the parties' representatives, foremen and shop stewards, applied that ambiguous provision in the past does constitute material proof in determining what the parties had agreed to and how they intended such a provision to be interpreted," I said:

> But where the language of the provision clearly shows what the parties agreed to and how they intended it to apply, as the arbitrator finds in this case, the language controls; and the past practice that misinterpreted the language falls.
>
> A past practice that conflicts with the clear language of a written provision or contradicts what the parties reasonably intended under the language of that provision, does not constitute an agreement by the parties to change or modify that written provision. Neither party waives its contractual rights established by the written provision by any practice that misinterprets the written provision; nor does either party relinquish its contractual rights under a written provision by failing to enforce those rights in the past.

Finding that if in the past one party "had withheld enforcing its rights or the obligations of the other party under the written contract, such conduct does not stop either party from enforcing its rights under the written provision in the future for the balance of the contract term," I said:

> If in the past the representatives of one party, foremen or shop stewards, had given more or accepted less than the written provision called

161

for, the condoning party may be stopped from trying to retroactively adjust the past misinterpretation or violation. But such past practice does not have the force of changing the rights and obligations of either party under the written provision.

A contract misinterpretation or violation that in the past had been permitted or accepted may be voidable by either party; and has no binding effect upon the rights of either party stipulated by the written provision for the balance of the contract term. Either party can insist that the other thenceforth comply with the terms as agreed to by the written provision; and the arbitrator's office constrains him to enforce those rights and obligations as agreed to by the parties under that written provision. In such cases, the past practice falls; and gives way to the written provision, which then determines the parties' rights and obligations for the future balance of the contract term.

Applying that rule of contract construction to the facts in the case, I held that the "company did not violate Article IX, Section C 2 of the existing contract when it paid the grievant 3 days pay thereunder." Then, finding that "Section C 2 does not obligate the company to pay the grievant an additional day's pay," I said:

> Though the union claims otherwise, the arbitrator finds that the language of Section C 2 is unambiguous and clearly speaks what the parties agreed to and intended under it. Section C 2 clearly sets a limit of "up to three (3) days"—and no more. Then, in determining what should be included in figuring any of those 3 days, the parties agreed that in cases of extended travel, the day following the funeral would also be included.

The "Blanket" Past Practice Clause

"Many of the specific practices which underlie the agreement," said the U. S. Supreme Court in the Warrior and Gulf Navigation case, "may be unknown, except in hazy form, even to the negotiators."

To bridge that gap, negotiators sometimes, though with less frequency today, incorporate into the contract a blanket past-practice clause. By such an all-inclusive clause they agree that existing practices, benefits, and working conditions theretofore established shall continue during the term of the contract unless changed by mutual consent.

Historically, such blanket clauses served a real need; and even today, in some industries governed by master contracts, the blanket past-practice clause may still justify its use. Nontheless, a blanket past-practice clause creates pitfalls for the foreman and shop steward in administering the written contract and frequently gives rise to grievances during the contract term. Instead of finding out from you, Mr. Foreman, at bargaining time what, if any, practices you or your predecessor had established in your department, your negotiator buys a blanket past-practice clause that may cover benefits he never intended to agree to or some you may not have known about.

THE CASE OF THE YEAR-END BONUS

For more than ten years past, without break, the employer had paid year-end bonuses to all its employees, warehouse and general office employees in the bargaining unit referred to in schedule A of the contract as well as employees exempt from the contract coverage or covered by a contract with another union referred to in schedule B.

The amount of the bonus paid to individual employees varied, usually depending on an employee's length of service. During all those past years the union had not bargained with the employer as to the amount of any individual employee's bonus; and the contract did not refer to the payment of any bonus, as such.

Around Christmas time, prior to when the dispute in the present case arose, the employer informed the union's shop committee and all its employees that due to adverse business conditions it intended to discontinue bonuses for all its employees, within and without the bargaining unit. The employer also told the shop committee that if business conditions improved, it would reinstate the bonus for all employees, union and nonunion alike. The union accepted the employer's statement in good faith and didn't raise the subject until the following year.

Then, in the spring, the union shop committee discussed the question of the bonus several times with the employer but did not press the subject further until the fall of that year, when contract negotiations came up under an interim wage reopening clause.

The union then raised the payment of the bonus for the prior year as well as for the current year and called the attention of the employer's

163

negotiators to paragraph 11, subsections (d) and (e), both of which provided:

> It is specifically agreed that all weekly wages, salaries, and all other fixed financial arrangements of employees in effect at the date hereof or increased hereafter by mutual agreement, shall not be reduced.

The employer's negotiator told the union that payment of a year-end bonus constituted a separate matter the negotiators should not mix up with the negotiations for a general wage increase under the reopening clause. They then completed their wage negotiations and left in abeyance the subject of the bonus.

Christmas and the end of that year came and passed with no bonus payment to the employees in the bargaining unit. Then, in the spring of the following year, the union shop committee found out that the company had paid year-end bonuses for the two prior years to all its employees outside the bargaining unit.

The union filed a grievance claiming that by failing to pay its employees in the bargaining unit the year-end bonus for the two prior years the company had violated the foregoing paragraph 11 as well as paragraph 18 of the contract, which provided:

> 18. *No discrimination.* It is understood that the Employer shall show no discrimination against or favoritism among its employees for Union activities or otherwise.

The company denied the grievance, and the union appealed to arbitration.

At the arbitration hearing the employer contended that "no formal bonus plan existed or had been agreed upon by the parties . . . as an integrated part of the wage structure of employees in the bargaining unit . . . that the year-end payments to its employees were not bonus payments, but represented gratuities, voluntarily made by the employer, in its sole discretion . . . and that it reserved the right to discontinue said payments to any of its employees."

In support of its position, the employer argued that the parties did not intend the year-end payments to be fixed financial arrangements of employees in the bargaining unit; that "it is not restricted by the contract in making voluntary payments to any of its other employees, who are outside the bargaining unit and not covered by the contract; and that it has not discriminated against nor shown favoritism among its employees by continuing to pay its other employees year-end payments."

The union claimed:

Such bonus payments constituted part of the employees' wages and wage structure . . . that bonus payments had been paid by the employer at the time that the first collective bargaining contract had been entered into by the parties, more than ten years ago; that they were an established part of the wages of employees in the bargaining unit and were incorporated into the existing contract as fixed financial arrangements under subsections (d) and (e) of paragraph 11 . . . and that the employer's unilateral action in discontinuing bonuses to employees in the bargaining unit violated said subsections of the contract.

In support of its position the union claimed:

The conduct and acts of the employer, in discontinuing bonus payments to union members only, who are the employees in the bargaining unit, while continuing to pay bonuses to all its other employees, not members of the union herein, and those in exempt jobs under schedule "B" of the contract, violates paragraph 18 of the contract; and that the reason given by the employer to the union members for discontinuing their bonus payments—adverse business and financial conditions—was untrue and misleading and was a subterfuge to discriminate against union members.

Finding that the employer had violated paragraphs 11 and 18 of the contract by failing to pay the year-end bonuses to employees in the bargaining unit for the two prior years, I sustained the union's grievance, and in my award I said:

The proof establishes that for more than ten years . . . and ever since the parties entered into their first contract, the employer paid all employees in the bargaining unit a year-end bonus. The employer disputes that these year-end payments were bonuses. The evidence establishes that they were. They were so called by the employer itself. The canceled checks, which the employer was directed to produce, upon the union's demand, by which the payments to the employees in the bargaining unit were made, show that these year-end payments were bonus payments. The checks . . . have the legend "Bonus" written on their face.

Noting that though the contract "does not refer to any bonus payment or plan, as such" but that by paragraph 11 the parties intended to cover them, I said:

The arbitrator finds that the bonus payments do, in fact, constitute fixed financial arrangements of the employees in the bargaining unit, in effect at the date of the contract. They are covered by subsections (d) and (e) of paragraph 11. They cannot be reduced or discontinued unilaterally by the employer during the term of the contract.

As to the employer's argument that by paragraph 11 the parties had only intended to cover weekly fixed financial arrangements and not any other kind, I said:

Subsections (d) and (e) expressly state: "and other fixed financial arrangements." They do not state, as the employer would have it construed, "and other weekly fixed financial arrangements." Language, which is clear and unambiguous on its face, speaks for itself. It establishes undisputed facts. The parties, by the language they used, did not say that the "other fixed financial arrangements" was to mean "other weekly fixed financial arrangements." To construe these subsections in that way, would be to do violence to the clear thought they express. The arbitrator cannot, under the guise of construing a clause, change its clearly expressed meaning. The arbitrator has no authority to interpolate words into contract clauses and thereby try to find a meaning which is contrary to the plain meaning of the words themselves.

Noting that the union had no knowledge of the basis upon which the employer had computed the individual employee's bonus in the past years but that such knowledge resided exclusively with the employer, I said:

The proof shows that over the years, the individual's bonus generally increased with his length of service. The lack of more detailed proof

166

on this point cannot serve to defeat the union's just claim. The employer knows the facts on this point. It voluntarily refrained from offering any proof on it. It kept silent. A party in arbitration cannot be heard to complain that facts which it considers material to the dispute are not brought out, when the failure to bring them out is due to that party's silence.

Then, referring to paragraph 18, which provided that the "employer shall show no discrimination against or favoritism among its employees for union activities or otherwise," I said:

Generally, such nondiscrimination clauses express in contractual language that which the law provides. A contract clause, unless otherwise expressed, refers to employees within the bargaining unit, covered by the contract. The parties, however, may enlarge certain rights and extend the contract coverage to employees outside the bargaining unit.

By paragraph 18, the employer agrees to show no favoritism among its employees. The contract refers to employees in the bargaining unit, schedule A, and employees outside the bargaining unit, schedule B. Employees under schedule A are all members of the union. None of the employees under schedule B are members of the union. All employees outside the bargaining unit did receive their bonuses . . . employees in the bargaining unit, members of the union, did not . . .

The arbitrator, therefore, finds from the proof offered, that the employer's action in failing and refusing to pay the year end bonuses . . . to those employees in the bargaining unit, who had been receiving them in the years prior thereto, as fixed financial arrangements, violated subsections (d) and (e) of paragraph 11 and paragraph 18 of the contract between the parties.

New Conditions Necessitate New Rules

The grievance may concern a situation not spelled out by the contract because of the new elements introduced in the plant after the contract was negotiated—new machinery or new processes, for example. These new conditions may require new rules.

That's what the IUE *Leadership Manual For Shop Stewards* says. What about the effect of new machines and new processes on existing

167

past practices? Do such new conditions make such past practices "no longer feasible or appropriate"? Yes! Since an established practice does not stand alone but attaches itself to the written contract as a supplement, it follows that the presumption that past practices would continue falls when the conditions out of which they arose no longer exist.

As Arthur J. Goldberg said in his paper "Management's Reserved Rights: A Labor View":

> To the extent that present conditions and methods for change are not revised, they [past practices] are accepted . . .
>
> Therefore, each party has the right to assume that changes in wages, hours, or working conditions not provided for by contract can be made only by mutual agreement or by following practices for making changes which have existed during the collective bargaining relationship or by virtue of management's exercise of an exclusive right (such as, introduction of new product, new machine, new material, new method of manufacture, etc.).

The rule of presumption, that established past practices continue only as long as the underlying conditions or methods remain unchanged, applies equally to a blanket past-practice clause. If new products, new machines, new materials, or new methods of manufacture necessitate revising the circumstances out of which the past practice arose, then the blanket clause no longer protects that practice.

Here's what Arthur J. Goldberg said about the past-practice clauses in the steel contracts:

> One thing is certain: These clauses, no matter how they differ among the various steel agreements, all agree on the right of the company to abandon a practice when the circumstances underlying the practice are eliminated. In other words, they are based on the right of the management to make changes in product, material, machinery, etc. This consideration is important to the industry.

THE CASE OF THE NEW PLASTIC TANK LINERS

The union filed a grievance claiming that the company had violated the contract by assigning maintenance and repair work on newly installed plastic liners of the electrolytic tanks to tank-house employees classified as miscellaneous laborers instead of assigning such work to employees in the leaderburner classification. The company denied the grievance, and the union appealed to arbitration.

Since 1898, when it started the electrolytic process of refining copper in its Raritan plant, the company had used lead sheets to line the sides and bottom of the concrete tanks, where the process took place. These concrete tanks, totaling 3,456, operate in sections of twenty-six tanks located in two tank houses. Lead tank linings required regular skilled maintenance work to repair breaks that occurred while installing and removing the cathodes and anodes during the process in order to prevent leakage of electric current and escape of the refined copper to the concrete sides of the tank.

Lead liners lasted an average of about fifteen years, from a low of about four to a high of about thirty years. When the company had to replace or rebuild a lead liner, tank-house laborers performed the preliminary installing work. Then journeymen leadburners and apprentice helpers took over, doing the final fitting and welding of the seams of the lead sheets and, thereafter, undertaking any maintenance and repair work that arose. Laborers performed other maintenance and repair work in the tank houses; and their job rate fell in the lower end of the wage scale. The leadburner job required much higher skills and experience and stood among the top jobs in the rate structure.

About a year before the present dispute arose, the company began to substitute prefabricated seamless plastic liners for lead liners when it had to rebuild a tank or repair the lining. At the time this case came to arbitration, the company had fitted about 275 tanks out of a total of 3,456 with the new plastic liners.

Formerly, when the company had to replace lead liners, it took six laborers about fifteen man-days to do the preliminary work of installing the sheets in one section of twenty-six tanks. After the laborers finished the preliminary work, a leadburner and helper would spend about twenty-six man-days doing the final dressing, fitting, and seam welding of the lead liners.

In contrast, to completely install and fit a prefabricated plastic liner, ready for the operating process, it takes six laborers a total of about four and a half man-days to perform the entire job.

Expressed in total man-hours, it took six laborers and one leadburner and helper about 328 man-hours to completely install the lead liner on a section of tanks, whereas it takes only six laborers a total of about thirty-six man-hours to do the same job.

Repairing the prefabricated plastic liners requires no seaming or welding work, because they consist of one piece, and the laborers simply iron out any breaks. Consequently, the repair work required no higher skills than the regular repair and maintenance work laborers normally did in their other jobs. Since laborers had assisted in the former lead-lining operations, the union did not protest the company having them install the plastic liners; but it did protest the company's action in assigning the repair and maintenance work to them instead of to the leadburners.

At the arbitration hearing the union claimed that "since employees in the leadburner classification had in the past performed repair and maintenance work on liners, the changeover to plastic liners should not upset that long-established past practice; that by reason of such past practice, employees in the leadburner classification have jurisdiction over such work and are better qualified to perform it."

In support of its claims the union relied on the working conditions clause, article XI of the contract, which provided:

Local rules or regulations covering working practices and working conditions of employees which have been established by custom or local agreement and were in effect prior to the execution of this agreement, shall not be changed during the life of this agreement without mutual consent. It is understood, however, that the company or the union, through their representatives, or committees, or in such manner as they may elect, may at any time discuss and negotiate for changes in said local rules or regulations covering working practices and working conditions of employees in the plant which have been established by custom or local agreement, were in effect prior to the execution of this agreement, and are not in conflict with this agreement.

The company claimed that the "contract does not restrict it from assigning work on new jobs, due to changes in means, methods or processes of production, to employees in already established classified jobs who are qualified to do the new or changed job." The company

170

relied upon the management rights clause, article III of the contract, which provided:

> Section 1. The management of the plant and the direction of the work forces, including the right to hire, discipline, suspend and discharge for just cause, and the right to lay-off employees because of lack of work are exclusive rights and functions of the company subject to the terms of this agreement.
>
> Section 2. The establishment of new jobs, abolishment of or changes in existing jobs, the type of products to be manufactured, the location of the operations, the schedules or restrictions of production, the schedules of work, and the method, process and means of manufacturing are exclusive rights and functions of management subject to the terms of this agreement.

Finding that the "changeover from lead to plastic liners constitutes a material change in the means, methods and processes of production that materially distinguishes the former job of repair and maintenance of lead liners from the new job of repairing and maintaining plastic liners," I denied the union's grievance, and in my award I said:

> The evidence shows that tank house employees perform maintenance and repair work on a variety of jobs in the tank house, fully comparable to the repair and maintenance work of plastic liners; that their skills, experience and responsibilities fully qualify them to do such work on the plastic liners; and consequently, the company did not violate the labor agreement between the parties by assigning such repair and maintenance work to them.

As to the union's claim that "employees in the leadburner classification have jurisdiction over the maintenance and repair work, because they had always in the past performed the work on liners," I found that the blanket past-practice clause of the contract did not support such claim and held:

> Article XI, relied upon by the union, fails to support its claim of jurisdiction over the new work. On the contrary, the very language of article XI shows that the parties intended that article to apply to working

171

practices and working conditions that "were in effect prior to the execution of this agreement." The company first installed plastic liners in September . . . and the working practices under which the union claims that the maintenance and repair work belongs to employees in the leadburner classification and over which they assert jurisdiction were not in effect prior to that date.

But more than that, the arbitrator finds that the parties did not intend article XI to apply to those working practices eliminated or changed as a result of setting up new jobs or making changes in existing jobs due to improved methods of production or changes in the process or means of production. Article XI must be construed in context and not in conflict with article III of the contract. Article III expressly recognizes the right of the company to establish new jobs, abolish or make changes in existing jobs, and improve the method, process and means of manufacturing. By article XI the parties intended to maintain working practices and working conditions where the work or jobs continued to exist and be performed in the same way; and where they have not been abolished or changed by technological improvements in means or methods of production.

The Case of the Union's Past Practice

About three years before the dispute in the present case arose, the company had initiated a "policy grievance," complaining about the local union's action in "inducing its membership to refrain from working a reasonable amount of previously scheduled overtime, after proper notice to employees had been given." In its grievance, the company had requested the union to "desist from interfering on the company's right to schedule reasonable and sufficient overtime to meet production requirements and customer commitments."

The union answered the company's grievance with a letter in which the union "denied that its officers induced its members to refrain from working overtime in contravention of the labor agreement"; and the letter further stated:

The officers of Local 116 do not question the right of the company to schedule overtime, nor do they propose to interfere with the scheduling of overtime. Since the inception of contractual relations between both parties it has been the union's past practice, conceded by the company, that it is the right of the individual employee to determine for himself whether or not he will work overtime. The local union leadership is subject to the will of the membership of the union.

The company did not reply to the union's letter and took no further action on its "grievance." About three years later the company disciplined, by written reprimands, two employees who had refused to work overtime "unless the union committee granted them permission." Following a meeting with the union's shop committee the parties agreed to submit to arbitration the company's "right to schedule and require employees to work sufficient and reasonable amounts of overtime and to discipline individual employees for refusing to work such overtime."

At the arbitration hearing the company claimed:

It has the right under the labor agreement to require employees to work a reasonable amount of overtime and to discipline an employee who refuses to work the overtime, unless he has an acceptable excuse not to work a particular overtime assignment . . . that the company did not relinquish its rights under the agreement to compel employees to work the required overtime, either by any understanding or past practice as claimed by the union . . . that the company did not waive its right to require employees to work overtime because it withheld taking disciplinary action in the past against employees who failed or refused to work overtime when assigned; and the agreement expressly provides against any such waiver.

The union claimed:

Overtime work is voluntary on the part of any individual employee or group of employees . . . that under the written agreements, including the union's letter . . . in answer to the company's "policy grievance," the company has the right to schedule overtime work but not compel employees to work overtime . . . and that during all the past years under the prior agreements the company did not discipline any employee who refused to work overtime, thereby acknowledging the understanding that the company did not have the right to compel an employee to work overtime or to discipline him for his refusal to work overtime.

173

Finding that under the contract the "company has the right . . . to discipline employees who, without a reasonable excuse, refuse to work such overtime, I said:

> The very words used in the overtime provisions of the labor agreement clearly show the parties agreed to and intended that the company had the right to require employees to work overtime upon meeting the advance notice to the individual employee or employees involved and to the steward having jurisdiction . . .
>
> Those provisions contain not a word giving the union's shop committee the right to decide when overtime work is required. Neither do those provisions nor any other written agreements between the parties require the union shop committee's approval for employees to work overtime, when required. Those provisions do not leave it to any individual employee to decide for himself whether he wants to work the required overtime; nor do those provisions allow an employee to refuse to work the required overtime without a reasonable, valid reason to excuse him from working a particular assigned overtime.

Then, finding that the union's letter sent three years earlier in answer to the company's "policy grievance" did not "make working the required overtime voluntary or optional on the part of any individual employee or group of employees," I rejected the union's argument that by that letter the company had "conceded (the) union's past practice . . . that it is the right of the individual employee to determine for himself whether or not he will work overtime." In my award I said:

> The language of the June 29th letter must be read in context with the dispute that was then being considered, namely, whether the union had induced employees to refrain from working overtime. The union had denied the company's charge; and to prove that its officers had not induced employees not to work overtime, the union pointed to the union's past practice, namely, that it was up to the individual employee to determine this question for himself. It was the union's past practice to keep hands off that the company had conceded; and not that it was the right of the individual employee to refuse to work the required overtime without a valid reason to excuse him.
>
> The arbitrator finds that the union's plea in defense against the

174

company's charge at that time cannot be construed to mean as the union now seeks to do that the union's past practice relieved the individual employee from the responsibility of working required overtime. If this were so, then a self-serving declaration by the union of its own practice or policy could relieve every individual employee from fulfilling any of the other duties required of him in his job under the collective bargaining agreement. Thus, the union could send the company a letter denying that its officers induced employees to refuse to comply with any of the established plant rules; and state in proof of such denial that it was the union's past practice for the individual employee to determine for himself whether he wanted to comply with the established plant rules. Would such a union's past practice conceded by the company relieve an employee of his responsibilities under the written agreement? Clearly not.

Noting that the "company withheld enforcing its rights and the employees' and the shop committee's obligations under the labor agreement," I said:

> The fact that the company in the past refrained from enforcing its rights to require employees to work overtime does not establish a past practice; nor does it constitute a recognition of an unwritten understanding that can be held to be a waiver of the rights established by the written provisions themselves.
>
> Likewise, the fact that the company, during all the past years, withheld disciplining any employee who refused to work the required overtime assigned to him does not constitute a waiver of the company's right to enforce, in the future, the employees' obligations under the agreement and to discipline an employee who fails or refuses to fulfill the duties required of him in his job.

Holding that neither party "relinquishes or waives its contractual rights established by the written provisions, by failing to enforce those rights or by allowing the other party to violate their obligations under them," I said:

> If in the past either party had condoned the other party's action in violating any of the written provisions or in the past withheld enforcing

its own rights and the obligations of the other party, such conduct does not estop either party from enforcing its rights under the written provisions for the future balance of the contract term.

The condoning party may be estopped from trying to retroactively adjust or undo the past violation. A violation that in the past had been permitted or condoned may be voidable by either party, as to its binding effect for the future of the contract term. Either party can insist that the written provisions be thenceforth complied with and enforced. In such case, the past practice falls and gives way to the written provisions, which then determine the parties' relations for the future balance of the contract term.

In the present case, that rule of contract construction finds itself explicitly expressed in the existing written agreement between the parties.

Article XVIII of the agreement expressly provides: "The waiver by either party of any provisions or requirements of this agreement shall not be deemed a waiver of such provisions or requirements for the future and shall not constitute a modification of this agreement."

6

Four Ways to Eliminate Inefficient or Restrictive Past Practices

Yes, Mr. Foreman, you can help yourself and your fellow foremen by eliminating past practices that have become "no longer feasible or appropriate." That's as much a part of your supervisory job as maintaining production quotas and employee discipline.

Just as you exercise your right of administrative initiative in initially interpreting the written clauses and initially applying the contract's benefits, so you exercise that same administrative initiative in removing restrictive or inefficient past practices. You have available four ways to do that, each of which demands your professional skills as a member of your management's team in running your department along lines of excellence.

The first two ways, the technological way and the corrective rule way, offer you the best chances of succeeding. The remaining ways, the voidable way and the negotiating-out way, will require greater effort on your part with less chance of success. But when you play the game of labor relations as a professional and follow the rules of collective bargaining, you surely increase your chances of winning.

177

Of course, when you initiate action to eliminate a practice the shop steward or the employees have enjoyed for a long time, because the practice has become no longer feasible or appropriate, you must expect the shop steward to protest your action. That doesn't mean that you violated the contract or that you have a weak case. The shop steward's only doing the job the employees elected him to do, namely, to protect the workers' and the union's rights under the contract.

The Technological Way

New or improved methods or new administrative procedures that revise the production base out of which a practice arose eliminate the need for the past practice to continue. When new machines, new materials, or new products come into your department, or you institute changes in storage facilities, schedules, or administrative procedures, review your record, Mr. Foreman, of restrictive or inefficient past practices to see if you should revise or discontinue any of them.

Does the new machine eliminate the need for the extra clean-up time required by the former machine? Does the new method warrant the consolidation of several jobs into one, thereby reducing the need for past wash-up time? Does the new air conditioning of the cab of the overhead crane justify eliminating the helper who in the past had to relieve the operator for breathing spells? Does the new operating procedure justify discontinuing the past practice of operators keeping their own records or spending time in other nonproductive activities? What effects do new shift schedules have upon eliminating costly past practices in scheduling, distributing, or equalizing overtime?

New or improved methods may justify reevaluating formerly existing production standards, work loads, size of crews, job content, wage rates, and incentive bonuses or taking up slack and idle time during the contract term. So, too, those changes may in turn justify you, Mr. Foreman, in reevaluating restrictive past practices that attached to the former job or way of doing the work. New or improved methods or procedures that materially distinguish the former job from the new job may call for new conditions in place of inefficient old past practices.

To repeat what the professional, Arthur J. Goldberg, said about past-practice clauses and management's right to eliminate past practices that changed conditions make "no longer feasible or appropriate":

> One thing is certain: These clauses, no matter how they differ among the various steel agreements, all agree on the right of the company to abandon a practice when the circumstances underlying the practice are eliminated. In other words, they are based on the right of the management to make changes in product, material, machinery, etc. This consideration is important to the industry.

Technological improvements or changes in methods of production offer you, Mr. Foreman, a guaranteed way to eliminate restrictive or inefficient past practices when they become no longer feasible or appropriate. When changes take place in your department, look into your existing practices and initiate action to eliminate those that no longer serve the need that formerly brought them into being.

The Corrective Rule Way

If the inefficient or restrictive past practice arose out of the absence or dormancy of a plant rule, establish and make known to the employees and the shop steward a new rule, or reestablish the dormant one!

Yes, that seems so simple; but that's the way the professional plays the game of labor relations. If the inefficient practice arose because you didn't have a plant rule prohibiting it, or if you did have a plant rule but had neglected to enforce it in the past, why, then, establish a new rule or republish the old one.

Suppose in the past employees in your department had, after clocking in at the beginning of their shift, spent, say, five minutes making coffee before beginning work or had stopped work five minutes before lunch or before the end of their scheduled shift. Would that past practice constitute an agreement reducing their regularly scheduled working hours? Not if it came about because of laxness or neglect on your part.

To correct such conduct, establish the following rule, in writing, giving each employee and the shop steward a copy and mailing a copy to the union's place of business:

> EMPLOYEES MUST BE AT THEIR APPOINTED WORK
> PLACES, READY TO WORK, AT THE REGULAR STARTING
> TIME AND SHALL REMAIN AT SUCH WORK PLACES AND
> AT WORK UNTIL THE REGULAR QUITTING TIME.

If the shop steward believes the new or reestablished rule violates the contract's set of working conditions as supplemented by a claimed past practice, he can file a grievance and protest your action in an orderly way through the grievance procedure. Even though he may feel that some of the employees have in the past avoided meeting fully their job duties, he may still have to file a grievance, since he must protect the rights of all employees under the contract. As the Glass and Ceramic Workers manual, *So You're A Grievanceman!* tells its shop stewards:

> The problems of management are not your problems. It is not up to you to make the workers toe the line or to increase efficiency. That's the employer's worry. Your job is to protect the workers and to get their grievances settled quickly and satisfactorily.

Suppose your department runs on a continuous shift basis and operating or safety conditions require that employees remain at their work stations until the next shift workers take over. But in the past you've been lax, allowing them to leave at the end of their shift. To correct such neglect, establish the following rule:

> WHERE THE OPERATIONS ARE CONTINUOUS, AN EM-
> PLOYEE SHALL NOT LEAVE HIS POST AT THE END OF
> HIS SCHEDULED SHIFT UNTIL HE IS REPLACED BY THE
> NEXT SHIFT EMPLOYEE OR UNTIL HE IS RELIEVED BY
> HIS SUPERVISOR.

Suppose for ten years past you had not insisted that every employee in your department undertake overtime work when it arose, as part of his regular job. Or suppose you never inquired of anyone who didn't want to work overtime when you assigned it to him his reason for refusing, or if he gave you the blanket excuse "personal reasons," you accepted it and didn't ask him to explain what those personal reasons consisted of each time he refused.

Would such past practices prohibit you in the future from requiring all employees to work a reasonable amount of overtime in the absence of a justifiable excuse? Or would such a past practice prevent you from inquiring into the facts making up the excuse of "personal reasons" so you could judge whether the personal reasons given each time supported a justifiable excuse? No, unless the written contract made working overtime optional or voluntary on the part of each employee.

To remove any doubt your past practice may have created in the minds of your employees or the shop steward and to enforce equally the job responsibilities of each employee under the contract, establish in writing the following rules:

> AN EMPLOYEE MUST BE AVAILABLE AND REPORT FOR WORK AS SCHEDULED OR OVERTIME WORK AS REQUIRED OR ASSIGNED TO HIM.

> IF AN EMPLOYEE IS UNABLE TO REPORT FOR OR PERFORM WORK DUE TO ILLNESS OR OTHER JUSTIFIABLE CAUSE, HE MUST REPORT HIS EXPECTED ABSENCE IN ADVANCE (TO HIS FOREMAN OR OTHER DESIGNATED PERSONNEL) AND GIVE THE REASONS FOR HIS INABILITY TO WORK.

CORRECTING ABUSE OF SHOP STEWARD'S OFFICE, TIME, AND PAY ALLOWANCES

Suppose in the past you had allowed the shop steward to neglect his regular job duties, shutting your eyes to his engaging during working hours in union business or other activities not directly related to his representative office of processing grievances in accordance with the grievance procedure set up by the contract.

To correct your past laxness and to put a stop to abuse by the shop steward of his regular job duties, publish and make known, in writing, the following rule:

> AN EMPLOYEE SHALL NOT NEGLECT HIS JOB DUTIES AND RESPONSIBILITIES OR REFUSE TO PERFORM WORK ASSIGNED TO HIM.

Bear in mind that a shop steward's union office doesn't relieve him of his responsibilities to perform his regular production job, for which the company pays him, except for such time his representative office reasonably requires him to spend in processing grievances according to the grievance procedure provided for by the contract.

Suppose in the past you have allowed the shop steward to leave his place of work and go into another department without bothering to ask him why he needed to take time off from his job at that time. Such past practice would not preclude you requiring the shop steward in the future to get your permission first and give you the reasons for his request, so you can judge the necessity for his leaving your department at that time. The shop steward must balance the responsibilities of his regular job against the responsibilities of his representative office at any given time. You, Mr. Foreman, must balance the reasonable needs of his representative office against the production and personnel needs in operating your department, without abuse of job responsibilities by any employee.

To correct any such practice or laxness on your part, that may have occurred in the past, publish and make known, in writing, to the shop steward and the union the following rules:

AN EMPLOYEE SHALL NOT RESTRICT PRODUCTION OR INTERFERE WITH OTHERS IN THE PERFORMANCE OF THEIR JOBS OR ENGAGE OR PARTICIPATE IN ANY INTERRUPTION OF WORK OR PRODUCTION.

AN EMPLOYEE SHALL NOT LEAVE HIS DEPARTMENT OR THE PLANT BEFORE THE END OF HIS SHIFT OR GO INTO ANY OTHER DEPARTMENT WITHOUT WRITTEN PERMISSION FROM HIS FOREMAN.

Then, to avoid in the future any dispute over whether the shop steward failed to give you the reasons, or the true reasons, for his request to stop his production job or to leave his department at that time, and to make effective the foregoing rules, establish a new administrative procedure for keeping time records in your department; and have the shop steward give you the particulars of his request by filling out a time recording form like the following:

TIME RECORDING FORM

Shop Steward Activities:
Written Request for Permission to Leave Department

_____ _____ _____
Employee's Name   Title (Union Office)   Department

I Request Permission To Leave My Department for the Following Reasons:

  1. State the purpose for your request: _____

_____

  2. State the person(s) you wish to speak to: _____

  3. Does your request concern a _pending_ Grievance? _____ If so:
     a. Give date Grievance submitted: _____
     b. Employee (or Employees) involved: _____

     c. Nature of Grievance: _____

  4. Give approximate time you expect to be absent from your regular job:

_____

     Date _____ Signature _____
                                Shop Steward (or Union Committeeman)

If Permission Granted, Respective Foremen Will Note & Sign the Following:

Date _____ Time Leaving Dept. _____ Time Returning _____

               Signature _____
                          Foreman of Department

Dept. Visited _____ Date _____ Time Entering _____ Time Leaving _____

               Signature _____
                        Foreman of Department Visited

Note: Article VII of the Labor Agreement (or Plant Rules or established practices) provides:

"Neither the Union nor employees shall engage in Union activities on the Plant premises during working hours . . . An employee shall not leave his Department or the Plant before the end of his shift or go into any other Department without written permission from his Foreman . . . An employee shall not restrict production or interfere with others in the performance of their jobs or engage or participate in any interruption of work or production."

CORRECTING PAST ABUSE OF CONTRACT BENEFITS

WRITE IT DOWN. There are a lot of reasons for this:

1. A worker isn't as likely to come to you with an unimportant or unfounded complaint if he knows he has to sign a statement putting it "on the record."
2. It reduces disagreements over the facts in deciding the merits of the case to have them down clearly and simply in black and white.

That's what the IAM *Pocket Guide* tells its shop stewards to do before taking up a grievance. Yes, that's how the professional shop steward determines whether the worker has a legitimate grievance. You too, Mr. Foreman, should have the employee sign a statement putting his claim for a contract benefit on the record in order to reduce disagreements over the facts in deciding the merits of his case and to allow you to determine whether he has a legitimate claim under the contract.

"Get all the facts," the Aluminum Workers manual tells its shop stewards in getting the employee to put his grievance in writing. "Be sure you have all the details and are not passing on rumors, opinions or half-truths. Facts can't be argued against."

"Once the worker has given you the facts," the International Chemical Workers *Handbook* tells its shop stewards, "and you have written them down, you don't have to worry about the worker changing his story."

Written records serve you and your employees as well as the company and the union. In investigating the merits of a claim or an excuse for absence, Mr. Foreman, you would do well to follow the professional advice given by the Printing Pressmen's manual to its shop stewards in investigating the merits of a grievance:

Sometimes a worker may not be convinced that he does not have a just grievance. In this event, an International Union Officer with 20 years of experience has offered this suggestion:

"One of the best strategies of a shop steward when investigating a grievance that has little if any merit, is to ask the individual to write out

184

a complete and detailed explanation of his grievance. If he generalizes, go back and ask him for more facts and details. Usually the grievance does not seem as conclusive when written as it does when told with emotion . . . This procedure usually serves to weed out the non-meritorious grievance from the real grievance."

You'll find it works if you try it. When a grievance that lacks merit is reduced to cold words, the truth is revealed to the worker.

So, too, Mr. Foreman, when an employee makes a claim for sick leave allowance or other benefits under the contract, get him to give you the facts of his claim, in writing. In the past you may have taken the employee's word that he was sick the day before or after the holiday and you excused him from meeting those eligibility requirements. Or in the past you may have accepted a doctor's certificate without making further inquiry of the employee about the facts that would help you verify his claimed sickness.

Such past practices do not prevent you from having the employee file his claim in the future "in black and white" and sign a statement putting it "on the record" to help you decide the validity of his claim.

Even if the contract requires an employee to furnish a doctor's certificate, that doesn't mean the negotiators agreed that you had to accept a certificate as the sole proof, exclusive of any other supporting proof you judge necessary to determine the validity of his claim. Too frequently, experience shows, employees obtain doctor's certificates as accommodating notes that often omit the details of the claimed illness; and leave you to consider "rumors, opinions or half-truths."

So, to prevent abuse in the future and to correct any restrictive past practice regarding supporting proof of an employee's claim for benefits, set up a new administrative procedure for processing such claims. As the Communication Workers *Steward's Manual* says: "The worker takes more care in stating his facts when he sees them in writing."

Requiring the employee to submit a signed written claim, such as the following form of employee report, will help you, Mr. Foreman, in deciding the merits of each case.

FORM OF EMPLOYEE REPORT

Claim for Sick Leave Allowance or Other Benefit

_____   _____   _____
Employee's Name   Address   Clock Number

Please *Write Out* the Following Information in Support of Your Claim for Sick Leave Allowance or for Holiday Pay.

1. State date (or dates) that you were sick: _____

2. Describe fully your illness: _____

   _____

   _____

3. Did your sickness on that day (or days):
   a. Confine you to your bed? _____ b. Confine you to your home? _____

4. Did you leave your home or engage in any outside activity on that day (or days)? _____ If so, explain the reason and the activity: _____

   _____

5. Did a doctor attend you? _____ If so, give doctor's name and address: _____

6. Give any other facts which will help your Supervisor determine the validity of your claim _____

   _____

   _____

(If additional space required, use reverse side)

I affirm that my answers and statements above are true and will be relied upon by my Supervisor in determining the validity of my claim for sick leave or other benefit.

Date: _____ Employee's Signature _____

Note: Article 23—Sick Leave—of the Labor Agreement (or Company Policy) provides:

"An employee claiming said sick leave allowance shall give to the Company a signed written claim of sickness (in addition to any other substantiating proof the Company may require) for each day(s) of sick leave allowance claimed.

"There shall be no abuse of sick leave allowance, which shall be for bona fide sickness only, physically preventing the employee from reporting for and performing his job. Any abuse of said sick leave allowance, or the filing of an invalid claim, shall subject the employee to disciplinary action.

"To be eligible for pay for one of said paid holidays, an employee must have worked the day before and the day after each of said holidays, unless excused for bona fide sickness."

186

The Voidable Way

THE CASE OF THE AFTERNOON SHIFT BONUS

About a year and a half prior to the time the dispute in this case arose, the union filed a grievance claiming the company had violated article XII of the contract by "withdrawing payment of the shift bonus to coal unloaders for the hours worked between 12:00 noon and 4:00 P.M." In its grievance the union claimed that all hours worked on a shift commencing at 12:00 noon constituted the afternoon shift and that the company had applied the article that way in the past.

The company answered that grievance by a letter, in which it denied that a shift starting at 12:00 noon constituted an afternoon shift and stated that traditionally and by common understanding between the parties the afternoon shift commenced at 4:00 P.M. and the night shift at 12:00 midnight, those being the regular turns on the rotating shifts connected with the continuous operation of the plant. The company admitted that for a long time in the past it had paid coal unloaders a shift bonus for the hours worked between 12:00 noon and 4:00 P.M. but said it had made such payments by error. The company further said that it would continue to pay only those individuals who continued to work such hours but would not pay the shift bonus for the hours between 12:00 noon and 4:00 P.M. to any employees who replaced those individuals in that job in the future.

The union replied to the company's letter, stating that it was "not in accord that shift differentials should not also apply to future coal unloader employees." Since the union did not proceed further with its grievance, the parties apparently settled that grievance on the basis of those letters.

During the year and a half that followed the company did not pay any coal unloaders who replaced the former individuals a shift bonus for any hours worked between 12:00 noon and 4:00 P.M.; and in no case had the union filed a grievance protesting the company's action. During that same period the company did not pay any other employees in other classifications any shift bonus for the hours worked between 12:00 and 4:00 P.M. but only paid the afternoon shift bonus for the

187

hours worked after 4:00 P.M. Then the union filed a grievance in the present case, claiming payment for shift bonus for the hours between 12:00 noon and 4:00 P.M. for three grievants, one of whom had replaced a former coal unloader. The company denied the grievance, and the union appealed to arbitration.

Article XII of the contract, relied upon by both parties to support their respective positions, provided:

> The Company shall pay shift bonuses . . . for work done on the afternoon and night shifts respectively as provided below.
> 1. Only those employees in job classifications which require regular rotating or fixed assignment on the afternoon and night shifts shall receive the shift bonus applicable for all hours worked on such shifts.

At the arbitration hearing the union claimed that "under article XII any scheduled shift starting at 12:00 noon or after constitutes an afternoon shift; and that article XII obligates the company to pay the afternoon shift bonus for all hours worked on such shift, from 12:00 noon on."

In support of its claim the union argued the "Company had applied article XII in that way in the past; and the company's unilateral action . . . stating that it would discontinue the payment of the afternoon shift bonus for the hours worked between 12:00 noon and 4:00 P.M. to employees who replaced coal unloaders, did not bind the union and thereby violated the contract."

The company claimed "under article XII the parties intended the afternoon shift to apply only to employees scheduled for the regular shift starting at 4:00 P.M.; and the night shift, starting at 12:00 midnight, which two shifts constituted traditionally the regularly rotating and fixed shifts in operation in the plant; and the union itself had in the past acknowledged that article XII was intended to apply in that way."

In support of its position the company argued that following the exchange of letters a year and a half before:

> The company had properly corrected its error of paying the shift bonus for the hours 12:00 noon to 4:00 P.M. thereby eliminating the past practice in the coal unloaders case for future replacements . . . the

union had acquiesced in the company's action . . . [and] since that time the company had not paid any employees who had replaced coal unloaders, nor any employees in any other classifications, the afternoon shift bonus for the hours worked between 12:00 noon and 4:00 P.M.; and the union had not protested the company's action in any such instance nor had the union filed any grievance in any case, until the grievances in the present case.

The company further argued that during the period following its corrective action a year and a half ago:

The parties had negotiated and executed their renewal collective bargaining contract without changing article XII; that at no time during negotiations had the union questioned the propriety of the company's action in eliminating the past practice of paying the afternoon shift bonus for hours worked between 12:00 noon and 4:00 P.M.; and that consequently the union had acquiesced in the way the company had interpreted and applied article XII.

Finding that the parties intended the phrase "afternoon and night shifts" under article XII to apply to the regular rotating or fixed assignments starting at 4:00 P.M. and 12:00 midnight, respectively, and did not intend paying the afternoon shift bonus for hours worked between 12:00 noon and 4:00 P.M., I denied the union's grievance, and in my award I said:

The proof offered by the union fails to support its claim that past practice obligated the company to pay the afternoon shift bonus for the hours between 12:00 noon and 4:00 P.M. The only evidence offered by the union of any past practice for paying the afternoon bonus for hours worked from 12:00 noon related solely to the coal unloaders' grievance . . . which the parties had settled.

Noting that since the grievance submitted by the union a year and a half ago the "company did not pay any operators who replaced coal unloaders the afternoon shift bonus for hours worked between 12:00 noon and 4:00 P.M.; nor did the company pay any other employees, in any other classifications, the shift bonus for those hours"; and during that period the union "did nothing further and the parties apparently settled that grievance," I said:

> The contract does not restrict the company from correcting an error, if in fact an error existed, in applying a contract provision; nor does the contract prohibit the company from eliminating for the future a past practice which stemmed from an error of interpretation . . .
>
> The union had the opportunity at that time to exercise its administrative right to protest and appeal through the grievance and arbitration provisions of the contract, the propriety of the company's action in eliminating for the future the past practice of paying coal unloaders, who filled those jobs as replacements, the shift bonus for the hours worked between 12:00 noon and 4:00 P.M., as well as the company's interpretation that article XII did not obligate the company to make such payments.
>
> Though the union informed the company in the . . . [prior] grievance that it was "not in accord" with the company's action, the union did not proceed further through the grievance and arbitration provisions of the contract to challenge the company's action; and the parties' settlement of that . . . grievance apparently rested on the company's action taken.

Then, finding that the "actions of both parties following the settlement of that . . . [prior] grievance constrain the arbitrator to find that the union had acquiesced in the company's action in eliminating the past practice of paying the afternoon shift bonus for the hours worked between 12:00 noon and 4:00 P.M. to employees who replaced coal unloader operators," I said:

> Thus, the proof shows that during the period of over one year following the [prior] grievance, 4 employees, at different times, had replaced coal unloader operators and the company had not paid any of such replacements the afternoon shift bonus for hours worked between 12:00 noon and 4:00 P.M. The union did not protest any of those cases during that period; nor did any of said employees file any grievance, establishing to that degree, at least, that the union had accepted and acquiesced in the company's action in eliminating whatever past practice had previously existed and the propriety of the way it construed article XII following the [prior] grievance.

190

Finding that during the entire period of a year and a half since the union had raised but had not further proceeded with its prior grievance the "company in no instance paid those employees the afternoon shift bonus for any hours worked prior to 4:00 P.M. and in none of those cases . . . did the union protest the company's action; nor did the employees affected file any grievance"; and that the practice that existed before the prior grievance did not continue to exist thereafter until the union filed the grievances in the present case, I said:

Where the language of a contract provision does not clearly reveal what the parties intended under it, the way the parties themselves interpreted and applied that ambiguous provision in the past provides material facts to guide the arbitrator in construing the language and in determining how the parties intended that provision to be applied.

To warrant a finding of a fixed, established past practice that binds both parties, the proof must show:

1. That the past practice relied upon by either party was unequivocal —that is, that the parties had followed and applied it consistently at all times in the past;
2. That such past practice was clearly enunciated and acquiesced in;
3. That it was readily ascertainable and had existed uniformly over a reasonably long period of time; and
4. That it was accepted and acted upon by both parties up to the time when one party challenged it.

The evidence offered in this proceeding does not satisfy these standards which the arbitrator follows; and fails to support the union's claim of an unequivocal past practice, that has been clearly enunciated and acquiesced in or that has existed uniformly during the period of time in question.

On the contrary, the past practice since the settlement of the [prior] grievance, apparently acquiesced in and accepted by the union up until the present grievances in this proceeding, differs materially from the past practice that existed prior [thereto]; and consequently the conflict between contrary past practices constrains the arbitrator to resolve the dispute independently of the conflicting past practices, relying upon the language of the provision and the circumstances under which the parties negotiated that language, to gather what the parties intended thereunder.

191

Then, finding that the "negotiating history of the present contract, under which the grievances in this proceeding arose, lends further support to the company's position in this case," for during those negotiations the "union did not question the propriety of the company's action taken . . . and consistently applied since then, in eliminating the past practice that had existed prior to the grievance settlement," I said:

> These facts, coupled with the fact that the renewal contract executed by the parties continued the language of article XII unchanged, constrain the arbitrator to find that the union had acquiesced in the propriety of the company's action in eliminating the past practice that had existed prior [thereto]; and thereby accepted the way the company had interpreted and applied article XII since then.

USING THE VOIDABLE WAY DURING THE CONTRACT TERM

You see, Mr. Foreman, neither party relinquishes nor waives its contractual rights, as agreed to under the written contract provisions, for the balance of the contract term because that party:

1. misinterpreted, misconstrued or wrongly applied its rights in the past;
2. failed to enforce its rights in the past; or
3. allowed the other party to violate its obligations under the contract in the past.

You cannot, Mr. Foreman, give more, nor the shop steward accept less, than the written contract calls for. If in the past you or the shop steward misinterpreted a written clause, by giving more or accepting less, either of you may be stopped from retroactively undoing the past practice that misinterpreted the written clause. Neither of you, however, forfeits the right to properly interpret and apply the written clause during the rest of the contract term.

As I said in the arbitration case of the "Written Provision vs. Past Practice" referred to earlier:

> A contract misinterpretation or violation that in the past had been permitted or accepted may be voidable by either party; and has no

binding effect upon the rights of either party stipulated by the written provision for the balance of the contract term. Either party can insist that the other thenceforth comply with the terms as agreed to by the written provision; and the arbitrator's office constrains him to enforce those rights and obligations as agreed to by the parties under that written provision. In such cases, the past practice falls; and gives way to the written provision, which then determines the parties' rights and obligations for the future balance of the contract term.

You use the voidable way, Mr. Foreman, by initiating action during the contract term to end a practice that has misinterpreted a written contract provision or that contradicts what you claim the negotiators reasonably intended under it. You also use the voidable way to stop a past practice that creates an unintended intraplant inequity, such as one that unequally distributes benefits or unequally treats employees covered by the same contract.

You also use the voidable way to stop a past practice that no longer meets the three standards of a fixed and established past practice, namely, where breaks have occurred in the past practice that show the parties have not applied it consistently, regularly, and uniformly so that it no longer survives as:

1. an unequivocal practice,
2. clearly enunciated and existing over a reasonably long period of time, and
3. accepted and acted upon in administering the written contract provisions.

Don't wait until the time for negotiating the renewal contract comes around to put a stop to a voidable past practice. Your chances of succeeding during the contract term through the grievance and arbitration steps, where the merits of the case finally determine the issue, far exceed your chances at the negotiating table, where the threat of a strike prevails.

If the shop steward files a grievance protesting your action ending a practice he claims you or your predecessor had established, the no-strike pledge constrains him and the employees affected to follow the grievance and arbitration steps, to finally resolve your differences in a peaceful way. Arbitration, not strikes, serves the union's interests as well as your own management's interests in settling disputes arising during the contract term.

As the IAM *Pocket Guide* cautions its shop stewards:

> Don't get upset and make empty threats that both you and the foreman know you can't carry out. Angrily saying that you'll call a strike immediately if he doesn't settle the grievance on your terms is absurd —and may be illegal according to the contract. If you and the foreman can't come to an agreement there are further steps to be followed before the question of a strike even comes up. If the contract provides for arbitration, the question of a strike is out of the picture entirely.

ARBITRATING THE MERITS OF A PAST PRACTICE

Your action eliminating a past practice you consider no longer feasible or appropriate, together with the shop steward's protest through a filed grievance, frames the material issue: Did your action violate the contract?

A past practice, if fixed and established, serves as material evidence that helps the arbitrator determine how the parties intended to interpret a written contract clause or apply a contract benefit. Still, the essential issue the grievance raises and the arbitrator decides remains the same: Did the action that the union protests violate the contract?

In arbitration the contract determines the merits of the grievance; and the arbitration tribunal finally settles that issue on its merits under the contract, not under the threat of a strike, which so often substitutes for the merits at the negotiating table.

As the United Glass and Ceramic Workers manual, *So You're A Grievanceman!* tells its shop stewards:

> In most instances it is lots cheaper and better to arbitrate a grievance during a contract year than it is to have a work stoppage. Usually grievances that are referred to arbitration on the basis of a principle are ones which the members in the shop or plant would not want to strike over.

194

You may lose the case in arbitration, but then again, you may win it. Even though you lose in arbitration, you at least will have an experience factor that may help your management's team negotiate out that past practice at contract renewal time. As the International Chemical Workers *Handbook For Stewards* advises its shop stewards:

> A written record of grievances—especially those you lose—is good to have when the contract comes up for negotiation. The record will remind you of your trouble spots, and indicate where changes in the contract should be made to avoid losing some of the grievances in the future.

Without an experience factor, which you can get only through a case you lose in arbitration, trying to bargain out an established past practice at the negotiating table will prove hopeless, if not impossible. Why?

The Negotiating Way

Did you ever sit at the negotiating table, Mr. Foreman, when your management tried to eliminate a past practice? Do you know of one instance—just one—when your management succeeded? Chances are, not once! Why? Because in trying to bargain out a past practice at the negotiating table, your management faces the same task as trying to reduce the number of paid holidays, the existing vacation schedules, the number of days of sick leave allowance, or any other benefits your employees or the union receive under the existing contract.

You see, Mr. Foreman, it's one thing for the union, as a politically structured organization, not to get more in the next contract for the workers it represents. It's an entirely different thing for the union to give up in the next contract a benefit or working condition the workers enjoyed under the prior contract. That would be committing political suicide, particularly in a competitive union market; and no union gives up what it claims it has without a strike.

Did you ever wonder how the overtime clause grew from a few simple paragraphs to five pages or more in successive contracts? That happened because the union's negotiator demanded explanatory sections to fill in loopholes in the prior contract that came about because the union had given up grievances or had lost arbitration cases during the preceding contract term.

But what kind of dry powder have you or your fellow foremen given your management's negotiator when he attempts to bargain out an inefficient or restrictive past practice at the negotiating table if you or they did nothing about that practice during the contract term? You didn't even try to eliminate it; you kept silent and let it go on and on. You didn't act to put an end to it, leaving it then to the union to challenge your claim that that past practice no longer remained feasible or appropriate or that it no longer met the standards of an established past practice.

You didn't lose an arbitration case over it, which would at least give your negotiator an experience factor to fortify his demand at the bargaining table. Because you took no action during the contract term, the union's negotiator says, "What's wrong with the practice? Why bring it up now? Your men didn't say anything about it during the past contract term."

Consequently, not having any dry ammunition to go on, your management's negotiator settles the renewal contract after bargaining on the union's demands for more benefits and improved working conditions, and his demand to eliminate the restrictive past practice gets lost in the shuffle.

The negotiating way nowhere near substitutes for one of the three other ways available during the contract term to eliminate a past practice that changed conditions make no longer feasible or appropriate.

The year-end negotiator who initiates a demand to eliminate inefficient, costly, or restrictive past practices at the bargaining table in no way substitutes for you, Mr. Foreman, the year-round administrator. When you initiate action during the contract term to eliminate a past practice no longer feasible or appropriate, the merits of your case under the existing contract will determine the propriety of your action through the grievance and arbitration process. When your negotiator attempts to bargain out a past practice at contract renewal time, the threat of a strike determines the outcome. When you do your job, Mr. Foreman, in managing with a union along lines of excellence, you fortify your management's negotiator in doing his job at the bargaining table.

Summing Up the Rules of Past Practice

Rule 1. An established past practice

1. Shows what the parties meant or intended by a word, phrase, or clause in the written contract by the way they themselves interpreted, construed, or applied it in the past; or

2. Is a benefit or working condition not set forth in the written contract that the company, through its supervisors, granted or allowed the employees to enjoy.

Rule 2. Management, through its supervisory personnel administering the written contract, initiated or acquiesced in every past practice that arises in the plant.

Rule 3. No employee, no shop steward, and no arbitrator created a past practice that you or your predecessor started or allowed to come into being in your department.

Rule 4. Past practices necessarily arise when you exercise your right of administrative initiative by initially interpreting the language of the written clauses and initially applying the benefits and working conditions under the contract.

Rule 5. In doing your job of managing, consider the future operating needs of your department as well as the operating needs of your fellow foremen in their departments who administer the same contract. Twenty-seven foremen administering one contract don't make twenty-seven companies or twenty-seven different contracts!

Rule 6. In administering the written provisions and handling grievances under them, set up sound practices that retain

197

and protect your flexibility in meeting your operating and personnel needs. Avoid establishing restrictive, inefficient, or costly past practices; and avoid abuse of contract benefits.

Rule 7. An established practice binding on both parties must satisfy three standards. It must be
1. Unequivocal—granted or allowed, interpreted, or applied, consistently, regularly, uniformly and without break.
2. Clearly enunciated—freely and openly allowed or acquiesced in and readily ascertainable as existing over a reasonably long period of time.
3. Accepted and acted upon—by the parties themselves through their authorized agents in administering the written contract and settling grievances under it during the contract term.

Rule 8. A past practice that satisfies those three standards becomes a fixed and established past practice that supplements—adds to or modifies—the written contract.

Rule 9. If the language of a written provision clearly shows what the parties agreed to or how they intended to apply it, then the written provision controls, and a contrary past practice that misinterpreted or misapplied that written provision falls.

Rule 10. If the language of a written provision does not, on its face, clearly show what the parties agreed to or how they intended to apply it, then the way the parties themselves, through their authorized representatives—foremen and shop stewards—interpreted or applied that ambiguous written provision in the past provides material facts to determine what they had agreed to or intended thereunder.

Rule 11. The single exception to the foregoing rules of contract construction is that if one party accepts and retains benefits under an established past practice that more liberally construes a written clause, that party cannot be heard to complain that the literal language of the written clause has not been followed; and in such case the established past practice constitutes an agreement that modifies the written clause.

Rule 12. The rules of equity apply in the arbitration process just as under any other system that dispenses justice. In seeking equity both parties must come in with clean hands. Equity does not permit one party to unjustly enrich itself by its own conduct.

Rule 13. An established past practice forms part of the backdrop of the negotiations of a written contract. If during contract negotiations both parties remain silent about an existing established past practice, the renewal contract serves as an "umbrella" under which it carries over that past practice into the succeeding contract term.

Rule 14. If one party demands at the negotiations for the renewal contract that an established past practice be eliminated or modified and that demand gets washed out during bargaining, the renewal contract more emphatically carries that established past practice into the succeeding contract term.

Rule 15. The Labor Management Relations Act (Taft-Hartley Law), which covers collective bargaining affecting interstate commerce, does not require the parties to execute a written contract setting forth the set of rules that govern their relations. The law only requires the parties to execute a written contract incorporating any agreement reached "if requested by either party."

Rule 16. The law does not require a written document for collateral agreements or past practices the parties may have entered into before or after negotiations. Past grievance settlements, understandings, customary benefits, or precedents that have become fixed as established practices need not be reduced to writing or signed by the parties' representatives.

Rule 17. In processing a grievance based on a claimed past practice under the grievance machinery or in arbitration, the same material issue prevails: Did the company violate the contract as modified or supplemented by the past practice?

Rule 18. The grievance record provides material facts to prove an established practice. Keep a written record of grievances and settlements of grievances in your department. Ask your predecessor for his written record. Pass your record along to your successor.

Rule 19. A past practice that conflicts with the clear language of a written provision or that contradicts what the parties reasonably intended under the language of that provision does not constitute an agreement by the parties to change or modify that written provision.

Rule 20. Neither party waives its contractual rights established by the written provision by any practice that misinterprets that written provision; nor does either party relinquish its contractual rights under a written provision by failing to enforce those rights in the past.

Rule 21. Your failure in the past to enforce established plant rules governing attendance or other personal conduct of employees in your department would not establish a past practice preventing you from strictly enforcing those plant rules in the future—after giving reasonable advance notice to your employees and the shop steward.

Rule 22. The foreman cannot give more, nor the shop steward accept less, than the written contract calls for.

Rule 23. If in the past the representatives of one party—foremen or shop stewards—gave more or accepted less than the written provision called for, the condoning party may be stopped from trying to retroactively adjust the past misinterpretation or violation. Such past practice does not change the rights and obligations of either party under the written provision.

Rule 24. A past practice that misinterprets, misapplies, or violates a written contract provision may be voided by either party for the balance of the contract term. Either party can insist that the other thenceforth comply with the terms as agreed to by the written contract; and the arbitrator's office constrains him to enforce those rights and obligations as agreed to by the parties under the written contract.

Rule 25. A blanket past-practice clause that incorporates by reference existing practices, benefits, and working conditions creates pitfalls in administering the written contract and gives rise to grievances during the contract term.

Rule 26. New operating conditions necessitate new rules. When the conditions out of which an established past practice arose no longer exist because of the introduction of new products, new machines, new materials, new methods of manufacture, or new administrative procedures, the past practice falls and the presumption that such past practice continues no longer exists.

Rule 27. The rule of presumption that established practices continue only as long as the underlying methods are not revised applies equally to a blanket past-practice clause.

Rule 28. If new products, machines, materials, or methods of manufacture necessitate revising the conditions or cir-

201

cumstances upon which the past practice had been based, then the blanket past-practice clause falls.

Rule 29. Past practices that have become no longer feasible or appropriate may be eliminated in four ways: (1) technological or method changes, (2) corrective rules, (3) voidable action, and (4) negotiating out.

The Technological Way

Rule 30. New or improved methods or new administrative procedures that revise the production or operational base out of which a past practice arose eliminate the necessity for that past practice to continue.

Rule 31. When new machines, new materials, new products, new storage facilities, new processes, new schedules, or new operating or administrative procedures come into your department, review your record of restrictive or costly past practices to see if they should be revised or discontinued.

Rule 32. Technological or methods of production changes provide the guaranteed way to eliminate restrictive or costly past practices when they become no longer feasible or appropriate.

The Corrective Rule Way

Rule 33. If the inefficient or restrictive past practice arose out of the absence or dormancy of a plant rule, establish and make known to the employees and the shop steward a new rule, or reestablish the dormant one!

Rule 34. If the costly past practice arose because you didn't have a plant rule prohibiting it, or if you did have a plant rule and had neglected to enforce it in the past, establish a new rule or republish the old one.

Rule 35. To enforce equally the job responsibilities of each employee under the contract and to remove any doubt a conflicting past practice may have created in their minds, establish and make known—in writing—to your employees and the shop steward corrective rules to eliminate that past practice.

Rule 36. The representative office of a shop steward does not relieve him of his responsibilities to perform his regular production job for which the company pays him except for the time the contract allows for processing grievances under the grievance procedure.

Rule 37. The shop steward must balance the responsibilities of his representative office in processing grievances against the responsibilities of his regular production job under the contract.

Rule 38. You must equate the needs of the shop steward's representative office in processing grievances with the production and personnel needs at all times in operating your department without abuse of job responsibilities by any employee.

Rule 39. To correct abuse by a shop steward of his office, time, or pay allowances provided for by the contract and to eliminate any conflicting past practice, publish and make known in advance—in writing—to the shop steward and the union rules and new administrative procedures to correct or eliminate such past practice.

Rule 40. To correct abuse of contract benefits and to eliminate any restrictive past practices regarding supporting proof of claims for benefits, establish—in writing—and make known to the employees and the shop steward in advance corrective rules and a new administrative procedure requiring employees to submit written claims for such benefits.

The Voidable Way

Rule 41. Neither party relinquishes nor waives its contractual rights as agreed to under the written contract provisions for the balance of the contract term because that party:

1. Misinterpreted, misconstrued or by error misapplied its rights in the past.

2. Failed to enforce its rights in the past.

3. Allowed the other party to violate its obligations under the contract.

Rule 42. You cannot give more, nor the shop steward accept less, than the written contract calls for.

Rule 43. If in the past the foreman or the shop steward misinterpreted a written clause by giving more or accepting less, neither may retroactively undo the past practice that misinterpreted the written clause. But neither the foreman nor the shop steward forfeits his right to properly interpret and apply the written clause in the future during the contract term.

Rule 44. A contract misinterpretation or violation that in the past had been permitted or accepted may be voided and thereafter has no binding effect upon the rights of either party stipulated by the written contract.

Rule 45. The foreman or the shop steward can insist that the other thenceforth comply with the terms of the contract; and in such cases the past practice falls and gives way to the written provisions, which then determine the parties' rights and obligations for the balance of the contract term.

Rule 46. The arbitrator's office constrains him to enforce the rights and obligations of each party as agreed to by them under the written provisions of the contract.

Rule 47. You use the voidable way by initiating action during the contract term to end a past practice that has misinterpreted a written contract provision or contradicts what you claim the negotiators reasonably intended under it.

Rule 48. You use the voidable way to stop a past practice that creates an unintended intraplant inequity, such as unequally distributing benefits or unequally treating employees covered by the same contract.

Rule 49. You use the voidable way to eliminate a past practice that no longer meets the three standards of a fixed and established past practice, namely: where breaks have occurred in the past practice that show that it has not been consistently, regularly or uniformly applied so as to no longer be deemed:

1. An unequivocal practice;
2. Clearly enunciated and existing over a reasonably long period of time; and
3. Accepted and acted upon in administering the written contract provisions.

Rule 50. Don't wait until the time for negotiating the renewal contract comes around. Your chances of succeeding during the contract term at the arbitration table, where the merits of the case prevail, far exceed your chances at the negotiating table, where the threat of a strike prevails.

Rule 51. Arbitration of grievance disputes arising during the contract term—not strikes—serves both the union's and management's interests.

Rule 52. The foreman's action eliminating a past practice deemed no longer feasible or appropriate, together with the shop steward's protest through a filed grievance, frames the material issue: did the foreman's action violate the contract?

Rule 53. In arbitration the written contract determines the merits of the grievance; and the arbitration tribunal finally settles that issue on its merits under the contract, not under the threat of a strike, which so often substitutes for the merits at the negotiating table.

Rule 54. You may lose the case in arbitration, but then again, you may win it. Even though you lose in arbitration, you at least will have an experience factor that may help your management's team negotiate out that past practice at renewal contract time.

The Negotiating Way

Rule 55. Without an experience factor, which you can get only by a case you lose in arbitration, trying to bargain out an established past practice at the negotiating table will prove difficult—if not impossible.

Rule 56. At the negotiating table the threat of a strike overshadows the merits of the demand to eliminate a past practice. If in the settlement the demand to eliminate an inefficient or restrictive past practice gets washed out, the renewal contract carries over that past practice into the succeeding term—more firmly acknowledged—as part of the renewal contract.

Rule 57. The negotiating way no where near substitutes for one of the three other ways available during the contract term to eliminate a past practice that changed conditions make no longer feasible or appropriate, namely: the technological way, the corrective rule way, or the voidable way.

Rule 58. The year-end negotiator in no way substitutes for the year-round administrator. Initiating action during the contract term to eliminate inefficient, costly, or restrictive past practices serves the interest of both parties because the orderly grievance and arbitration provisions and not the strike or the threat of a strike allow the parties to finally settle the action on its merits under the contract's set of working conditions.

SECTION THREE

The Rules of Overtime

7

Assigning and Distributing Overtime Work

Let's look at the subject of overtime work first within the framework of collective bargaining and the collective bargained contract.

The Labor Management Relations Act (Taft-Hartley Law), which covers collective bargaining affecting interstate commerce, requires the employer and the union representing the workers in the bargaining unit to confer in good faith over "wages, hours, and other terms and conditions of employment." Although the Act does not specifically enumerate the mandatory subjects of bargaining, as distinguished from permissive subjects, overtime practices and work schedules are mandatory subjects.

The Act obligates the parties to confer in good faith on mandatory subjects but "does not compel either party to agree to a proposal or require the making of a concession." Mandatory subjects include paid holidays and vacations, rest periods, health, welfare, and pension plans, seniority, discipline, management's rights, grievance machinery and arbitration, union security, dues checkoff, and no-strike-no-lock-out clause or pledge.

The parties may discuss other subjects outside the scope of wages, hours, and other conditions of employment, not otherwise unlawful, referred to as nonmandatory or permissive subjects, if both parties agree to confer on them. Permissive or nonmandatory subjects include performance bond against possible breach of contract, strike ballot before calling a strike or refusing a final offer, or employer contributions to an industry promotion fund.

Illegal subjects, that the law decrees unlawful for either to insist the other bargain on, include unlawful union security clauses, such as closed shop (requiring union membership before hiring), union shop with less than thirty-day grace period, insisting upon withdrawal of pending unfair labor practice charges, hot cargo, or other work jurisdiction clauses.

Since the law does not compel the parties to reach an agreement on mandatory subjects, good-faith bargaining may result in a deadlock on any mandatory subject. On nonmandatory or permissive subjects or on illegal subjects neither party can insist that the other bargain on them or have its position create an impasse over such subjects. Work schedules and overtime practices being mandatory subjects, the Act requires the parties to bargain on them in good faith without obligating them to reach agreement.

While other statutes, including state laws, may cover different areas of wages, hours, and working conditions, the Fair Labor Standards Act, referred to as the Wage-Hour Law, sets the "minimum wage, overtime and child labor standards" that apply to employees engaged in interstate commerce. That Act, with some few exceptions, requires time and a half pay for overtime in excess of forty hours worked in each work week. The Act does not:

1. Limit the number of hours of work in a day or in a week;

2. Require payment for days or hours not worked, such as holidays, vacations, sick leave; or

3. Provide for different rates of pay for work on Saturday, Sunday or holidays as such.

In bargaining over work schedules and overtime practices, negotiators may, and usually do, agree upon additional overtime and other
premium pay provisions, such as (1) time and a half over eight hours
in a day, (2) premium pay for working on Saturday, Sunday or holidays, as such, (3) reporting, call-in, or call-back premium pay, (4)
shift differentials, (5) counting a paid holiday as if worked in computing weekly overtime pay, and, in some cases, (6) shorter work day
and work week, with overtime thereafter.

The negotiators may also agree upon methods for (1) assigning,
(2) distributing, and (3) equalizing overtime, (4) shop steward
representation during overtime work periods, and other collateral
subjects dealing with work schedules and overtime practices. Then,
during the contract term, if a dispute arises as to which employees
overtime work belongs to or whether the negotiators intended to make
working overtime mandatory or voluntary, the language of the clauses,
the reasonable intent of the negotiators under them, and the negotiating
history become material facts in settling such disputes.

The Case of the Wrong Assignment of Overtime

The union filed a grievance claiming that the company's supervisors
had violated the contract by taking away overtime work from employees classified as structures mechanics and assigning it to employees
classified as sheet metal workers.

The contract set forth the job descriptions of each classified job and
provided that an employee's job classification governed his seniority
rights upon layoff and recall after layoff.

Structures mechanics ordinarily worked on the flight line doing the
repair work on in-service airplanes, generally situated on the field or
in hangars. Sheet metal workers worked inside the shop doing bench
work on sheet metal parts, and that job rated a lower wage than the
structures mechanic's job.

For some time prior to February 25th the company had assigned
structures mechanics to perform repair work on an Avianca plane
scheduled to depart on Saturday, February 27th. On Thursday, Feb-

213

ruary 25th, an outer wing panel of the plane exploded, damaging it beyond repair. The company had to remove the panel and replace it with a new one.

On Friday, February 26th, some of the structures men asked the supervisor in charge of the repair work if he wanted them to work overtime on the Saturday and Sunday. The supervisor said he didn't need them.

On Saturday the supervisor assigned the Avianca repair work to sheet metal workers; and they worked on the plane for a period of five days, including overtime hours. The union complained about the supervisor assigning the work to sheet metal men; but the supervisor refused to change the assignment. The union then filed a grievance claiming that the supervisor had improperly denied structures men work in their classification. The company denied the grievance, and the union appealed to arbitration.

At the arbitration hearing the union claimed that the "company does not have the right under the contract to disregard the established job descriptions in assigning work to employees in the bargaining unit; nor to assign to employees in a lower rated classification, work that properly belongs to employees in the higher rated classification, when employees in the latter classification are available."

In support of its claim the union argued:

The reasons given by the company for assigning the work to sheet metal workers instead of to structures mechanics—that an emergency existed, that it was not practical to assign the work to structures mechanics, and that timely completion of the work and customer relationship necessitated the company in making the assignment—had not been the reasons given by the company's supervisor nor the company's representatives in the answers to the grievance in the first and second steps; and further, said reasons were not valid nor do they justify the company in violating the contract.

The company claimed:

The job descriptions were not intended to limit work assignments but only to provide the basis for proper classification and rates of pay under the rate structure; that in the past comparable work had been assigned

214

to sheet metal workers; and since all the employees concerned are in a single, all-inclusive bargaining unit, no one group of classified employees can properly assert jurisdiction over work assigned to employees in other classifications.

In support of its claim the company argued that the accident had created "an emergency and under the circumstances, the company assigned the work to sheet metal men who were readily available, and who could work uninterruptedly and as a unit on the job, in order to meet the time schedule and maintain proper customer relations."

The company further argued the "grieving employees . . . did not suffer any loss of regular work; and that although the assignment to the sheet metal workers permitted them to obtain more overtime than was currently being assigned to structures mechanics, this action in no way violated the overtime provisions of the contract."

Finding that the "established job description of the structures mechanic classification expressly covers the work in question—and that the job classification of the lower rated job of sheet metal workers does not," I sustained the union's grievance, and in my award I said:

> The arbitrator finds no merit to the company's claim that the job descriptions were not intended to limit work assignments, but only to provide a basis to properly classify employees and determine their rates of pay.
>
> Article VIII expressly provides that the ". . . job descriptions . . . in effect on the date of the execution of this agreement . . . shall be a part of this agreement." The parties thereby made the established job descriptions a part of the contract for all purposes under the contract.

Then, noting that under the seniority provisions of the contract an employee's "job classification seniority" governed his seniority rights of layoff and recall, I said:

> Thus, it is clear that under their contract, the parties intended the separate job classifications to determine not only an employee's proper classification and rate of pay, but also his seniority preference and priority to available work covered by his job classification. Otherwise, the security offered by his job classification would be rendered valueless . . .

215

Insofar as the established job classifications under the contract restrict the employee's seniority preference to available work in his classification, so to the same extent those established job classifications restrict the company in assigning the available work to available employees classified in those separate jobs. The job classification system the parties voluntarily established under their contract restricts the flexibility of an employee in exercising his seniority preference for available work as it restricts the flexibility of the company in assigning available work. Any other conclusion would render meaningless the job classification system established by the contract.

Rejecting the company's argument that "since the contract sets up a single all-inclusive bargaining unit, it precludes jurisdictional disputes within the bargaining unit," I said:

The conflict between assignment and priority to available work arises out of the job classification system the contract sets up—not from the all-inclusive bargaining unit. The job classification system under the contract determines the intrabargaining unit jurisdiction of employees in the bargaining unit to available jobs and available work in those jobs —and conflicts over available work assignments have to be resolved in accordance with the job classification system the parties agreed upon under their contract.

As to the company's claim that on prior occasions it had assigned comparable work to sheet metal men and the union had not raised any protest, I found the proof failed to show "any established past practice whereby the parties intended to modify or change the clear and unambiguous provisions of the contract, which the arbitrator finds controlling in this case." In my award I said:

Though the company had on occasions in the past assigned comparable work to sheet men, the proof shows that on some of the jobs both structures and sheet men worked intermittently; and on others, the work assigned fell properly under the sheet metal job description.

The proof does not meet the objective standards upon which a finding can be made of the existence of an established past practice to change or modify the clear and unambiguous contract provisions. The arbitrator does not find (1) an unequivocal practice; (2) that has been clearly enunciated and acquiesced in; and (3) readily ascertainable over a reasonably long period of time as a fixed and established practice accepted by both parties.

Then, referring to the overtime clause of the contract, which provided that "Where questions arise regarding overtime, they shall be subject to the grievance procedure. It is the intent of the Company, where practicable, to divide overtime equally among affected employees," I held that the fact that the "work in question involved overtime work assignments does not make any material difference in this case," and I said:

Clearly, this provision does not license the company to assign available overtime work, expressly covered by the job description of one classification in which employees are available for that work, to employees of another classification, whose job descriptions do not cover that work. To the contrary, that provision expressly requires the company to divide overtime equally among "affected" employees—and under the facts in this case, the grievants herein were the affected employees to whom the overtime work should have properly been assigned . . . The fact that the assigned work complained of arose out of overtime work, does not change the union's claim. The company's action caused the affected employees to lose opportunity for work called for by their job classification.

The issue is not whether the company had divided the overtime work equally—but rather whether the company had violated the contract by improperly assigning the available work. The arbitrator finds the company had violated the contract by assigning the Avianca repair work to employees classified as metal workers, instead of to the grievants herein, classified as structures mechanics. The damages the grievants claim for that contract violation flow from the overtime hours actually worked by the sheet metal men.

Overtime Work Constitutes Part of an Employee's Regular Job

You see, Mr. Foreman, available work on overtime hours or days does not differ from available work during an employee's normal hours and days of work. Both make up part of an employee's regular job,

217

and consequently the duties of the regular job include the responsibility to work a reasonable amount of overtime. That leads us to the first two rules of overtime.

RULES ONE AND TWO OF OVERTIME

Rule 1. The normal hours and days of work, as well as a reasonable amount of required overtime, make up an employee's regular job.

Rule 2. The duties of an employee's regular job include responsibility to work, when required, a reasonable amount of overtime in that job.

If an employee's job security depends on available work during his normal hours of work, then his job security equally extends to available work during overtime hours for which he's qualified. If, Mr. Foreman, you can take away overtime work, which when available constitutes part of his job, then you could take away part or all of his normal hours of work and lay him off. But if you give those normal hours of work to other employees who have less seniority under the contract, you violate the seniority rights of the employee whom you laid off, because the contract gave him priority to available work.

Correspondingly, since overtime work constitutes part of an employee's regular job, it follows that performing a reasonable amount of overtime when required constitutes part of the duties of that job. And since the duties of an employee's regular job require him to be available for the normally scheduled hours of work, it follows that the responsibilities of his regular job require him to be available for and undertake a reasonable amount of overtime in that job. When you, Mr. Foreman, make available a reasonable amount of overtime, over and above an employee's normal hours of work and you assign that overtime to him, the duties of his regular job require that he be available for and undertake that overtime as part of his job.

To impose responsibility on an employee to undertake a reasonable amount of overtime as part of his regular job, you must accept the fact that that overtime constitutes part of his regular job. Conversely, if available overtime constitutes part of an employee's regular job, then he has the responsibility to undertake overtime as part of that job. Neither you nor your employees can have the one without the other. That leads to the third rule of overtime.

RULE THREE OF OVERTIME

> *Rule 3.* When you assign a reasonable amount of available overtime to one of your employees, the duties of that employee's regular job require that he undertake the overtime as part of his job.

THE CASE OF COMPULSORY VS. VOLUNTARY OVERTIME

On May 17th the company posted the following notice on the bulletin board:

The entire Shop, including the Maintenance and Toolroom Departments, will work 45 hours per week, beginning Monday, May 21st. Employees will work from 8:00 A.M. until 5:30 P.M. from Monday to Friday inclusive, with the exception of the Supercharger Department, which will retain their present working hours.

The union did not object to the company scheduling overtime work; and with few exceptions, the employees did not object. Some employees left their jobs after eight hours of work without permission and without giving their foremen any reason for failing to work the added hours of overtime, as scheduled. The company did not take disciplinary action in those cases, but the foremen handled them on an individual basis.

In September, during a grievance meeting, the union notified the company that under the contract it "had no right to require overtime work, namely, work in excess of 8 hours per day or 40 hours per week, but that any participating in such overtime work could only be voluntary on the part of the employee or employees."

The company answered the union's statement, claiming "it has the right to require such overtime work, provided it compensates the employees who work in excess of 8 hours per day or 40 hours per week in accordance with Article III of said contract and the Fair Labor Standards Act."

Then the company initiated arbitration, submitting as the issue it wanted arbitrated the "right of the employer to require overtime." The union objected to the company's demand for arbitration, claiming the issue not arbitrable under the contract.

The parties then agreed to allow the board of arbitration provided for by the contract to first decide the preliminary issue of arbitrability raised by the union; and the parties further authorized the board to issue an interim award on that preliminary issue before deciding the merits of the dispute.

In January of the following year the board of arbitration held a hearing on the preliminary issue of arbitrability. At the hearing the union argued "overtime work is optional and voluntary on the part of any individual employee, and the failure or refusal of an employee to work the scheduled overtime hours should be raised by the company in a specific grievance case against such employee," and that therefore the company did not raise an arbitrable issue.

The company claimed that its demand raised an arbitrable issue, arguing:

> It has the right under the contract to schedule overtime work and all employees in the bargaining unit are obliged to work the scheduled overtime hours, unless a proper and reasonable excuse is given; and rather than have the conflicting positions of the parties on this basic issue resolved after the company has taken disciplinary action against one or more employees for their failure or refusal to work overtime . . . the differences between the parties and their respective rights under the contract on this issue be determined by arbitration.

Following the hearing on arbitrability, the majority of the board of arbitration, including myself as chairman, issued an interim award holding that the company had raised an arbitrable issue, under Articles VIII and IX of the contract, which provided that "Whenever any grievance, dispute or controversy arises between the company and the union . . . and is not settled satisfactorily between the parties, then such dispute shall be referred to a Board of Arbitration . . ."

Following the interim award and up through May of that year the board of arbitration held further hearings on the merits of the issue raised by the company. At those hearings the company claimed "it has the right to schedule overtime hours of work on a regular basis and that employees in the bargaining unit are obliged to be available for and to work the regularly scheduled overtime hours, unless an individual employee presents a reasonable and justifiable excuse for not being able to work the overtime hours as scheduled."

The company challenged the union's position that "overtime work is optional and voluntary with the employees in the bargaining unit or that an employee or all the employees in the bargaining unit can refuse to work overtime and may not be subject to disciplinary action for their failure or refusal to work overtime."

Article II of the contract, hours of work, provided:

1. The working day shall consist of eight (8) consecutive hours of work, and the work-week shall consist of forty (40) hours, five (5) consecutive days each week, Monday through Friday.

Article III, overtime, provided:

1. All work in excess of eight (8) hours per day, or forty (40) hours per week, shall be paid for at the rate of time and one-half the regular base rate per hour for the number of hours worked.

2. Any work performed on Saturdays shall be paid for at the rate of one-and-one-half times the regular base rate per hour for the number of hours worked.

3. All work performed on Sundays shall be paid double the regular base rate per hour for the number of hours worked.

The company claimed that Article II referred "only to the regular or normal working day and work-week, for which the agreed upon contract rates of pay apply; that it does not refer to or restrict the scheduling of a longer or shorter working day or work-week; and in the past, the parties have . . . applied Article II in this way."

The company argued that "Article II must be read in context with Article III; that under Article III, the parties expressly provide the conditions and rates of pay under which employees are to work overtime; and that by its very purport, the parties contemplated and intended the company could schedule overtime work."

The union claimed:

Article II expressly provides the working day shall consist of eight (8) consecutive hours of work, and the work-week shall consist of forty (40) hours, five consecutive days each week; that this is the limit of the working day and work-week the parties agreed upon and contracted for; that this is the limit of the working day and work-week the employees are obligated to be available for and to work; and any work in excess of eight hours in a day or forty hours in a week is not compulsory but solely voluntary on the part of the employees . . . [that]

Article III, providing for overtime rates of pay, does not enlarge the working day or working week, agreed upon by the parties under Article II; it only sets forth what the rates of pay shall be, if employees were to work, at their option or voluntarily, any overtime hours; and Article III does not, expressly or impliedly, give the company the right to require employees to work overtime or to discipline them, if they fail or refuse to work overtime.

The parties relied upon other clauses in the contract to support their respective positions, including the management's right clause, Article X, which provided:

1. The operation of the plant and the direction of working forces, including the right to hire, suspend, or discharge for proper cause, or transfer, and the right to relieve employees from duty because of lack of work, or for other legitimate reasons, is vested exclusively in the company, subject, however, to the terms of the contract.

The company argued that "scheduling overtime work is a management function and responsibility and directly concerns the operation of the plant and the direction of working forces."

The union argued that Article X "does not expressly nor impliedly give the company the right to require employees to work overtime";

that Article X makes those reserved "managerial rights . . . subject, however, to the terms of the contract"; and that the company cannot use Article X to change the expressed agreement of the parties under Article II, which establishes the length of the working day and work-week during which the contract obligates employees to perform available work.

Article XIV, Subdivision 1, of the contract, also relied upon by each party, provided:

> Employees will not be requested to work overtime on the one (1) day of each month scheduled for shop meetings of the union, except in cases of emergency.

The company claimed that this section implicitly recognized its right to schedule overtime work.

The union claimed that the wording of that section showed that the company could only "request" overtime work, which the parties deemed voluntary and not obligatory.

The union further argued:

> Past practice of the parties over the years shows that overtime work had been voluntary on the part of the employees and that no employee, who for personal reasons did not want to work overtime, was compelled to do so, and no disciplinary action was taken against him; and in the past, no employee was required to give any specific reason or excuse for not working overtime, but to merely state "personal reasons," which excuse had been accepted by the company without question.

Following the close of the hearings on the merits of the dispute the parties agreed to withdraw their respective appointees on the board of arbitration and authorized me as chairman to decide the dispute and render the award as sole arbitrator.

Finding that the contract did not prohibit the scheduling of overtime work but that on the contrary, "these clauses show the parties intended that overtime work could be scheduled," in my award I said:

> The arbitrator finds and awards that the company has the right under the existing contract to schedule a reasonable amount of overtime work

223

on a regular basis, when its business and production needs reasonably require overtime work and where the amount of overtime work required does not unreasonably interfere with the health and welfare of the employees concerned, or with the legitimate objectives of the union. Where these qualifying requisites exist, as the arbitrator finds they do in this case, the employees in the bargaining unit are constrained to be available for and to work the scheduled overtime hours, unless an employee in any particular instance has a reasonable, valid or justifiable excuse for not working overtime. The arbitrator further finds and awards that the standards to be used by the parties in determining whether in any particular instance an employee's excuse for not working the scheduled overtime hours is reasonable, valid or justifiable, shall be the same standards customarily used to determine excusable absences from working the normal or regular scheduled working day of eight hours or work-week of forty hours. Where "personal reasons" are asserted by an employee, to excuse him from working overtime, in any particular instance, the company may inquire into the nature of such personal reasons and the employee is constrained to state them. An employee who is or may be unable to work the scheduled overtime hours on any particular day, shall, when able to, give prior notice thereof to his department foreman or supervisor, reasonably in advance as he is able.

Then, finding that the company based its action in scheduling regular daily overtime work of one hour "upon considerations of business and production necessities," I said:

The scheduled overtime work is found to be reasonable in amount and consonant with the normal function and responsibility of the company in managing the plant and controlling its operations. No proof has been offered to show that the scheduling of one hour overtime work per day adversely affects the health or welfare of the employees in the bargaining unit; nor does it appear that the scheduling of such reasonable overtime work, in the present period of national defense, derogates the union's goal of limiting the normal work day and work week, in line with its legitimate, historical objective.

Referring to Article II which established the normal or regular work day of eight hours and work week of forty hours, I said:

224

It is a common clause and is included, in one form or another, quite generally, in collective bargaining contracts, particularly in industries engaged in interstate commerce. This Article embodies, as a contractual right, the historical gain made by American wage earners, through collective bargaining, in establishing as a norm, an eight hour work-day and a forty-hour work-week in American industry. Its principal purpose is to protect wage earners from the necessity of working excessive hours to secure a fair wage, sufficient to maintain a fair standard of living, without endangering their health and well-being. The proof in this case fails to show that the overtime work, as scheduled, is excessive, or would, in any wise, work to the detriment of the health or well-being of the employees or the legitimate objective of the union.

Then, noting that Article II "does not prescribe a scheduled work-day or work-week," I said:

Article II does not explicitly nor impliedly prohibit or restrict the company from scheduling overtime work that may reasonably be required, depending upon the varying business necessities and production requirements of the plant. The succeeding Article III of the contract prescribes the overtime rates of pay for work beyond the normal eight hours per day or forty hours per week. Article II must be read in context with Article III. The latter Article clearly contemplates that under certain conditions reasonable overtime work may be required by the company. Article III, as well as some of the other above quoted clauses of the contract, shows the parties anticipated that the need for overtime work may arise during the contract term.

Far from prohibiting the scheduling of overtime work, these clauses show the parties intended that overtime work could be scheduled. They make provision regulating the conditions and pay therefor, when overtime work is scheduled, as well as providing certain exceptions to the scheduling, as instanced by Article XIV, Subdivision 1, above quoted.

Rejecting the union's claims that the "company cannot require any individual employee to work overtime; that overtime work is optional or voluntary with each employee; and that if an employee, for any personal reason, without further explaining the reason, fails or refuses to work overtime, the company cannot discipline him," I said:

225

Clearly, such a position, if sustained, would negate the very issue decided in this dispute. If the company has the right to schedule a reasonable amount of overtime work, when reasonably deemed necessary by business and production requirements, as the arbitrator finds it has under the facts in this case, then that right cannot be nullified or rendered meaningless by the simple device of allowing overtime work to be voluntary or optional on the part of each employee in the bargaining unit.

Reason and equity require that a contractual right or benefit be enjoyed, not frustrated. In this case, the preponderant majority of the employees in the bargaining unit want the overtime work and have performed it, without objection. Efficiency of plant and production operations, as well as protection of jobs and earning capacity, require planning and multiple-employee cooperation and endeavor.

To allow overtime work to be optional or voluntary with each individual employee would make difficult, if not fruitless, planning for and securing efficiency of operations; it would adversely affect the job and earning benefits of other employees in the bargaining unit, who want the overtime work and who are available to perform it.

Then, finding that the contract did not restrict the company in scheduling or requiring employees to work overtime, I said:

In the absence of an explicit contract provision to the contrary, the arbitrator is constrained to find and award that the employees in the bargaining unit are obligated to be available for and to work the overtime work that has been scheduled in the plant, unless in any particular instance, an employee has a reasonable, valid or justifiable excuse not to work the scheduled overtime.

Since the contract clauses showed that the parties intended a reasonable amount of overtime to constitute part of an employee's regular job, I held that the same standards to excuse an employee from working his normal hours of work would apply, including personal reasons, and I said:

The company may inquire, in any particular instance, into the nature of the personal reasons asserted by an individual employee and the employee involved will be obliged to state them.

226

The standards to be used by the parties in determining whether, in any particular instance, an employee's excuse for not working the scheduled overtime hours is reasonable, valid or justifiable, shall be the same standards customarily used to determine excusable absences from working the normal or regular scheduled work-day of eight hours or work-week of forty hours.

Pitfalls in Not Following the Rules of the Game

Let's review the facts and actions of the company and the union in the foregoing case and see how they square with the rules of labor relations the professional follows.

The company posted its notice of overtime in May. The union did not object to the company scheduling overtime and did not protest the company's action through the grievance and arbitration machinery. With few exceptions, the employees did not object and undertook the overtime work as scheduled. The few employees who refused to work the overtime didn't give any reason for refusing. The foremen handled those cases on an individual basis without taking disciplinary action. The company failed to follow the rules of equality of treatment.

ENFORCING EQUALLY THE RESPONSIBILITIES OF EACH EMPLOYEE UNDER THE LABOR CONTRACT AND PLANT RULES GUARANTEES EQUALITY OF TREATMENT FOR ALL AND AVOIDS PREFERENTIAL TREATMENT TO ANY SINGLE EMPLOYEE.

THE UNION CANNOT COOPERATE WITH MANAGEMENT IN MANAGING THE EMPLOYEES. THE SHOP STEWARD CANNOT COOPERATE WITH THE FOREMAN IN SUPERVISING THE EMPLOYEES. THE BURDEN OF MANAGING AND MAINTAINING EMPLOYEE DISCIPLINE RESTS WITH THE FOREMAN ALONE.

MAKE THE UNWRITTEN RULE OF THE SHOP AND SOCIAL PRESSURE WORK FOR YOU, MR. FOREMAN. AVOID PREFERENTIAL TREATMENT BY MAKING EACH EMPLOYEE RESPECT THE RESPONSIBILITIES OF HIS JOB EQUALLY WITH HIS FELLOW WORKERS.

227

Instead of initiating disciplinary action against the few employees who refused to work overtime, foremen extended preferential treatment to those employees who offered no valid reason to excuse them from working the overtime.

In September, four months later, at a meeting with the company's representatives the union claimed that overtime was voluntary on the part of any employee and said the company "had no right to require overtime work." The company replied, saying it "had the right to require employees to work the overtime."

The union, following the rules of the game, didn't pursue its oral protest further. The union had spoken, and the company had answered! The union didn't file a grievance or take the company to arbitration!

The union knew the rules for administering the contract:

TO ASSURE ORDER IN ADMINISTERING THE LABOR CONTRACT DURING ITS TERM, THERE IS A CLEAR PROCEDURAL LINE DRAWN: THE FOREMAN DIRECTS AND THE SHOP STEWARD GRIEVES IF HE OBJECTS, WITHOUT IMPLYING ANY GREATER WEIGHT TO THE DIRECTION THAN TO THE GRIEVANCE.

THE FOREMAN AND THE SHOP STEWARD POSSESS EQUAL STATUS IN EXERCISING THEIR RESPECTIVE ADMINISTRATIVE RIGHTS—TO DIRECT AND TO GRIEVE—IN THE BARGAINING PROCESS, IN HANDLING GRIEVANCES, AND BEFORE THE ARBITRATOR.

The union refrained from filing a grievance challenging the company's action in scheduling overtime because the union wanted to defend the interests of all employees in the bargaining unit, those who wanted and those who didn't want to work the overtime. By orally stating its position and not grieving, the union protected its own interests as a political organization by publicly announcing that the contract didn't give the company the right to compel employees to work overtime. Then the company breached the first two rules of collective bargaining:

THE SUPERVISOR NEVER GRIEVES UNDER THE LABOR CONTRACT.

MANAGEMENT NEVER INITIATES ARBITRATION TO ENFORCE ITS ORDER!

Note: Under the rules of collective bargaining there's only one case when management initiates arbitration against the union, namely, when the union violates its no-strike pledge during the contract term. The company disciplines those employees who engage in the strike and initiates arbitration against the union for money damages to retroactively compensate for the losses the company suffered.

The company grieved and initiated arbitration against the union! In grieving and initiating arbitration the company failed to follow the negotiating rules of labor relations:

COLLECTIVE BARGAINING AGREEMENTS REGULATE OR RESTRICT THE EXERCISE OF MANAGEMENT'S RIGHTS. THEY DO NOT PROHIBIT MANAGEMENT FROM PERFORMING THEM.

THE CONTRACT DOESN'T GIVE OR SPELL OUT MANAGEMENT'S SUBSTANTIVE RIGHTS IN CONDUCTING ITS BUSINESS. MANAGEMENT RETAINS AS RESERVED RIGHTS ALL THOSE RIGHTS THAT HAVE NOT BEEN EXPRESSLY REGULATED OR RESTRICTED BY THE AGREED-UPON SET OF WORKING CONDITIONS SET FORTH IN THE CONTRACT.

By submitting and framing the issue as the "right of the employer to require overtime," the company breached the following rules of labor arbitration:

FRAME THE ISSUE AND SUBMIT AND ARGUE YOUR CASE BEFORE THE ARBITRATOR ON THE MATERIAL ISSUE: DID THE COMPANY'S ACTION (OR THE UNION'S ACTION IN STRIKING) VIOLATE THE CONTRACT?

HE WHO INITIATES ACTION HAS THE BURDEN OF JUSTIFYING HIS ACTION. WHOEVER STARTED THE "CHAIN OF

EVENTS" TAKES ON THE BURDEN OF ANSWERING THE
QUESTION "WHY?"

WHEN THE FOREMAN ACTS, HE MAKES HIS MANAGE-
MENT RESPONSIBLE FOR HIS ACTIONS. WHEN THE SHOP
STEWARD ACTS BY VIOLATING THE NO-STRIKE PLEDGE,
HE MAKES HIS UNION RESPONSIBLE FOR HIS ACTIONS.

The union didn't initiate action. The company did, by scheduling overtime work. The union didn't violate its no-strike pledge; and the union didn't protest the company's action through the grievance machinery. The company voluntarily submitted its own action to review by the board of arbitration. Instead of waiting until the union challenged the company's action through grievance and arbitration, the company asked the arbitration board for what amounted to a declaratory judgment to advise the company whether or not it had the right to manage its business in scheduling overtime work.

The union, following the professional rules of the game, didn't want to have a board of arbitration advise the parties of their respective rights under the contract. Since the company, by initiating arbitration to review its own actions, had, in effect, joined issue on management's rights vs. union rights, the union objected, claiming the issue submitted by the company not arbitrable.

Arbitrable or not arbitrable, the union tried to protect the interests of every employee in the bargaining unit it represented, even those who didn't want to work overtime. As the United Rubber Workers manual advises its shop stewards in the rules of labor relations, "A steward has the responsibility of enforcing the contract in the best interests of all the workers."

"The problems of management," says the UAW *Steward's Guide,* "are not the steward's problems. It is not up to the stewards and committeemen to make workers toe the line or to increase efficiency."

Another four months went by after the company initiated arbitration before the board of arbitration decided the preliminary issue of arbitrability. The majority of the board, the union representative dissenting, held the company's "grievance" arbitrable.

Then the union let out all stops, even though most of the employees wanted the overtime. The company, by not following the rules of the game, forced the union to take a position on management's rights vs. union rights to protect a few of the employees at the expense of the preponderant majority of employees. The union had avoided challenging the company's right to compel employees to work the scheduled overtime because most of the employees wanted it. The union could not discipline the few employees who didn't want to assume equally their responsibilities with all the other employees. The union did not give preferential treatment to those few employees; the company did by not disciplining those employees who had refused without a reasonable excuse to work the scheduled overtime, thereby failing to enforce the job responsibilities equally upon all employees. If the company had taken disciplinary action, it would have avoided putting the interests of the majority of the employees, as well as the union's interests as the representative of all the employees, in jeopardy.

Then, another four months passed until May, when the board completed the hearings on the merits of the company's grievance. Then in June, more than a year since the company had posted its notice, the company won, but so had the great majority of employees. However, during that year, those who wanted to, worked the overtime; and those who didn't, the company did not discipline; and they received preferential treatment.

Why did the arbitration take about a year? Because the company did not follow the rules of the game. If the company had initiated corrective disciplinary action by written reprimands against the few dissidents who wanted preferential treatment, the board of arbitration provided for by the contract would have speedily settled the rights of the parties by deciding the just cause of the company's action. The union would have defended the rights of the few without jeopardizing its own rights or the rights of the many.

As a professional, Mr. Foreman, follow the rules of the game of labor relations in handling grievances and disciplinary cases during the contract term. Exercise your right to manage by initiating action; and leave it to the shop steward to exercise his right to protest your action but not your right to initiate the action. Then you'll be managing with a union along lines of excellence.

231

Did the Negotiators Intend Overtime Work?
That's the Question

In bargaining out the hours of work and overtime clauses, as mandatory subjects, the negotiators for both sides had full latitude to discuss the issue of compulsory vs. voluntary overtime work. Some contracts call overtime work voluntary on the part of the individual employee; others require the union's prior consent; and some expressly make overtime work mandatory.

In most contracts the negotiators agree upon the conditions to govern overtime—when required, scheduled, assigned, or performed —without explicitly dealing with the issue of compulsory vs. voluntary overtime. At the bargaining table both sides usually skirt that issue; and to avoid a locking of horns that could lead to a strike, they leave the issue, if it should arise during the contract term, for the parties' representatives or the arbitrator to settle on its merits under the other agreed-upon clauses dealing with overtime.

You see, Mr. Foreman, the union faces the horns of a dilemma on the question of compulsory overtime. It recognizes that production needs during the contract term may at times require employees to work overtime because of the lateness or absence of other employees, when a continuous manufacturing process requires uninterrupted manning, or when production difficulties that management could not reasonably anticipate arise. The union equally recognizes that many employees want, or need, overtime work to supplement their earnings and thus avoid taking on a second "moonlight" job.

On the other hand, unions set a goal for a shorter work day and work week to improve employees' working conditions as well as to spread the work for employees on layoff or unemployed and to increase the dues-paying membership in the bargaining unit. In some cases the union raises the compulsory overtime issue during the contract term as a pressure tactic to compel favorable grievance settlements or to fortify its bargaining position in forthcoming negotiations for the renewal contract.

So, when a dispute arises during the contract term over the issue of compulsory vs. voluntary overtime, the question arises: What did the negotiators reasonably intend under the clauses governing overtime work?

Look at your contract, Mr. Foreman, and see how many of the following clauses it contains:

1. Overtime rates for daily overtime hours as well as for more than forty hours a week.
2. Time and a half for Saturdays (or the sixth day) and double time for Sundays (or the seventh day), as such.
3. One and a half or two times the regular rate for work on holidays in addition to holiday pay.
4. Time and a half for the first day following an unscheduled change in an employee's shift or working hours, in the absence of prior notice.
5. Time and a half on the starting day of the succeeding scheduled work week when less than 48 hours intervenes after the preceding scheduled work week.
6. Shop steward representation during overtime hours.
7. Prohibiting work on certain specified holidays, such as Labor Day.
8. Giving overtime preference to shop stewards or to senior employees.
9. Requiring supervisory personnel to equally distribute overtime among qualified employees in the department or operating group when the need for overtime arises.

These clauses, as well as others your contract may contain, specifying the rates of pay and conditions governing overtime, reasonably show that the negotiators anticipated that the need for a reasonable amount of overtime may arise during the contract term; and consequently, you can reasonably conclude, Mr. Foreman, that under those clauses the negotiators intended a reasonable amount of mandatory overtime depending on operational needs or production difficulties prevailing at the time. The absence of an explicit statement making overtime voluntary supports this conclusion; and the rule of equality of treatment, each employee sharing equally the responsibilities as well as the benefits of his job, lends further support. So, in the absence of a contrary intent, we come to the next rules of overtime.

Rules Four to Six of Overtime

Rule 4. Unless the contract explicitly makes working overtime voluntary or optional, the duties of an employee's regular job constrain him to be available for and undertake a reasonable amount of overtime work when business, operational needs or production difficulties reasonably require the overtime work unless an employee in any particular instance has a reasonable excuse for not working the overtime.

Rule 5. The reasonableness of an employee's excuse for not working overtime in any particular instance should be judged by the same standards customarily used by you to determine excusable absences from working the normal or regular hours of work in that employee's job.

Rule 6. When an employee asserts "personal reasons" to excuse him from working the required overtime, you, Mr. Foreman, should inquire into the facts constituting such personal reasons; and the responsibilities of an employee's job constrain him to give you those facts.

8

Contractual Obligations Under the Hours of Work and Overtime Clause

The normal, regular, basic, or standard hours of work clause establishes substantive contractual rights and obligations that mutually bind the company and the union. Unless the contract provides otherwise, the hours of work and overtime clause does not guarantee that work will be available, does not commit the company to make work available, and does not guarantee any specific number of hours or days of work to any employee.

Consequently, Mr. Foreman, the hours of work and overtime clause does not prevent you from consolidating jobs, reducing crews, taking up slack or idle time due to technological changes or improved methods or facilities, eliminating abuse of pay for time not worked, subcontracting production or maintenance work, laying off workers—or cutting out overtime work. Hours of work and overtime depend upon work being available for employees in the bargaining unit. Then, in what way does the hours of work and overtime clause obligate you? What contractual commitment does each party give the other under the normal or regular hours and days of work clauses?

The Case of the Extra-Board Employees' Work Week

The union filed a grievance claiming that the company had violated the contract by failing to provide a forty-hour work week for those employees in the bargaining unit referred to as "extra-board" employees. The company denied the grievance, and the union appealed to arbitration.

For several years prior to the time this dispute arose the company had experienced difficulty in manning full-time skilled jobs in some of its departments operating on a seven-day continuous production schedule due, in part, to an excessive amount of absenteeism. To meet its production needs, the company had to hold over or call back regular production employees after they had completed a full shift of work. The regular employees complained about the necessity of consistently working overtime, finding it burdensome; and the company, finding the overtime costly, complained about the difficulty of securing sufficient skilled employees to man all the shifts.

The company proposed to the union setting up "boards of extra employees" in some of the departments to serve as spare hands when regular production employees were absent, out on sick leave, or on vacation. Having such a pool of spare employees would reduce the need for overtime work, conserve payment for overtime, and assure the company of sufficient skilled employees to fill its production schedules.

For several months the company conferred with the union trying to obtain its consent. The union's officers refused to agree to a plan that would bring more employees into the bargaining unit than available full-time jobs. The union feared that extra employees would threaten the gains in hours and working conditions it had secured for all regular employees under the contract. Some of the union officers recognized the need of some such plan to meet the problem and wanted to go along with it. Others opposed it. The union refused to give its consent "officially"; but because the union's officers differed among themselves,

236

the union did not protest the company's action in putting the plan into effect.

The company set up special rules to govern the hours and working conditions of extra-board employees; and although the company discussed these rules with the union, the union refused to formally consent to or approve them. Since extra-board employees worked only when substituting for regular employees absent or on vacation, they did not enjoy the earning opportunities and other benefits the contract accorded regular employees. During the three years the plan operated, up to the time of the present case, regular employees in some of the departments had filed grievances claiming that the plan violated the contract and demanded that the company terminate it. Since the union's officials continued, during this period, to differ among themselves about the plan, the union did not process any of those grievances beyond the third step of the grievance procedure—except one.

In that one, raised about a year after the company had put the plan into effect, employees in one of the departments filed a grievance claiming that the contract entitled extra-board employees to reporting pay. The company denied the grievance, claiming that the rules governing extra-board employees did not provide for reporting pay and that the company had employed extra-board employees "upon the understanding and with their individual consents that they would not be entitled to reporting pay." The majority of the board of arbitration in that case sustained the grievance and held that the company "is obligated by the terms of the contract to pay reporting pay to extra board employees on the same basis as other employees."

Thereafter, employees in the departments affected by the plan continued to raise grievances questioning the validity of the plan or some part of its operation; but the union did not process any of these later grievances beyond the third step until the last one leading up to the present case. During this period of about three years prior to the time the present dispute arose, the parties executed two renewal contracts. At no time during the negotiations of those renewal contracts did either party raise the subject of extra-board employees; and none of the renewal contracts, including the one under which the present dispute arose, referred to extra-board employees or the company's plan covering them.

237

At the arbitration hearing the union claimed that the contract entitled extra-board employees to all the working conditions and benefits regular employees enjoyed, including those under Article III, Subdivision A, which "establishes a forty-hour work week as the norm; that extra board employees are entitled to the guarantee of a forty-hour per week regular working schedule, as is provided for all other employees under the contract; and that the company is violating said Article by scheduling extra board employees for less than forty hours per week of work, with consequent loss to them in earnings, holiday and vacation benefits and job security."

The union argued, "it did not under any contract, including the present one, consent to the extra board employee set up, as a permanent part of the employee structure, . . . and were the board to disallow the union's grievance it would result in destroying the forty-hour week which the union has secured through collective bargaining."

The union demanded the company employ extra-board employees on a forty-hour work week schedule in accordance with Article III of the contract and discontinue the extra-board plan.

Article III, Subdivision A, material to the principal issue in the case, provided:

A. The normal work day shall be eight (8) consecutive hours in any one work day, and the normal work week shall be forty (40) hours in any one week . . .

1. When necessary the Company may schedule more than eight (8) hours in any one work day, and more than forty (40) hours in any one work week, and the employee so scheduled agrees to meet the same.

The company claimed that "Article III, Subdivision A, of the contract does not guarantee forty hours work a week to any employee, regular or extra board; that said Article only establishes the basis upon which overtime rates are regulated; that extra board employees are employed only for extra available work, and their working schedules are governed by the rules established for them and consented to by the union."

The company argued:

It cannot schedule forty hours' work for extra board employees under present operating conditions; that the real reason for the present grievance is to compel the company to provide and pay for overtime work, which would be inequitable and would cause the very conditions to recur, for which the plan was originally established to correct; (and) the extra board plan is the only practical and fair method for distributing available work.

The board of arbitration sustained the union's grievance, holding that the company had violated Article III, Subdivision A "in failing to provide a forty (40) hour work week for extra board employees."

In my accompanying opinion, written as chairman of the board, I found that the union did not under any of the contracts, including the present one, "agree to the extra board employee set-up as a permanent part of the employee structure." Then, noting that the union did not "bind itself to accept the plan as an amendment or auxiliary part of any contract," I said:

> The extra board plan was purposely not made part of the contract. It was never incorporated, directly or by reference, into any of the renewal contracts, including the existing one. It is clear why this subject was not raised by the union or by the company in any of the contract negotiations . . . Both parties were aware, that were it raised, agreement would not have been reached. Both parties deemed it best to allow the plan to continue, not as a contractual right or obligation, but as one, outside the contract, and therefore, "at will."

Finding that the union "did not waive its contractual right to insist that extra board employees be accorded the same rights and benefits accorded all other employees in the bargaining unit," I said:

> The extra board employee plan is not and never was a part of any contract between the parties. The proof shows that it was expressly not made a part of any contract. It cannot be made a part of the existing contract, under the guise of an arbitration proceeding . . .
>
> This board has not the authority or function to add to the contract that which the parties themselves, by their acts and conduct, refrained from adding during three contract negotiations and renewals. It follows, therefore, that if the extra board plan was never a part of the contract, the award in this case upholding the union's grievance does not "eliminate" the plan from the contract, as the company claims.

Then, referring to the union's claim that Article III, Subdivision A, "guarantees a forty-hour work week to all employees" and the company's counterclaim that Article III "does not guarantee any number of hours to any employees, and that said Article simply sets up what is known as the normal work week, beyond which are overtime hours and paid for accordingly," I said:

> Article III, Subdivision A is a common provision in collective bargaining contracts. It does not, as the union contends, guarantee any number of specific daily or weekly hours of work to any employee in the bargaining unit. Yet, it is not merely, as the company contends, a measure for determining when overtime pay shall be paid . . .
>
> The "normal" work-day and work-week provision does not guarantee that work will be available or that any employee in the bargaining unit is assured of work during that normal period. The scheduling of work and employees for work is usually dependent upon varying business necessities and production requirements. The right of employees in the bargaining unit to be scheduled for available work is governed by a number of provisions in the contract, seniority, layoff and recall . . . One of those provisions is the normal work-day and work-week clause. It is a substantive provision and creates, within the limits of the contract, mutual rights and obligations.

Then, noting that the "normal work-day and work-week provision obligates employees to be available for work when scheduled," I said:

> The normal work-week and work-day provision obligates the company to schedule hours of work in any one day consecutively . . . It also obligates the company that when work is available and it schedules work, the opportunity of working a normal work day and work week will be accorded to all employees in the bargaining unit, subject to the other expressed terms of the contract . . .
>
> Extra board employees are entitled to this right of opportunity to available work, equally with other employees in the bargaining unit. Under the company's present extra board plan, extra board employees do not get this right. As a result, they suffer certain inequities . . .
>
> Some of the extra board employees have seniority standing of up to five years. Yet, by reason of their status as extra board employees, they

they have less job security and opportunity than regular production employees with less seniority in the bargaining unit—although, as the company concedes, they are covered by the same seniority provisions of the contract.

Finding that the company violated Article III, Subdivision A, by failing to provide the same opportunity of a normal forty-hour work week to extra board employees in the bargaining unit covered by the same provisions of the contract as regular employees, but to avoid the hardship that would flow from abruptly discontinuing the extra board employee plan, the board of arbitration unanimously awarded as follows:

> That no additional extra board employees be hired by the company; that the company shall proceed to schedule as many of the present extra board employees for a regular 40-hour work week as there are or may be production jobs available, in accordance with the seniority standing of the present extra board employees and the seniority provisions of the contract . . .
>
> That present extra board employees shall be absorbed into regular production jobs, as they become available, in accordance with their present seniority standing and the seniority provisions of the contract, to the end that the existing extra employee plan shall be discontinued and terminated.

THE COMPANY'S CONTRACTUAL COMMITMENT

When you, Mr. Foreman, make work available to your employees, the normal or regular or basic or standard hours of work clause contractually commits you to schedule that work so that your employees will normally or regularly work, let's say, an eight-hour five-day work week and not normally or regularly work a shorter or longer work day or work week!

You see, Mr. Foreman, the negotiators agreed upon what normally or regularly would constitute a work day and work week, depending upon work being available. If you have available work, that clause commits you to schedule it so that those qualified employees whose seniority rights give them priority to such available work will have the opportunity of normally or regularly working the normal or regular work day and work week as agreed upon.

If an employee has seniority rights to work that will normally afford him the normal agreed-upon hours and days of work, you would violate his rights if you compelled him to share that normal work with other employees. Employees don't want to "share the poverty." If there's not enough work available to provide all the employees in your department with the normal work day and work week as agreed upon, then those whose seniority rights give them priority to such work want that normal day's or week's work. To spread the available work by taking some of it away from those who have seniority rights to it and giving it to others would violate the agreed-upon normal hours of work clause. In the absence of other provisions the negotiators may have agreed upon to spread available work, the normal hours of work clause commits you to schedule the normal hours and days of work for those employees who have seniority rights to that work and to lay off the remaining employees for whom available work does not exist.

The "normal" clause also restrains you, Mr. Foreman, from stretching the agreed-upon norm of a work day or work week into a consistently longer work day or work week so that the agreed-upon normal work day or work week becomes permanently abnormal.

Conversely, however, by establishing the norm of a work day and work week the negotiators anticipated the need for some longer or shorter days and weeks, abnormal ones—above or below the norm. Auxiliary clauses governing the conditions of working less than the norm (reporting, call-in, or call-back clauses) or working more than the norm (overtime and premium rates of pay and methods for distributing overtime) show the parties intended employees would work some abnormal hours or days—below or above the norm.

THE UNION'S CONTRACTUAL COMMITMENT

By agreeing to a normal or regular work day and work week clause, the union contractually agrees that when you, Mr. Foreman, schedule qualified employees according to their seniority rights to work the normal or regular hours and weeks of work, those employees will be available for and undertake that work. The inability of an employee

242

to report regularly and on time for his normal scheduled hours of work because of absences due to chronic sickness (even though supported by doctor's certificates) does not relieve that employee from meeting the normal days and weeks of work the contract commits him to.

Unexcused absence or lateness or stoppage of work for union business, including abuse by a shop steward of his representative office, does not relieve any employee from meeting the union's contractual commitment. Likewise, by agreeing to the normal hours of work clause the union implicitly recognizes that abnormal days and weeks of work may occur—below or above the norm. Consequently, when operational or personnel needs or production difficulties require a reasonable amount of overtime over and above the norm, the union commits each qualified employee assigned such overtime to make himself available for and undertake that overtime as part of his regular job.

Rules Seven to Thirteen of Overtime

To sum up these further rules of overtime:

Rule 7. Unless the contract provides otherwise, the hours of work and overtime clauses do not guarantee that work will be available and do not commit the company to make work available; nor do those clauses guarantee any specific number of hours or days of work or overtime to any employee.

Rule 8. When work becomes available, the normal or regular or basic or standard hours of work clause contractually commits the foreman to schedule that work so that qualified employees whose seniority rights give them priority to such available work will have the opportunity to work the normal or regular work day and work week, and not normally or regularly work a shorter (sharing the poverty) or longer (permanently abnormal) work day or work week.

Rule 9. When the foreman schedules qualified employees according to their seniority rights to work the normal or regular

243

hours and days of work, the union commits, under the normal or regular or basic or standard hours of work clause, those employees to be available for and undertake that work.

Rule 10. The inability of an employee to be available for his normal scheduled hours of work because of absences due to chronic sickness (even though supported by doctor's certificates) does not relieve that employee from meeting the normal days and weeks of work that the contract obligates him for.

Rule 11. Unexcused absence or lateness or stoppage of work for union business, including abuse by a shop steward of his office, does not relieve an employee from meeting his normal or regular hours of work.

Rule 12. Auxiliary clauses governing the conditions of working less than the norm (reporting, call-in, or call-back clauses) or working more than the norm (overtime and premium rates of pay and methods for distributing overtime) show that the negotiators intended employees to work some abnormal days or weeks below or above the norm.

Rule 13. When operational or personnel needs or production difficulties require a reasonable amount of overtime over and above the norm, the hours of work and overtime clauses commit each qualified employee assigned such overtime to be available for and undertake that overtime as part of his regular job.

The Case of Whose Overtime Work:
Day or Shift Pipefitters?

The union filed a grievance protesting the foreman's action in assigning certain construction work, on a Saturday, to two shift pipefitters, claiming that the work "was outside of the shift pipefitters' job, as agreed to by the parties." The union demanded that the company pay day pipefitters at overtime rates for the hours spent by the shift pipefitters on the work. The company denied the grievance, and the union appealed to arbitration.

Under the contract both day and shift pipefitters carried the same job rate, with a shift differential for the latter. A single seniority roster covered both classified jobs; but each one had its own separate overtime roster.

Some time before this case arose, both shift and day pipefitters had helpers assisting them in the work. Then, when the company removed the helper from shift pipefitters, the union protested the change. The company justified its action in a letter to the union whereby it limited the job duties of shift pipefitters to what the parties called "emergency and general maintenance" work and "performing jobs that do not require the assistance of a helper." Day pipefitters continued to do construction work assisted by helpers. The union accepted this change in job duties for shift pipefitters and dropped its protest.

Then, on a Saturday, the foreman called in, at overtime rates, a day pipefitter and helper to do some construction work. They worked a full day shift, 7:30 A.M. to 4:00 P.M.

On that Saturday a shift pipefitter reported for his regularly scheduled shift, 7:00 A.M. to 3:00 P.M. His foreman assigned him to do part of the construction work the day pipefitter and helper were then doing. He protested, claiming that the work was not part of his regular job. The foreman insisted that he do the work, and he did, spending five hours on the job. He left at 3:00 P.M., the end of his shift. The day pipefitter and his helper continued with the work until 4:00 P.M., the end of their day shift. On that same Saturday the foreman had assigned another shift pipefitter to do incidental work related to the construction job that didn't require the assistance of a helper. He spent three hours doing that incidental work, which the union also claimed constituted construction work.

At the arbitration hearing the union claimed:

The company's letter constituted an agreement limiting the shift pipefitters' job to emergency and general maintenance work only; the union relied upon that agreement, in allowing the company to remove helpers from the shift pipefitters' job; and the company violated that agreement, by assigning construction work . . . that should have been assigned to day pipefitters, who were assisted by helpers.

The union demanded that the company pay eight hours pay at overtime rates to day pipefitters whom the foreman should have called in to work, for the time spent by the two shift pipefitters on construction work that Saturday.

The company claimed:

Its letter did not limit shift pipefitters to emergency and general maintenance work only; and it did not restrict the company from assigning to shift pipefitters any type of work pipefitters normally performed, including incidental construction work, that had been performed by day pipefitters and had either been left over or could not have been completed by the latter during their day shift.

The company further argued that the "contract reserves to the company the right to assign work of any type to employees classified as pipefitters, irrespective of the shift they worked on; and the established past practice supports the company's right in making the assignments."

Finding that the company's letter constituted an agreement under which the "parties intended to delineate the duties and responsibilities of the shift pipefitters' job, as distinct from the day pipefitters' job . . . [and] the parties intended to confine shift pipefitters to emergency and general maintenance work [that did not] require the assistance of a helper," I sustained the union's claim as to the shift pipefitter who had worked five hours on the construction job but denied its claim for the three hours worked by the other shift pipefitter who did incidental work related to the construction job left over by the day pipefitter.

As to the five-hour claim, I found that that work "had not been left over from the day shift. It was construction work . . . then being performed by a day pipefitter with a helper." In my award I said:

The arbitrator finds that that was the type of construction work the parties intended to exclude from the shift pipefitters' job under the . . .

agreement. A contrary finding . . . would in effect render meaningless that agreement. The essential purpose justifying the company's action in removing helpers from shift pipefitters would be nullified. The union relied on the description of the shift pipefitters' job the company itself described. The union accepted that description as constituting the regular job content of shift men, namely, they were to perform emergency or general maintenance work. That constituted a material change in the former job of shift men. It was upon that basis the union acquiesced in the company's action in removing helpers from shift men. To construe the . . . agreement otherwise . . . would do violence to the very objective the parties intended and put into effect by that agreement.

As to the three-hour claim, the proof showed that the "work he performed had been left over by the day pipefitter who had been unable to complete it by the end of the latter's shift; and the foreman assigned it to him to complete it." Finding that the past practice supported the assigning of such incidental work left over by the day pipefitters, I said:

His foreman . . . had always assigned shift men to complete jobs the day men could not finish on their shift, which did not require the use of a helper . . . [and] that he had followed this past practice for years and that neither the men nor the union had raised any complaint.

I denied the three-hour claim and awarded that the "company shall pay for five hours of work, computed at time and a half of the regular pipefitters' rate, which sum shall be distributed to the appropriate day pipefitters as damages for said violation."

DISTINGUISHING BETWEEN INCIDENTAL WORK AND CLASSIFIED JOBS

The normal hours of work and overtime clauses do not obligate you, Mr. Foreman, to provide overtime work in any job; nor do those clauses prevent you from eliminating overtime work if the need for the overtime no longer exists.

"Pipefitters' work is pipefitters' work," you may say. True, but "an agreement is an agreement" that sets up different classified jobs. In the foregoing case the company itself had separated the job of day pipe-fitter from that of shift pipefitter, had distinguished the duties between each of those jobs, and had, in effect, made each of those jobs separate classified ones. The union had acquiesced in the company's action of removing the helper from the shift pipefitter's job based on the changed duties in those two jobs.

Assigning construction work to one of the shift pipefitters during his regular scheduled hours of work, at straight-time rates, had deprived day pipefitters of the available five hours of overtime work covered by their classified job. To that extent, the company had violated the agreement made with the union. In assigning the other shift pipefitter, at his straight-time rate, to do the leftover incidental work that did not require a helper, the foreman acted in the way the parties intended under their agreement.

You may find it difficult at times, Mr. Foreman, to distinguish between work that belongs to a classified job and work that's incidental or only indirectly related to that job. Reasonable people may disagree with your judgment; and the shop steward may protest your action in assigning the work. As long as you observe the set of working conditions of the contract without subterfuge or abuse, your employees will respect your judgment even though the shop steward challenges it.

The Case of Who Services the Air Compressor?

An employee classified as helper in the Maintenance Department who regularly worked on the first shift filed a grievance claiming that he had been deprived of overtime work on the second shift on two days during his work week. During the week in question, on his regularly scheduled first shift he helped service an air-compressor machine the company had rented to use in certain repair work.

On two separate days during that week the company continued to use the air compressor on the second shift. On each of those days a maintenance mechanic or helper on the first shift checked the compressor for mechanical needs shortly before the end of the first shift. During the second shift on those days the compressor required no repairs or mechanical servicing. Available employees on the second shift fed the necessary gasoline or water required to keep the machine running.

The grievant claimed that the foreman should have kept him over on overtime on the second shift to service the air compressor. The foreman denied the grievance on the ground that he had not deprived the grievant of any overtime work opportunity under the contract. The union then appealed to arbitration.

At the arbitration hearing the union claimed that since the grievant "had serviced the air compressor on the first shift, the company should have kept him over onto the second shift on those two days, at overtime, to continue to service it; and the company violated the contract in allowing employees on the second shift, other than maintenance mechanics . . . crew, to service the air compressor."

The company claimed, "no employee was assigned to service the air compressor, at overtime, on the second shift; no repair or mechanical service work had been performed on the air compressor by any other employees in the department; the services of a maintenance mechanic or helper were not required to service the machine on the second shift on those days; and none had been assigned to perform such work."

Finding that the "work performed on the air compressor during the second shift on the two days in question did not require the services of a maintenance mechanic or helper," I denied the union's grievance. In my award I said:

No maintenance mechanic or helper had been assigned to overtime work on the second shift on those two days. Regularly scheduled employees on the second shift fed gasoline or water, as needed, to the compressor to keep it operating. This work was incidental to the normal functioning of the compressor and was not the kind of work that required the services of a maintenance mechanic or helper.

Section 8 of Article II, relied upon by the union to support its position, provided:

8. Insofar as practicable, overtime worked shall be equally divided among the employees in the crew and, pursuant to this policy, said overtime worked shall be rotated among said employees.

249

Finding that section "not material to the issues in this case," I said:

> No overtime work was available nor was any assigned, which could be equally divided among the employees in the crew. The arbitrator finds the parties intended that section to apply to situations where overtime work is available and employees are assigned to such overtime work. Such facts were not present in this case . . . The proof establishes that no mechanical work was performed on the air compressor during the second shift; and the company did not transfer any employee from a different crew to do any mechanical servicing work on the compressor . . . The arbitrator therefore finds the company did not violate Section 8, when it allowed regularly scheduled employees on the second shift to feed to the air compressor gasoline or water, as required, in order to keep the machine functioning in the normal course of its use.

Eliminating Overtime by Changes in Shifts or Hours of Work

When you take away work, Mr. Foreman, formerly performed by some employees at overtime rates and give it to qualified employees working during their regular scheduled hours at straight-time rates, you're bound to have your employees and the shop steward react against the change.

Suppose for the past year or so you had some of your maintenance repair men come in, say, at 6:00 A.M.—two hours before the start of their regularly scheduled shift of 8:00 A.M. to 4:30 P.M. You paid them a premium rate of, say, time and a half for those two hours; and they worked until 4:30 P.M., the end of their regularly scheduled shift. You needed those two hours before the morning shift of production workers came on at 8:00 A.M. to repair some equipment or to make ready certain changeovers on some of the machines. The rest of the maintenance repair men reported at their regularly scheduled shift time, 8:00 A.M., and the full crew worked until 4:30 P.M.

The need to have two or three maintenance men report two hours earlier each day continues pretty consistently, and you decide you can have better maintenance coverage by setting up a regularly scheduled shift for those two or three maintenance men from 6:00 A.M. to 2:30

P.M. and have the remaining maintenance men continue on the 8:00 A.M. to 4:30 P.M. shift. You figure on paying a shift differential for the 6:00 A.M. to 2:30 P.M. shift; but then you cut out the overtime pay for the two hours from 6:00 A.M. to 8:00 A.M. and have the men on the new shift work at straight-time rates.

In the absence of any contrary contract provision, the normal hours of work and overtime clauses do not prevent you from setting up the new shift or changing the starting time on existing shifts to meet the operating needs of your department. Some of the maintenance men, who liked the former overtime opportunity, may grieve; and others may prefer the change in setting up two shifts. The shop steward may protest your right to set up the other shift, but you and the shop steward can handle that issue, as well as others dealing with the amount of shift differential and the staffing of the new shift under the grievance procedure; and if you can't settle those questions, then the shop steward can appeal to arbitration to have them finally settled.

The Case of the Special-Duty Occupational Group

The company had transferred a pipefitter from the East plant pipefitters occupational group to the special-duty occupational group to fill in for two other pipefitters in the special-duty group out on vacation for a period of six consecutive weeks. During that six-week period, the transferred pipefitter worked six Sundays and one holiday as a member of the special-duty group.

The union filed a grievance claiming that the company "violated the distribution of overtime provision of the contract and the long established past practice thereunder, thereby depriving employees in the West plant pipefitters occupational group of overtime work on said days to which they were entitled." The company denied the grievance, and the union appealed to arbitration.

Article XIV of the contract, dealing with overtime, provided:

Overtime and extra work in addition to the currently scheduled work week shall be divided on the basis of hours paid for, as impartially as possible, among employees in the same occupational group in the same

251

department . . . Such impartial distribution need not take place in the same week but may be spread over a period of time.

The foreman and the steward will jointly check the equalization of overtime and extra work lists at the end of each three-month period and wherever it is evident that certain employees are out of line, so far as overtime and extra work is concerned, every effort will be made to give these employees the opportunity to be brought into line.

For the purpose of distributing available overtime among employees performing certain repair and maintenance work, the parties set up, among others, the following occupational groups: East plant pipefitters, West plant pipefitters, and special-duty group.

Forty hours over five consecutive days, Monday through Friday, constituted the normal work week for pipefitters. When assigned to work on Sunday or one of the paid holidays under the contract, they received two times their regular rate of pay. Article XXII of the contract defined the special-duty occupational group as follows:

As this Agreement is signed a "Special Duty" man is an especially assigned employee of the Pipe Shop or Electrical Department whose regular working schedule normally includes one or more of the shifts on Saturday or Sunday and time-off instead during the week, or whose regular working schedule is normally rotated to include at least one Saturday and Sunday in each period of consecutive days worked.

Because the regular working schedule of a special-duty man included one or more shifts on Saturday or Sunday, employees generally considered a job in that group less desirable than other jobs with the normal weekday schedule of work. Consequently, when the company required an employee for the special-duty work, it usually had to pick the lowest man in seniority from one of the other occupational groups and assign him as a special-duty man.

To compensate for having Saturday or Sunday in their regular working schedule, the contract granted special-duty men ten cents per hour as added compensation to their regular rate of pay. In addition, special-duty men who worked on Sunday received overtime at the rate of one and a half times their regular rate of pay and, in effect, the same for working on a payroll holiday. Employees in the other occupational groups received overtime pay at the rate of two times their regular rate of pay for working on Sunday or a payroll holiday.

Just prior to the time the dispute in this case arose the special-duty group consisted of six employees. Special-duty men worked over all parts of the premises, including the East and West plants, maintaining oil pressures, temperatures, conditions of pumps and doing other kinds of special repair work in maintaining the plant and readying the equipment over the weekend for the following week's work.

In the past, in the absence of one of the six special-duty men the company had assigned another special-duty man to take his place, but since he had his own schedule to work, the company would have to assign an employee from the pipefitter occupational group to fill in for a Sunday shift. The company would pay the pipefitter double time for such Sunday work, whereas if the regular special-duty man had worked, he would have received time and a half.

With the mills located in the East plant the need for a greater amount of maintenance and repair work always existed there, making a greater amount of overtime work available in the East plant. To make up the difference in available overtime between the East and West pipefitters groups, when the company had to fill in for occasional Sunday work, it assigned such overtime to the West plant pipefitters.

Plant maintenance required six special-duty men to cover all shifts. Two were away on vacation, each for a three-week period, so that for a consecutive period of six weeks the special-duty group lacked one man. At first the company tried to have one of the special-duty men take over certain shifts; and he agreed to have his schedule changed. However, it turned out that he would have had to work sixteen consecutive hours; and the company encountered similar difficulties in trying to rearrange the schedules of the other four special-duty men to substitute for the two special-duty men off.

The company then decided to increase the number of special-duty men by adding another pipefitter to that occupational group and temporarily assigning him as a regular special-duty man, trained to take

253

over when a permanent opening arose in that group. The company first offered the special-duty assignment to a West plant pipefitter who had the lowest seniority in his group, but he refused to accept. The company then offered the assignment to an East plant pipefitter who had the lowest seniority in his group, and he accepted.

As a member of the special-duty group he filled the regular working schedules of each of the special-duty men off on vacation during the six-week period; and he worked during that period six Sundays and one holiday that the regular special-duty men would have worked.

At the arbitration hearing the union claimed:

> The company should have assigned the overtime work on those six Sundays and the payroll holiday to a man in the West plant pipefitter group to fill in for the special-duty men on vacation; that under the long established past practice for equalizing overtime opportunity, the company had always used men from the West plant group; [and] the company by assigning . . . an East plant pipefitter to work those overtime days departed from this long established past practice and violated the rights of the West plant pipefitters under the contract, as applied by the parties.

The union argued that the "company either should have rearranged the schedules of other regular special-duty men or have used a West plant pipefitter to work the overtime resulting from the men being away on vacation during that period; and that therefore, the company should pay the overtime lost by West plant fitters who were entitled to work the days in question."

The company denied violating the overtime provision of the contract or any established past practice under it by assigning an additional pipefitter "to the special duty group to train him as a member of that occupational group and had him perform the regular schedule of work of special duty men [and] that during the six week period that he was a member of the special duty occupational group, [he] performed the Sunday and holiday work as a regular part of his scheduled job and not as an East plant pipefitter."

The company argued:

254

It had sought, by rearranging the schedules of the remaining special duty men, to have them take over the Sunday work for the men on vacation, but scheduling difficulties prevented such rearrangement; the company had first offered the job of becoming a special duty man to a West plant pipefitter, but he had turned it down; and the company properly assigned the overtime work to [the East plant pipefitter] as part of his regular schedule of work as a member of the special duty occupational group in accordance with the overtime provision of the contract.

Finding that the company's action in transferring a pipefitter "to the special duty occupational group and scheduling him to work the six Sundays and holiday during the six-week period as part of his regular schedule as a special-duty man, did not violate either the contract or the practice followed by the parties in the past," I denied the union's grievance, and in my award, said:

Article XIV, Subdivision 15 of the contract expressly provides that overtime shall be divided "among employees in the same occupational group in the same department." During that six-week period [the East plant pipefitter] was a member of the special duty occupational group —and therefore, he was entitled to share in whatever overtime work became available for that group as well as any of the other members of the special duty group.

The past practice relied upon by the union does not apply to the facts present in this case. The arbitrator finds that that past practice applied when the company assigned overtime work regularly done by employees in one occupational group to employees in another, separate occupational group. In such case, the overtime work would be assigned to men in the West plant occupational group rather than the East plant occupational group. But in this case, [the East plant pipefitter] performed the Sunday and holiday work as a member of the special duty occupational group—and as part of his schedule of work in that group, in accordance with the requirements of Article XIV.

Then, finding that the "contract does not restrict the company in determining the number of employees in an occupational group and

... the facts in this case clearly demonstrate that [the East plant pipe-fitter] was temporarily made a member of the special duty group to meet operating and scheduling needs, present and future," I said:

> The proof shows that the company did at first seek to rearrange the schedule of the remaining special duty men but such rearrangement was not feasible nor practical; and further, the company did offer the job of being a special duty man to a West plant pipefitter . . . but he turned it down. These circumstances—coupled with the fact that the company wanted to train a replacement for regular employees in the special duty group who were approaching retirement age—eliminate any possible inference that the company sought to proceed contrary to the contract or the established past practice of affording available opportunity to employees in the West plant pipefitters' occupational group so as to equalize their overtime with men in the East plant pipefitters' group.

9

To Whom Does Available
Overtime Belong?

Since undertaking a reasonable amount of overtime work when required constitutes part of an employee's regular job, the duties of that
job require him to make himself available for that overtime work. If
you make overtime work available, then it follows that you can compel
the qualified employee in that job to undertake the overtime work as
part of his regular job; and, consequently, the overtime you make available belongs to the employee whom you can compel to work it.

By keeping an employee on his job during his regular hours of
work, you implicitly recognize, Mr. Foreman, that he's qualified for
that job. Therefore, when you make overtime available in that job,
you likewise implicitly recognize he's qualified to do the overtime
work.

Unless your contract provides otherwise, the overtime you make
available, Mr. Foreman, belongs to the qualified employee and not to
the best among the qualified employees. You will recall the three types
of seniority clauses:

1. Strict or straight seniority (Type I), which implies ability and qualifications to do the available work and gives the priority to the senior-in-length-of-service employee.

2. Modified or contingent seniority (Type II), which explicitly states the factors of ability and qualifications and gives the priority to the senior qualified employee.

3. Relatively-equal-in-ability seniority (Type III), which provides a relative evaluation between and among qualified employees and gives the priority to the best-qualified employee.

If your contract gives overtime to the senior employee, the overtime belongs to him, provided he's qualified to do the available work. If your contract requires you to distribute overtime equally among employees in a department or other operating unit, then you must allow those employees qualified to do the work to share in it. You cannot, Mr. Foreman, choose the best among the qualified employees.

Of course, if the overtime requires a journeyman, it belongs to the journeyman, not to the helper. If the overtime work relates to the skills and duties of a classified job, then the overtime belongs to the employees in that classified job.

How about employees on layoff? Do they have any rights to the available work you assign as overtime? Can you require employees working their scheduled normal hours to work overtime when other employees in those classified jobs remain out on layoff?

The Case of Overtime Rights of Laid-off Employees

The company had disciplined two employees classified as assemblers in the experimental model shop department 53, who had refused to work overtime because other assemblers were on layoff "unless the union committee granted them permission." The union protested the disciplinary action and the parties agreed to submit the dispute to arbitration.

At the arbitration hearing the union challenged the company's right to compel employees to work overtime on the ground, among others, that under the contract:

Overtime work is voluntary on the part of any individual employee or group of employees; that under the present and prior agreements an "unwritten understanding" had been established and followed requiring the company to get the approval of the union shop committee before an employee would work overtime when there was a layoff of other employees in his classification or department . . . [and] the company's action in disciplining the two employees—who refused to work over- time because at the time other employees in their classification were on layoff—was improper and violated the provisions of the written agree- ments between the parties.

The company claimed that the "overtime provisions of the agree- ment clearly show the parties intended overtime work to be com- pulsory, when required, and not voluntary on the part of any employee or group of employees . . . whether or not other employees were on layoff at the time."

The company also claimed:

The overtime required of the two assemblers on April 30th and May 1st was reasonable to meet the company's needs in the experimental and development work the two assemblers had been engaged in and were familiar with; that even though there may have been other assemblers in other departments on layoff at that time, it would not have been practical or efficient to recall and train them in the required experimental work that was being carried on; and the agreement does not obligate the company to do so.

The agreement set up the procedure and conditions to govern over- time work. Subdivision (i) provided:

(i) The Employer agrees to rotate overtime within a department equally among employees working on similar work, provided that the employees are capable of performing the work for which overtime is required. The term similar being defined as work which can be per- formed by employees holding the same occupation and having the same calibre of skill within the occupation, in relation to the work for which overtime is necessary. Disputes as to the application of this clause shall be subject to the grievance procedure.

259

Other subdivisions specified the necessary advance notice and the number of union stewards and committeemen assigned for "required" overtime work.

Finding that under the agreement the "company has the right to schedule and require employees to work sufficient and reasonable amounts of overtime and to discipline individual employees who, without a reasonable excuse, refuse to work such overtime," I said:

> Eight times in the overtime provisions, the parties explicitly use the word "require." In Subdivision (i) the company agrees to rotate overtime within a department . . . "for which overtime is required." Subdivision (j) stipulates the advance notice to be given—whenever "overtime work is required." Subdivision (k) stipulates the number of stewards to be included when "overtime work is required," depending upon "the number of employees required" to work such overtime. Subdivision (l) provides: "Whenever overtime work is required," a duly elected shop committeeman, selected by the union, "shall work overtime" for every major fraction of 100 employees "required to work overtime."

Then, finding that the overtime provisions did not "require the union shop committee's approval for employees to work overtime, when required . . . nor do those clear provisions distinguish between working the required overtime when other employees may be on layoff or not," I said:

> On the contrary . . . the parties expressly provided and intended that when the company's business or production needs reasonably necessitated overtime work, the company could require—order—employees to work overtime, irrespective of whether at the time other employees were on layoff in the classification or department, unless any particular employee had a reasonable, valid reason to excuse him from working the required overtime in any particular instance.

Finding that the "company had good business and operational reasons to require these two employees to work overtime, even though at the time other assemblers in other departments were on layoff," I said:

[The two] assemblers . . . had been engaged on experimental work in department 53. They worked alongside of design engineers and model shop mechanics, experimenting on new types of machines. They did not work on regular production assemblies. They were engaged in making test runs on experimental machines which they had been working on for several months, and with which they were familiar.

Engineers and mechanics, whom they worked alongside of, orally directed them in their work. There were no formal procedures which could be followed in making the test runs. No assemblers were on layoff from their department at the time.

The proof does not show that there were assemblers on layoff from other departments who were qualified to do the work in the experimental model shop. The union simply claims an "unwritten understanding"—which the arbitrator finds has not been established—that employees could not be required to work overtime when other employees were on layoff without the union shop committee's approval. The agreement reserves to the company, not to the union's shop committee, the right to determine the necessity for overtime work, depending upon the company's business and operational needs.

The management's rights clause, Article X of the agreement, provided:

The management of the plant and the direction of the working force, including the right to hire, suspend or discharge for cause, to assign to jobs, to transfer employees within the plant, to increase and decrease the working force, to determine products to be handled, produced or manufactured, the schedules of production and the methods, processes and means of production or handling is vested exclusively in the Employer, provided this will not be used for the purpose of discrimination against any employee or to avoid any of the provisions of this agreement.

Noting that that "provision reserves to the company the right to determine the business or operational need for overtime work even if other employees at the time may be on layoff," with seniority rights of recall, I said:

The agreement doesn't circumscribe that right; nor does the agreement give the union shop committee the right to judge or decide the necessity for overtime work. The union has the right to challenge the company's action in an orderly way through the grievance and arbitration procedures provided by the agreement, if the company's action, in requiring employees to work overtime, was "used for the purpose of discrimination against any employee or to avoid any of the provisions of this agreement."

Then, finding that the "company has the responsibility in requiring employees to work overtime when other qualified employees may be on layoff at the time, to see that its action does not discriminate against the rights of those qualified employees on layoff or violate any of the provisions of the agreement," I said:

Article IV of the agreement, hours of work, establishes the regular work day and work week for employees in the bargaining unit. Employees on layoff with recall rights continue to be in the bargaining unit. Article IV contemplates that there may be shorter, or longer, work days and work weeks than the regular ones, depending upon the availability of work, the availability of qualified employees, the business necessities then prevailing, or the production difficulties present at the particular time. Some employees may be on layoff and others required to work overtime, depending on those operational needs and qualifications of available employees.

Then, finding that "Article IV shows the parties intended overtime work to be part of an employee's regular job by providing for overtime rates of pay for work in excess of the regular work day or work week; by providing to rotate overtime within a department equally among employees working on similar work; by requiring advance notice; and by providing for the employment of shop stewards and committeemen on the overtime," I said:

Whether the company's action in scheduling and requiring employees to work overtime when other employees in the bargaining unit qualified to do the available work are on layoff, violates the rights of those qualified laid-off employees to be recalled, depends upon the reason-

262

ableness of the company's action in the light of the business and operational necessities prevailing at the time. The company must equate its operating needs with the job rights of all employees in the bargaining unit, as agreed to by the collective bargaining agreement. The necessity for the overtime in light of the business, operational or production difficulties then present; the availability of qualified employees; and the extent of the overtime required—in the absence of any contrary written provision—make up the criteria which the company must consider in equating its needs to schedule overtime with the job rights of qualified employees to be recalled and given opportunity to work under the collective bargaining agreement.

Under the agreement between the parties, the union retains the right to challenge the company's action in requiring employees to work overtime beyond the regular work day or work week, if the union believes the rights of other employees on layoff are being violated. That challenge, however, must be made in an orderly way through the grievance and arbitration procedures, not by the union shop committee countermanding the supervisor's order. The agreement does not give the union shop committee the right to give or withhold its approval for employees to work overtime, when ordered. The agreement gives the union shop committee the right to protest the supervisor's order and seek redress under the grievance and arbitration provisions.

Finding that "no assemblers were on layoff in the experimental department 53 . . . [or] on layoff from other production departments who were qualified to do the experimental work . . . [and] business reasons and operational necessities present at the time in the experimental work being done in department 53 warranted the company in requiring assemblers . . . to work overtime," I said:

The arbitrator therefore finds the company's action in assigning and requiring these two assemblers to work overtime did not violate any of the rights of other assemblers who may have been on layoff at the time; nor violate the rights of the union under the labor agreement. The arbitrator further finds that since working a reasonable amount of overtime constitutes part of an employee's regular job, he must be available for and work required overtime, unless he has a justifiable, valid reason at the time to excuse him from working.

263

Then, finding that the two assemblers "did not give any justifiable or valid reason to excuse them from working the required overtime," I said:

> The arbitrator finds that under the labor agreement between the parties, an employee who fails or refuses without a reasonable, valid excuse to work a reasonable amount of required overtime, subjects himself to disciplinary action. Article XI of the labor agreement provides that employees "are subject to disciplinary action or discharge for just cause." The failure or refusal of an employee to work the required overtime, in the absence of a valid reason to excuse him, constitutes just cause for disciplinary action. The arbitrator finds the company had just cause for disciplining these two employees by written reprimands for their refusal to work the required overtime on April 30th and May 1st.

The Three Reasonable Rules of Overtime

> But often the contract does not provide a clear-cut "yes" or "no" answer to a grievance. If the contract says, for example, that the workers must work a "reasonable" amount of overtime, and the men in your department don't want to work, the settlement of the grievance depends on just what the word "reasonable" means in this situation. This may be a grievance. The men think they are being treated unfairly and if you can make a good case that the company is being "unreasonable" you should take the case up. If you can't convince the company it is being unreasonable, maybe an arbitrator will agree with you.

That's what the AFL–CIO manual advises shop stewards. You see, Mr. Foreman, the shop steward judges your supervisory action by the same rules you follow in performing your supervisory job, namely:

> IN ADMINISTERING CONTRACT CLAUSES, SUPPORT YOUR JUDGMENT BY THE FACTS OF THE CASE AND JUSTIFY YOUR ACTION BY THE RULE OF REASON OF WHAT A RESPONSIBLE, PRUDENT FOREMAN WOULD DO UNDER THE PRODUCTION, OPERATIONAL, OR PERSONNEL CIRCUMSTANCES PREVAILING AT THE TIME.

NEVER USE THE WORD "EMERGENCY" TO SUPPORT OR JUSTIFY ANY ACTION YOU TAKE IN INTERPRETING OR APPLYING CONTRACT CLAUSES! BE PREPARED TO SUPPORT YOUR ACTION BY THE PRODUCTION, OPERATIONAL OR PERSONNEL DIFFICULTIES YOU HAD TO OVERCOME.

In assigning, distributing and enforcing overtime work, your employees judge your actions by the same rules: Did you act reasonably when you required your employees to work overtime in this situation? Did you act reasonably in applying the benefits and enforcing the job responsibilities under the hours of work and overtime clauses equally among your employees and without preferentially treating anyone?

"Reasonable" means free from bias, prejudice, or discrimination; reasonable means supervising without fear or favor; reasonable means acting without subterfuge or abuse. Yes, when you come right down to it, Mr. Foreman, reasonable means the same as "just cause." The rule of reason applies when you impose corrective discipline, when you establish and enforce plant rules, when you judge the personal conduct of your employees, and in arbitration, when the arbitrator reviews the cause for your disciplinary action.

When you discipline employees who refuse to work the required overtime, prepare yourself, Mr. Foreman, to meet the challenge of the following three reasonable rules of overtime:

1. Reasonable in amount.
2. Reasonable advance notice.
3. Reasonable excuse not to work the overtime.

WHAT CONSTITUTES A REASONABLE AMOUNT OF OVERTIME?

Unless your contract provides otherwise, the normal hours of work and overtime clauses contemplate that employees will undertake a reasonable amount of overtime work as part of their regular jobs. A reasonable amount of overtime work depends upon: (1) business or operational necessities, (2) production difficulties, or (3) availability of qualified employees at the time.

Since you have the burden of managing, Mr. Foreman, you have the responsibility of deciding initially the reasonableness of the amount of the overtime work required. Tested against those standards of (1) business or operational necessities, (2) production difficulties, and (3) availability of qualified employees, the overtime work, daily or weekly, should not stretch over such a continuous period of time that it tends to breach the ceiling of the contract's normal or regular work day or work week.

To put that another way, the overtime should not extend uninterruptedly for such a long period of time that it converts the contractual normal or regular work day or work week into an abnormal, permanently longer work day or work week. Though the negotiators may have intended a reasonable amount of overtime as part of each employee's job, you can't construe the normal hours of work and overtime clauses, in the absence of a contrary intent, to allow you to lengthen the normal work day or work week beyond a reasonable period, or to such an extent that the overtime turns the normal work day or work week into permanently longer ones.

If you find that you need overtime work pretty regularly and rumblings start, look into the causes. Perhaps you have a lot of absenteeism or chronic sick cases in your department. Start correcting that situation. Maybe changes in operating methods call for you to consolidate jobs, take up slack or idle time, rearrange work schedules, institute new shifts, or put on more workers!

Under the normal hours of work and overtime clauses each employee's job responsibilities constrain him to undertake a reasonable amount of overtime work as part of his job. Your supervisory job responsibilities constrain you, in scheduling a reasonable amount of overtime work, to respect the normal work day and work week the negotiators intended under those clauses.

You, Mr. Foreman, initially decide the reasonableness of the overtime in light of the operational necessities, production difficulties, or availability of qualified employees prevailing at the time. If the shop steward disagrees with your decision, he can protest it through the steps of the grievance procedure; and if not satisfied, he can appeal to arbitration. Meanwhile, the shop steward and your other employees follow your order and look for redress through the orderly grievance machinery your contract sets up.

GIVING REASONABLE ADVANCE NOTICE

Some contracts stipulate the amount of advance notice required when the foreman assigns overtime work. Sometimes the duties of the job itself implicitly carry advance notice of required overtime, such as completing repair work on breakdowns or overcoming production difficulties to get the equipment back into operation as quickly as possible to avoid layoff of production workers. In a 24-hour seven-day continuous shift operation, plant rules may make overtime mandatory by providing as follows:

> IN DEPARTMENTS OF CONTINUOUS OPERATIONS, AN EMPLOYEE SHALL NOT LEAVE HIS POST AT THE END OF HIS SCHEDULED SHIFT UNTIL THE NEXT SHIFT EMPLOYEE REPLACES HIM OR UNTIL HIS SUPERVISOR RELIEVES HIM.

If your contract, Mr. Foreman, does not specify the advance notice required for overtime work, you may consider, as a rule of thumb, the following as reasonable advance notice.

1. For occasional daily or weekly overtime, notice given before or at the end of an employee's prior day's shift of work.
2. For occasional Saturday or Sunday overtime, sixth or seventh day, notice given one full intervening day or shift of work prior thereto.
3. For scheduled overtime work, daily or weekly, in the succeeding work week, notice given during or before the end of the employee's work or shift in the prior week.

Production difficulties may at times prevent you from giving such advance notice. In those cases you may have to give shorter notice; and then the production difficulty will determine the reasonableness of the notice you gave.

Here again, you balance the production necessities of your department against your employees' personal necessities; and when the situation prevents you from giving reasonable advance notice, you evaluate an employee's excuse not to work the overtime in light of the extent of the advance notice you gave. A shorter advance notice may justify you in accepting an employee's excuse that a longer advance notice would justify you in rejecting.

WHAT'S A REASONABLE EXCUSE?

Subject to unforeseen personal difficulties he may meet with, an employee's excuse not to work the required overtime should consist of the same reasons and meet the same standards that you would ordinarily accept as reasonable to excuse him from working his normal hours or days of work.

Bona fide illness that would excuse an employee from finishing up his normal working hours would customarily excuse him from staying on for the required overtime work. If an employee asks you to excuse him from working one of his normal days of work because of a "personal reason" and you're satisfied his personal reason constitutes a valid excuse, then you may accept the same kind of personal reason to excuse him from working overtime on the day you requested him. If you do not accept as a justifiable reason an employee's excuse for absence on one of his normal days, such as to take care of some personal business, attend the opening ball game, go hunting or work a "moonlight" job, then you would not accept such reasons to excuse him from undertaking a reasonable amount of overtime equally with all the other employees in your department.

If an employee complains about fatigue, eye strain, or feeling sick during his normal hours of work, you may accept such excuses as reasonable ones to relieve him from completing his normal hours of work on that day. But you expect him to take corrective measures to remedy his vision or to put himself into a fit physical condition to perform his job, including a reasonable amount of overtime since it constitutes part of his regular job. If several of your employees give you the same kind of excuse on a day you require overtime work, such as not well,

268

feeling sick, too tired, you can pretty much tell they're engaging in concerted action to avoid meeting their job responsibilities. In such cases, have each employee write out in black and white his reason for refusing to work the overtime, and have each one sign a statement putting it "on the record"!

The Case of the Doctor's Certificate

An industrial relations director who participated in my workshop seminar program reported the following incident that happened at one of his company's plants.

An employee told her foreman she couldn't work overtime any more and gave him a doctor's certificate that simply stated she was "not physically able to work overtime." Her foreman took her to the plant manager, who shortly before had attended one of the workshop seminars.

He listened to the employee's reason why she couldn't work overtime any more, and after reading the doctor's certificate, threw it aside and said to her:

> We can't accept these doctor's certificates to excuse you from doing your job. For five bucks you can get all of them you want. Now, look, if you're not able to work overtime as the other employees in your department, we can't continue to employ you in your regular job. If I make a special case for you, I'll have to do it for all the others. Now, either you are well enough to do your full job or you're not—and unless you can work overtime along with the other employees, we'll have to let you go.

The employee didn't say anything and left. About an hour later, after the lunch break, the shop steward in her department came into the manager's office and said: "Mary was quite upset after that speech you gave. But any way, I've talked to her and she said she'll work the overtime when needed. But," said the shop steward with a twinkle in his eye, "what bothers her and me is—how'd you know she paid $5.00 for the doctor's certificate?"

Here again, Mr. Foreman, to avoid the pitfall of a blanket medical

269

excuse unsupported by facts you or your company's doctor can verify, have the employee write out his reason for not being able to work overtime and have him sign a statement putting it on the record. In that way, the "truth will out."

Handling the "Personal Reasons" Excuse

If you believe, Mr. Foreman, the negotiators intended under the normal hours of work and overtime clauses of your contract that working a reasonable amount of overtime constituted part of each employee's job, then you should apply the same rules to excuse an employee from working a reasonable amount of overtime that you follow to excuse him from working his normal hours of work. If an employee gives "personal reasons" as an excuse to relieve him from working the required overtime, ask him to give you the facts supporting his personal reasons, noting them on your record as he gives them to you, so that you can determine whether he has a justifiable excuse.

As pointed out in the arbitration case of "Compulsory vs. Voluntary Overtime" cited earlier, unless your contract provides otherwise:

> The standards to be used by the parties in determining whether, in any particular instance, an employee's excuse for not working the scheduled overtime hours is reasonable, valid or justifiable, shall be the same standards customarily used to determine excusable absences from working the normal or regular scheduled work day of eight hours or work week of forty hours . . .
>
> Where "personal reasons" are asserted by an employee, to excuse him from working overtime, in any particular instance, the company may inquire into the nature of such personal reasons and the employee is constrained to state them. An employee who is or may be unable to work the scheduled overtime hours on any particular day, shall, when able to, give prior notice thereof to his department foreman or supervisor, reasonably in advance as he is able.

If in the past you have accepted the blanket statement of "personal reasons" to excuse employees in your department from working a reasonable amount of overtime, does that past practice preclude you from inquiring in the future as to the facts to verify the reasonableness of the employee's excuse? No! Does a past practice of excusing employees from working overtime without requiring a reasonable excuse make working overtime voluntary or optional on the part of each employee in your department? No again!

The Written Contract vs. Conflicting Past Practices—What Prevails?

The written contract! A past practice of excusing employees for a personal or no reason or of allowing employees to refuse without a reasonable excuse to work a reasonable amount of overtime, which conflicts with otherwise clear, normal hours of work and overtime clauses, does not make working a reasonable amount of overtime in the future voluntary or optional on the part of any employee; and it does not bar you, Mr. Foreman, from requiring qualified employees in the future to work a reasonable amount of overtime as part of their regular job duties.

As I said in the award in the arbitration case of the "Union's Past Practice" in which the union argued that the company had waived its right to require employees to work overtime because the company had in the past not taken disciplinary action against those who had refused to work overtime:

> The fact that the company in the past refrained from enforcing its rights to require employees to work overtime does not establish a past practice; nor does it constitute a recognition of an "unwritten understanding" that can be held to be a waiver of the rights established by the written provisions themselves.
>
> Likewise, the fact that the company, during all the past years, withheld disciplining any employee who refused to work the required overtime assigned to him does not constitute a waiver of the company's right to enforce, in the future, the employees' obligations under the agreement—and to discipline an employee who fails or refuses to fulfill the duties required of him in his job.

271

You see, Mr. Foreman, a past practice that conflicts with a clear contract provision or contradicts what the negotiators reasonably intended under the written provision becomes voidable as to its binding effect for the future of the contract term. Either party can insist that the other thenceforth comply with the written provisions. In such case, the past practice falls and gives way to the written provisions, which then determine the parties' relations for the balance of the contract term.

By initiating action during the contract term you use the voidable way to end a past practice that has misinterpreted a written contract provision or that contradicts what you claim the negotiators reasonably intended under it. Neither party waives its contractual rights under the written contract provisions because that party (1) misinterpreted, misconstrued, or by error misapplied its rights in the past, (2) failed to enforce its rights in the past, or (3) allowed the other party in the past to violate its obligations under the written provisions of the contract.

You also use the voidable way to stop a past practice that by unequally distributing the benefits or unequally enforcing the job responsibilities among your employees creates an intraplant inequity. To remove any doubt that a past practice relieves any employee from working a reasonable amount of overtime in the absence of a reasonable excuse and to enforce equally the job responsibilities of each employee under the contract, follow the corrective rule way by establishing, in writing, the following plant rules.

> AN EMPLOYEE MUST REPORT FOR WORK AS SCHEDULED OR OVERTIME WORK AS REQUIRED OR ASSIGNED TO HIM.
>
> IF AN EMPLOYEE IS UNABLE TO REPORT FOR OR PERFORM WORK DUE TO ILLNESS OR OTHER JUSTIFIABLE CAUSE, HE MUST REPORT HIS EXPECTED ABSENCE IN ADVANCE (TO HIS FOREMAN OR OTHER DESIGNATED PERSONNEL) AND GIVE THE REASONS FOR HIS INABILITY TO WORK.
>
> AN EMPLOYEE SHALL NOT NEGLECT HIS JOB DUTIES AND RESPONSIBILITIES OR REFUSE TO PERFORM WORK ASSIGNED TO HIM.

Equitably Distributing Available Overtime

If your contract requires you to distribute overtime equally, then when you have overtime available, Mr. Foreman, it belongs to those qualified employees in the classified jobs or other operating group in which the need for the overtime work arises. Since each employee's regular job contemplates a reasonable amount of overtime, you distribute available overtime equally among all the employees qualified in that job and not to or among the best-qualified employees. If an employee in a classified job does not possess the skills needed to do the required overtime work, then he's not qualified to do the work, and you distribute the overtime equally among the remaining qualified employees.

When you distribute overtime equally, you take into account the business or operational necessities, the production difficulties, and the availability of qualified employees prevailing at the time the need for the overtime work arises.

If you excuse one of your employees from working overtime because you accept as valid the excuse he offers, you count the overtime opportunity against his record in the overtime roster as if he had worked it, unless your contract provides otherwise. If an employee refuses to work a reasonable amount of overtime you assign to him without offering an excuse you can accept as reasonable, you count the overtime opportunity offered him against his record in the overtime roster as if he had worked it; and in addition, you follow corrective discipline, warning him that in the future he must undertake a reasonable amount of overtime as part of his regular job.

You see, Mr. Foreman, you breach the rule of equality of treatment when you allow one of your employees, without a reasonable excuse, to evade part of the job responsibilities you require of his fellow employees. If you fail to take corrective disciplinary action, he suffers only the detriment of having the overtime opportunity charged against him. That's just the price he expected to pay for receiving preferential treatment! You have not corrected his failure to undertake his job responsibilities equally with his fellow employees.

When an employee without a reasonable excuse refuses to work a

273

reasonable amount of overtime, you warn him that in the future you expect him to meet his job responsibilities and undertake overtime work when required, equally with his fellow employees. If he fails to heed your warning and later again refuses, without a reasonable excuse, to work the required overtime, you apply the rules of corrective discipline by sending him a letter of reprimand, delivering a copy to his shop steward or union committee chairman, and mailing a copy to the union's place of business. Use the following type of letter of reprimand.

LETTER OF REPRIMAND

Refusal to Work Overtime: Insubordinate Conduct

April 12, 19_____

Mr. Leo Harolds
(Home Address)

Dear Sir:

I am giving you this Written Reprimand, as disciplinary action, for your insubordinate and improper conduct on April 10, 19_____ in refusing to undertake and failing to perform the necessary overtime work I had assigned to you.

On that day, at about 10:30 A.M., I informed you and three other machine operators in your department that due to production difficulties we had experienced that morning, I would require you and the three other employees to work overtime that day for about one and a half hours commencing at 4:30 P.M., the end of your shift. You said you "didn't want to work overtime." When I asked you "Why?" you said it was a "personal reason" and refused to explain further.

I told you then as I had previously told you that working a reasonable amount of overtime, when required by operational needs or production difficulties, constituted part of the duties of your job—and unless you had a valid reason I could accept to excuse you from working overtime that day, I expected you would fulfill your responsibilities.

274

On March 22, 19_____ when I had then asked you to work overtime that day you said you "didn't want to." I did not insist then that you work overtime, as I had enough employees to cover the work. But I did orally warn you that your job responsibilities required you to be available for and undertake a reasonable amount of overtime when required unless you had a reasonable excuse not to.

This time, on April 10, 19_____, you said you had "some other personal business to take care of." When I asked you to explain what that personal business was, you refused to do so. I again told you that working a reasonable amount of overtime when required by production needs was not voluntary or optional on the part of any employee and that unless you gave me a valid reason why you could not work the overtime that day, I could not excuse you and I expected you to do this part of your job.

At 4:30 P.M. on that day, at the end of your shift, you left your place of work and went to the locker room. You did not return thereafter to your machine but clocked out and left the plant.

Though two of the other machine operators in your department did remain after 4:30 P.M. that day and worked overtime—I having excused Tom Roscoe since he had a valid excuse—your failure to work the required overtime created difficulties for me, your foreman, and put an extra burden upon the other employees in your department, who met the requirements of their jobs. Your failure to work the required overtime also affected the production needs of the department upon which your job and the jobs of your fellow employees depend.

I point out to you, by this Written Reprimand, that the duties of your job require you to work overtime as part of your regular job equally with all your fellow workers. As you well know, our plant rules, a printed copy of which you and all the other employees had received—provide:

> An employee must be available and report for work as scheduled or overtime work as required or assigned to him.
>
> An employee shall not neglect his job, duties and responsibilities—nor refuse to perform work assigned to him.

Since you did not offer at the time I instructed you to work overtime that day any valid reason I could accept to excuse you, your refusal to work the required overtime violated your duties and the responsibilities of your job and constituted improper and insubordinate conduct on your part.

275

I am by this Written Reprimand giving you an opportunity to correct your improper conduct in the future and I expect that hereafter you will fully perform and meet all the duties and responsibilities required of you in your job. Should you fail to do so, you will subject yourself to further disciplinary action.

Very truly yours,

_____

Foreman

cc: Mailed to the Union's place of business
cc: Given to the Union Shop Steward or Committee Chairman

THE CASE OF THE ERROR IN DISTRIBUTING OVERTIME

The union filed a grievance claiming that the foreman had bypassed an operator in the "doubles" overtime roster and demanded eight hours' pay at time and a half for the overtime he had lost. The company denied the grievance, and the union appealed to arbitration. Article 11, Subdivision (e), of the contract provided:

(e) Overtime shall be distributed as equally as possible among those who have earned seniority.

In applying that provision to the operating needs of the acid recovery department, the general foreman and the shop stewards in the department had agreed to a procedure whereby they set up two duplicate seniority lists of operators. One list, referred to as the doubles roster, listed the operators on each shift separately. The foreman used that roster for doubling from one shift to the other, that is, for an employee working over to a second shift, succeeding the one he had completed, when an employee scheduled for the succeeding shift failed to report for work.

The second list, referred to as the scheduled and call-in roster, listed all the operators in the department according to seniority. The foreman used that one for two purposes: (1) scheduled overtime work, that is, overtime the company could anticipate and schedule in advance; and (2) call-in, that is, employees called in to handle special production problems or difficulties. The contract provided premium pay for such call-in work.

Due to an error the company claimed arose because of a misunderstanding in applying the two rosters during certain short-work weeks, the foreman charged the grievant's call-in assignment to the doubles roster instead of to the scheduled and call-in roster. Then, when another doubles opened up, the foreman passed over the grievant and gave it to the next lower man on the doubles roster.

At the arbitration hearing the union claimed:

The company admits in its written answers in this case that it made an error; its offer to correct its error by making changes in the rosters would not remedy the loss of overtime [the grievant] suffered; and further, in the past, the company had corrected such errors in making overtime assignments by paying for the amount of overtime lost; and the company is bound by such past practice and cannot now substitute a different method to correct its error.

The company claimed that the grievant:

had not, in fact, been deprived of any overtime work, but only in the order of receiving overtime assignments . . . the company has fulfilled its obligation under Article 11, Subdivision (e), which only requires that "overtime shall be distributed as equally as possible . . ."; and that contract provision does not obligate the company to equalize distribution of overtime by making payment to two employees for overtime worked only by one.

The company acknowledged:

In the past, in some cases and in some departments, it has paid an employee, who for some clerical error or oversight, has been passed on his regular turn, for the overtime hours he missed; [but] it has in this department, and in other cases in the past, corrected an error of

277

assigning overtime by giving the next turn to the complaining employee; and the union has acquiesced in and did not raise any objection to such practice.

Finding that the foreman's error in charging the grievant's call-in turn to the doubles roster arose "from a misunderstanding on the foreman's part, following the discussion between the foreman and the union steward in that department earlier that month," I denied the union's grievance; and in my award I said:

> The crux of this case rests on the method available to the company to correct this error in distributing overtime.
>
> During the discussions in the grievance steps, the company offered to correct its error by eliminating [the grievant's] charge on the "doubles" roster and transferring it to the "Scheduled—Call-In" roster. The union refused to accept this method. The union claims that since the grievant had lost a turn in overtime, the past practice of the parties obligates the company to pay him for the overtime turn he lost.
>
> The company denied the grievant in fact had lost or been deprived of any overtime opportunity; and neither the contract provision, Article 11, Subdivision (e), nor the past practice of the parties, obligates or compels the company to remedy the error by paying for the February 13th overtime turn.

Then, finding that the "procedure the parties set up . . . to apply Article 11, Subdivision (e), of the contract in this department, did not include or refer to any method to correct any errors in the procedure agreed upon," I said:

> Subdivision (e) of Article 11 does not prescribe any method—it simply provides that "overtime shall be distributed as equally as possible." Unless the parties had agreed to a single method to apply that contract provision, the method offered by the company in this case satisfies that provision equally, as does the method sought by the union. How the parties themselves have construed or applied a contractual provision, which is ambiguous or which is stated in general terms, as Article 11, Subdivision (e) is, in this case, constitutes an important factor in find-

278

ing out what they intended under that provision. Past practice in applying such a provision provides material facts to determine what the parties intended.

Finding that a past practice, "to be binding on both parties, must be (1) unequivocal, (2) clearly enunciated and acted upon, (3) readily ascertainable over a reasonable period of time as a fixed and established practice accepted by both parties" and that the "evidence in this case fails to satisfy those objective standards," I said:

> The union's evidence of past practice shows that in some cases in the past, the company corrected an error in assigning overtime, by making payment . . . No instance was shown that payment had been made for an error in the department concerned with in this case.
>
> On the other hand . . . the general foreman in this department testified he could not recall a single instance where pay had been given to an employee who had been improperly passed over for an overtime turn. Affirmatively, he testified there had been prior instances in the department where the company had rectified an error in assigning overtime by giving the employee passed up the next opportunity to pick up the overtime. That was the same solution that was offered by the company in [the grievant's] case.

Then, finding that the "evidence shows that there was a variation in the method by which the parties agreed to correct errors under Article 11, Subdivision (e) in the assignment of overtime . . . and the company could properly, under Article 11, Subdivision (e) of the contract, correct said error by changing the charge of overtime turn in the rosters and by allowing [the grievant] to make up subsequently the overtime turn he lost," I said:

> The proof does not establish nor does the arbitrator find an unequivocal, clearly enunciated past practice as claimed by the union in applying Subdivision (e) of the contract, existed; or that such a past practice had been accepted by the parties as fixed or established practice, obligating the company to correct any errors in overtime assignments by paying the employee passed up, overtime pay.

279

On the contrary, the solution offered by the company in the grievance steps finds equal support in the past practice of the parties and satisfies the dominant intention of the parties under Article 11, Subdivision (e) of the contract.

EQUALIZING OVERTIME OVER A REASONABLE PERIOD

Under the normal hours of work clauses the regular hours of work, say forty hours per week, belong to those employees who by their seniority rights have priority to those hours of work. So if you deny an employee's priority to any part of those regular hours of work by laying him off, by failing to recall him after layoff, by assigning those hours to employees outside his classified job, or by any other error, you violate that employee's seniority rights. He thereby loses those regular hours of work; and you can correct your error only by paying him money as damages to retroactively make him "whole" for the time he lost.

But the clause calling for equally distributing overtime differs widely from the regular hours of work clause because it does not give priority to any one employee to available overtime but requires you to distribute the overtime equally among all the employees in the classified job, operating group, or other agreed-upon roster in which the overtime need arises. Of course, in initially starting off to distribute the available overtime among the employees in the roster you may begin with the most senior man, but then you rotate the overtime down the line as it arises. No one in the roster has priority to any particular overtime since the negotiators specifically agreed to equally distribute it among all the employees irrespective of anyone's seniority.

So if you make an error by passing over the next man whose turn came up in the roster, you have not, Mr. Foreman, denied him his equal distribution of overtime. Unless your contract provides otherwise, instead of paying money damages you correct your error by using future overtime opportunities to distribute equally the overtime work. Phrases such as "where practicable," "if possible," or "when feasible," which negotiators often use in equal-distribution clauses, show that they did not intend you, Mr. Foreman, to equalize overtime every day, every hour, or every week but over a reasonable period of time—say, three, six, or twelve months, depending on how often overtime opportunities arise in your department.

Here again, Mr. Foreman, you follow the rule of reason in determining a reasonable period of time within which to equalize the available overtime so that you equitably distribute it without favor, subterfuge, or abuse. What constitutes a reasonable period of time depends upon the frequency with which overtime arises in your department as well as the operational necessities, the production difficulties, or the availability of qualified employees at the time. You, Mr. Foreman, initially determine what would constitute a reasonable period of time within which to equalize overtime in your department; and if the shop steward disagrees, he can protest your action in an orderly way through the grievance procedure.

Pyramiding of Overtime
and Premium Pay

Overtime pay for working beyond the normal daily or weekly hours of work represents one type of premium pay. Other types of premium pay include shift bonus or differentials, pay for working on holidays, or working on Saturday or Sunday "as such"; penalty pay for a succeeding work day following change in an employee's weekly scheduled shift or hours of work, penalty pay for reporting (if not previously told not to report for work), for call-in (before the start of an employee's regular shift), and for call-back (recalled after completing his regular shift).

Historically, premium pay for working overtime was intended, among other objectives, to discourage management from extending the normal work day and work week and to spread employment opportunities. But as with overtime pay, the other types of premium pay equally serve to compensate employees for working an onerous number of hours or days in a week, for working inconvenient shifts, or on a holiday, Saturday, or Sunday, which interferes with the workers' normal pursuit of personal or family life.

In administering overtime and other premium pay clauses you may find, Mr. Foreman, that two or more types of premium pay apply to the same hours worked. Thus, your contract may provide for double time for hours worked on a holiday in lieu of holiday pay. If one of your employees works nine hours on that holiday, does he receive double time for the ninth hour? Or time and a half of double time for that ninth hour?

If your contract provides for an overtime rate for working beyond the normal daily as well as weekly hours of work and for other types of premium pay for some of those same hours, you must decide whether the negotiators intended to pyramid the different types of premium pay, that is, whether they intended to count the same hours twice in computing overtime pay or to pay two or more types of premium pay for the same hours.

The Case of Pyramiding Holiday and Penalty Pay

The union filed a grievance claiming that the company had violated the contract by failing to schedule-off certain shift employees for two consecutive days within a seven-consecutive-day period on two different occasions and demanded time and a half for the days of June 6th and July 11th worked by them. The company denied the grievance, and the union appealed to arbitration.

The contract between the parties consisted of two parts. Part I, a master contract, covered nine of the company plants, including the Peekskill plant. Part II, a local contract, covered employees in the bargaining unit at the Peekskill plant.

Part I, Subdivision (e) of Section 3, obligated the company to schedule "at least five (5) days work" within the week in which a holiday falls. That section provided:

> (e) Employees eligible to receive idle holiday pay shall be scheduled for at least five (5) days work within that week, which may include the holiday, if worked, and shall not be laid off in that week, subject to such exceptions as may be agreed to by the respective Local Unions and Plant Managers.

In complying with that provision, Section (h) of Article 4 of Part I of the contract exempted premium pay for a Saturday if the company scheduled Saturday as one of the five days in the holiday work week.

283

Part II, Article 3, Section 1 d, obligated the company to schedule employees "for two consecutive days off within a seven-consecutive-day period." That section provided:

> All employees shall be scheduled for two consecutive days off within a seven-consecutive-day period. Exceptions may be made by mutual consent of the parties hereto. Forty-eight (48) hours shall constitute two days.

The grievant's regular weekly schedule ran from Monday through Friday, 4:00 P.M. to midnight. The contract named May 30th and July 4th as paid holidays. Each of those holidays that year fell on a Monday. The company advanced the weekly work schedule in the grievant's departments from Tuesday to Saturday for the two weeks in which those holidays fell. The company did not schedule production work for the Monday holidays.

For the week immediately following each of those holidays and thereafter, the regular weekly schedule, Monday through Friday, again became effective. As a result, the grievants returned to work on those Mondays (June 6th and July 11th) after an interval of only twenty-four hours from their prior shift and, consequently, within less than forty-eight hours (or two consecutive days) following the end of their last scheduled shift, as provided for by Section 1 d of Part II of the contract.

At the arbitration hearing the union claimed:

> Section 1 d obligates the company to schedule employees off for two consecutive days, within a seven consecutive day period, unless the parties mutually agree to an exception; since the union was not consulted and did not consent to any exception, the company violated this section; and the company should pay the affected shift employees time and a half for the hours of work on the two Mondays following the holiday weeks, as the company has done in the past when similar contract violations occurred.

The company claimed:

> Section 1 d does not apply nor did the parties intend it to apply to the type of change in weekly schedules involved in this case; the company

advanced the weekly work schedule in the weeks in which the paid
holidays fell, from Tuesday through Saturday, in order (a) to accommodate the holidays and allow the employees off, with pay and (b) to
allow the company to comply with the other provisions of the contract
which obligate the company to schedule five working days in any week
in which a paid holiday falls; and the company has followed the same
scheduling practice in all similar cases in the past and neither the union
nor any of the affected employees have complained or raised a grievance.

Finding that the parties "intended Section 1 d to apply to individual
employee cases where operational requirements in the different departments did not allow for scheduling all employees on a regular basis," I
denied the union's grievance; and in my award I said:

The arbitrator finds the parties did not intend Section 1 d to apply to
such a situation, as arose in this case. The proof shows that when the
parties had previously negotiated changes in schedules, following a re-
duction in the regular work week from seven to five days, no mention
was made of the effect upon the schedules of a holiday falling within a
scheduled work week. The proof shows the company followed the
same procedure in the past, in all other instances, when rescheduling
weekly work following a paid holiday, without complaint by the union
or the affected employees.

Finding that Section 1 d must be read "in context with the other provisions of the contract and in light of the contractual history which led
up to Section 1 d," I said:

Subdivision (e) of Section 3 (Part I) obligates the company to schedule "at least five (5) days work" within a week that a holiday falls . . .
No question has been raised as to the propriety of the company's
action in not scheduling work on the two holidays, on which the employees were off, with pay. Section (e), above, obligated the company
to schedule work for the Saturday of that holiday week, which it did.
Then, in order to get the regular weekly schedules back on the track
following the holiday week, the employees reported for work on the
following Monday, the beginning of the next regularly scheduled work
week. Of necessity, some employees did not have two consecutive days

285

off. Some had less than forty-eight hours but more than twenty-four hours; others had only twenty-four hours off. But such a result had to be reasonably anticipated by the parties if the company was to accommodate the paid holiday off, schedule five working days for employees during the holiday week, and then get back to the regularly scheduled work week, following the holiday.

Then, finding that the "company followed this procedure on all past occasions in other departments of the plant when holidays necessitated the same change in weekly schedules, and no objection had been made at any time that such scheduling, or the result flowing therefrom, violated Section 1 d of the contract," I said:

> These uncontroverted facts constrain the arbitrator to find the parties did not intend Section 1 d to apply to a change in weekly schedules, made necessary to accommodate a holiday falling in a prior work week . . . Were the arbitrator to find otherwise, it would result in imposing an obligation upon the company, either (1) to schedule work on a paid holiday which the contract does not compel or (2) to pay premium pay for the Saturday, the fifth working day, which the contract (a) obligates the company to provide and (b) for which the contract expressly exempts premium pay, Section (h) of Article 4 (Part I).

THE SINGLE STANDARD RULE

Unless your contract, Mr. Foreman, provides otherwise, you avoid counting the same hours twice, or pyramiding different types of overtime, premium, or penalty pay for the same hours worked. If your contract calls for different or more than one overtime, premium, or penalty rate for the same hours or days, you apply only one rate of pay—the single highest overtime, premium, or penalty rate.

The Case of the Overtime Lunch Hour

Section 6 of Article II of the contract provided:

6. Employees held over four or more hours overtime consecutive with their regularly scheduled work shift shall receive one hour for lunch

with pay. The company also agrees to furnish such held-over employees a meal or, at company's option, allow one dollar and fifty cents ($1.50) in lieu thereof.

The union filed a grievance claiming that the company had violated that section by failing to pay one hour for lunch and the meal allowance to three employees engaged in piece-rate work who had performed the hourly equivalent of twelve or more hours of work on certain days. The company denied the grievance, and the union appealed to arbitration.

The three employees, classified as mud men, worked in the tank room of the electrolytic department. The company paid them on a piece-rate basis computed on the basis of a standard daily number of tanks mudded. The company counts and carries on its records the number of tanks mudded as the equivalent of hours worked by those employees. Thus, if two men mud eight tanks in one day, as the established norm, the company pays them for eight equivalent hours of work at straight time. If they finish the eight tanks in less than eight hours, they are free to go home. If the company requires piece-rate employees to work overtime, the company pays them at overtime rates for each tank completed over the established norm.

For accounting purposes, the company records the completed tanks as hours worked on the accounting cards. The employees' time cards, however, show the actual hours worked by each on each day regardless of the number of equivalent hours credited them on the company's accounting cards for computing their pay.

On the days in question their foreman assigned the three grievants to work overtime in their jobs. They finished and received pay for twelve tanks. For accounting purposes the company credited each employee with the equivalent of twelve hours. Each of those employees, however, worked less than twelve hours on any day, as shown by their time cards.

At the arbitration hearing the union claimed that "under Section 6, all piece workers who do the hourly equivalent of twelve or more hours a day are entitled to receive one hour for lunch with pay and $1.50, in lieu of a meal."

The company claimed:

Parties intended Section 6 to reimburse employees who actually work in point of time twelve or more hours on any one day; and the parties did not intend to have that section apply to piece workers who actually work less than twelve hours in a day but who, for purposes of computing their pay, are credited with the hourly equivalent of twelve hours or more; and since none of these employees actually worked twelve consecutive hours on any of the days in question, the company is not obligated under Section 6 of Article II to pay them the additional hour and the meal allowance, as claimed by the union.

Finding that none of the grievants had been "held over four or more hours on the days in question, as specified in Section 6 of Article II," I denied the union's grievance; and in my award I said:

Their time cards of hours actually worked establishes this.

In the absence of any facts showing a contrary intention, the clear language of Section 6 constrains the arbitrator to find the parties intended it to apply to an employee who actually works or is held over on his job for four or more hours consecutive with their regularly scheduled work shift.

That the company carried on its books for computing pay purposes the hourly equivalent of work performed does not enlarge the clear purpose the parties intended and sought to achieve under Section 6. The arbitrator finds the parties intended that section to apply to employees actually held over on their jobs. The proof fails to show the parties intended that section to apply to employees who are not held over on their jobs or who, for methods of bookkeeping, are credited on the payroll with the equivalent of hours worked.

Concerted Refusals to Work Overtime

When two or more employees refuse to work a reasonable amount of overtime without a reasonable excuse after reasonable advance notice, their conduct constitutes a concerted action that violates the responsibilities of their regular job and breaches the no-strike pledge under the contract. Concerted refusals to work overtime challenge your authority to manage, Mr. Foreman; and each employee in the group subjects himself to corrective disciplinary action.

If the shop steward engages in the concerted action by refusing with the other employees in the group to undertake the overtime work required of him, he not only subjects himself to disciplinary action but also makes the union liable for the breach of its no-strike pledge of the contract. In some cases the shop steward uses the concerted refusal of employees to work overtime as a political pressure tactic to strengthen his bargaining position on pending grievances or to fortify the union's strategy in forthcoming renewal contract negotiations.

You counter such tactics immediately, Mr. Foreman, by cautioning your employees and the shop steward that if they want to challenge your action, the contract provides an orderly way in which to do so. In the words of Arthur J. Goldberg: "That challenge is made through the grievance procedure, not through rebellion"!

THE CASE OF THE UNPREDICTABLE OVERTIME

At about 11:30 P.M. an operator in the manual cable operating section on the 5:00 to 1:00 A.M. shift told his supervisor he felt sick and would not be able to complete his tour of duty. According to the established procedure, the overtime schedule called for a certain operator on the 4:00 to 12 midnight shift to work one hour overtime, from 12:00 to 1:00 A.M. The supervisor so informed that operator. He refused, claiming a stomach disorder. The next operator regularly scheduled for overtime also refused, claiming he had a heavy cold. A third operator refused to work the overtime, claiming physical fatigue. The fourth and remaining operator on the shift also refused, claiming severe eyestrain. As a result, since all the operators refused to work the required one hour overtime, the supervisor had to close the circuit and it did not operate for that hour.

Two days later in the same section the same thing happened again. On that day weather conditions had interrupted radio circuits, piling up traffic. At about 11:00 P.M., the supervisor found over 500 messages on hand. To transmit them he had to use additional channels for one hour overtime, from 12:00 to 1:00 A.M. Each of the seven operators working on the 4:00 to 12:00 shift refused to work the additional hour of overtime. Five of them said they felt "too fatigued" to work

289

overtime; a sixth said he had an "early appointment with his dentist"; and the seventh said he was "unable to work."

The following night a similar situation arose. The supervisor required overtime after 1:00 A.M. because about 500 messages had again piled up after 11:00 P.M. due to interrupted cable lines. The seven operators on the 5:00 P.M. to 1:00 A.M. tour of duty refused to work overtime. One said he did not "feel well"; another said he had to go to the hospital with his wife; the third said he felt "fatigued"; the fourth said he was "not well"; the fifth said his eyes were "tired"; the sixth said he had "a headache"; and the seventh was "not feeling well."

Two days later, at a meeting with the union officials, the company charged that the "action of the men constituted a concerted refusal to follow the established procedures in accepting and working overtime assignments, which their jobs called for." The union complained that the "mid-watch shift was understaffed to meet the normal work load." The parties had discussed and differed upon this subject for several years.

In the manual cable operating section the company schedules operators on regular continuous shifts staggered over twenty-four hours a day and seven days a week. Operators service both cable and radio circuits to transmit messages. Each operator's scheduled shift changes every week and rotates from day work to evening work. The supervisor maintains rotating rosters of overtime in the section, from which he makes overtime assignments when required. Sometimes operators change shifts and overtime assignments among themselves, but the responsibility rests with the one assigned to see that someone fills his shift or undertakes the overtime.

During normal operations radio and cable circuits clear southbound traffic at about midnight or 1:00 A.M. and northbound traffic at about 2:00 A.M. Due to unavoidable physical conditions, breaks occur from time to time in the ocean cables and radio circuits. Cable breaks generally continue for longer periods, requiring more time to repair and put the cable back into operation, because it takes more time to locate and get a cable repair ship to the break. A cable break increases the work load on the radio circuits, which also meet with unavoidable breaks due to frequency changes and atmospheric conditions. When a

290

cable breaks or atmospheric conditions interrupt radio circuits, which the company cannot anticipate, traffic piles up. Overtime work then becomes necessary to clear traffic as quickly as possible in order to meet the next day's traffic.

Both parties have always accepted overtime work as an "inescapable part of the industry"; and both have recognized that breaks in cable and radio circuits, being unpredictable, require operators to work overtime in order to keep operations adequately staffed and traffic going. Although the job subjects every operator to the possibility of working overtime, the effect of breaks bears more heavily upon operators on the evening and midwatch shifts, due, in part, to the types of messages the men have to transmit during those shifts.

At the meeting with the union officials the company told the union the concerted refusal of the operators to work overtime violated the no-strike-no-lockout clause, Article VII of the contract, and said that if the operators did not correct their misconduct, the company would proceed with disciplinary action. Article VII of the contract provided:

> The company agrees that during the life of this agreement there shall be no lockouts, and the union agrees that during the life of this agreement there shall be no strikes, sitdowns, slowdowns, walkouts or stoppage of work, or impeding the conducting of operations of the company for any reason whatsoever.

About four weeks later three operators scheduled on the 5:00 P.M. to 1:00 A.M. tour again refused to work overtime without giving any reasonable excuse. One operator said he felt "too fatigued," another, "too tired," and the third "not feeling well." The following day the company posted a general bulletin that stated:

> Effective immediately, when overtime is required in any Section, Supervisors will make the assignment on the basis of the overtime procedure now in effect. After the overtime posting is made it will be the responsibility of the individual so assigned to either work the overtime as scheduled or get a substitute.
>
> Henceforth, Supervisors will not accept any notes, regardless of cause, declining overtime.

291

The union filed a grievance claiming that the bulletin violated Section 9 (b) of the overtime provisions in Article XIV of the contract, which provided:

(a) Due to the necessity for continuity of public service, employees may be required to work shifts around the clock, to work on Sundays and Holidays and to work overtime, whether in the form of an addition to a regular work day as provided in sub-section (b) herein, or in the form of sixth day duty.

(b) Due to the necessity for meeting unpredictable requirements for staffing operations, an employee may be required by the company to work overtime in addition to scheduled periods of duty.

(c) The company agrees to assign overtime as equitably as possible.

During the grievance meetings the union claimed that supervisors did not give operators sufficient advance notice of required overtime assignments. The company agreed to modify the bulletin and reposted it with the following additional sentence:

Overtime assigned with less than one hour advance, except for absentee coverage, will be on a voluntary basis.

The union filed another grievance, again claiming the revised bulletin violated Section 9(b) of the overtime provisions. The company denied both grievances, and the union appealed them to arbitration.

At the arbitration hearing the union claimed:

Section 9 (b) limits the company's right to require operators to work overtime except when it is necessary to meet "unpredictable requirements" for staffing operations; Section 9 (b) does not give the company the right to regularly and consistently require operators to work overtime on the mid-watch (12 midnight to 7:00 A.M. and 1:00 A.M. to 8:00 A.M.) when the conditions requiring such overtime work become predictable, or could have been reasonably anticipated by the company in advance; and under the latter circumstances the working of overtime is voluntary on the part of the individual operator . . . and the company's action in issuing the general bulletins and thereby making overtime work mandatory and denying employees the right to decline overtime for sickness or other legitimate reasons, as in the past, violated the contract.

The company claimed:

Necessity for overtime work has long existed in the company's operations and in the industry and has been acknowledged by the union, as expressly set forth in the contract, and has been accepted by the employees, as part of their regular jobs; Section 9 expressly gives the company the right to schedule and assign overtime work regularly to all employees, whenever overtime work is required; Section 9(b) does not limit the company's right to schedule, assign and require employees to regularly work overtime, as the union contends, nor did the parties intend such limitation when they negotiated the contract; and neither Section 9(b) nor any other part of Section 9 or of the contract allows nor was it intended to allow an employee to voluntarily determine whether or not he would work the assigned overtime.

The company further claimed that the "refusal of employees, during the period preceding the posting of General Bulletins 51 (c), to work the overtime required and assigned to them, was deliberate, without cause, and constituted a concerted refusal on their part that violated Section 9 of Article XIV and Article VII [the No-Strike-No-Lockout clause] of the contract."

Finding that the "company did not violate Section 9(b) by scheduling and assigning overtime work to employees on the mid-watch during the period in question; and that the company did not violate Section 9(b) or any other provision of the contract, in posting General Bulletins 51 (c)," I denied the union's grievance; and in my award I said:

The proof establishes and the arbitrator finds that the refusal of the employees to work overtime on the mid-watch on December 1st, 3rd and 4th . . . and on January 4th . . . was without cause or justifiable reason; constituted a concerted refusal on their part; and violated Section 9 of Article XIV and Article VII of the contract.

293

The arbitrator further finds the company's action in issuing General Bulletins 51 (c) was warranted in light of the actions of the employees in refusing to work the overtime assigned to them on said dates.

Then, finding that the company had posted the general bulletins "as corrective warnings to employees with respect to their obligations under Section 9 of Article XIV and Article VII," I said:

> Section 9(a) expressly recognizes the need for overtime work in the company's operations, because of necessity for continuity of public service. Overtime work has always been required in the company's operations; and overtime work has always been scheduled and assigned by the company in the past.
>
> Section 9, read as a whole, contractually expresses the need for and the responsibility of employees to work the overtime the company schedules and assigns. Section 9 (b) does not, as the union contends, limit the company in scheduling and requiring employees to work overtime. When read in context with Section 9(a), it extends the company's right to require employees to work overtime in those areas not covered by Section 9 (a).

Noting that "Section 9 (a) requires employees to work shifts around the clock; to work on Sundays and holidays, and to work overtime whether in the form of an addition to a regular day as provided in Subsection (b) herein, or in the form of sixth-day duty," I said:

> Thus, the clear language of Section 9 (a) shows the parties intended an employee's regular tour of duty, as well as his regular work day and work week, may be extended by required overtime work.
>
> Section 9 (b) then explicitly sets forth the reason for overtime work, as an addition to a regular work day, referred to in Section 9 (a). Section 9 (b) provides:
>
> "Due to the necessity for meeting unpredictable requirements for staffing operations, an employee may be required by the Company to work overtime in addition to scheduled periods of duty."

Finding that the "language of Sections 9 (a) and 9 (b), when read as a whole, expressly requires employees to work overtime whenever the necessity for such overtime arises," I said:

294

No part of those sections limits the company's right to require employees to work overtime. Nowhere does it reserve to the employee the right to voluntarily determine for himself to work or refuse to work the required or assigned overtime. Section 9 only restricts the company to assign overtime work as equitably as possible. No question has been raised by the union that the overtime work complained of in this case has not been equitably assigned.

I rejected the union's argument that:

The phrase "unpredictable requirements" in Section 9 (b) limits the company's right to schedule and assign overtime work as an addition to an employee's regular work day . . . only to "abnormal requirements which cannot be reasonably foreseen" . . . [such as] unexpected absenteeism, interruptions in radio circuits, and initial periods following cable breaks . . . [and] that after a reasonable period of time has elapsed, following the initial period of these unpredictable requirements, the conditions which gave rise initially to the necessity for overtime no longer continue to be "unpredictable"; and that during that ensuing period, the company cannot require employees to work overtime; and an employee has the right voluntarily to accept or reject overtime assignments.

I said:

The proof fails to establish these claims. On the contrary, the proof establishes and the arbitrator finds the parties intended the phrase "unpredictable requirements" to cover and apply to the very kind of overtime required during the period out of which the two grievances in this case arose.

The union takes the phrase "unpredictable requirements" out of context and urges a meaning which the language of Section 9, when read as a whole, negates. The evidence fails to show the parties intended the phrase "unpredictable requirements" to cover two kinds of situations: namely, that the same conditions which, concededly, are unpredictable in their initial stages and continue for some time in the future to be unpredictable, and under which, concededly, the company has the right to assign and the employees are obligated to perform overtime work, become "predictable" at some point in the future. Neither the past history of the parties involving overtime work nor the negotiations leading up to acceptance of Section 9 in the contract support such intention.

Noting that the "evidence discloses that there have been long standing differences between the parties as to adequate staffing of the midwatch by regularly scheduled employees," I said:

> Though these differences color the conflict of the parties under the present grievances, the arbitrator finds they are not material to the issues in this case. The parties must assume responsibility for resolving those differences by collective bargaining. The arbitrator has no authority under the guise of arbitrating the present grievances to change or modify the contractual provisions which the parties themselves have agreed upon and which bind the arbitrator, as they do both parties.

Then, finding that the general bulletins "continued unchanged the long established procedure of scheduling and assigning overtime work," I said:

> Under this long established procedure, if an operator because of bona fide illness was not able to fulfill his scheduled overtime work, he would so notify his supervisor, and the overtime work would be assigned to the next operator, in accordance with the rotating schedule in the section. If an operator for other than bona fide illness could not or did not want to work the overtime, it was up to him personally to get another operator to substitute for him. Operators exchanged or traded overtime assignments among and between themselves, but the overtime work required had to be filled. The operator scheduled for overtime work was responsible to serve the overtime or to get a substitute. Overtime work assignments were not voluntary on the part of any individual operator. They were necessary and mandatory as part of the operator's job, as pointed out above.

The union also challenged the propriety of that sentence of the bulletins that stated: "Henceforth, Supervisors will not accept any notes, regardless of cause, declining overtime," claiming that "this instruction to supervisors does not allow employees to decline overtime for sickness or other legitimate reasons, as in the past." As to that claim, I said:

As pointed out above, insofar as this instruction to supervisors makes the operator responsible for working overtime assigned to him or to get a substitute, it does not violate either Section 9 (b) of Article XIV or the previously established practice.

The prior incidents of concerted refusals of employees in the section to work the assigned overtime, referred to above, gave rise to the need for this instruction . . . as it warns employees of their obligations under Section 9 of Article XIV and Article VII of the contract . . . The proof shows that since these bulletins were issued employees have not improperly refused to work the scheduled and assigned overtime. No instance has been shown that these bulletins have been improperly applied to any particular employee, so as to violate his rights under the contract or under the long established practice of the parties, in assigning and performing overtime work.

In the absence of such proof, the arbitrator has no authority in this proceeding to determine, in advance, whether the contents of General Bulletins 51 (c) could be improperly applied in the future so as to violate the rights of any employee, nor does the arbitrator have authority under the contract to pass upon the instructions the company deems fit to give to its supervisors in enforcing the contract provisions.

Summing Up the Rules of Overtime

Rule 1. The normal hours and days of work, as well as a reasonable amount of required overtime, make up an employee's regular job.

Rule 2. The duties of an employee's regular job include responsibility to undertake, when required, a reasonable amount of overtime in that job.

Rule 3. When you assign a reasonable amount of overtime to one of your employees, the duties of that employee's regular job require that he undertake the assigned overtime as part of his job.

Rule 4. Unless the contract explicitly makes working overtime voluntary or optional, the duties of an employee's regular job constrain him to undertake a reasonable amount of

297

overtime work when business, operational needs, or production difficulties reasonably require the overtime work unless an employee in any particular instance has a reasonable excuse for not working the overtime.

Rule 5. The reasonableness of an employee's excuse for not working overtime in any particular instance depends on and should be judged by the same standards you use to determine excusable absences from working the normal or regular hours of work in that employee's job.

Rule 6. When an employee asserts "personal reasons" to excuse him from working the assigned or required overtime, you should inquire into the facts of such personal reasons; and the responsibilities of an employee's job require him to give you those facts.

Rule 7. Unless the contract provides otherwise, the hours of work and overtime clauses do not guarantee that work will be available and do not commit the company to make work available; nor do those clauses guarantee any specific number of hours or days of work, or overtime, to any employee.

Rule 8. When work becomes available, the normal or regular or basic or standard hours of work clause contractually commits the foreman to schedule that work so that qualified employees whose seniority gives them priority to such available work will have the opportunity to work the normal or regular work day and work week and not normally or regularly work a shorter (sharing the poverty) or longer (permanently abnormal) work day or work week.

Rule 9. When the foreman schedules qualified employees, according to their seniority, to work the normal or regular hours and weeks of work, the union commits, under the normal or regular or basic or standard hours of work clause, those employees to be available for and undertake that work.

Rule 10. The inability of an employee to be available for his normal scheduled hours of work because of absences due to chronic sickness (even though supported by doctors' certificates) does not relieve that employee from meeting his normal days and weeks of work the contract obligates him for.

Rule 11. Unexcused absence or lateness or stoppage of work for union business, including abuse by the shop steward of his office, does not relieve an employee from meeting his normal or regular hours of work.

Rule 12. Auxiliary clauses governing the conditions of working less than the norm (reporting, call-in, or call-back clauses) or working more than the norm (overtime, penalty and premium rates of pay and methods for distributing overtime) show that the negotiators intended employees to work some abnormal days or weeks, below or above the norm.

Rule 13. When operational or personnel needs or production difficulties require a reasonable amount of overtime over and above the norm, the hours of work and overtime clauses commit each qualified employee assigned such overtime to undertake that overtime as part of his regular job.

Rule 14. The normal hours of work and overtime clauses do not obligate the foreman to provide overtime work in any job; nor do those clauses prevent the foreman from eliminating overtime work if the need for overtime ceases or no longer exists.

Rule 15. In determining the need for overtime, you distinguish between work that belongs to a classified job and work that's incidental or only indirectly related to that job.

299

Rule 16. If you have available qualified employees working at straight time to do such incidental or indirectly related work, unless your contract provides otherwise, you assign such work to those employees working at straight time rates.

Rule 17. The shop steward may disagree with your judgment and may protest your action in assigning work. As long as you observe the set of working conditions under the contract, without subterfuge or abuse, your employees will respect your judgment even though the shop steward challenges it.

Rule 18. Unless your contract provides otherwise, the normal hours of work and overtime clauses do not restrict you in setting up new shifts or changing the starting time on existing shifts to meet the operating needs of your department or to overcome personnel or production difficulties.

Rule 19. The shop steward negotiates with you after he protests your action and files a grievance under the grievance procedure over your right to set up another shift as well as over the amount of shift differential you initially set and whether you followed your employees' seniority rights under the contract in staffing the new shift.

Meanwhile, your actions stand, and if the shop steward disagrees with them, he appeals to arbitration to have those questions finally settled.

Rule 20. A reasonable amount of overtime constitutes part of an employee's regular job. The duties of that job, in the absence of a reasonable excuse, require him to be available for and undertake that overtime work.

Rule 21. If you make overtime work available, the rule of equality of treatment constrains you to compel each qualified employee in that job to undertake the overtime work; and consequently, the overtime work you make available belongs to the employees whom you can compel to work it.

Rule 22. By keeping an employee on his regular job, you implicitly recognize that he's qualified for that job, including overtime work you make available in that job.

Rule 23. If your contract provides that overtime shall be given to the senior employee, then the overtime belongs to him providing he's qualified to do the available work.

Rule 24. If your contract provides that overtime shall be equally distributed, you assign available overtime among employees qualified to do the available work and not to the best-qualified employees.

Rule 25. The normal hours of work clause establishes the regular work day and work week for all employees in the bargaining unit.

Rule 26. Employees on layoff with recall rights continue to be in the bargaining unit.

Rule 27. Depending on (1) business necessities, (2) operational needs, (3) production difficulties, and (4) availability of qualified employees prevailing at the time, some employees may be on layoff and others assigned to work overtime.

Rule 28. In requiring employees to work overtime when at the time other qualified employees may be on layoff, you balance your operating needs against the job rights of those laid-off employees who retain recall rights to work opportunity.

Rule 29. Unless your contract provides otherwise, in scheduling or assigning overtime work while other qualified employees with recall rights may be on layoff you consider: (1)

business or operational needs, (2) production difficulties, (3) availability of qualified employees, and (4) the extent of the overtime required at the time.

Rule 30. In distributing, assigning, and enforcing overtime work, your employees judge your actions by the rule of equality of treatment, namely, whether you apply the benefits and enforce the job responsibilities under the hours of work and overtime clauses equally among your employees and without preferential treatment to anyone.

Rule 31. An employee who refuses without a reasonable excuse to work a reasonable amount of overtime after having been given reasonable advance notice subjects himself to corrective disciplinary action.

Rule 32. "Reasonable" means free from bias, prejudice, or discrimination; "reasonable" means supervising without fear or favor; "reasonable" means acting without subterfuge or abuse.

The Three Reasonable Rules of Overtime

Rule 33. Reasonable in amount or extent: depending upon (1) business or operational necessities, (2) production difficulties, or (3) availability of qualified employees at the time, the scheduled or assigned overtime work, daily or weekly, should not be of such a regularity or consistency that it tends to breach the ceiling of the normal or regular work day or work week established by the contract or of such a degree or extent that it tends to convert the contractual normal or regular work day or work week into a permanently abnormal longer work day or work week.

Rule 34. Reasonable advance notice: subject to operational, personnel or production difficulties that may arise in your department, you may consider, as a rule of thumb, the following as reasonable advance notice:

1. For occasional daily or weekly overtime—notice given before or at the end of an employee's prior day's shift.

2. For occasional Saturday or Sunday overtime, 6th or 7th day—notice given one full intervening day or shift of work prior thereto.

3. For scheduled overtime work, daily or weekly, in the succeeding work week—notice given during or before the end of the employee's work or shift in the prior week.

Rule 35. Reasonable excuse: subject to unforeseen personal difficulties an individual employee may experience, an employee's excuse not to work the required overtime should be of the same kind and meet the same standards that you would ordinarily accept as a reason for excusing him from working his normal or regular hours of work.

Rule 36. Avoid the pitfall of a blanket medical excuse unsupported by any facts! Have the employee write out his reason for refusing to work the overtime in "black and white"; and have him sign a statement putting it "on the record."

Voidable Past Practices

Rule 37. A past practice of excusing employees for personal reasons or of allowing employees to refuse, without a reasonable excuse, to work a reasonable amount of overtime, that conflicts with otherwise unambiguous, normal hours of work and overtime clauses, does not make working a reasonable amount of overtime in the future voluntary or optional on the part of any employee and does not bar you from requiring a qualified employee in the future to be available for and work a reasonable amount of overtime as part of the duties and responsibilities of his regular job.

Rule 38. Use the voidable way, by initiating action during the contract term, to end a past practice that has misinterpreted

303

the hours of work and overtime clauses or that contradicts what you claim the negotiators reasonably intended under them.

Rule 39. Neither party waives its contractual rights under the written provisions because that party (1) misinterpreted, misconstrued or by error misapplied its rights in the past, (2) failed or neglected to enforce its rights in the past, or (3) allowed the other party in the past to violate its obligations under the written provisions of the contract.

Rule 40. Use the voidable way to stop a past practice that creates an unintended intraplant inequity or to remove any doubt that a past practice relieves any employee from working a reasonable amount of overtime in the absence of a reasonable excuse by establishing, in writing, plant rules that enforce equally the job responsibilities of each employee to be available for and undertake a reasonable amount of overtime as part of his regular job.

The Rules of Equal Distribution

Rule 41. If your contract provides for equal distribution of available overtime you distribute available overtime equally among all qualified employees in the classified jobs or other operating group in which the need for the overtime work arises.

Rule 42. If you excuse an employee from working overtime because you accept the excuse he offers, you count the overtime opportunity offered him in the overtime roster as if he had worked it, unless your contract provides otherwise.

Rule 43. If an employee refuses to work a reasonable amount of overtime required of him without offering a reasonable excuse, you count the overtime opportunity offered him in the overtime roster, as if he had worked it; and in addition, you follow the corrective discipline way, warning him that in the future he must be available for and undertake a reasonable amount of overtime, equally with his fellow employees.

If thereafter he again refuses to work a reasonable amount of overtime without a reasonable excuse, you apply the rules of corrective discipline, sending him a written reprimand and giving a copy to his shop steward or union committee chairman and mailing a copy to the union's place of business.

Rule 44. Unless your contract provides otherwise, you equalize the distribution of available overtime over a reasonable period of time, such as three, six, or twelve months; and you correct errors by using future overtime opportunities to distribute the overtime work equally within a reasonable period.

The Rules Against Pyramiding of Overtime, Penalty and Premium Pay

Rule 45. Unless your contract provides otherwise, you avoid counting the same hours twice for overtime, penalty or premium pay; and you avoid pyramiding for the same hours the different types of overtime, premium, or penalty pay.

Rule 46. If your contract provides for different or more than one overtime, premium, or penalty rate for the same hours or days worked, apply only one—the single highest overtime, premium or penalty rate of pay.

Concerted Refusals to Work Overtime

Rule 47. If two or more employees refuse to work a reasonable amount of overtime after reasonable advance notice without a reasonable excuse, their conduct constitutes a concerted action that violates the responsibilities of their regular jobs and breaches the no-strike pledge under your contract.

Rule 48. Concerted refusals to work overtime challenge your authority to manage; and each employee engaging in concerted action subjects himself to corrective disciplinary action.

Rule 49. A shop steward who engages in concerted action by refusing with other employees to undertake overtime work assigned to him subjects himself to disciplinary action and, in addition, makes the union liable for damages arising out of the breach of the no-strike pledge under your contract.

Rule 50. If two or more of your employees, in concerted action, offer the same kind of excuse on the same day that you require them to work overtime, such as eyestrain, fatigue, not feeling well, too tired, headache, unable to work— excuses that the sensory facts you observe fail to support —have each one of them write out his reason for refusing to work the overtime, in "black and white," and have each one sign a statement putting it "on the record."

Rule 51. Apply corrective discipline to each employee who engages in concerted action in refusing to work the overtime required of him in his job; and apply corrective discipline to the shop steward who uses the concerted refusal of employees to work overtime as a political pressure tactic during the contract term.

The Rules of
Labor Arbitration

I I

The Supreme Court Speaks
on Labor Arbitration

Plainly the agreement to arbitrate grievance disputes is the quid pro quo for an agreement not to strike. Viewed in this light, the legislation does more than confer jurisdiction in the federal courts over labor organizations. It expresses a federal policy that federal courts should enforce these agreements on behalf of or against labor organizations and that industrial peace can be best obtained only in that way.

From its decision in the Lincoln Mills case, quoted in part above, decided in 1957, to the Drake Bakeries case, decided in 1962, the United States Supreme Court firmly established the rules of arbitration under collective bargaining contracts affecting interstate commerce. In that short span of five years the Court put to rest a host of troublesome questions that had arisen over the enforceability of arbitration, the relation between arbitration and the no-strike pledge, and the jurisdiction and authority of the arbitrator to make final and binding settlements of grievances arising during the contract term.

The U.S. Supreme Court also resolved many conflicting positions between lower federal courts and state courts on enforcing arbitration under labor contracts. Although other questions will arise in the future, in the principal cases decided in those five years the Supreme Court firmly established the rule that the courts will enforce arbitration freely contracted for as the method for finally settling grievances during the contract term.

"If the grievance is appealed to the higher stages of the grievance procedure," the IUE *Leadership Manual* tells its shop stewards, "it is still your grievance. Don't lose track of it."

Your job, Mr. Supervisor, doesn't end when the grievance or disciplinary case passes through your step in the grievance procedure. It's still your case; and a fuller understanding of the arbitration process should help you in preparing your case for the higher steps of the grievance procedure and for arbitration if the union appeals to arbitration.

The Supreme Court Revokes the Common Law Doctrine

On June 3, 1957, the U.S. Supreme Court handed down its decision in the Textile Workers Union vs. Lincoln Mills case. In that historic decision the Court held that under Section 301 of the Labor-Management Relations Act of 1947, as amended, referred to as the Taft-Hartley Law, the agreement to arbitrate grievance disputes contained in collective bargaining agreements would be specifically enforced.

What makes that decision so historic? Prior to 1957 no federal law governed labor arbitration under collective bargaining contracts covering employees in an industry affecting interstate commerce. The Federal Arbitration Statute excluded jurisdiction over arbitration under collective bargaining contracts. The common law, derived principally from the English common law as it developed under Magna Carta and other historic doctrines, continued to govern labor arbitration.

The common law recognized arbitration voluntarily agreed to as a substitute for court action but only over disputes that existed at the time the contracting parties agreed to go to arbitration. That is, the common law would not enforce an agreement between contracting parties to submit to arbitration a dispute arising in the future. The

310

common law regarded an agreement to arbitrate future disputes as an executory agreement. In such cases, if one party demanded and the other refused to go to arbitration, the court would not compel arbitration. The only relief available to the party demanding arbitration was to start an action for breach of agreement to arbitrate, and the aggrieved party would get only a nominal money judgment of six cents.

Prior to 1957 some of the states had modified the common law rule that refused to enforce executory agreements to arbitrate. In those states statutes made valid and enforceable a provision in a collective bargaining contract under which the parties had voluntarily agreed to settle by arbitration a controversy arising during the contract term. Then came the Supreme Court's decision in the Lincoln Mills case, which overturned the common law rule against enforcing executory agreements to arbitrate. Said the Supreme Court:

> It seems, therefore, clear to us that Congress adopted a policy which placed sanctions behind agreements to arbitrate grievance disputes, by implication rejecting the Common-law rule, discussed in Red Cross Line v. Atlantic Fruit Co. 264 US 109, 68 L ed 582, 44 S Ct 274, against enforcement of executory agreements to arbitrate. We would undercut the Act and defeat its policy if we read Section 301 narrowly as only conferring jurisdiction over labor organizations.

Arbitration—the Quid Pro Quo for the No-Strike Pledge

Thus, by one stroke, the Supreme Court made an arbitration agreement voluntarily entered into by contracting parties to a collective bargaining contract covering employees in an industry affecting interstate commerce enforceable against either party and subject to federal, not state, law.

In the Lincoln Mills case the union had instituted a suit under Section 301 of the Taft-Hartley Act to compel the company to arbitrate grievances over the company's action in changing work assignments and increasing work loads. The union demanded money damages and an order directing the company to restore the former work loads and job assignments. The collective bargaining contract prohibited strikes

311

or work stoppages and set up a grievance procedure to handle grievances arising during the term, with arbitration as the final step.

The Federal District Court ordered the company to comply with the arbitration provision. The Federal Court of Appeals reversed, by a divided vote, holding that the District Court had no authority under federal or state law to grant the relief the union sought. The U.S. Supreme Court reversed the Court of Appeals and directed the company to arbitrate the monetary claim the union asserted.

Mr. Justice William Douglas wrote the majority opinion, which held that the "agreement to arbitrate grievance disputes, contained in this collective bargaining agreement, would be specifically enforced." The Court quoted the following from the Senate Report of the legislative history of Section 301 of the Taft-Hartley Law:

> If unions can break agreements with relative impunity, then such agreements do not tend to stabilize industrial relations. The execution of an agreement does not by itself promote industrial peace. The chief advantage which an employer can reasonably expect from a collective labor agreement is assurance of uninterrupted operation during the term of the agreement. Without some effective method of assuring freedom from economic warfare for the term of the agreement, there is little reason why an employer would desire to sign such a contract.

Holding that the "agreement to arbitrate grievance disputes was considered the *quid pro quo* of a no-strike agreement," the Court said:

> Plainly the agreement to arbitrate grievance disputes is the quid pro quo for an agreement not to strike. Viewed in this light, the legislation does more than confer jurisdiction in the federal courts over labor organizations. It expresses a federal policy that federal courts should enforce these agreements on behalf of or against labor organizations and that industrial peace can be best obtained only in that way.

The Court further held that the "substantive law to apply . . . is federal law; law which the courts must fashion from the policy of our national labor laws"; that the "range of judicial inventiveness will be determined by the nature of the problem"; that "federal interpretation of the federal law will govern, not state law . . . but state law, if compatible . . . may be resorted to in order to find the rule that will best effectuate the federal policy"; and that "any state law applied, however, will be absorbed as federal law and will not be an independent source of private rights."

Referring to the fact that while the case was pending the company had terminated its operations and contracted to sell its mill properties and that all work in the mill had ceased, the Court held:

> Insofar as the grievances sought restoration of work loads and job assignments, the case is, of course, moot. But to the extent that they sought a monetary award, the case is a continuing controversy.

The Arbitration Trilogy of 1960

On June 20, 1960, the U.S. Supreme Court decided three cases simultaneously, which have since become known as the "trilogy on arbitration," the Warrior and Gulf Navigation Company, American Manufacturing Company, and Enterprise Wheel and Car Corporation cases. In each of those cases the United Steelworkers of America represented the employees in the respective bargaining units.

In the first two cases the union had asked the Court to enforce arbitration, which the parties had agreed to, and to compel the company to arbitrate the union's claim that the company had violated the contract. In each case the company had resisted arbitration, claiming that the grievance was not arbitrable. In the third case, Enterprise Wheel and Car Corporation, the union asked the Court to enforce an arbitrator's award rendered after the contract had expired. The company refused to comply with the award, claiming that the arbitrator had exceeded his authority.

WARRIOR AND GULF NAVIGATION COMPANY CASE

In the first case the company had contracted out maintenance work previously performed by employees in the bargaining unit, which had resulted in the layoff of a number of employees. The subcontractors used the company's supervisors to lay out the work, hired some of

313

the laid-off employees at reduced wages, and assigned some of the laid-off employees to work on the company's barges.

The union protested the company's action, claiming that it violated the contract by inducing a partial lockout of the affected employees. The contract contained a no-strike-no-lockout clause and a grievance and arbitration procedure that covered differences over the "meaning and application of the provisions" of the contract or "any local trouble of any kind" but excluded from arbitration "matters which are strictly a function of management."

The Federal District Court dismissed the union's action to compel the company to arbitrate the grievance. That court, "after hearing evidence, much of which went to the merits of the grievance," held that the contract did not "confide in an arbitrator the right to review the defendant's business judgment in contracting out work" and that "the contracting out of repair and maintenance work, as well as construction work, is strictly a function of management not limited in any respect by the labor agreement involved here." The Circuit Court of Appeals, by a divided vote, affirmed, the majority holding that the contract had withdrawn from the grievance procedure "matters which are strictly a function of management," including subcontracting.

Arbitration Is "Part and Parcel" of Collective Bargaining

The U.S. Supreme Court, by a divided vote, reversed and ordered the company to arbitrate the union's grievance. In his majority opinion Mr. Justice William Douglas distinguished between commercial and labor arbitration, saying:

> In the commercial case, arbitration is the substitute for litigation. Here arbitration is the substitute for industrial strife. Since arbitration of labor disputes has quite different functions from arbitration under an ordinary commercial agreement, the hostility evinced by courts toward arbitration of commercial agreements has no place here. For arbitration of labor disputes under collective bargaining agreements is part and parcel of the collective bargaining process itself.

Noting that the "grievance machinery under a collective bargaining agreement is at the very heart of the system of industrial self-government" and that the "processing of disputes through the grievance machinery is actually a vehicle by which meaning and content is given to the collective bargaining agreement," the Supreme Court said:

> The collective bargaining agreement states the rights and duties of the parties. It is more than a contract; it is a generalized code to govern a myriad of cases which the draftsmen cannot wholly anticipate . . . The collective agreement covers the whole employment relationship. It calls into being a new common law—the common law of a particular industry or of a particular plant . . . Gaps may be left to be filled in by reference to the practices of the particular industry and of the various shops covered by the agreement. Many of the specific practices which underlie the agreement may be unknown, except in hazy form, even to the negotiators.

Holding that "apart from matters that the parties specifically exclude, all of the questions on which the parties disagree must therefore come within the scope of the grievance and arbitration provisions of the collective agreement," the Court said:

> The grievance procedure is, in other words, a part of the continuous collective bargaining process. It, rather than a strike, is the terminal point of a disagreement . . .
>
> The labor arbitrator's source of law is not confined to the express provisions of the contract, as the industrial common law—the practices of the industry and the shop—is equally a part of the collective bargaining agreement although not expressed in it . . .
>
> The parties expect that his [the arbitrator's] judgment of a particular grievance will reflect not only what the contract says but, insofar as the collective bargaining agreement permits, such factors as the effect upon productivity of a particular result, its consequence to the morale of the shop, his judgment whether tensions will be heightened or diminished. For the parties' objective in using the arbitration process is primarily to further their common goal of uninterrupted production under the agreement to make the agreement serve their specialized needs.

315

In stating that the "labor arbitrator's source of law is not confined to the express provisions of the contract, as the industrial common law —the practices of the industry and the shop—is equally a part of the collective bargaining agreement although not expressed in it," the Court expressed that doctrine too broadly. In the companion case, Enterprise Wheel and Car Corporation, the Court corrected that statement and properly limited it to the particular agreement under which the dispute arose, saying:

> Arbitrators under these collective agreements are indispensable agencies in a continuous collective bargaining process. They sit to settle disputes at the plant level—disputes that require for their solution knowledge of the custom and practices of a particular factory or of a particular industry as reflected in particular agreements.

If the bargaining history reasonably shows that the negotiators intended a particular written provision to be construed according to the custom or practice in the industry, such custom or practice then properly serves the arbitrator as a source of law in deciding the dispute. So too with practices that arise in the plant covered by the contract that show how the parties themselves through their representatives, foremen and shop stewards, interpreted a particular provision in the past or applied a particular benefit under the contract. Such past practices contribute to the arbitrator's source of law. So too with industry or plant practices reflected in the contract. But practices under contracts other than the one under which the dispute arose do not serve the arbitrator as a source of law.

Arbitration Coextensive with the No-Strike Pledge

Then, holding that an "order to arbitrate the particular grievance should not be denied unless it may be said with positive assurance that the arbitration clause is not susceptible to an interpretation that covers the asserted dispute. Doubts should be resolved in favor of coverage . . . Every grievance in a sense involves a claim that management has violated some provision of the agreement," the Court said:

Collective bargaining agreements regulate or restrict the exercise of management functions; they do not oust management from the performance of them. Management hires and fires, pays and promotes, supervises and plans. All these are part of its function, and absent a collective bargaining agreement, it may be exercised freely except as limited by public law and by the willingness of employees to work under the particular, unilaterally imposed conditions. A collective bargaining agreement may treat only with certain specific practices, leaving the rest to management but subject to the possibility of work stoppages. When, however, an absolute no-strike clause is included in the agreement, then in a very real sense everything that management does is subject to the agreement, for either management is prohibited or limited in the action it takes, or if not, it is protected from interference by strikes.

Question of Contract Violation Decided by the Arbitrator, Not the Court

In the absence of any express provision excluding a particular grievance from arbitration we think only the most forceful evidence of a purpose to exclude the claim from arbitration can prevail, particularly where, as here, the exclusion clause is vague and the arbitration clause quite broad. Since any attempt by a court to infer such a purpose necessarily comprehends the merits, the court should view with suspicion an attempt to persuade it to become entangled in the construction of the substantive provisions of a labor agreement, even through the back door of interpreting the arbitration clause, when the alternative is to utilize the services of an arbitrator.

Finding that the union's grievance alleged that the contracting-out violated the agreement, the Court concluded:

There was, therefore, a dispute "as to the meaning and application of the provisions of this Agreement" which the parties had agreed would be determined by arbitration. Whether contracting-out in the present case violated the agreement is the question. It is a question for the arbiter, not for the courts.

317

AMERICAN MANUFACTURING COMPANY CASE

In the second case of the trilogy, two weeks after an employee had settled a compensation case against the company, in which his doctor had expressed the opinion that the injury had made him "25 percent permanently partially disabled," the union filed a grievance claiming that the seniority provisions of the contract entitled him to return to his job. The company refused to arbitrate, claiming "(1) the [employee] is estopped from making his claim . . . on the basis that he was permanently partially disabled, (2) . . . not physically able to do the work, and (3) that this type of dispute is not arbitrable under the collective bargaining agreement in question."

The Federal District Court held that the employee "having accepted the settlement on the basis of permanent partial disability was estopped to claim any seniority or employment rights." The Court of Appeals affirmed the District Court's decision but for different reasons. It held, after reviewing the evidence, that the grievance was "a frivolous, patently baseless one, not subject to arbitration under the collective bargaining agreement."

The Supreme Court unanimously reversed the lower courts' decisions and directed the company to arbitrate the union's grievance. Mr. Justice William Douglas, writing the opinion for the Court, said:

> There is no exception in the "no-strike" clause and none therefore should be read into the grievance clause, since one is the *quid pro quo* for the other. The question is not whether in the mind of a court there is equity in the claim. Arbitration is a stabilizing influence only as it serves as a vehicle for handling every and all disputes that arise under the agreement.

The Arbitrator, Not the Court, Decides the Merits

Holding that the "function of the court is very limited when the parties have agreed to submit all questions of contract interpretation to the arbitrator," the Court said,

> . . . whether the moving party is right or wrong is a question of contract interpretation for the arbitrator. In these circumstances the

318

moving party should not be deprived of the arbitrator's judgment, when it was his judgment and all that it connotes that was bargained for.

The courts therefore have no business weighing the merits of the grievance, considering whether there is equity in a particular claim, or determining whether there is particular language in the written instrument which will support the claim. The agreement is to submit all grievances to arbitration, not merely those the court will deem meritorious. The processing of even frivolous claims may have therapeutic values which those who are not a part of the plant environment may be quite unaware.

Stating that "when the judiciary undertakes to determine the merits of a grievance under the guise of interpreting the grievance procedure of collective bargaining agreements, it usurps a function which under that regime is entrusted to the arbitration tribunal," the Court said:

The union claimed in this case that the company had violated a specific provision of the contract. The company took the position that it had not violated that clause. There was, therefore, a dispute between the parties as to "the meaning, interpretation and application" of the collective bargaining agreement. Arbitration should have been ordered.

You will note that in each of these cases the Court did not decide that the union had an arbitrable grievance and the Court did not decide that the company had violated the contract. The Court held, in effect, that the parties had agreed under the grievance and arbitration provisions, coupled with the no-strike clause, to submit those questions to the arbitrator. The Court declined to weigh the merits or consider the equity of a grievance in determining whether the grievance and arbitration provisions covered the union's claim of breach of contract. The arbitrator had the authority to decide those questions.

ENTERPRISE WHEEL AND CAR CORPORATION CASE

In the final case of the trilogy, the company had refused to arbitrate a grievance protesting the discharge of eleven employees. The Federal

District Court ordered arbitration. About four months after the contract had expired, the case went to arbitration. About eight months later the arbitrator rendered his award, finding that the misconduct did not justify the penalty of discharge. He reduced the discharge penalty to a ten-day suspension and directed the company to reinstate the eleven employees with back pay to the date of reinstatement, less money they may have received from other employment. The company refused to comply with the award, claiming that the contract did not authorize the arbitrator to award reinstatement or wages for any period after the contract had expired.

The Federal District Court confirmed the arbitrator's award and directed the company to comply with it. The Circuit Court of Appeals agreed that the District Court had jurisdiction to enforce the award but held the failure to specify the amounts to be deducted from the back pay rendered the award unenforceable and, further, that an award for back pay and reinstatement after the contract had terminated could not be enforced because the contract had expired.

The U.S. Supreme Court agreed with the Court of Appeals that the judgment of the District Court should be modified "so that the amounts due the employees may be definitely determined by arbitration." In all other respects, the Supreme Court affirmed the District Court's judgment enforcing the arbitrator's award ordering the company to reinstate the discharged employees. Mr. Justice William Douglas, in his opinion written for the majority of the Court, said:

> The refusal of courts to review the merits of an arbitration award is the proper approach to arbitration under collective bargaining agreements. The federal policy of settling labor disputes by arbitration would be undermined if courts had the final say on the merits of the awards.

The Court held that the arbitrator had not exceeded his authority in setting aside the discharge and ordering the company to reinstate the eleven employees with back pay even though the contract had expired. The mere ambiguity in the arbitrator's opinion accompanying his award as to the amount of back pay, the Court held, constituted no reason "for refusing to enforce the award."

320

The Contract Determines the Arbitrator's Authority

Arbitrators under collective bargaining contracts, the Court said, serve as "indispensable agencies in a continuous collective bargaining process. They sit to settle disputes at the plant level—disputes that require for their solution knowledge of the custom and practices of a particular factory or of a particular industry as reflected in particular agreements." Then, speaking on the arbitrator's authority in interpreting and applying the contract, the Court said:

> Nevertheless, an arbitrator is confined to interpretation and application of the collective bargaining agreement; he does not sit to dispense his own brand of industrial justice. He may of course look for guidance from many sources, yet his award is legitimate only so long as it draws its essence from the collective bargaining agreement. When the arbitrator's words manifest an infidelity to this obligation, courts have no choice but to refuse enforcement of the award.

Emphasizing that the question of interpretation of the contract is "a question for the arbitrator," the Court said:

> It is the arbitrator's construction which was bargained for; and so far as the arbitrator's decision concerns construction of the contract, the courts have no business overruling him because their interpretation of the contract is different from his.

Arbitrability and Merits Decided by the Arbitrator, Not the Court

You will note that in the last case, Enterprise Wheel and Car Corporation, the union had protested the discharge of the eleven employees during the contract term before the contract had expired. The fact that the processing of the grievance took many months and the fact that the arbitrator handed down his award after the contract had expired did not relieve either party from honoring its agreement to arbitrate grievances arising during the term of the contract. Nor did those facts oust the arbitrator from jurisdiction and authority to decide the issues of reinstatement and back pay. Having found that the company had violated the contract during its term by discharging the eleven employees, the arbitrator's award made the employees "whole" by ordering the company to reinstate them into their former jobs with back pay for the loss in earnings they had suffered less pay for a ten-day suspension, which he found the appropriate penalty for the offense they had committed.

In the two preceding cases, Warrior and Gulf Navigation and American Manufacturing, the Court restrained itself from considering the merits of a grievance or whether "in the mind of a court there is equity in the claim" in determining the arbitrability of a grievance. In this third case, Enterprise Wheel and Car Corporation, the Court also refrained from reviewing the merits of an arbitrator's award because a "review by a court of the merits would make meaningless the provisions that the arbitrator's decision is final, for in reality it would almost never be final." In these cases the Court established the rule of labor arbitration that the "question of interpretation of the collective bargaining agreement is a question for the arbitrator."

THE ARBITRATOR'S JURISDICTION AND AUTHORITY

How does an arbitrator serve under a collective bargaining contract? What makes up the office he fills? How does he exercise his jurisdiction and authority in performing his job duties?

An arbitrator serves essentially as the agent of both parties, jointly appointed by them, to settle finally the differences they submit to him and to make a binding "contract of settlement" for them. As the court in the case of Ballance vs. Underhill put it:

> [An award] partakes of the nature of a contract between the parties, which they have, by their submission, authorized the arbitrator to make for them and by which they are conclusively bound . . . It is in this latter character alone [a contract of settlement] that an award is treated when courts of equity have interfered to enforce a specific performance of it.

An arbitrator serves as the mutual agent of the parties who appointed him. His award, deciding the dispute, constitutes a contract of settlement that binds both parties, just as if they themselves had signed the settlement. An arbitrator's jurisdiction to make a contract of settlement for the parties extends only to those matters the parties by their contract or submission agreement empowered him to make for them in their stead. If the contract or submission agreement does not empower him to make a contract settlement of the dispute, he lacks jurisdiction to make one, and to that extent the dispute is not arbitrable. Arbitrability means, did the parties agree to make arbitration available for a particular dispute under their contract or arbitration clause? To put that another way, does the contract make a particular dispute arising during the contract term subject to the arbitration system the parties have set up?

If the contract gives the arbitrator jurisdiction, that is, makes the particular dispute subject to arbitration, then the question of the arbitrator's authority to decide the merits of the dispute within the framework of the contract comes up. An arbitrator exercises only the authority the contract or submission agreement delegates to him. If in exercising his jurisdiction in the case he goes beyond his delegated authority, then his award, his contract of settlement, becomes a voidable one. In either case:

1. Whether the contract gives the arbitrator jurisdiction over a dispute; or
2. Whether the arbitrator exceeded his delegated authority in deciding the dispute and making his contract of settlement—

his jurisdiction and authority as the mutual agent for the parties are properly subject to court review unless the parties expressly agreed otherwise. As the court in Halstead vs. Seamon said:

> It is for the Court to judge whether arbitrators have exceeded their powers or refused to exercise them. The [contract] is the foundation of their jurisdiction and they are not the exclusive judges of their own powers.

If the parties agree that an arbitrator's award shall be final and binding, it becomes final and binding so long as the arbitrator does not exceed his delegated authority in deciding the dispute; and his award becomes final and binding upon the parties as any other contract of settlement that they themselves enter into.

The courts uphold the sanctity of a contract of settlement made by an arbitrator to the same extent that the courts uphold the sanctity of any other contract voluntarily entered into by the parties. As the court in the case of Lehman vs. Ostrovsky said:

> In the absence of fraud or other wrongful act on the part of another contracting party, he who signs or accepts a written contract is bound by the stipulation and conditions expressed in it.

To the extent that strict rules of law or evidence do not circumscribe the power of the parties to enter into a contract, strict rules of law or evidence do not bind their agent, an arbitrator, in making a contract for them. Just as the law does not require the parties to give the reasons why they entered into a contract, so the law does not require their arbitrator to give the reasons why he made his contract of settlement for them. As the Court said in the Enterprise Wheel and Car Corporation case, "Arbitrators have no obligation to the court to give their reasons for an award."

On the other hand, whatever breaches of conduct would nullify a contract, such as fraud, undue influence, or corruption, would nullify an arbitrator's award. As the court in the case In re Wilkins said:

> Where the merits of a controversy are referred to an arbitrator selected by the parties, his determination as to the law or the facts is final and conclusive . . . The award of an arbitrator cannot be set aside for mere errors of judgment either as to the law or as to the facts. If he keeps within his jurisdiction and is not guilty of fraud, corruption or other misconduct affecting his award, it is unassailable, operates as a final and conclusive judgment, and however disappointing it may be the parties must abide by it . . . Otherwise the court would substitute its own judgment in place of the judgment of arbitrators freely chosen by the parties to settle the controversy and the award would thus become the commencement instead of the end of litigation.

Now do you see why, Mr. Supervisor, courts refrain from reviewing the merits of an arbitrator's award? Since the parties voluntarily chose the arbitrator as their mutual agent to make the contract of settlement for them, neither one can welch on that contract of settlement however disappointing it may find it. The parties voluntarily made their bargain through their mutual agent, the arbitrator; and that bargain binds them just as any other contract of settlement they themselves make.

The Retroactive Remedy for Violation of the No-Strike Pledge

> If the union did strike in violation of the contract, the company is entitled to its damages; by staying this action, pending arbitration, we have no intention of depriving it of those damages. We simply remit the company to the forum it agreed to use for processing its strike damage claims. That forum, it is true, may be very different from a courtroom, but we are not persuaded that the remedy there will be inadequate. Whether the damages to be awarded by the arbitrator would not normally be expected to serve as an "effective" deterrent to future strikes, which the company urges, is not a question to be answered in the abstract or in general terms. This question, as well as what result will best promote industrial peace, can only be answered in the factual context of particular cases.

In the Drake Bakeries case, quoted above, together with two others, Lucas Flour Company and Sinclair Refining Company cases, all decided in 1962, the U.S. Supreme Court set the rules of labor arbitration governing the parties' legal duties under their agreement to arbitrate grievance disputes during the contract term, the legal remedy available to redress or deter a violation of their agreement to arbitrate, and the appropriate forum, court or arbitration, in which to obtain relief.

In the case between Lucas Flour Company and Local 174, Teamsters, Chauffeurs, Warehousemen & Helpers of America, the U.S. Supreme Court held that a strike the union called during the contract term violated the collective bargaining contract even though the contract did not contain a no-strike clause, and the Supreme Court affirmed a money judgment against the union for the damages suffered by the company as a result of the strike.

In the case between Sinclair Refining Company and Oil, Chemical and Atomic Workers Int'l Union, AFL–CIO–CLC, decided the same day as the Drake Bakeries case, the Supreme Court held that the company's complaint in a court suit properly stated a cause of action against the international and local unions for money damages because the union had violated its no-strike pledge over grievances arising during the contract term. The Court rejected the union's contention that the company should have submitted its claim to arbitration.

In the Sinclair Refining Company case the Court held that under their contract the parties did not make arbitration available as the forum in which the company could pursue its claim for damages against the union for its alleged violation of its no-strike pledge and accordingly upheld the company's complaint for damages against the union in its court suit. The Supreme Court distinguished its decision in the Sinclair Refining Company case from the Drake Bakeries case, handed down the same day, in which the Court held that under the contract in the latter case the parties had made arbitration available as the forum in which the company could pursue its claim for damages arising from the union's breach of its no-strike pledge. In the Sinclair case the Supreme Court dismissed two other counts in the company's complaint, for money damages against committeemen of the local union and for an injunction enjoining the union from striking in the future over grievances even though the parties had agreed to submit those grievances to arbitration.

LUCAS FLOUR COMPANY CASE

In that case the company had discharged an employee after he had damaged a new fork-lift truck by running it off a loading platform and onto some railroad tracks. The company told the union's business agent, who had protested, that it had discharged the employee because of unsatisfactory work. The union then called a strike to force the company to rehire the employee. The strike lasted eight days, after which the union agreed to submit the employee's discharge to arbitration. About five months later the board of arbitration rendered its award, upholding the company's action in discharging the employee and denying him reinstatement.

In the meantime, the company had sued the union in court in the state of Washington, demanding damages for business losses caused by the strike. After a trial the court granted the company a judgment against the union of $6,501.60. The court held that the "strike was a violation of the collective bargaining contract, because it was an attempt to coerce the employer to forego his contractual right to discharge an employee for unsatisfactory work." The union appealed to the U.S. Supreme Court, but the Court upheld the judgment of damages.

Union Liable for Damages Even in the Absence of a No-Strike Clause

The Supreme Court, with Mr. Justice Hugo Black strongly dissenting, rejected the union's claim that "there could be no violation in the absence of a no-strike clause in the contract explicitly covering the subject of the dispute over which the strike was called." The Court held:

> The collective bargaining contract expressly imposed upon both parties the duty of submitting the dispute in question to final and binding arbitration. In a consistent course of decisions the Courts of Appeals of at least five Federal Circuits have held that a strike to settle a dispute which a collective bargaining agreement provides shall be settled exclusively and finally by compulsory arbitration constitutes a violation of the agreement. The National Labor Relations Board has reached the same conclusion . . . We approve that doctrine. To hold otherwise would obviously do violence to accepted principles of traditional contract law. Even more in point, a contrary view would be completely at odds with the basic policy of national labor legislation to promote the arbitral process as a substitute for economic warfare.

The Court held that the state court had jurisdiction to decide the case but that federal labor law, not state law, controlled. Although it upheld the money judgment, the Supreme Court refused to adopt the reasoning of the state court and held:

> Insofar as the language of that [State] court's opinion is susceptible to the construction that a strike during the term of a collective bargaining

327

agreement is *ipso facto* a violation of the agreement, we expressly reject it.

Enforcing the Union's Implied Pledge Not to Strike

Finding that the union's strike action violated its agreement to submit grievances to final and binding arbitration, by which it had "impliedly" agreed not to strike, the Court held:

> What has been said is not to suggest that a no-strike agreement is to be implied beyond the area which it has been agreed will be exclusively covered by compulsory terminal arbitration. Nor is it to suggest that there may not arise problems in specific cases as to whether compulsory and binding arbitration has been agreed upon, and, if so, as to what disputes have been made arbitrable. But no such problems are present in this case. The grievance over which the union struck, was, as it concedes, one which it had expressly agreed to settle by submission to final and binding arbitration proceedings. The strike which it called was a violation of that contractual obligation.

Voluntary Enforceable—Not Compulsory—Arbitration

You will note, Mr. Supervisor, that the Court refers to "compulsory terminal" arbitration. It uses the term in the sense of enforceable arbitration. Since the parties had voluntarily agreed to submit the dispute in question to arbitration, the Court enforced that agreement by finding that the union had violated its contractual obligation not to strike.

Our federal labor law, unlike the law in some other countries, does not compel management or unions to agree to use arbitration to settle disputes arising between them. The Taft-Hartley Act encourages the use of arbitration as a "desirable method for settlement of grievance disputes arising over the application or interpretation of an existing collective-bargaining agreement." In interpreting the Taft-Hartley Act the Supreme Court, starting with the Lincoln Mills case, held that once the parties had voluntarily agreed in their collective bargaining contract to arbitrate grievance disputes arising during the contract term, they would be bound by their agreement; and the court would enforce that agreement to arbitrate against the party who tried to evade its promise to arbitrate. In some other countries the law imposes compulsory arbitration of grievance disputes arising during the term of a collective bargaining agreement and prohibits strikes or lock-outs during the contract term.

The law of the Province of Ontario, Canada, for example, requires that "every collective agreement . . . shall provide that there will be no strikes or lock-outs so long as the agreement continues to operate." And that law further provides:

> Every collective agreement shall provide for the final and binding settlement by arbitration, without stoppage of work, of all differences between the parties arising from the interpretation, application, administration or alleged violation of the agreement, including any question as to whether a matter is arbitrable.

As you can see, the law there equates the no-strike-no-lock-out prohibition with compulsory arbitration of grievance disputes arising during the contract term over the "interpretation, application, administration or alleged violation of the agreement." Further, the Ontario law empowers the arbitration tribunal to decide "any question as to whether a matter is arbitrable."

By holding that the "agreement to arbitrate grievance disputes is the *quid pro quo* for an agreement not to strike," the Supreme Court, in effect, arrived at the same balance by equating the no-strike pledge with the arbitration clause over grievances arising during the contract term the parties had agreed to settle by binding arbitration.

ARBITRATION ENFORCED EVEN IN THE
ABSENCE OF A NO-STRIKE CLAUSE

The Supreme Court had anticipated its decision in the Lucas Flour Company case, decided in 1962, holding the union liable for money damages for violating its agreement to arbitrate even in the absence of a no-strike clause in the contract explicitly covering the subject of the dispute over which the union called the strike. In the three cases decided in 1960, the arbitration trilogy, the Supreme Court held that arbitration was the *quid pro quo* for the no-strike clause. The opinion of the Justices who concurred in the decision clearly showed that the Court would enforce the parties' agreement to use final and binding arbitration to settle disputes arising during the contract term even in the absence of a no-strike clause in the contract. In his concurring opinion, referring to the *quid pro quo* relationship between the no-strike clause and the arbitration clause, Mr. Justice William J. Brennan, Jr., said:

> The Court makes reference to an arbitration clause being the quid pro quo for a no-strike clause. I do not understand the Court to mean that the application of the principles announced today depends upon the presence of a no-strike clause in the agreement.

In the next two cases, decided in 1962, the Supreme Court laid out the ground rules that govern the union's duty to honor its contractual pledge not to strike during the contract term. The Court in effect held:

1. The conduct of union shop stewards and committeemen who violate the union's agreement not to strike during the contract term subjects the union to liability for money damages for breach of its pledge not to strike;

2. That money damages constituted the remedy available to the company for the union's action in striking over grievances the parties agreed to settle by final and binding arbitration;

3. That the law did not empower the court to enjoin by an injunction disputes the parties had agreed to submit to arbitration;

4. If the contract limits the company's right to seek damages through the arbitration forum, then the court will entertain a suit and determine the damages;

5. If, however, the parties' contract contemplates arbitration as the forum for the company's claim for damages, because the union allegedly violated its no-strike pledge, either by an expressed no-

strike clause, or an "implied" agreement to submit the dispute to final and binding arbitration, or both, the court will enforce that agreement to arbitrate; and will, accordingly, stay a court action until the company has submitted to arbitration its claim for money damages.

SINCLAIR REFINING COMPANY CASE

In that case 999 employees had engaged in a work stoppage because the company had docked three employees a total of $2.19 from their pay. The company filed a court suit asking for money damages and for an injunction, naming the international and local unions and twenty-four employees as defendants. The company's complaint set forth three counts.

Count I: The company claimed that the unions caused the strike over the three pay claims, which were properly subject to the grievance procedure, thereby violating the unions' agreement "not to strike over any cause which could be the subject of a grievance" under the contract. The company asked for damages in the sum of $12,500 from the international and local unions.

Count II: The company asked judgment in the same amount against twenty-four employees who served as union committeemen.

Count III: The company asked for an injunction enjoining the union from striking in the future over grievances the contract made subject to grievance and arbitration.

The union moved to dismiss the company's complaint and to stay the suit, claiming that (1) the contract made arbitration the forum for all of the issues raised in the company's complaint, and that (2) grievances of employees then pending in arbitration involved similar issues.

The Supreme Court upheld the company's complaint under Count I for money damages against the international and local unions. It dismissed the company's claim under Count II for money damages against the twenty-four committeemen and dismissed its demand under Count III for an injunction enjoining the union from striking in the future over grievances the contract made subject to arbitration.

Arbitration Not Made Available to the Company

The Supreme Court found that the contract did not obligate the company to arbitrate its claim, finding that the "contract here involved is not susceptible to a construction that the company was bound to arbitrate its claim for damages against the union for breach of the undertaking not to strike." The contract precluded "arbitration boards from considering any matters other than employee grievances." The Court said:

> There is not a word in the grievance and arbitration article providing for the submission of grievances by the company. Instead, there is the express, flat limitation that arbitration boards should consider only employee grievances. Furthermore, the article expressly provides that arbitration may be invoked only at the option of the union. At no place in the contract does the union agree to arbitrate at the behest of the company. The company is to take its claims elsewhere, which it has now done.

The Court distinguished its decision in the Drake Bakeries case, in which it had directed the company to go to arbitration for money damages, stating that in the Drake Bakeries case the "question of arbitrability of a damages claim for breach of a no-strike clause is considered and resolved in favor of arbitration in the presence of an agreement to arbitrate 'all complaints, disputes or grievances arising between them involving . . . any act or conduct or relation between the parties.' "

Responsibilities of the Union and Its Committeemen

The Court dismissed the company's claim for damages against the twenty-four committeemen, holding that the "union is liable for the acts of its agents, under familiar principles of the law of agency" as well as under the provision of the Taft-Hartley Act, which expressly provides that "in determining whether any person is acting as an 'agent' of another person so as to make such other person responsible for his acts, the question of whether the specific acts performed were actually authorized or subsequently ratified shall not be controlling."

332

The Court held that the conduct of the twenty-four committeemen who participated in work stoppages subjected them to disciplinary action but not to a claim for money damages. Said the Supreme Court:

> The union itself does not quarrel with the proposition that the relationship of the members of the bargaining unit to the employer is "governed by" the bargaining agreement entered into on their behalf by the union. It is universally accepted that the no-strike clause in a collective agreement at the very least establishes a rule of conduct or condition of employment the violation of which by employees justifies discipline or discharge . . . The conduct charged in Count II is therefore within the scope of a "violation" of the collective agreement.

In its decision the Court referred to the congressional history of Section 301 of the Taft-Hartley Act, which showed that "only the union was to be made to respond for union wrongs, and that the union members were not to be subject to levy; . . . makes unions bound by the acts of its agents according to conventional principles of agency law; . . . exempts agents and members from personal liability for judgments against the union; . . . and that liability for damages will lie against union assets only . . . to 'prevent a repetition of the Danbury Hatters case, in which many members lost their homes.' "

In the Danbury Hatters case the Court noted the "legislative determination that the aftermath of that decision was not to be permitted to recur." The Supreme Court said:

> In that case, an antitrust treble damage action was brought against a large number of union members, including union officers and agents, to recover from them the employer's losses in a nationwide, union-directed boycott of his hats. The union was not named as a party, nor was judgment entered against it. A large money judgment was entered, instead, against the individual defendants for participating in the plan "emanating from headquarters," by knowingly authorizing and delegating authority to the union officers to do the acts involved.

In dismissing Count II, against the local's twenty-four committeemen, the Court held:

The national labor policy requires and we hold that when a union is liable for damages for violation of the no-strike clause, its officers and members are not liable for these damages. Here, Count II, as we have said, necessarily alleges union liability but prays for damages from the union agents. Where the union has inflicted the injury it alone must pay.

Money Damages, Not Injunction, for Violating the No-Strike Pledge

Under Count III the company claimed that the union had violated the "no slowdowns, no strikes or work stoppages" clause of the contract by engaging in a series of work stoppages and strikes on nine separate occasions over a period of nineteen months, each of which grew out of a grievance that the union could have submitted to arbitration under the contract and "fell squarely within the unions' promises not to strike."

In a footnote the Court summarized those occurrences in which employees stopped work or refused to cross a picket line in support of grievances alleging that "riggers were entitled to do certain work along with machinists . . . and boilermakers"; that "pipefitters could not dismantle and remove certain pipe coils without riggers being employed on said work also"; concerning "employment by the Company of an independent contractor to operate a contractor owned crane"; that "burners and riggers would not dismantle a tank roof without employment of boilermakers at the said task"; and that about 999 employees stopped work over a grievance "on behalf of three riggers that they should not have been docked an aggregate of $2.19 in their pay for having reported late to work."

The District Court granted the unions' motion to dismiss this count, finding the controversy a labor dispute, which barred the federal court from issuing the injunction sought. The Circuit Court of Appeals affirmed the order of dismissal; and upon appeal, the Supreme Court also affirmed, holding that the case involved a labor dispute within the meaning of the Norris-LaGuardia Act and that Section 301 of the Taft-Hartley Act did not narrow or repeal the Norris-LaGuardia Act.

334

Mr. Justice Hugo Black wrote the opinion for the majority of the Court, from which Mr. Justices Brennan, Douglas and Harlan dissented in a separate opinion. The Court held:

> It is especially significant that the section (301) contains no language that could by any stretch of the imagination be interpreted to constitute an explicit repeal of the anti-injunction provisions of the Norris-LaGuardia Act in view of the fact that the section does expressly repeal another provision of the Norris-LaGuardia Act dealing with union responsibility for the act of agents.

The Supreme Court distinguished the company's action for an injunction against future strikes from its decision in the Lincoln Mills case, where it held that the Norris-LaGuardia Act did not prohibit the Court from ordering arbitration "to compel the parties to a collective bargaining agreement to submit a dispute which had arisen under that agreement to arbitration where the agreement itself required arbitration of the dispute."

The Supreme Court found that the congressional history of Section 301 showed no intent to modify, repeal, or accommodate the prohibition in the Norris-LaGuardia Act in order to make Section 301 effective and held:

> Obedience to the congressional commands of the Norris-LaGuardia Act does not directly affect the "congressional policy in favor of the enforcement of agreements to arbitrate grievance disputes" at all for it does not impair the right of an employer to obtain an order compelling arbitration of any dispute that may have been made arbitrable by the provisions of an effective collective bargaining agreement. At the most, what is involved is the question of whether the employer is to be allowed to enjoy the benefits of an injunction along with the right which Congress gave him in Section 301 to sue for breach of a collective agreement. And as we have already pointed out, Congress was not willing to insure that enjoyment to an employer at the cost of putting the federal courts back into the business of enjoining strikes and other related peaceful union activities.

335

DRAKE BAKERIES CASE

In that case the company instituted an action for damages in the Federal District Court against Local 50, American Bakery & Confectionery Workers International, AFL–CIO, claiming that the union had violated the no-strike clause of the contract.

On December 16 the company notified the union and its employees that because Christmas and New Year's Day would fall on Friday, in order to have fresh bakery products to sell on the Monday following the holiday, employees would not work on the Thursdays before Christmas and New Year's but would work on the Saturdays following those holidays. The union objected, claiming that the proposed work schedule violated the contract and that the contract did not obligate employees to work on those two Saturdays. The company claimed that it was exercising its management's rights in rescheduling work. For the December 26 Saturday the parties worked out an arrangement whereby eighty out of the 190 employees reported, which allowed the company to produce its goods. However, following further conferences, only twenty-six employees reported on Saturday, January 2, thereby preventing the company from producing its bakery products. The company then instituted court action for damages, and the union moved to stay it.

Arbitration, Not Court, Is the Forum for Damages

The Federal District Court held the company's claim an "arbitrable matter under the contract" and stayed the court action pending completion of arbitration. The Circuit Court of Appeals affirmed by a divided vote. The Supreme Court, Mr. Justice John Harlan dissenting, affirmed and held that the grievance and arbitration provision of the contract "obligates the company to arbitrate its claim for damages from forbidden strikes by the union." Mr. Justice Byron White, writing the opinion for the majority of the Court, noted the broad coverage of Article V, the grievance and arbitration provision, and said:

> The company asserts that there was a strike by the union in violation of the no-strike clause. It therefore has a "complaint" against the union

336

concerning the "acts" or "conduct" of the union. There is also involved a "dispute" between the union and the company, for the union denies that there was a strike at all, denies that it precipitated any strike, denies that the employees were obligated under the contract to work on that January 2, and itself claims that the employer breached the contract in scheduling work for the holidays. Article V on its face easily reaches the employer's claim against the union for damages caused by an alleged strike in violation of the contract.

The Court distinguished the limited arbitration clause in the Sinclair Refining Company case, which expressly excluded claims by the company, from the broad coverage of the grievance and arbitration clause in this Drake Bakeries case, which covered "questions of interpretation or application of any clause or matter covered by this contract or any act or conduct or relations between the parties hereto, directly or indirectly."

The Supreme Court also distinguished the Lucas Flour Company case, where it upheld a court judgment for money damages against the union, saying:

> In Local 174 v. Lucas Flour Co., it was held that a clause requiring the parties to submit disputes to final determination by arbitration implied an obligation not to strike over such disputes. Accordingly, the Court upheld an employer's Section 301 breach of contract suit against the union for strike damages due to a walkout over an arbitrable dispute. In that case, unlike the present one, the union conceded that there had been a strike over a grievance which the union had agreed to submit to arbitration. The only question in dispute was liability *vel von* [whether or not]. The union did not contend that, and the Court did not consider whether, the employer's damage claim should have been taken to an arbitrator.

Finding that the contract obligated the "company to arbitrate its claim for damages from forbidden strikes by the union," the Supreme Court said:

> If the union did strike in violation of the contract, the company is entitled to its damages; by staying this action, pending arbitration, we

337

have no intention of depriving it of those damages. We simply remit the company to the forum it agreed to use for processing its strike damage claims. That forum, it is true, may be very different from a courtroom, but we are not persuaded that the remedy there will be inadequate. Whether the damages to be awarded by the arbitrator would not normally be expected to serve as an "effective" deterrent to future strikes, which the company urges, is not a question to be answered in the abstract or in general terms. This question, as well as what result will best promote industrial peace, can only be answered in the factual context of particular cases . . . The dispute which this record presents appears to us to be one particularly suited for arbitration, if the parties have agreed to arbitrate. We hold that they did so agree and will hold the company to its bargain.

Management's Rights Under the Arbitration Process

15,000 STRIKE BUICK OVER JOB STANDARDS

About 15,000 members of Local 599 of the Auto Workers Union walked off the job at Buick's main plant . . .

Buick officials said a total of 19,000 workers, including 4,000 at other General Motors plants in the area, would be affected by the walkout.

That strike, as reported in the New York *Times,* took place during the term of the contract over work standards the company wanted to set up. The company said the strike "was completely unnecessary and unwarranted," and the union countered by claiming that the company was trying to establish work standards "on some jobs that exceed twice the capacity of workers and machines." You may properly question whether the right to strike during the contract term over certain types of disputes, instead of having them finally settled by arbitration, serves the interests of either management or the union. That policy question, of course, the parties themselves have to answer.

The overwhelming majority of labor contracts provide for final and binding arbitration of grievance disputes over changes in production standards, as well as over evaluating new or changed jobs and the ap-

338

propriate rates for such jobs. In a few industries, however, such as the automotive industry, some labor agreements expressly exclude grievances over production standards from arbitration. Generally, those grievances come about because of technological changes in the means, methods, or processes of production. The union then claims that the change in production standards results in a speed-up, an increase in work loads, or an improper reevaluation of existing job or incentive rates. In those cases the contract usually provides a grievance procedure to handle such grievances, but it does not include final and binding arbitration as its terminal step. If the parties fail to settle grievances over production standards in the grievance procedure, neither one can take the other to arbitration since the contract makes such grievances not arbitrable; and the union reserves the right to strike over them during the contract term.

David R. Jones reported in the New York *Times:*

Ford Motor Company, assuming a tough posture in negotiations with the United Automobile Workers, demanded changes . . . in the present grievance procedure. It said the union had abused the special grievance procedure and that this had become "the most troublesome part" of the contract. The company said it was a "matter of high urgency" to change things, and that it was "determined" to do so.

The present contract permits a union local to strike if there are grievances on production standards, new job rates and health and welfare. No other grievances can result in strikes because binding arbitration is provided.

Ford charges, in essence, that under the special grievance provision the local has tried to pressure the company into concessions on other matters. The international union, he asserted, "often lends a form of encouragement to the abuse" as an outlet for local militancy instead of trying to halt it.

Grievances over production standards and job rates for new or changed jobs during the contract term do not differ essentially from grievances dealing with consolidating jobs, taking up slack, eliminating idle time, or reducing size of crews that result from improved methods of production or changes in the former way of doing the job that warrant reevaluating the former job. The real issue in such cases is the value of the resulting new or changed job, including new production standards, in relation to the value of existing jobs in the existing wage structure, depending upon the increase or decrease in employees' effort, skill, duties, responsibilities, or working conditions, brought about by the new or improved methods of production.

SLOTTING THE NEW OR CHANGED JOB
IN THE EXISTING WAGE STRUCTURE

When the parties agree to submit such cases to arbitration, the arbitrator does not initially set the new production standard or the new rate for the new or changed job; nor does the arbitrator decide independently of the contract's wage structure, the new production standard, or the new rate. The arbitrator reviews the new rate or the revised production standard that management initially sets for the new or changed job to determine whether it bears the proper relationship, in terms of job value, to the existing rates of other unchanged jobs in the existing wage structure.

The agreed-upon existing wage structure, with its peg points of rated job values the parties themselves agreed upon and the existing level of earnings under that wage structure serve the arbitrator as guideposts in comparing the job value of the new or changed job with the job value of the remaining unchanged jobs in that wage structure. In other words, the arbitrator decides, unless the contract expressly gives him wider authority, whether the company has properly slotted the new or changed job into the existing wage structure.

Although the arbitrator does have some latitude in reviewing the value the company or the union claims for the new or changed job, the existing wage structure circumscribes his authority to determine whether the company had properly slotted the new or changed job. The value of unchanged existing jobs provides a reasonably effective safeguard for both parties that limits the arbitrator, in reviewing the rate for the new job, to see that he does not disturb the balanced wage structure the parties themselves agreed to for the remaining contract term. Although the arbitrator may err in reviewing management's action in slotting the new or changed job or in assessing the union's claims, his error, I suggest, falls within the area of probable expectancy and certainly gives rise to less havoc for either party than a strike, or the threat of a strike, during the contract term.

Both management and the union need the arbitration process, or some comparable quasi-judicial system, to help them regulate their affairs and finally settle differences arising during the contract term. The alternative, a strike that interrupts production and jobs during the contract term, is a poor substitute for arbitration.

Does Arbitration Take Away Management's Right to Manage?

No, Mr. Supervisor, arbitration of grievances during the contract term does not take away your management's right to manage! On the contrary, arbitration strengthens your management's right to manage during the contract term.

The working conditions of the contract circumscribe the rights your management could exercise freely before your employees organized and joined a union to represent them. Once management and the union have agreed upon the set of working conditions to govern their relationship during the contract term, you, Mr. Supervisor, manage by exercising your administrative right to initially interpret and initially apply those agreed-upon working conditions. Arbitration of grievances and disciplinary cases during the contract term serves management as much as it serves the union. The professional manager recognizes that arbitration protects his right to manage during the contract term; and without arbitration, no union worth its salt would forego the right to strike during the contract term. Only the uninitiated management representative, the week-end bargainer, or the do-gooder who hasn't learned the rules of the game of labor relations complains that arbitration usurps management's right to manage.

Does Arbitration Take Away the Union's Right to Grieve?

No, Mr. Supervisor, arbitration of grievances does not take away the union's right to grieve! On the contrary, arbitration strengthens the union's rights under the contract and gives substance to its right to grieve against any action of management during the contract term. Arbitration relieves the union of the necessity of using the strike or the threat of a strike to back up its protest in defending the set of working conditions and the employees it represents. Final and binding arbitration assures the union that management will remedy any action that violates the workers' or the union's rights under the contract. Arbitration assures the union of equal status with management in administering the contract's set of working conditions and handling grievances and disciplinary cases that may arise.

ARBITRATION SUBSTITUTES FOR THE STRIKE
DURING THE CONTRACT TERM

> We would not willingly sign an agreement without an arbitration clause. An arbitration clause is necessary if we are to agree to a no-strike clause.

That's a professional, John P. Burke, president of the Pulp, Sulphite and Paper Mill Workers Union talking, and he knows that arbitration serves the interests of the union and the employees it represents. How could a union agree to a no-strike clause without providing some method, independent of management, to back up its right to grieve and make it meaningful? Obviously, Mr. Supervisor, the union can't, and won't, let you be the sole judge of any action you take in interpreting or applying the contract's set of working conditions. You can't retain the right to initiate action unilaterally in applying the contract's working conditions without consulting or negotiating with the shop steward —and then serve as the judge and jury in assessing the propriety of your action!

Precisely because the labor contract makes arbitration available as the method to settle grievance disputes arising during the contract term, the union leaves to you the right to initiate action without consulting or negotiating with the shop steward and foregoes the right to strike to back up its grievance. Precisely because the labor contract provides for binding arbitration, the union pledges not to strike. Instead, the union agrees to use the orderly machinery to settle differences arising over the way the negotiators intended to apply the contract's set of working conditions. Precisely because the labor contract makes arbitration available, you, Mr. Supervisor, direct, leaving the shop steward to grieve if he objects to your action. Arbitration of grievances and disciplinary cases during the contract term reviews the propriety of your action under the agreed-upon set of working conditions—but not your right to initiate the action.

"1,000 Walk Out at G. E. Plant," headlines a news item in the New York *Times*.

> About 1,000 day-shift workers walked out . . . at the General Electric Company's electronic plant. A union official said a machine maintenance man had been ordered to oil a machine in violation of the company-union contract. A company spokesman said the man had been asked to oil the machine as part of a preventive maintenance program.

Arbitration or the right to strike during the contract term, that is the question! What best serves management's and the union's interests in uninterrupted production and jobs during the contract term—the arbitration method or the strike method?

Why Unions Buy Arbitration

Why, you may ask, do unions buy arbitration? Would not the strike or the threat of a strike achieve better results for the union in getting favorable settlements of grievances, just as the threat of a strike at the negotiating table so frequently serves the union in getting better contract settlements? Certainly, arbitration comes nowhere near matching the bargaining power of the threat of a strike. That's the principle reason why unions almost universally refuse to use arbitration to set the terms of a first or renewal contract. Using arbitration to negotiate the labor contract would weaken the union's bargaining position, because arbitration would then substitute for the strike threat; and the union would lose the most potent weapon it commands. As Henry Ford II, chairman of the board of the Ford Motor Company, put it:

343

I am convinced that responsible bargaining is most unlikely if the very possibility of a strike is ruled out from the beginning . . . A strike is never a good thing. When one occurs, it means that at least one party has overreached the bounds of reason and responsibility. But the best and probably the only effective way to prevent overreaching is to preserve the possibility that a strike may occur.

As the Lapointe Machine Tool Company case study reported:

Although the strike threat does not dominate negotiations, it is in the background. "We haven't had to show our power but we never forget that we have it," was the way one union representative expressed it. For its part, the company cannot be bluffed too easily; in fact, this statement probably summarizes management's attitude: "If the people are talked up to a strike and want it, you might as well have it—to clear the air."

As George W. Brooks, former Director of Research and Education of the Pulp, Sulphite and Paper Mill Workers Union, in talking about collective bargaining and the strike, said:

It is not the strikes that occur which are important; the important thing is that the idea of strike is present at every negotiation. What gives a settlement its final sanction in the minds of the employees is not that it was "fair" or "generous" or "correct" but rather that it was "all we could get without striking."

Then why do unions buy arbitration to settle grievance disputes? Why do unions readily agree to give a no-strike pledge and in its place, substitute binding arbitration?

ARBITRATION PROTECTS THE UNION'S FINANCIAL SECURITY!

Yes, that's why most unions buy arbitration and forego the right to strike over grievances and disciplinary cases. A union cannot afford, yes, financially afford, to require its treasury to support strikes over grievances or disciplinary cases arising during the contract term. A union, no matter how financially stable it may be, no matter how much

344

money it may have in its strike fund, must guard that strike fund to finance a strike that may come about in bargaining for the renewal contract to improve the wages, hours, and working conditions of the employees it represents. The top leaders of the union cannot chance giving the power to threaten to strike over a grievance during the contract term to each of the thousands of shop stewards and then have to back up each shop steward's threat by making strike benefits available.

The need to preserve its financial stability constrains unions to forego the strike during the contract term. The necessity of protecting its own union security in the competitive labor market compels the vast majority of unions to substitute arbitration for the strike to settle grievances and disciplinary cases. Even in those few industries, such as the automotive industry, in which the union reserves the right to strike during the contract term over production standards, the top union officers use the strike selectively and sparingly. And even in those limited cases the union's constitution or policy generally requires the consent of the international union before a strike can take place.

With thousands of grievances arising each year under the more than 100,000 collective bargaining agreements, you see, Mr. Supervisor, what a bind the top officers of a union would put themselves in if they allowed the individual shop stewards or committeemen to call a strike over a grievance, say, for four hours reporting pay for one employee. Think what would happen to a union's treasury if each of the 270,000 or more shop stewards and committeemen, representing eighteen million or more organized employees represented by international, unaffiliated, or independent unions in the United States and Canada, had the power to call a strike over an unsettled grievance?

You can see how a strike over a grievance demanding eight hours pay for overtime work for one employee, multiplied a hundred times under different contracts, could deplete a union's treasury. The stakes wouldn't warrant opening up the union treasury to support a thousand employees in striking over such an issue. A union cannot chance a shop steward saying to a foreman, "If you don't settle this grievance by promoting the senior employee you passed over, we'll strike!" And the union cannot chance a foreman replying to such a threat, "No, we'll not settle the grievance on the terms you demand!"

The shop steward threw the gauntlet down and the foreman joined the issue by challenging the shop steward to strike. The drain of a strike on a union's treasury, local or international, would involve too great a risk. Arbitration becomes the lesser evil and the more acceptable alternative for the union. That's why unions buy arbitration to settle grievances and disciplinary cases arising during the contract term. To protect its financial security, a union gives on behalf of itself and the employees it represents a pledge not to strike and substitutes binding arbitration.

THE SHOP STEWARD'S UNION RESPONSIBILITY

"NO EMPTY THREATS," cautions the Aluminum Workers International Union *Shop Steward's Manual:*

> Don't get upset and make empty threats that both you and the foreman know you can't carry out. Angrily saying that you'll call a strike immediately if he doesn't settle the grievance on your terms is absurd—and actually illegal according to the contract. If you and the foreman can't come to an agreement there are further steps to be followed, including arbitration, before the question of a strike even comes up.

"Don't make silly threats," says the AFL–CIO *Manual for Shop Stewards.*

> In most cases you are bluffing when you tell the foreman the men will walk out. Most contracts do not permit strikes over grievances, and in any case the grievance has to go through further steps in the grievance procedure before there is any question of strike.

And the UAW *Steward's Guide* says:

> A steward or committeeman who blows up and threatens to shut down his department is looking for trouble. If he pulls a wild cat, he may be subject to discipline from both the union and the company.

The International Association of Machinists *Pocket Guide for Shop Stewards* bluntly states, "If the contract provides for arbitration,

346

the question of a strike is out of the picture entirely." It warns its shop stewards against irresponsible action that may make the union liable for money damages, saying:

> It is entirely conceivable that a single irresponsible act on the part of a steward or committeeman could bankrupt his Union. The enumeration of specific duties and responsibilities of a steward or committeeman in the agreement does not release the Union from responsibility for other acts which he may commit.

TO GRIEVE, NOT REBEL!

Labor-management relations have progressed far since the early days of unionization with its bitterness and jungle warfare. Modern labor laws have outlawed the "yellow dog" contract and have strictly limited the court injunction. The labor contract curbs the earlier arrogance of many managements in dealing with employees' legitimate economic and social needs. The former bull of the woods approach has given way to respect for the individual worker's dignity and job rights. Likewise, the incubating period of union leadership has long since passed. Union leaders have matured in technical training, experience, and professional know-how. Today union leaders easily match management leaders in negotiating the labor agreement. At the plant level local union shop stewards and committeemen often excel management's supervisory personnel in administering the labor agreement and handling grievances and disciplinary cases under it.

Having achieved equal status with the foreman in administering the labor contract, the shop steward is responsible for protecting the union's rights as well as those of the employees he represents. As Arthur J. Goldberg said in his paper, "Management's Reserved Rights: A Labor View":

> But the union has rights too; the worker has rights. In fact, the union has the duty and as a union man the employee has the duty as well as the right to challenge the company's acts when they violate the workers' rights. That challenge is made through the grievance procedure, not through rebellion.

347

That's the rule of conduct governing the shop steward's representative office that the labor contract contemplates. That's the duty the union delegates to the shop steward in challenging the company's actions when it violates the workers' rights.

THAT CHALLENGE IS MADE THROUGH THE GRIEVANCE
PROCEDURE, NOT THROUGH REBELLION.

A shop steward's conduct that, directly or indirectly, leads, encourages, or silently permits employees to use self-help instead of the orderly grievance and arbitration machinery threatens the very industrial peace the labor contract tries to protect during the contract term.

To grieve, not rebel! That's the rule of conduct that governs the shop steward's union responsibility in handling grievances and disciplinary cases. Employees, including the shop steward, who take matters into their own hands by concerted action destroy the continuity of relations the negotiators intended in setting up the orderly grievance procedure. Excuses such as the workers "reacted emotionally"; management "goaded them into walking out"; they're "only human and could stand just so much"; or "we just couldn't control them"—such excuses no longer justify the shop steward's or the employees' violation of the no-strike pledge the union's negotiators agreed to on their behalf.

A shop steward's leadership carries responsibilities, as well as benefits of prestige, time off with pay for handling grievances, and super-seniority—the last to be laid off from his department. He cannot justly relieve himself of the no-strike pledge the contract imposes upon him by shrugging his shoulders and saying, "It's up to the men themselves." He owes a duty to the union, in leading those he represents, to follow the orderly grievance procedure and not rebel. Slowdowns, quickies, work stoppages, group refusals to work overtime, or other concerted activities that violate the contract's no-strike pledge open up his union to claims for money damages.

Contract Violation: the Material Question
in Arbitration

Every case appealed to arbitration presents the material question: Did the action grieved against violate the contract? When management claims money damages against the union, the arbitrator decides whether the union, through the actions of its representatives, violated the contract's no-strike pledge. The case may also raise collateral issues, such as the amount of damages suffered or other appropriate relief that the contract may authorize the arbitrator to award.

Similarly, when the union appeals a case to arbitration, the arbitrator decides whether management, through the actions of its representatives, violated the contract's set of working conditions the parties agreed to. Here again, the union's case may raise collateral issues such as the amount of damages suffered by the union or the employees affected or other appropriate relief the contract may authorize the arbitrator to award. But in all cases appealed to arbitration the parties join, frame, submit, and argue the material issue: Did the action protested violate the contract? Arguing a claimed contract violation on any other ground clouds the real issue before the arbitrator.

As the U.S. Supreme Court said in the Enterprise Wheel and Car Corporation case:

> . . . an arbitrator is confined to interpretation and application of the collective bargaining agreement; he does not sit to dispense his own brand of industrial justice. He may of course look for guidance from many sources, yet his award is legitimate only so long as it draws its essence from the collective bargaining agreement. When the arbitrator's words manifest an infidelity to this obligation, courts have no choice but to refuse enforcement of the award.

The arbitrator does not decide what's best for the parties according to his own dictates; nor does he "sit to dispense his own brand of industrial justice." The arbitrator, as the mutual agent of the parties, dispenses justice according to the agreed-upon terms of the contract. He does not decide between right and wrong as an abstract question but only right or wrong under the contract. He does not decide what's fair or unfair according to his own feelings but according to what the parties agreed to as fair or unfair by their contract. The contract establishes the law of the shop, which binds the arbitrator as well as the parties. The arbitrator decides the equities of a claim according to the contract, and the contract governs his authority to make a final settlement of the dispute submitted to him.

349

As Ben Fischer, international representative of the United Steel-workers of America, said in his paper on "What and When and How to Arbitrate," delivered before the National Academy of Arbitrators:

> Most of us would suggest that in the long run we are best served by ad-herence to the contract terms as the guide for *all* arbitration. Although the parties may make their own settlements without feeling restricted by contract limitations, the arbitrator cannot properly superimpose his judgment on the basis that he "knows best" what the parties should do. He should know best only in terms of what the contract means, and he can know best if he lives with its interpretation day-in and day-out. He is not there to appease either side; in the long run he is there to convince both parties that he is competent as an interpreter of the agreement, as a fact finder, and as an able practitioner with the com-petence to apply the facts to the contract and the contract to the facts.
>
> It is true that arbitration may reveal that the contract, as read and interpreted by the arbitrator, is deficient or unfair in some respects. This is for the parties to correct if they agree to do so, not for the arbitrator to deal with. To an arbitrator, the agreement must be the industrial law whether he likes it or not.

Summing Up the Rules of Labor Arbitration

Arbitration: the Quid Pro Quo
for the No-Strike Pledge

Rule 1. An agreement contained in a collective bargaining con-tract affecting interstate commerce to arbitrate grievances during the contract term is the *quid pro quo* for an agree-ment not to strike during the contract term.

Rule 2. The courts will specifically enforce an agreement to arbi-trate grievances during the contract term on behalf of or against unions.

Rule 3. Where there is no exception in the no-strike clause, none should be read into the grievance or arbitration clause, since one is the *quid pro quo* for the other.

350

Federal Law, Not State Law, Governs

Rule 4. Federal law and federal interpretation of federal law will govern, not state law.

Rule 5. State law, if compatible with federal law, may be resorted to in order to find the rule that will best effectuate federal policy.

Rule 6. Any state law applied will be absorbed as federal law and will not be an independent source of private rights.

Grievance Machinery and Arbitration

Rule 7. Arbitration of labor disputes under collective bargaining agreements is part and parcel of the collective bargaining process itself.

Rule 8. Apart from matters that the parties specifically exclude, all questions on which the parties disagree come within the scope of the grievance and arbitration provisions of the collective bargaining contract.

Rule 9. The processing through the grievance procedure and arbitration of "even frivolous claims may have therapeutic values."

Rule 10. Grievance procedure and arbitration, not a strike, is the terminal point of a disagreement.

Judicial Inquiry on Arbitrability

Rule 11. Arbitration is a matter of contract, and a party cannot be required to submit to arbitration any dispute he has not agreed to submit.

Rule 12. The judicial inquiry under Section 301 of the Taft-Hartley Law must be strictly confined to the question of whether

351

the reluctant party did agree to arbitrate the grievance or to give the arbitrator authority to make the award he made.

Rule 13. The question is not whether in the mind of a court there is equity in the claim or whether the court may deem the claim to be meritorious; nor should the court weigh the merits of a grievance to determine if it is arbitrable.

Rule 14. An order to arbitrate a particular grievance should not be denied unless it may be said with positive assurance that the arbitration clause is not susceptible to an interpretation that covers the asserted dispute. Doubts should be resolved in favor of coverage.

Rule 15. In the absence of any express provision excluding a particular grievance from arbitration, only the most forceful evidence of a purpose to exclude the claim from arbitration can prevail.

Rule 16. Whether the moving party is right or wrong is a question of contract interpretation; and the moving party should not be deprived of the arbitrator's judgment when it was that judgment and all it connotes that was bargained for.

Arbitrator's Jurisdiction and Authority

Rule 17. Arbitrators under collective bargaining agreements serve as indispensable agencies in a continuous collective bargaining process. They sit to settle disputes at the plant level—disputes that require for their solution knowledge of the customs and practices of a particular factory or of a particular industry, as reflected in particular agreements. Flexibility in meeting a wide variety of situations is needed. The draftsmen may never have thought of what specific remedy should be awarded to meet a particular contingency.

Rule 18. An arbitrator is confined to interpretation and application of the collective bargaining agreement. He does not dispense his own brand of industrial justice. He may, of course, look for guidance from many sources, but his award is legitimate only as long as it draws its essence from the collective bargaining agreement. When the arbitrator's words manifest an infidelity to this obligation, courts have no choice but to refuse enforcement of the award.

Rule 19. Arbitrators have no obligation to give their reasons for an award. A mere ambiguity in the arbitrator's opinion accompanying his award, which permits the inference that the arbitrator may have exceeded his authority, is not a reason for refusing to enforce his award.

Rule 20. The question of interpretation of the collective bargaining agreement is a question for the arbitrator. It is the arbitrator's construction the parties bargained for. As far as the arbitrator's decision concerns construction of the contract, the courts have no business overruling him because their interpretation of the contract differs from his.

Rule 21. An arbitrator's award constitutes a contract of settlement by the parties themselves, which they have by their submission authorized the arbitrator to make for them and by which they are conclusively bound.

Since the parties voluntarily chose the arbitrator as their mutual agent to make a contract of settlement for them, courts refrain from reviewing the merits of an arbitrator's award. Neither party can welch on the contract of settlement made for them by the arbitrator.

Rule 22. Where the parties refer the merits of a controversy to an arbitrator selected by them, his determination as to the law or the facts is final and conclusive.

353

Rule 23. The award of an arbitrator cannot be set aside for mere errors of judgment either as to the law or as to the facts. If he keeps within his jurisdiction and is not guilty of fraud, corruption, or other misconduct affecting his award, it is unassailable, operates as a final and conclusive judgment, and, however disappointing it may be, the parties must abide by it.

The Legal Duty to Abide by the Agreement to Arbitrate

Rule 24. When the parties agree to settle a grievance by final and binding arbitration, that agreement imposes upon both parties the duty to submit the grievance to arbitration.

Rule 25. A strike by the union to settle a grievance that the collective bargaining agreement provides shall be settled exclusively and finally by arbitration constitutes a violation of the agreement even in the absence of a no-strike clause in the contract explicitly covering the subject of the grievance over which the union called the strike.

Rule 26. A contractual clause requiring the parties to submit disputes to final determination by arbitration implies an obligation not to strike over such disputes and makes the union liable for damages due to a walkout over an arbitrable dispute.

Rule 27. A no-strike agreement is not to be implied beyond the area that has been agreed will be exclusively covered by enforceable terminal arbitration.

Responsibilities for Violating the No-Strike Pledge

Rule 28. The collective bargaining agreement governs the relationship of employees in the bargaining unit to the employer.

354

Rule 29. The no-strike clause in a collective bargaining agreement at the very least establishes a rule of conduct or condition of employment the violation of which by employees justifies discipline or discharge.

Rule 30. The union is bound by and is liable for the acts of its agents under familiar principles of the law of agency; and under Section 301 of the Taft-Hartley Law, the question of whether the specific acts performed were actually authorized or subsequently ratified will not be controlling.

Rule 31. When a union is liable for damages for violation of the no-strike clause, its officers and members are not personally liable for those damages. When the union has inflicted the injury, it alone must pay.

The Forum for Damages: Court or Arbitration

Rule 32. When the collective bargaining contract is not susceptible to a construction that the company was bound to arbitrate its claim for damages against the union for breach of the undertaking not to strike, the court must decide whether the company is entitled to damages from the union for breach of contract.

Rule 33. When the contract obligates the company to arbitrate its claim for damages from forbidden strikes by the union, the court will enforce the bargain to arbitrate and will stay a court action until the claim for damages is presented to arbitration.

Money Damages Is the Remedy, Not Injunction

Rule 34. Section 301 of the Taft-Hartley Law did not modify, repeal, or accommodate the anti-injunction provision of the Norris-LaGuardia Act, although it did expressly repeal that provision dealing with union responsibility for the acts of its agents by providing that in determining whether any person is acting as an agent of another person in order to make such other person responsible for his acts, the question of whether the specific acts performed were actually authorized or subsequently ratified will not control.

Rule 35. A mandatory injunction to carry out an agreement to arbitrate and to compel the parties to a collective bargaining agreement to submit a dispute which had arisen under that agreement to arbitration, where the agreement itself required arbitration of the dispute, did not violate the anti-injunction provisions of the Norris-LaGuardia Act.

Rule 36. Courts do not have jurisdiction to grant an injunction enjoining a union from striking in the future over grievances a collective bargaining contract makes subject to arbitration. The company has the right to sue for breach of contract and for damages in that forum—court or arbitration—that the parties have agreed to use under their contract.

Management's and Union's Rights
Under the Arbitrable Process

Rule 37. Arbitration does not take away management's right to manage. Arbitration of grievances and disciplinary cases during the contract term strengthens the supervisor's right to initiate action.

Rule 38. Arbitration does not take away the union's right to grieve. Arbitration of grievances and disciplinary cases during the contract term strengthens the shop steward's right to protest any action initiated by the supervisor—but not the supervisor's right to take the action.

Rule 39. Arbitration substitutes for the strike during the contract term, thereby protecting the interests of both management and the union.

Rule 40. Arbitration assures the shop steward of equal status with the supervisor in administering the agreed-upon set of working conditions and in handling grievances and disciplinary cases.

Rule 41. The union buys arbitration during the contract term to protect its financial security, to avoid depleting its union treasury, and to save its financial resources to back up its threat of a strike in negotiating the terms of the renewal contract.

Rule 42. Management buys arbitration as the *quid pro quo*—something for something—for the union's agreement not to strike during the contract term.

Arbitration and the Shop Steward's
Responsibilities

Rule 43. The no-strike pledge binds the shop steward as well as the employees he represents.

Rule 44. The shop steward's office makes him responsible to the union for following the orderly grievance machinery, including arbitration if provided for, in handling grievances and disciplinary cases.

Rule 45. In exercising his representative office, the no-strike pledge imposes upon the shop steward the rule of conduct to grieve—not rebel!

Rule 46. A shop steward who blows up and threatens to shut down his department is looking for trouble. If he pulls a wildcat, he may be subject to discipline from both the union and the company.

Rule 47. The shop steward and the employees he represents have the duty, as well as the right, to challenge the foreman's actions if they violate the workers' rights under the contract. That challenge is made through the grievance procedure, not through rebellion!

The Material Issue: Contract Violation

Rule 48. Appealing a dispute to arbitration during the contract term raises the material question: Did the action grieved against violate the contract?

Rule 49. When management claims money damages against the union, the arbitrator decides whether the union through the actions of its representatives violated the contract's no-strike pledge.

Rule 50. When the union appeals a case to arbitration, the arbitrator decides whether management through the actions of its representatives violated the contract's conditions.

Rule 51. The parties join, frame, submit, and argue the material issue: Did the action protested violate the contract?

Rule 52. As the mutual agent of both parties, the arbitrator dispenses justice according to the agreed-upon terms of the contract. He does not dispense his own brand of industrial justice.

Rule 53. The contract establishes the law of the shop, which binds the arbitrator as well as the parties; and the contract governs his delegated authority in finally settling the dispute submitted to him.

Rule 54. Although the parties may make their own settlements without feeling restricted by the contract limitations, the arbitrator cannot superimpose his judgment on the basis that he knows best what the parties should do.

Rule 55. To an arbitrator, the contract must be the industrial law whether he likes it or not.

Rules of Evidence and Procedure in Arbitration

Rule 56. Unless the contract provides otherwise, strict rules of evidence or procedures of court action do not apply in the arbitration process. Arbitration constitutes a voluntary, private system to dispense justice under the contract during its term, and the parties exercise essential control in setting up and administering their arbitration tribunal.

Rule 57. Both parties come before the arbitrator as equals and maintain their equal status throughout the proceeding. Each party offers to the arbitrator, as their mutual agent, whatever evidence it wishes and by which it hopes to justify its action or support its claim.

Rule 58. The foreman has the burden of proof in every grievance raised by his employees or the shop steward in his department. He who initiates action must justify his action! Whoever started the chain of events takes on the burden of answering the question "why?"

Rule 59. When the foreman acts, he makes his management responsible for his actions. When the shop steward acts by violating the no-strike pledge he makes his union responsible for his actions.

Rule 60. If the union appeals the grievance to arbitration, frame the issue and submit and argue your case before the arbitrator on the question: Did the company's action violate the contract?

Rule 61. No judgment by default in arbitration! Neither party has the burden of making out a prima facie (at first sight) case. Neither party must go first or prove its case by a preponderance of evidence or beyond a reasonable doubt. The arbitrator looks to each party to offer its evidence and renders his award upon the total evidence presented to him.

Rule 62. Unless the contract provides otherwise, once the parties have appointed their arbitrator and he exercises jurisdiction over the proceeding, neither party retains the right to withdraw without prejudice its claim from that arbitration proceeding without the consent of the other party.

Rule 63. The arbitrator's oath of office charges him with the duty to faithfully and fairly hear and examine the issues in controversy in accordance with the arbitration agreement and render a final and binding decision.

Rule 64. The union's withdrawal of its grievance from arbitration constitutes a final settlement of that grievance on its merits —on the basis of the company's answer given in the last step of the grievance procedure.

Rule 65. In the absence of a contrary contract provision, once the arbitrator acquires jurisdiction over the dispute, neither party, over the objection of the other, retains the right to frustrate the arbitration proceeding by its own default or by withdrawing its claim without prejudice.

Rule 66. When you're taken to arbitration, remember it's still your case, and go to win!

Rules for Handling Technological Changes and Improved Production Methods

12

New Conditions During
the Contract Term

The grievance may concern a situation not spelled out by the contract because of the new elements introduced in the plant after the contract was negotiated—new machinery or new processes, for example.

These new conditions may require new rules.

That's what the IUE *Leadership Manual* tells its shop stewards. Technological changes during the contract term create new conditions for you, Mr. Foreman, as well as for the shop steward. New machines, new products, and improved methods give rise to legitimate grievances over whose job, whose work, whose overtime, or who gets laid off.

Changes in means, methods, or procedures of operation or subcontracting of production or maintenance work may require you to eliminate some jobs, consolidate others, reduce crews, take up slack or idle time, reevaluate work loads, set new job or incentive rates, or reevaluate existing ones.

Sometimes the shop steward may file a grievance objecting to your action in unilaterally initiating such changes without first consulting, negotiating with, or getting the union's prior approval. More often, he will file a grievance protesting a change in rates of pay, working conditions, or seniority rights of the affected employees. How well you handle such grievances, Mr. Foreman, directly affects your control over costs of production, including labor costs, in your department.

The Case of the Change in Storage Facilities

About nine months before this dispute arose, the company had consolidated its assembly operations into one location of the plant, where it had converted a former subassembly area into a storage area. The company then transferred drive shafts, formerly stored in the main assembly area, to the new storage area and assigned the task of cleaning the drive shafts to the grievant, classified as helper, checking and stamping, in labor grade 4, whom the company had transferred to the new storage area. Prior to the change in its assembly operations and storage facilities employees classified as assemblers, in the higher labor grades of 7 and 9, had done the cleaning work on those drive shafts before installing them on equipment or, at that time, storing them in their own area.

The work of cleaning drive shafts consisted essentially of removing burrs from inside holes and from the keyseat with a steel rod and file, blowing chips with an air hose, wrapping friction tape around threaded parts of the shaft and grease holes, and putting plugs in the ends of the shafts.

The union filed a grievance claiming that the company "violated the contract between the parties by unilaterally transferring the work of cleaning drive shafts, formerly performed by assemblers in a higher labor grade, to the grievant herein, classified as a helper, checking and stamping, in a lower labor grade." The company denied the grievance, and the union appealed to arbitration.

Article VIII of the contract, upon which both parties relied to support their respective positions, provided:

> If the Company establishes new classifications, or revises existing classifications to a significant degree, the rate for the new or revised

classification will be subject to negotiation. If no agreement is reached, the Company may assign a temporary rate of pay. If the matter remains unresolved for a period of thirty (30) days the temporarily assigned rate will become the accepted rate of the job, unless the Union requests that the matter be processed through arbitration prior to the expiration of the thirty (30) day period.

The union claimed:

The company violated Article VIII by unilaterally removing the work of cleaning drive shafts from the assembler's job, classified in the higher labor grades of 7 and 9, and assigning that work to the grievant classified in the lower labor grade 4 . . . that Article VIII does not give the company the right to make such changes in job content between existing job classifications without prior negotiation between the parties; and the transfer of the work of cleaning drive shafts resulted in a substantial change in job duties and responsibilities of the helper, checking and stamping, classification.

The union demanded that the "company be directed to reinstate the work of cleaning drive shafts to the assembler's classification and pay the grievant the assembler's B rate for the time he worked on drive shafts . . . or in the alternative, that the company be required to negotiate with the union on a new job classification resulting from the transfer of such cleaning work and an appropriate rate therefor."

The company claimed:

Its action in transferring the work of cleaning drive shafts from the assembler's job, for reasons of efficiency in operations, to the helper, checking and stamping, job did not violate the contract, but on the contrary Article VIII expressly recognizes the right of the company to unilaterally make such revision in existing classifications without prior negotiation with the union; and the transfer of such cleaning work did not dilute the skills and responsibilities of the assembler classification nor did it increase to a significant degree the job, duties, responsibilities or required skills of the helper, checking and stamping, classification and therefore the contract does not obligate the company to negotiate a revised rate of pay for the helper, checking and stamping, classification.

365

Finding that the "company did not violate the existing contract by transferring the work of cleaning drive shafts out of the assembler's classification and work area; revising the helper, checking and stamping, classification to include such cleaning work; and assigning said work" to the grievant, I denied the union's grievance and in my award said:

> The proof establishes and the arbitrator finds that Article VIII of the existing contract does not restrict the company from unilaterally establishing new classifications or revising existing ones during the contract term. Nor does said Article VIII obligate the company to negotiate with the union on revised classifications resulting from the transfer of duties or work from one classification to another during the contract term.
>
> The unambiguous language of Article VIII . . . only obligates the company to negotiate with the union on the rate for the revised classification if revised to a significant degree.

Noting that "Article VIII of the existing contract differs materially . . . from Article VIII in the prior contract and clearly shows the parties intended the present Article VIII to require the company to negotiate with the union on the rate for the job, if changed to a significant degree, and not upon the revision of the job classification itself," I said:

> Under this clear language (of Article VIII), the arbitrator finds the parties intended that the company could exercise the right to revise existing classifications without being subject to negotiations and agreement as the prior contract required. In light of this clear language of Article VIII in the existing contract, the arbitrator has no authority under the guise of interpreting a contract clause to find a meaning different than the language of the clause itself speaks of or a meaning different than that clearly intended by the parties themselves.

Then, finding that the grievant had in the past "performed comparable cleaning work on other kinds of shafts and machine parts which required the use of similar tools and materials, and involved comparable skills, duties and responsibilities to those involved in the cleaning of drive shafts," I said:

366

The proof establishes that for many years . . . the company had assigned and the grievant had performed cleaning work on a variety of other types of shafts and machine parts comparable to the cleaning work of drive shafts as part of the duties and responsibilities of the classification of helper, checking and stamping. The proof further shows such cleaning work required the use of similar tools and materials and in some cases greater skills, duties and responsibilities to those involved in the cleaning of drive shafts . . . (and) transferring the cleaning of drive shafts from the assembler's classification and area of work and assigning that work to the classification of helper, checking and stamping, did not dilute the skills, duties and responsibilities of the assemblers job; nor did it revise the classification of helper, checking and stamping, to a significant degree; therefore, the arbitrator finds the resulting revision does not warrant a new rate for the helper, checking and stamping, classification.

The Administrative Rights: to Manage and to Protest

Unless your labor contract provides otherwise, Mr. Foreman, you retain the right during the contract term to make changes in the means, methods, processes, materials, and schedules of production in your department, unilaterally, without consulting, negotiating with, or getting the shop steward's prior approval. That's part of your management's retained rights and your right of administrative initiative—to improve the operating facilities and procedures in your department by new means, methods, or processes of operations.

Unless your contract provides otherwise, the shop steward retains the right to question, by protest and appeal through the grievance procedure and arbitration, if provided for, whether your action in unilaterally initiating changes in means, methods, processes, or materials of production violated any of the provisions of the contract. That's part of the shop steward's administrative right in policing the contract—to protest any action he believes violates the employees' or the union's rights under the contract's set of working conditions.

What Displaces Jobs or Employees?

Changes in means, methods, processes, or materials of production reduce available work or eliminate jobs or employees in the bargaining unit. New operating or storage facilities, improved production schedules or administrative procedures, or consolidating operations may necessitate eliminating former departments or discontinuing existing crafts or jobs. New machines, new methods, or improved facilities constitute a new way of doing the job, craft, work, or service. Instituting new jobs, consolidating classified jobs or crafts, reducing crews or complement of the work force, eliminating slack or idle time, and reevaluating existing work loads, job, or incentive rates, necessitated by the new way of doing the job, displace employees in the bargaining unit.

HOW DO YOU DISTINGUISH THE "NEW WAY" FROM THE "OLD WAY"?

By demonstrable facts, showing that a material, substantial, significant, or major change has taken place in the way of doing the job. Not just any kind of "paper" change but a change in means, methods, operating facilities, or procedures that clearly distinguishes the new way of doing the job from the former way.

How do you prove a material, substantial, significant, or major change in means, methods, or processes? Well, that depends on what brings about the change. You can prove technological changes by new machines or new facilities more readily because of observable facts. The less mechanical the change, the greater the degree of proof required. Must the change take place at a fixed, definite time or in one integrated, completed unit? No, the change may occur in a single unit of equipment or time, or it may consist of a series of separate or multiple changes taking place over a reasonable period of time that accumulatively result in a material change. But no matter what the change, the burden rests on you, Mr. Foreman, to prove by demonstrable facts that a material change has taken place that materially or significantly distinguishes the new way of doing the job from the old way!

That's the key to sustaining your action in eliminating work, jobs, or employees in the bargaining unit during the contract term. Unless you can show that a change has occurred that materially distinguishes

368

the new job from the former one, your effort to take up slack, eliminate idle time, reevaluate work loads, job, or incentive rates, reduce crews, consolidate existing jobs, or transfer work from one classified job to another will meet with little success!

"Why," you may ask, "can't I take one man off the crew when there isn't enough work for three of them to do? The job only requires two men. Why must I keep on a third man when he's not needed and pay him for eight hours for doing no work?"

Because when your negotiator, Mr. Foreman, bargained out the contract's set of working conditions, he knew or should have known that the job employed three men, not two. The size of the crew, the work load, and the working conditions then prevailing formed the backdrop for negotiating the wages, hours, and working conditions for the ensuing contract term. The union's negotiator accepted those working conditions and the rates of pay based upon them in agreeing to the contract for the new term.

"What has taken place," the shop steward asks, "that gives you the right, Mr. Foreman, to remove one man from that job and make the other two do the work that formerly three had been employed to do?"

Yes, Mr. Foreman, the burden rests on you to answer the shop steward's question; and unless you can show that something has changed—a new facility or an improved method—that materially distinguishes the old job or the old way of doing it from the new job or the new way of doing it, the negotiated hours of work, rates of pay, and working conditions bind you during the contract term.

THE CASE OF THE ACCUMULATED MINOR CHANGES

Starting about five years before this dispute arose, the company began making major changes in its papermaking machines and operating processes and installing new and additional equipment. These changes resulted in increased duties, skill requirements, and responsibilities for the operating personnel in the department, including the beaterman helper. The company completed the major machine changes prior to September of the year in which the parties negotiated the existing contract but continued to install additional new equipment and make minor changes in operating procedures after September and during the contract term, effecting changes in the duties of the beaterman helper's job.

The beaterman helpers, two on each shift, prepare and haul bales of stock and raw materials to the two papermaking machines in the department, load them onto the conveyors, remove waste materials from the area, clean the operating equipment, and at times relieve the head beaterman. During the years in which the major changes occurred the company had increased the rate of the changed jobs of all the employees, including the beaterman helpers.

About five months after September, when the parties had negotiated their existing contract, the union filed a grievance demanding an increase in the beaterman helper's rate, claiming that changes had taken place in the working conditions of that job.

After restudying the job the company denied the grievance on the ground that the "minor" changes that had occurred during the existing contract term did not justify any increase in the beaterman helper's rate. The union then appealed to arbitration.

Article V, Section C, of the contract provided:

C. 1. It is recognized that changing conditions and circumstances may from time to time require the installation of new base and incentive rates, adjustment of existing base and incentive rates, or modification of wage payment plans because of major changes in equipment or methods. An accumulation of minor changes occurring during the term of this agreement will be construed as a major change. Under these circumstances the following procedure shall apply.

At the arbitration hearing the union claimed that the "changes that have accumulated after September . . . the effective date of the existing contract, constitute a major change in the duties and responsibilities of the beaterman helper's job, as intended by the parties under Section C of Article V; that these changes must be considered as continuous changes necessarily related to those changes that continued to accumulate before and after September" and that the "resulting increase in duties, responsibilities and skills now required of the beaterman helper warrant that his rate be increased."

370

The company claimed that "although changes have taken place in the department after September . . . effecting the beaterman helper's job, they were minor changes and cannot be construed as an accumulated major change as intended by the parties under Section C of Article V . . . and the minor changes in equipment and operating processes and job duties that have occurred since September . . . do not warrant any further increase in the beaterman helper's job at this time."

Finding that "changes in equipment and production methods in the papermaking department have brought about changed conditions that warrant an increase in the base rate of the beaterman helper's job," I sustained the union's grievance. In my award, I said:

> The company concedes that changes have taken place in the beaterman helper's job during the existing contract term, but argues that those changes were minor and do not constitute in the aggregate a major change occurring during this contract term . . .
>
> The arbitrator . . . finds the minor changes in equipment and production methods occurring after September . . . though in some respects continuous and related to those occurring prior thereto, can properly be construed as constituting a major change during the contract term as intended by the parties under Section C of Article V of the existing contract.

As to the company's claim that no major change in the beaterman helper's job had occurred after September, the cutoff date stipulated in the existing contract, I said:

> As pointed out above, the company concedes that changes have occurred after that date, though the company terms them "minor." But the arbitrator finds that those minor changes accumulated sufficiently during the existing contract term to constitute a major change in the beaterman helper's job as intended by the parties under Section C.
>
> In the same way, in a case where the company seeks to reevaluate a job or piece rate due to a series of related and continuous changes over an extended period of time, some of which may have started in the term of a prior contract, the final accumulation of minor changes may only result in a major change in a succeeding contract term when it then may properly warrant that the rate be reevaluated.

371

Reevaluating the New or Changed Job

After making the change in the method, machine, or procedure of work, you, Mr. Foreman, or other representatives of your management, reevaluate the new, changed, or consolidated job, craft, or work in terms of its new job value.

Any increase in the evaluating factors of effort, skills, duties, responsibilities, or working conditions required in the new or changed job, craft, or work you credit to the job in terms of increase in its job value as compared to the job value of other comparable jobs, crafts, or work in the existing wage structure.

Likewise, any decrease in the evaluating factors of effort, skills, duties, responsibilities, or working conditions resulting from reduced requirements in the new or changed job, craft, or work, you debit to the job in terms of decrease in its job value as compared to the job value of other comparable jobs, crafts, or work in the existing wage structure.

Having found the job value of the new or changed job in relationship to the job value of other comparable jobs in the existing wage structure, you set a new rate and slot it into its proper place in the existing wage structure under the contract.

The new rate, whether lower, the same, or higher than the old one, should reflect any increase or decrease in job value of the new, changed, or consolidated job, work, or craft.

Whatever method you use in evaluating any new job you follow in reevaluating a job changed during the contract term. Avoid short cuts in evaluating the changed job or glossing over the changes in job value by saying: "Well, the rate should be about the same as either of the two other jobs that had been consolidated. In fact, the job is easier to do now, and I don't know what the beef is all about!"

That approach, Mr. Foreman, usually creates a pitfall for you in handling grievances dealing with rates for new or changed jobs during the contract term. You, as manager of your department, initially set the rate for the new job, and if challenged, you must demonstrate by objective, evaluating criteria that the rate you set bears a proper relationship in terms of job value to other existing comparable jobs and that you have slotted the job into its proper place in the existing wage structure under the contract. After setting the new rate you notify the shop steward and the employees affected of the new rate, the new production standards, and the new job duties required.

THE SHOP STEWARD'S RIGHT TO PROTEST

The shop steward retains the administrative right, unilaterally, without asking, consulting with, or getting your prior approval, to protest the rate you set and any change in production standards, work loads, size of crew, or other working conditions of the new job; and he has the right to question whether the employees in the bargaining unit, retained or assigned, had seniority rights under the seniority clauses of the contract to the new or changed job.

THE CASE OF LEADBURNERS VS. TANK HOUSE EMPLOYEES

In this arbitration case, the union claimed that the company had violated the contract "by assigning maintenance and repair work on the newly installed plastic liners of the electrolytic tanks to tank house employees, classified as miscellaneous laborers, instead of assigning such work to employees in the leadburner's classification."

The company claimed:

The change from lead liners to plastic liners constitutes a material improvement in method, process and means of production; that the change to plastic liners has eliminated the need for the higher skills, experience and responsibilities of leadburners in maintaining and repairing the new plastic liners; that the level of skills and responsibilities of tank house employees rather than those employees in the leadburner classification compares more appropriately to the level of skills and responsibilities required in maintaining and repairing the plastic liners and, therefore, warrants the company in assigning such work to them.

In my award, denying the union's grievance, I found that the changeover from lead to plastic liners constituted a material change in

373

the methods of production that materially distinguished the former job of repairing lead liners from the new job of repairing plastic liners, and I said:

> The arbitrator finds that the repair and maintenance work of plastic liners does not require the level of skills, experience or responsibilities of employees in the leadburner classification, as required in the work of maintaining and repairing lead liners; and the level of skills, experience and responsibilities of tank house employees compares more accurately and bears the proper relationship to the level of skills, experience and responsibilities required in doing the maintenance and repair work on plastic liners.

Then, finding that "using plastic liners in place of lead liners constitutes an improved method of production, results in abolishing a previously existing job, establishes a new job, and necessitates changes in working conditions and practices that attached to or arose out of the previously existing job and way of doing the work," I said:

> In determining to which classified employees the contract obligates the company to assign new or changed jobs, resulting from technological changes in production methods, the level of skills, duties and responsibilities of the new or changed job serves as the standard—the determining criterion. The level of skills required in a new or changed job determines the value of that job under and its place in the wage structure of the contract. In setting the value of a new or changed job and in determining to what classified employees the new or changed job should properly be assigned, the level of skills, duties and responsibilities required in the new or changed job must be compared to those of other existing classified jobs in the wage structure. The relative relationship between the new job and other existing jobs in the wage structure determines not only the value of the new job but also what employees in other classified jobs in the wage structure may be qualified to be assigned to the new job.

Finding that the "change from lead to plastic liners resulted in a material change of job content and value in the new maintenance and repair work as compared to the value and level of skills and responsibilities required in the former repair work," I said:

374

The level of skills and the value of the new job of maintaining and repairing plastic liners compare fully with and bear the proper relationship to the level of skills and responsibilities of employees in the tank house classification. The level of skills of tank house employees qualifies them to do the maintenance and repair work on the plastic liners; and since the new job no longer requires the higher level of skills of employees in the leadburner classification, the arbitrator finds the company properly assigned such maintenance and repair work to tank house employees.

DOES THE RATE FOR THE CHANGED JOB DEPEND ON INCREASED PRODUCTIVITY?

No, and unless your contract otherwise provides, the rate for the new or changed job does not reflect any increase in productivity or any resulting savings in labor or production costs. The existing wage structure set up by the contract and the rates for comparable jobs in that wage structure serve as guidelines in setting the rate for the new or changed job during the contract term.

Increased productivity and savings in production costs accruing from method changes during the contract term become bargainable subjects in negotiating the terms of the renewal contract. The new rates of pay and increased economic benefits in the renewal contract may reflect increases in productivity during the prior contract term, depending, of course, on the prevailing economic climate and strength of each side at negotiating time. The value of the changed job relative to the value of other comparable jobs in the existing wage structure, and not any resulting increase in productivity, determines the rate for the new or changed job during the contract term.

The Case of the Tracdrill Operator's Rate

The company installed a new piece of equipment, a tracdrill, to drill holes for blasting in its quarry area. The tracdrill operates as a mobile unit powered by compressed air furnished by a diesel engine; and one employee operates it. In setting the rate for the new job the company used the rates for comparable drilling jobs in the wage structure.

The union filed a grievance claiming that the company had not properly evaluated the tracdrill job because the company had not taken into account the savings in labor costs accruing from the new equipment.

The company denied the grievance, and the union appealed to arbitration.

At the arbitration hearing the union claimed:

In determining the proper rate for a new job established by the company during the contract term, the elements of savings in labor costs resulting from the new machine and area or going rates paid for similar jobs by other companies should be considered as proper factors in determining the rate for the new job.

The company claimed:

The value of the new job should be determined solely in relation to the value and established rates of other comparable jobs in the existing rate structure . . . (and) neither the increase in productivity or savings in labor costs accruing from the new machine nor area rates that may be paid for comparable jobs by other companies, which factors the union has advanced and relies upon, are material factors to be considered by the arbitrator in determining the rate for a new job established during the contract term—and should be disregarded.

Although I sustained the union's grievance in part, finding that the company had not properly evaluated the new tracdrill job in relation to other drilling jobs in the wage structure, I rejected the union's claims that savings in labor costs and area rates constituted proper guideposts in setting the rate for new or changed jobs during the contract term. In my award I said:

In the absence of a contractual provision providing otherwise, increase in productivity or resulting savings in labor costs, due to technological improvements during the contract term, are not material, evaluating factors for determining the proper rate for a new job or a change in an old job arising out of changes in methods, processes, materials, or schedules of production during the contract term. To the extent the technological improvement or change in methods or machines effects a change in the requirements and evaluating factors of the job—such as

376

training and experience required, mental and manual skills and effort involved, responsibility for new tools and equipment, change in surrounding working conditions, changes in hazards and degree of supervision and other similar evaluating factors—the rate for the new or changed job must reflect the value of the change in those evaluating factors—up or down.

Holding that "increase in productivity or resulting savings in labor costs, which flow from the technological change in production methods or machines during the contract term, do not constitute proper evaluating factors for determining the value of the new or changed job; nor for determining the proper rate for a new or changed job in relation to the rates of other comparable jobs in the existing wage structure established by the parties under the contract," I said:

The employees' opportunity to share in such increased productivity or savings in labor costs rests with the parties themselves—in mutually bargaining out the terms, wage structure, working conditions and other benefits in their renewal contract. The established wage structure, the level of earnings under that wage structure, and the relation in value between comparable jobs in that wage structure alone serve the arbitrator as material guideposts in evaluating a new or changed job and in fixing its proper rate during the contract term, unless the parties otherwise agree.

Noting that the "arbitrator's function is to determine whether the rate for the new job, which the company initially set, bears a proper relationship to the rates established for the other jobs; and whether the new rate has been properly slotted into the existing wage structure, without reference to rates that may be paid by other companies for comparable jobs under their established wage structures," I said:

Were the arbitrator to fix the rate for a new or changed job, resulting from a technological change in methods or machines during the contract term, irrespective of its relationship to other comparable jobs in the existing wage structure, the effect would be to upset the existing wage structure and the differentials between the jobs under it that the parties themselves agreed to, and would result in a chain reaction

377

among and between other jobs, thereby creating intra-rate inequities in existing job rates.

The arbitrator, in reviewing the propriety of a rate for a new or changed job during the contract term, does not substitute for collective bargaining—which only the parties can do. The arbitrator takes the existing wage structure and the value of comparable jobs set by the parties themselves under their own wage structure and determines whether the new rate has been properly slotted into that wage structure; and if not, determines the proper rate in relation to the rates for other comparable jobs in the existing wage structure.

Then, noting the contract defined grievances as "differences . . . as to the interpretation or application . . . of this Agreement," I said:

> The contract between the parties constrains the arbitrator to compare the challenged rate for the new job of tracdrill operator with the existing rates for comparable jobs in the existing rate structure agreed upon by the parties under their contract. Were the arbitrator to ignore the relationship of the new rate to the other existing rates in the established rate structure or consider such factors as increased productivity, savings in labor costs resulting from the technological improvement or what other companies under their wage structures pay for comparable jobs, he would in effect be altering the existing wage structure the parties themselves agreed to and set up. The contract between the parties clearly prohibits the arbitrator from doing so.

DOES EVERY METHOD CHANGE NECESSITATE REEVALUATING THE RATE?

No, only those changes that materially or substantially change the existing way of doing the job. Changes that only enforce existing methods or indirectly facilitate existing procedures would not warrant reevaluating the existing job or rate.

The Case of the Automatic Timing Governor

The company had installed a governor on its grinding machines that automatically controlled the machine's operations and prevented the individual operator from releasing the machined part before the machine had completed the cycles set for the job.

For some time the company's supervisors had experienced difficulty in getting individual operators to comply with the standard cycles set for various jobs. Some operators would release the part before the machine had completed its grinding cycles; and in this way the operator speeded-up his work and produced more pieces in the hour.

In some cases the experience and skill of the operator allowed him to maintain the standard quality of the job even though he released the part before the machine had completed the standard cycles. In others, cutting short the standard cycles resulted in poor quality, excessive down-time, and scrap. Speeding-up the machine also overloaded the wheels, thereby requiring the operator to make a greater number of wheel changes.

Earlier the company had tried out another type of automatic control; but some of the operators found that gently tapping the machine would jump the control, thus outwitting the control and cutting short the standard cycles set for the jobs. The company's supervisors had tried to enforce the cycle standards, and when the operators refused to comply, they had disciplined them. But the corrective disciplinary action proved ineffective.

The new automatic governor locked the machine and compelled the operator to allow it to complete the cycle set for each job. It prevented the operator from determining for himself the number of cycles each part should go through and made the operation uniform for all operators.

The union filed a grievance claiming that the automatic control governor substantially changed the existing piece-rate jobs and reduced the operator's former piece-rate earnings and demanded that the company reevaluate the jobs and retroactively adjust the operator's loss in earnings.

The company denied the grievance, and the union appealed to arbitration.

Article IX, Section F, of the contract, which the union claimed the company had violated, provided:

Section F. Piece work rates in effect . . . and all new or changed piece rates, after having become permanent, will not be changed unless substantial changes occur in equipment, method, or material.

A rate shall be considered permanent after having been worked on for a reasonable period after being set. Those parts of an operation affected by a substantial change in equipment, method, or material shall be retimed and the part of the piece work rate applicable to that part shall be set to yield not less than 130% of the incentive base rate. Time standards shall not be changed because of the efficiency of, or effort expended by, an employee.

At the arbitration hearing the union claimed:

The automatic governor, by controlling the cycles for each job, restricts the operator in the number of pieces he can produce . . . increases the time required to make wheel changes and get size, thereby substantially reducing his piece-rate earnings and incentive opportunity . . . (and) effects a substantial change in equipment, method, or material, requiring the job be reevaluated in order to maintain the incentive yield of 130% provided for by Section F of the contract.

The company claimed:

It has not changed the jobs, the incentive base rates or the incentive opportunity as established by the parties under the contract; that the automatic governor which the company has installed does not constitute a substantial change in equipment, method, or material, as intended by the parties under Section F, requiring that the jobs in question be reevaluated; the automatic control only enforces the required cycles of the machine operations and only makes the operator perform his job according to the standards set for his job and upon which the incentive base rates for the job had originally been set and established by the parties under their contract.

Finding that the "use of the governor to automatically control the cycles of the job, does not result in a substantial change in equipment, method, or material, as intended by the parties under Section F of the contract," I denied the union's grievance. In my award, I said:

380

On the contrary, the governor only mechanically enforces the established cycle standards for each job which the operator himself is bound to respect and upon which the incentive base rates and incentive earnings opportunity of the job had been established by the parties under their contract.

The company has not changed the established cycles for any job. Neither has it changed, nor has the governor effected any change in, the incentive base rates and the incentive opportunity yield under the incentive system established by the contract. The job and the incentive rates, long established, remain the same.

Noting "since the governors have been in use, there is no longer the need that previously existed for the company's supervisors and foremen to police the operators, to see that they maintain the machine cycles set for each job," I said:

The arbitrator inspected the machines in operation and observed the effect of the governor on the job. The arbitrator finds the governor does not materially increase the time required for getting size or making wheel changes than had been required before the governor was installed. Further, observing the required cycles for each job reduces the wear on the wheels, and thus requires fewer wheel changes during the production time. With or without the governor, the efficiency and effort expended by the individual operator largely determine the time required in getting size and making wheel changes. The operators' efficiency and effort still largely determine the operators' incentive earnings opportunity.

Then, finding that the automatic governor "does not prevent the operator from making out on the job as established by the contract," I said:

The arbitrator, therefore, finds that the company's action in installing the governors to control the established cycles of the machines does not violate Section F of the contract and was warranted under the facts which gave rise to its use . . . and does not warrant any retroactive adjustment in the piece rate earnings of the employees affected by the installation of the automatic governors.

Summing Up the Rules for Handling Technological Changes and Improved Production Methods

Rule 1. Changes in means, methods, processes, materials, or schedules of production or changes in administrative procedures reduce or eliminate available work or jobs or displace employees in the bargaining unit.

Rule 2. New operating or storage facilities or improved production schedules or procedures may necessitate eliminating former departments, consolidating operations, or discontinuing existing crafts or jobs.

Rule 3. New machines, new methods, and improved facilities constitute a new way of doing the job, craft, work, or service.

Rule 4. Consolidating classified jobs or crafts, reducing crews or size of the work force, eliminating slack or idle time, reevaluating existing work loads or job or incentive rates resulting from the new way of doing the job displaces work or employees in the bargaining unit.

Rule 5. You prove the new way by demonstrable facts that show that a material, substantial, significant, or major change in means, methods, materials, operating facilities, or procedures has taken place that clearly distinguishes the new way of doing the job from the former way.

Rule 6. Unless a change has occurred that materially distinguishes the new job from the former one, your effort to take up slack, eliminate idle time, reevaluate work loads or job or incentive rates, reduce crews, consolidate existing jobs, or transfer work from one classified job to another will hardly succeed.

Rule 7. The change in method, operating facilities, or procedure may take place in a single unit of equipment or time, or may consist of a series of separate or multiple changes taking place over a reasonable period of time that accumulatively result in a material, substantial, significant or major change.

Rule 8. Unless the contract provides otherwise, management retains the right to initiate and make changes in the means, methods, processes, materials, or procedures and to subcontract production or maintenance work during the contract term, unilaterally and without consulting, negotiating with, or getting the union's prior approval.

Rule 9. The management's rights clause, or the retained rights of management to manage, in the absence of any expressed provision in the contract limiting such rights, reserves to management the right to initiate and put into effect such changes during the contract term.

Rule 10. Unless the contract provides otherwise, the union retains the right to question—by protest and appeal through the grievance procedure and arbitration, if provided for— whether the action in unilaterally initiating changes of production or methods during the contract term violated any of the provisions of the contract.

Rule 11. Unless the contract provides otherwise, the union does not have the right to limit, circumscribe, or veto management's right to initiate such changes or to subcontract production or maintenance work during the contract term.

Rule 12. After making the technological, or methods, or procedural change, you, Mr. Foreman, or other representatives of your management, reevaluate the new, changed, or consolidated job, craft, or work in terms of its new job value.

Rule 13. Any increase in the evaluating factors of effort, skills, duties, responsibilities, or working conditions called for in

383

the new or changed job you credit to the job in terms of increase in its job value as compared to the values of comparable jobs in the existing wage structure.

Rule 14. Any decrease in the evaluating factors of effort, skills, duties, responsibilities, or working conditions called for in the new or changed job you debit to the job in terms of decrease in its value as compared to the values of comparable jobs in the existing wage structure.

Rule 15. The new rate, whether lower, the same as, or higher than the old one, should reflect any increase or decrease in job value of the new, changed, or consolidated job.

Rule 16. You set a new rate for the new or changed job in relationship to the job or work value of other comparable jobs in the existing wage structure under your contract; and you slot the rate into its proper place in that existing wage structure.

Rule 17. You must be prepared to demonstrate by objective evaluating criteria that the new rate you initially set bears a proper relationship in terms of job value to other comparable jobs in the existing wage structure.

Rule 18. Unless the contract provides otherwise, increase in productivity or resulting savings in labor costs due to changes in means, methods, materials, operating facilities, or procedures during the contract term do not constitute evaluating factors in determining the proper rate for the new or changed job.

Rule 19. The seniority provisions of the contract govern the seniority rights of employees in the bargaining unit to the new or changed job.

Rule 20. The skills, duties, and responsibilities of the new or changed job as compared to the skills, duties and responsibilities of other existing classified jobs under the contract determine to which classified employees the new or changed job should properly be assigned.

Rule 21. Unless the contract provides otherwise, the shop steward retains the right to protest unilaterally—without asking, consulting with or getting the foreman's prior approval— the job value and rate initially set for the new or changed job and changes in production standards, work loads, size of crew, or other working conditions of the new or changed job; and he may question whether the employees in the bargaining unit, retained or assigned, had seniority rights under the seniority provisions of the contract to the new or changed job.

Rules for Handling
the Subcontracting Case

13

The Issues and Pitfalls
in Subcontracting

What Does the Certification of a
Bargaining Unit Certify?

In the case of Carey vs. Westinghouse Electric Corporation, the
U.S. Supreme Court cited the policy of the National Labor Relations
Board on the effect of the Board's certification of a bargaining unit:

A Board certification in a representative proceeding is not a jurisdictional award; it is merely a determination that a majority of the employees in an appropriate unit have selected a particular labor organization as their representative for purposes of collective bargaining. It is
true that such certification presupposes a determination that the group
of employees involved constitute an appropriate unit for collective bargaining purposes, and that in making such determination the Board
considers the general nature of the duties and work tasks of such employees. However, unlike a jurisdictional award, this determination by
the Board does not freeze the duties or work tasks of the employees in
the unit found appropriate. Thus, the Board's unit finding does not
per se preclude the employer from adding to, or subtracting from, the

employees' work assignments. While that finding may be determined by, it does not determine, job content; nor does it signify approval, in any respect, of any work task claims which the certified union may have made before this Board or elsewhere. "Plumbing Contractors Assn., 93 N.L.R.B. 1081, 1087."

What Does the Recognition Clause Recognize?

The first question that arises in handling grievances protesting the company's action in subcontracting production or maintenance work during the contract term is, does the contract's recognition clause, per se, exceed the scope of a certification by the Board of the appropriate bargaining unit?

To put that another way, did your negotiators, Mr. Foreman, intend the recognition clause, which recognizes the union as the exclusive bargaining agent for the maintenance and production employees in the bargaining unit with respect to wages, hours, and other terms and conditions of employment, to constitute a jurisdictional award covering production or maintenance work available at the time the parties negotiated their contract or during the contract term? No, unless your contract provides otherwise.

The recognition clause serves the same purpose as the Board's certification. It recognizes the union as the representative for purposes of collective bargaining of those employees whose duties and work tasks the recognition clause describes. The recognition clause covers employees, not jobs, crafts, duties, or work tasks.

Unless your contract otherwise provides, the recognition clause does not serve as a jurisdictional award covering jobs, crafts, duties, or work tasks. Like the Board's certification, the recognition clause "does not freeze the duties or work tasks of the employees in the unit" and "does not per se preclude the employer from adding to, or subtracting from, the employees' work assignments." And further, like the Board's certification, while the recognition of the bargaining unit covered by the contract "may be determined by, it does not determine, job content; nor does it signify approval, in any respect, of any work task claims" the recognized union may have made before the Board or elsewhere.

390

THE RECOGNITION CLAUSE COVERS EMPLOYEES, NOT JOBS

Unless your contract provides otherwise, Mr. Foreman, the recognition clause applies to those employees who perform those jobs, crafts, or services as long as such work continues to exist and remains available to employees in the bargaining unit. The recognition clause does not guarantee that the company will have or will make available any particular jobs or work; nor does the recognition clause give employees in the bargaining unit at any time a proprietary interest in or to any jobs or work.

Subcontracting maintenance or production work during the contract term eliminates those formerly existing jobs, crafts, or work and makes them no longer available to employees in the bargaining unit; and unless your contract provides otherwise, the recognition clause describing the employees in the bargaining unit does not follow such eliminated jobs, work, or crafts.

What Displaces Bargaining-Unit Employees?

Subcontracting production or maintenance work during the contract term displaces employees in the bargaining unit. Just as new machines, new methods, or new procedures constitute a new way of doing the job, craft, work, or service, so the subcontracting of production or maintenance work constitutes *eo ipso,* of itself, a new way of doing the work. Just as technological changes or improved methods eliminate jobs, crafts, work, or services, so subcontracting eliminates those jobs.

As pointed out earlier, not every technological change or improved method constitutes a new way of doing the former job or work. The facts must demonstrate that a material—a substantial, significant or major—change has taken place that clearly distinguishes the new way of doing the job from the former way. That same key applies in determining whether the facts of the subcontracting demonstrate that a material change has taken place that clearly distinguishes the new way of doing the job from the former way.

In evaluating the facts of subcontracting production or maintenance work during the contract term to determine what displaces bargaining-unit employees, you use the following two guideposts:

1. Do nonbargaining-unit employees using the same method, means, materials, equipment or facilities displace bargaining-unit employees by "stepping into their shoes" and doing the job or work in the same way as formerly?
2. Does the new or changed way of doing the job or work due to changes in method, means, materials, equipment, or facilities displace bargaining-unit employees from that job or work?

If the material facts show that the subcontractor's employees do the work in the same way using the company's equipment and facilities, controlled or supervised by the company's supervisors, they would in fact be stepping into the shoes and filling the available jobs of bargaining-unit employees. In such a case the conclusion would be inescapable that the subcontractor's employees displaced bargaining-unit employees. And in such a case, in the absence of a contract provision permitting subcontracting during the contract term, the subcontracting would violate the commonly used recognition and seniority clauses and the classified job structure and wage schedules of the contract, just as if the company had assigned that work to nonbargaining-unit employees or used other employees outside the bargaining unit to fill bargaining-unit jobs.

If, on the other hand, the subcontractor's employees do the work by a different or improved method, use the subcontractor's facilities, equipment, materials, and supplies, and work under the control and supervision of the subcontractor's supervisors, one could reasonably conclude that the subcontractor's employees did not fill the former job or do the same work formerly done by bargaining-unit employees. In such a case the subcontracting would constitute a change in means, methods, or procedures that materially distinguishes the new way of doing the job from the former way. And in such a case, in the absence of any contract provision prohibiting subcontracting work during the contract term, the subcontracting would not violate the commonly used recognition or seniority clauses or the classified job structure or wage schedules of the contract.

392

THE TWO SUBCONTRACTING CASES,
GRIEVANCES NO. 27 AND NO. 28

The union filed two grievances protesting the company's action in subcontracting work on two different occasions. In both grievances the union claimed that the company had violated the recognition clause, the wage Schedule A, and Schedule B of the contract.

The recognition clause, Article I, provided:

The Employer recognizes the Union as the exclusive collective bargaining agent in matters pertaining to hours, wages, and other conditions of employment . . . for all production, maintenance, shipping and warehouse employees . . . excluding, however . . . spot and temporary employees as defined in Schedule B attached to and made a part of this agreement.

Schedule A set forth the minimum basic straight time rates per hour for permanent employees. Schedule B provided:

1. A Spot or Temporary employee is defined as any person hired for specific period of time, not to exceed sixty (60) days in any eight (8) month period.
2. Spot or Temporary employees shall not do production, warehousing, shipping or laboratory work unless approved by the Union.
3. Spot or Temporary employees shall not do repair and maintenance work at any time when the restrictions on sub-contracting contained in Article XXVIII apply, provided the work to be done by the Spot or Temporary employees can be done by a bargaining unit employee under the same conditions as outlined in Article XXVIII.

The company denied both grievances, claiming that it had acted in accordance with Article III, the management's rights clause, and Article XXVIII of the contract. Article III provided:

The management of the Employer's plant and business, including the direction of the working force and right to plan, direct, and control operation and use of all equipment and other property of the Employer is the exclusive right and duty of the Employer.

The Employer has the sole right to hire, lay off, promote, demote or transfer employees, to suspend or discharge employees for proper cause; the Employer has the exclusive right to control the type of product, volume of production, scheduling of operations, the right to determine the size and composition of the working force, the right to study and/or introduce new or improved methods or facilities, the right to determine what work will be performed by outside contractors, and the right to establish and maintain rules and regulations governing the operation of the plant, a violation of which shall be among the causes for discharge. These rights shall be exercised with due regard for the legal rights of the employees, and further the Employer shall not exercise these rights in violation of the specific provisions of this agreement.

The listing of specific rights in this article is not intended to be nor shall be considered restrictive of or a waiver of any of the rights of management not listed and not specifically surrendered herein whether or not such rights have been exercised by the Employer in the past. The Employer retains all rights not otherwise specifically covered by this agreement.

Article XXVIII provided:

The Employer agrees not to sub-contract any maintenance or repair work at any time when the number of its employees scheduled to work during a given work week, who are classified as welders or mechanics is less than four (4), provided said welders or mechanics can do the required maintenance or repair work and that the necessary facilities know how and equipment are available without further cost to the Employer. This is the one and only restriction on the sub-contracting of work intended by this agreement; all "make" or "buy" decisions shall be made exclusively by the Employer, solely on the economic and/or delivery-time, and/or quality basis as in the past.

The union appealed both grievances to arbitration.

Subcontracting Dust Collector Work:
Grievance No. 27

At the arbitration hearing the evidence established the following material facts.

394

On Saturday, March 13th, the company had hired from an employment agency three men to do manual work in cleaning the dust collector in department 102. The work required the men to install new bags, purchased by the company, in the dust collector or to take out the old bags that had collected dust and to hose down, wash, dry, and hang them back, using the hoses and washing equipment the company had on hand for that purpose.

Employees in the bargaining unit classified as laborers had performed that routine cleaning work in the past as part of their regular job. They had worked on the dust collector during the week preceding Saturday, March 13th; and on the following Monday, March 15th, they finished the cleaning work on the bags the three outside men had left over and didn't complete on the preceding Saturday. The company paid the employment agency its charges for the three nonbargaining-unit men at rates less than the contract laborers' rates and without the time and a half for Saturday work provided for by the contract.

The union claimed that the company had "hired spot or temporary employees to do work that belonged to bargaining-unit employees, qualified to do the work; and the company had thereby displaced bargaining-unit employees with spot or temporary employees, violating the recognition clause, the wage schedule and Schedule B of the contract." The union demanded pay at time and a half for "three senior laborers in the bargaining unit, for the hours worked that day."

The company denied that it had hired spot or temporary employees to do work prohibited by any subdivision of Schedule B and claimed:

> Outside contractors had supplied the employees to do the work; the need for outside help in cleaning and replacing the bags in the dust collector had arisen because of a fire during the week prior to March 13th requiring the company to buy new bags to replace those that had burned . . . (and) it had employed during the work week not less than four welders or mechanics as called for by Article XXVIII that the parties had agreed upon as the one and only restriction on subcontracting of work intended by this agreement.

The majority of the board of arbitrators, the union's member and myself as chairman, sustained the union's grievance. In my accompanying opinion, written as chairman of the board, I said:

The company hired the three new employees from an employment agency. They used the bags bought by the company; used the hose, tools and washing equipment owned by the company; and they did the work in the very same way with the same facilities that bargaining unit employees, classified as laborers, had performed previously in the same week; and had completed the work left over by the non-bargaining unit employees the following Monday. The non-bargaining unit employees had simply stepped into the shoes of the bargaining unit employees. That's the inescapable conclusion the material facts in this case compel.

Finding "no merit in the company's claim that the employment agency served as an outside contractor because the company paid the employment agency a lump sum payment for its charges; and in turn, the employment agency paid the three workers it had supplied at the request of the company," I said:

> The chairman finds the company had employed those three new workers as spot or temporary employees; and that Schedule B governs the conditions of their employment. The company's foremen supervised the three new employees; and the company directed and controlled their work—not the employment agency.
>
> Schedule B (2) of the contract prohibits spot or temporary employees from doing production, warehousing, shipping or laboratory work unless approved by the union. The union had not approved the employment of the three temporary employees.

I rejected the company's claim that "the three new employees did repair and maintenance work under Schedule B (3); and the company had complied with the condition required by Article XXVIII," saying:

> The chairman finds no merit in this claim, for clearly the skills and experience required by the repair and maintenance work Schedule B (3) speaks of, and the parties intended thereunder, did not encompass the routine manual work the three new employees had been hired for. The language of Schedule B (3), when read in context with Article XXVIII expressly referred to therein, shows the parties intended maintenance and repair work to cover the experiences and skills required

396

of employees classified as welders or mechanics; and not that of employees classified as laborers.

Considering the routine type of work performed and the skills and experiences required, the chairman finds the cleaning and replacing of bags in the dust collector, performed by employees classified as laborers as a regular part of their job, constituted indirect production work and not skilled maintenance or repair work performed by employees classified as welders or mechanics, as expressly stipulated by the parties in Article XXVIII.

I found no merit in the company's argument that "Article III of the contract expressly reserves to it the right to determine the size and composition of the work force . . . introduce new or improved methods or facilities, the right to determine what work will be performed by outside contractors . . . and it had the right to have the dust collector work performed by nonbargaining-unit employees supplied by the employment agency whom the company claimed acted as an outside contractor for that work." I said:

> The management's rights clause, Article III, by its very words makes the exercise of those retained rights of the company subject to the rights of the union and the employees as agreed to in the set of working conditions of the contract. Article III expressly provides "the Employer shall not exercise these rights in violation of the specific provisions of this agreement." The evidence satisfies the chairman that in employing temporary employees on that Saturday to do the work of bargaining unit employees, without benefit of any change in the means, method, equipment or facilities in doing that work, the company had violated Schedule B, one of the specific provisions of the contract.

Finding that the evidence did not support the company's claim that "the need to hire the three employees on Saturday came about because a fire, occurring in the early part of the week, had destroyed the bags on hand and the company had to buy new ones to replace them," I said:

> The proof fails to establish that a production difficulty had arisen that warranted the company in failing to use bargaining unit employees to continue to do that work on that Saturday.
>
> The proof establishes that regular employees, classified as laborers,

had performed the very work during that week after the fire had occurred; and they continued to do the remaining work on the Monday following the Saturday. The company does not question that their own employees were qualified and available to do the work on Saturday. The fact that the contract called for time and a half for bargaining unit employees working on Saturday, as such, did not create production or personnel difficulties that would justify the company denying regular employees available work, and substituting temporary employees in their place.

The award directed that the "company shall pay three senior laborers pay, computed at time and a half of each of said senior employees' regular rate, for the hours worked that day, March 13 . . . by said non-bargaining-unit employees."

Subcontracting Roof Ventilator Work:
Grievance No. 28

In this case, the evidence established the following material facts.

Prior to March 6th the company had contracted with an outside contractor to replace the ventilators on the roof of Department 102. On Saturday, March 6th, employees of the outside contractor installed the ventilators and performed the necessary related repair work. They used the materials, tools, and machinery supplied by the subcontractor, and the subcontractor supervised the work performed. The contract between the company and the subcontractor called for a package deal under which the subcontractor undertook to do the complete job of replacing the ventilators, supplying the materials and parts, using his own employees and equipment, and supervising and paying his employees. The company agreed to pay the subcontractor a lump sum payment for doing the complete ventilating job.

The company had not assigned to, nor at any time had any of the employees in the bargaining unit performed, any of the work of replacing the ventilators; nor did the company supervise the subcontractor's employees in doing that work. During the work week in which Saturday, March 6th, fell the company had employed in the bargain-

398

ing unit no fewer than four welders or mechanics, as provided for by Article XXVIII of the contract.

The union claimed that the company had used spot or temporary employees to do bargaining-unit work and demanded "equal hours of pay for that day at time and one half for the two senior maintenance men who did not work."

The company claimed that it had subcontracted the entire job "on a contract basis with an outside contractor" and that it had not hired any men as spot or temporary employees under Schedule B of the contract to do that work.

The majority of the board of arbitrators—this time the company's representative and myself as chairman—denied the union's grievance. In my accompanying opinion I said:

> The company did not violate the contract by contracting-out that job to a subcontractor on a package contract basis, under which the subcontractor's employees performed the whole job as an integrated unit, and as such, the sub-contracting constituted a material change in the means, method and way of doing the job; and consequently, the subcontracting method itself, and not the subcontractor's employees, displaced employees in the bargaining unit.

Finding that the company "had contracted-out on a contract basis with an outside contractor the entire job of replacing the ventilators," I said:

> The contract between the company and the subcontractor called for a package deal, under which the subcontractor undertook to do the complete job—using his own employees, his own equipment, and supervising and paying his employees. In turn, the company paid the subcontractor a lump sum payment for the entire job. At no time had the company assigned to nor had any of the employees in the bargaining unit performed any part of that job.

Then, finding that during the work week in which Saturday, March 6th, fell and on which the subcontractor's employees worked on the

399

job the company had employed in the bargaining unit no fewer than four welders or mechanics as provided for by Article XXVIII of the contract, I said:

> Under Article III of the contract, the management's rights clause, the union expressly recognizes the company's "right to determine the size and composition of the working force . . . introduce new or improved methods or facilities, the right to determine what work will be performed by outside contractors . . ." Unlike the facts in the dust collector case—here the company did not violate any of the specific provisions of this agreement in exercising its right to introduce new or improved methods or facilities, and the right to determine what work will be performed by outside contractors.
>
> On the contrary, the proof shows the company, in exercising its right to use outside contractors in this case, fully complied with the single condition the parties explicitly agreed to in Article XXVIII. Under that article, the company agreed not to sub-contract any maintenance or repair work at any time when the number of its employees scheduled to work during a given work week, who are classified as welders or mechanics, is less than four (4), provided said welders or mechanics can do the required maintenance or repair work and the necessary facilities, know-how and equipment are available without further cost to the employer.

I found no merit in the union's claim that the "company had violated the recognition clause (Article I); the seniority clauses (Articles XXIV, XXVI) and the wage Schedule A of the contract."

> The recognition clause in no way freezes jobs or work that may have previously been available to bargaining unit employees; or formerly had been assigned to and performed by employees in the bargaining unit. The recognition clause governs the hours, wages, and other conditions of employment of employees in the bargaining unit when they perform work made available to them. The recognition clause does not govern jobs or work that bargaining unit employees do not perform or no longer perform. Consequently, the recognition clause does not restrict the company from eliminating jobs or work previously performed by employees in the bargaining unit when due to new or

400

improved methods or facilities or sub-contracted to outside contractors. Neither the recognition clause, the wage schedule nor the seniority clauses of the contract extend to jobs or work that are not available to, nor performed by, bargaining unit employees.

Then, referring to the wage schedule and seniority clauses, I said:

Likewise, the wage Schedule A and the seniority clauses of the contract do not freeze jobs or work; nor give bargaining unit employees a proprietary interest to any particular job or work. The wage schedule sets forth the rates of pay the parties agreed upon to cover the jobs as long as they continue to be performed by bargaining unit employees. If they are no longer available to or performed by bargaining unit employees, then the wage schedule does not govern those jobs.

So, too, with the seniority clauses, that set forth a relative status of employment as between two or more employees to jobs or work available to and performed by bargaining unit employees. The seniority clauses of the contract do not prohibit the company from eliminating jobs or work; nor having jobs or work performed by outside contractors on a bona fide contract basis.

Noting that in the "dust collector case, the company had made available and assigned to bargaining-unit employees the cleaning and installing of the bags during the week previous to Saturday and in the week following Saturday . . . (and) the company had just sought to substitute nonbargaining-unit employees in doing that work," I said:

In the ventilator case, the company had in no way violated any of the clauses of the contract since it subcontracted that work to outside contractors on a bona fide contract basis. There the contracting-out constituted new or improved methods or facilities of doing the work; and though it resulted in removing work opportunities for bargaining unit employees, the contracting-out did not violate any of the clauses of the contract.

Collateral Issues in the Subcontracting Case

What about the site where the subcontractor's employees perform the work? If the subcontracting takes place off the premises, contiguous to the premises, or on the premises, do such elements raise a material issue? No, unless your contract provides otherwise.

The site where the subcontracting takes place may color the dispute by sharpening or lessening its immediate impact. Subcontractors' employees working at different rates of pay on the plant site, alongside the company's regular employees performing or qualified to perform similar work, tend to aggravate the dispute. When the subcontracting takes place off the plant site, at the subcontractor's place of business, the strain over job security tends to lessen. Regardless of where the subcontracting takes place, the relevant question remains: What displaces bargaining-unit employees or reduces work opportunities for present or new dues-paying bargaining-unit employees? In answering that question, the facts of the subcontracting in the particular case determine the material issue:

> DOES THE SUBCONTRACTING CONSTITUTE A SUBSTANTIAL, SIGNIFICANT OR MAJOR CHANGE THAT MATERIALLY DISTINGUISHES THE NEW WAY OF DOING THE WORK FROM THE FORMER WAY?

That same rule applies whether the subcontractor performs a part of the prime work or service of the company or only indirect work or an auxiliary service to its principal business, such as subcontracting cafeteria or eating facilities, truck delivery, plant security, utility disposal, window washing, or janitorial work.

How about loss of overtime work or opportunity? Does that factor carry any weight? No, unless, again, your contract provides otherwise. Overtime constitutes part of an employee's regular job; and if the subcontracting eliminates employees or opportunities for new employees in the bargaining unit, then whether or not the subcontracting reduces or eliminates overtime opportunities would not raise a material issue.

How about layoffs? If the subcontracting initially causes or subsequently results in layoff of employees qualified to do the work, or if the subcontracting lessens the recall rights of employees on layoff qualified to do the work, would those facts raise relevant issues in deciding whether the subcontracting violated the contract's set of working conditions? No, unless your contract provides otherwise.

None of these factors—the site where the subcontracting takes place, whether the subcontractor performs a part of the prime work or service of the company or only indirect or auxiliary work or service, whether the subcontracting eliminates overtime opportunity, or whether the subcontracting causes layoffs or affects recall rights—in the absence of any contrary contract provision, none of these factors raises material issues in determining whether the subcontracting does or does not violate the recognition or seniority clauses or classified job structure or wage schedules of the contract. The relevant question that decides the case still remains:

> DOES THE SUBCONTRACTING CONSTITUTE A CHANGE IN
> MEANS, METHOD, MATERIALS, PROCEDURES, OR FACIL-
> ITIES THAT MATERIALLY DISTINGUISHES THE NEW WAY
> OF DOING THE WORK FROM THE FORMER WAY?

THE CASE OF INTRACOMPANY PRODUCTION CHANGES

About two years before this dispute arose the company, engaged in the production and converting of textile goods at its Paterson, New Jersey, plant, acquired the ownership of another plant manufacturing the same product located in the state of Connecticut. The union represented the employees in the Paterson plant, and a different union represented the employees in the Connecticut plant.

The company then began to reorganize its production methods and facilities between the two plants. It discontinued production of goods in bulk at the Connecticut plant and transferred those operations to the Paterson plant, where it installed new machines and improved methods of production. Since the Connecticut plant had greater converting facilities and employed about three times more employees in those departments than the Paterson plant, the company discontinued its converting operations in the Paterson plant and transferred them to the Connecticut plant.

As a result of these intracompany transfers of operations the company laid off forty-seven employees at the Paterson plant who had been employed in the converting department.

The union representing the Paterson employees filed a grievance claiming that the company had violated Section XI of the contract "by giving out work to another mill, while forty-seven of its employees were laid off." The union demanded reinstatement of the laid-off employees with full pay for all time lost.

The company denied the grievance, and the union appealed to arbitration.

Section XI of the contract provided:

Outside Work—No work done in the plant shall be given out unless the mill giving out such work is filled to capacity on its normal shift operations. In any case where work may be given out, such work must be given to a mill having a contract with the Union. Workers shall not be required to perform any work for any mill or firm in which there is a strike.

At the arbitration hearing the union claimed:

Irrespective of the reason for change in operations between the Paterson and Connecticut plants, Section XI prohibits the company from giving out the converting work from the Paterson plant, with the consequent layoff of employees; that Section XI was designed to protect employees in the bargaining unit from losing their jobs, by taking away their work and giving it to other employees in another mill; and the company should be directed to reemploy the forty-seven employees laid off, with pay for all time lost.

The company claimed:

Section XI was never intended by the parties to restrict the company from changing its methods and processes of manufacturing or from eliminating or discontinuing any of its departments . . . that the clause was never intended as a means for the union to exercise control over the operations or equipment of the company; nor to require the company to retain facilities or processes where changed business conditions necessitated changes; nor was it intended to restrict the company from commencing new operations or methods or from eliminating or discontinuing old ones, as has been done in this instance.

The company further claimed:

404

Integrating the operations between the two plants was made in good faith, was necessitated by sound business judgment and has resulted in increased production work at the Paterson plant, thereby providing greater job security to a greater number of employees in the bargaining unit; and the layoff of employees in the converting departments did not violate Section XI of the contract.

Finding that the parties did not intend Section XI "to restrict the company in making reasonable and necessary changes in methods and processes of production, even though such changes result in permanently displacing some of the employees in the bargaining unit," I denied the union's grievance. In my award I said:

> The history and the language of Section XI support the company's position.
>
> The proof establishes that Section XI was intended to prevent a company from giving out work to "family" or non-organized plants in the early days of union organization in this industry. It was intended to prohibit the practice of sub-contracting production work normally done in the plant, where production facilities and jobs were available at the organized plant . . .
>
> Its purpose was to prevent a company or mill organized by the union, from avoiding, by subterfuge or under the guise of sub-contracting production work, its contractual obligations, to the detriment of the union and of the employees in the bargaining unit in the organized company or mill.

Then, noting that the parties intended Section XI "as its language shows, to prevent the company from giving out work, from subcontracting work, when production facilities and jobs were available at the company's plant," I said:

> That is the scope and intent of Section XI, which the arbitrator finds from the proof offered in this proceeding.
>
> Work that was done in the plant could not be given out unless the mill giving out such work is filled to capacity on its normal shift operations. Due to the reorganization between the company's two plants, converting work is no longer done in the Paterson plant; the

405

converting departments have been completely eliminated; converting facilities are no longer available in the Paterson plant; converting work is no longer part of that plant's normal shift operations . . . The language of Section XI is sufficiently clear to show the parties intended it to prevent the sub-contracting of work regularly done at the plant where there are facilities available for such work.

I found that the company "acquired the Connecticut plant in the normal movement of business expansion and development" and transferred all converting operations to the Connecticut plant and all production operations to the Paterson plant for operational reasons. I found:

The transfers were not undertaken as a subterfuge to avoid any contractual obligation between the parties under their contract.

Section XI of the contract between the parties does not restrict the company from making such intracompany transfers of operations. Although the exchange of operations affected the jobs of some of the employees in the bargaining unit, the exchange increased the available jobs in the production departments in the Paterson plant. The proof also shows the effect of these exchanges fortified the job security of the substantial majority of employees in the bargaining unit in the Paterson plant.

What Facts Support Subcontracting as a Material Change?

Demonstrable proof—written memoranda, facts, and figures that show:

1. A package deal under which the subcontractor undertakes to perform the entire job for a stipulated sum of money or value on a bona fide contract basis.
2. The subcontractor employs and uses his own employees and not any bargaining-unit employees in performing the work.
3. The subcontractor directs, controls, and supervises his own work force, and no bargaining-unit employees, in performing the work.

4. The subcontractor employs and pays his employees, withholding customary payroll taxes.

5. The subcontractor's employees use the tools, equipment, materials, supplies, machinery, or facilities owned or supplied by the subcontractor.

6. The subcontractor's employees perform and complete the entire subcontracted work as an independent, integrated job or unit of work.

7. The subcontracting results in economy—saving of time or money, either by overcoming production, operational, seasonal or personnel difficulties or by savings in production or labor costs.

In the absence of any contract provision restricting subcontracting during the contract term, proof of the foregoing facts would support a reasonable finding that the subcontracting constituted a substantial, significant, or major change in means, methods, materials, procedures, or facilities that materially distinguished the new way of doing the work or job from the former way.

The affirmative showing that the subcontracting saved time or money or that production, operational, seasonal or personnel difficulties necessitated the subcontracting, eliminates any inference of subterfuge, fraud, or antiunion bias. Savings in time or money would reasonably include availability of necessary facilities or funds to buy them and availability of qualified employees or the cost or delay in time to train new employees to do the necessary job.

Savings in time would also include having the subcontracting work done when it would least interfere with regular production or scheduled hours of work and a guarantee that the subcontractor would complete the work within a stated time or other warranties of prompt and satisfactory performance.

Just as savings in production time or labor costs motivate management to consolidate jobs, eliminate idle time, or reduce crews by undertaking technological or method changes in production facilities, so saving production time or labor costs or overcoming production difficulties motivates management to subcontract production or maintenance work during the contract term. In fact, unless the subcontracting demonstrates a saving of time or money or the need to overcome operational difficulties, a doubt arises about the bona fides of the subcontracting.

The Three Pitfalls in the Subcontracting Case

You must take the same care, Mr. Manager, in defending the subcontracting case that you would in defending your actions in making method changes in the operating facilities in your departments. Subcontracting per se casts no magic spell for either the shop steward or the arbitrator. You need hard facts to justify eliminating jobs or work opportunities for your bargaining-unit employees.

The burden of proof rests on you to demonstrate, by facts and figures, that the subcontracting adds up to a material change in the way of doing the work and that the changed way—and not nonbargaining-unit employees—displaced bargaining-unit employees or jobs.

In preparing and offering your proof avoid the following three pitfalls:

FRACTIONALIZING THE SUBCONTRACTED WORK
IN AREA OR TIME

You muddy the case when you subcontract the electrical work on two floors of the building and then assign your own electricians, when you can spare them from their regular jobs or at overtime, to do the same work on the third floor.

Similarly, you fractionalize the job when you assign one of your maintenance men to fill in for an absent subcontractor's employee, letting him work alongside employees of the subcontractor while you supervise and exercise control over him. You may try to justify having the work done in such piecemeal fashion because of expediency, wanting to get the job done quickly, or even wanting to give your own employees an opportunity to earn some overtime money. You may feel you're acting fairly, but the shop steward has to protect the contract rights of all the bargaining-unit employees and the union; and fractionalizing the work gives him an opening to dispute the bona fides of your whole subcontracting deal. Subcontract the entire job as an integrated unit or a package deal without splintering it into bargaining-unit and nonbargaining-unit work.

COMMINGLING TOOLS, EQUIPMENT, OR SUPERVISORS

"Why did you subcontract that job, Mr. Manager?" the shop steward will ask. "Didn't you have on hand the necessary bags, hose, tools and washing equipment? Did the subcontractor bring to the job any new materials, machines or equipment you didn't have available or didn't want to buy just for that job? Did you use his workers just to avoid paying overtime to your regular employees? Did you just lend the subcontractor your supervisors—to supervise his workers? Then, what did you need the subcontractor for?"

Yes, the shop steward will ask you those questions and many more if you lend the subcontractor your tools, your materials, your equipment, your employees—or your supervisors! Did the changed way of doing the job displace bargaining-unit employees? No! The subcontractor's employees did the work of bargaining-unit employees simply by stepping into their shoes!

Don't you see that such mixing up of men and machines gives your representatives in the higher steps of the grievance procedure or before the arbitrator wet ammunition, not dry powder, when they try to support your action under the basic issue the subcontracting grievance raises: Does the subcontracting constitute a substantial, significant or major change that materially distinguishes the new way of doing the work from the former way?

If you subcontract the job, Mr. Manager, let the subcontractor supply the needed materials, equipment, and workers and use his own supervisors to supervise the job and men doing the work.

CAMOUFLAGING THE BONA FIDES OF THE PACKAGE DEAL

You may have had a real need to subcontract the job, Mr. Manager, but taking short cuts casts doubt on the good faith of your action. You create suspicion of your ulterior motive by making a loan to a former employee to buy the materials or equipment needed and then subcontracting the job to him! The shop steward will hardly be taken in by such pretense. Avoid any action that camouflages the real deal. You won't get very far when you sell your trucks to former bargaining-unit employees, take back purchase-money mortgages, and then subcontract your delivery routes to them as independent contractors! That may constitute a legal change of ownership, but hardly a material change in the way of doing the job.

The affirmative proof of savings in time or money or the necessity of overcoming production difficulties eliminates the inference that subterfuge, fraud or antiunion bias motivated you in entering into the subcontracting deal. In subcontracting production or maintenance work during the contract term, Mr. Manager, you're on firm ground when you follow the rules of the game. Handle your case as a professional, and you'll be managing with a union along lines of excellence!

Summing Up the Rules for Handling Subcontracting Cases

Rule 1. The certification of a bargaining unit by the National Labor Relations Board does not constitute a jurisdictional award, does not freeze the duties or work tasks of the employees in the unit found appropriate, does not per se preclude the employer from adding to, or subtracting from, the employees' work assignments, and does not determine job content, or signify approval, in any respect, of any work task claims the certified union may have made before the Board or elsewhere.

Rule 2. Unless your contract expressly provides otherwise, the recognition clause, which recognizes the union as the exclusive bargaining agent for the described employees in the bargaining unit, does not constitute a jurisdictional award over work, does not freeze the duties or work tasks of employees in the bargaining unit, does not per se preclude the foreman from adding to or subtracting from employees' work assignments, does not determine job content, and does not signify approval in any respect of any work-task claims the recognized union may have made before the Board or elsewhere.

Rule 3. Unless your contract provides otherwise, the recognition clause covers employees, not jobs or work, and applies to employees who perform those jobs, crafts, work, or services as long as they continue to exist and remain available to employees in the bargaining unit.

Rule 4. The recognition clause per se does not guarantee that any particular jobs, tasks, or work will be available; nor does the recognition clause give bargaining-unit employees a proprietary interest in any jobs or work.

Rule 5. In the absence of any contrary contract provision the recognition clause does not follow jobs, crafts, work, or services that management has contracted-out and no longer makes available to bargaining-unit employees.

Rule 6. During the contract term the recognition clause obligating the parties to bargain collectively over wages, hours, and working conditions applies to any question arising under the set of working conditions negotiated and agreed upon in the contract; and the contract's set of working conditions determines the settlement of any question arising thereunder.

Rule 7. Unless your contract provides otherwise, where the contract speaks of particular classified jobs, work, or tasks as "belonging to" or to be "performed by" particular employees or specified groups or classifications of employees, the parties intend such descriptive words or assignments of classified jobs, or groupings of work, to apply to those jobs or work that exist and are available at the time to employees in the bargaining unit.

411

> *Rule 8.* Such descriptive assignments of work, tasks, or classified jobs, in the absence of any contrary provision, do not limit or circumscribe management's right to initiate technological changes or subcontract such jobs or work during the contract term.

Past Practices Give Way to Technological Changes and Subcontracting

> *Rule 9.* A past practice that conflicts with the clear language of a written provision or contradicts what the parties reasonably intended under the language of that provision does not constitute an agreement by the parties to change or modify that written provision.

> *Rule 10.* If a past practice limiting or circumscribing management's right to institute technological changes or subcontract during the contract term conflicts with clear and unambiguous written contract provisions, such as a management's right clause, the written contract governs the rights of the parties for the remaining term of the contract.

> *Rule 11.* Neither party waives its contractual rights established by a written provision by any practice that misinterprets that written provision; nor does either party relinquish its contractual rights under a written provision by failing to enforce those rights in the past.

> *Rule 12.* A past practice that misinterprets, misapplies, or violates a written contract provision may be voidable by either party for the balance of the contract term. Either party can insist that the other thenceforth comply with the terms as agreed to by the written contract; and the arbitrator's office constrains him to enforce those rights and obligations as agreed to by the parties under the written contract.

Rule 13. New operating conditions necessitate new rules. When the conditions out of which an established past practice arose no longer exist because of the introduction of new products, new machines, new materials, new methods of manufacture, new administrative procedures, or the bona fide contracting-out of work, the past practice falls and the presumption that such past practice continues no longer exists.

Criteria and Pitfalls in the Subcontracting Case

Rule 14. The bona fide subcontracting of production or maintenance work constitutes a new way of doing the work.

Rule 15. Subcontracting raises the key question: What displaces bargaining-unit employees?

1. Do nonbargaining-unit employees using the same method, means, materials, equipment, or facilities displace bargaining unit employees by stepping into their shoes and doing the work in the same way? Or:

2. Does the new or changed way of doing the job or work, due to changes in method, means, materials, equipment, or facilities, displace bargaining-unit employees from that job or work?

Rule 16. Where the subcontractor's employees do the job or work in the same way, using the company's equipment and facilities, controlled and supervised by the company's supervisors, the reasonable conclusion would be inescapable that the subcontractor's employees and not the new way of doing the job displaced bargaining-unit employees by stepping into their shoes.

Rule 17. Where the subcontractor's employees do the work by a different or improved method, use the subcontractor's facilities, equipment, materials, and supplies, and where the subcontractor's supervisors control and supervise his employees, the subcontracting would constitute a substantial, significant or major change that materially distinguishes the new way of doing the job from the former way.

Rule 18. Such collateral factors as:

1. The site where the subcontracting takes place—off, contiguous to, or on the premises;

2. Whether the subcontractor performs a part of the prime work or service or only the indirect or auxiliary work or service, such as subcontracting cafeteria facilities, truck delivery, plant security, utility disposal, window washing or janitorial service;

3. Whether the subcontracting eliminates overtime work or overtime opportunities for bargaining-unit employees;

4. Whether the subcontracting causes layoffs or affects recall rights of bargaining-unit employees—

These collateral factors, in the absence of any contrary contract provision, do not raise material issues in determining whether the subcontracting does or does not violate the recognition or seniority clauses or the classified job structure or wage schedules of the contract.

Rule 19. To support a reasonable finding that the subcontracting constituted a substantial, significant, or major change that materially distinguishes the new way of doing the work or job from the former way, the proof should demonstrate:

1. A package deal on a bona fide contract basis under which the subcontractor employs, pays for, directs, controls and supervises his own work force and not bargaining-unit employees or company supervisors; and

performs and completes the entire subcontracted work as an independent, integrated unit of work using his own tools, equipment, materials, supplies, machines, or facilities; and

2. The subcontracting results in economy, savings in time or money, by overcoming production, operational, seasonal or personnel difficulties or by savings in production or labor costs.

Rule 20. In subcontracting production or maintenance work during the contract term, Mr. Manager, avoid these three pitfalls:

1. *FRACTIONALIZING* the subcontracted work in area or time.
2. *COMMINGLING* tools, equipment, or supervisors.
3. *CAMOUFLAGING* the bona fides of the package deal.

Arbitrability and the Arbitrator's Jurisdiction

Rule 21. Unless your contract provides otherwise, the no-strike clause or the no-strike pledge implicit in the grievance steps and final and binding arbitration as the terminal step, or both, restrains the union from striking or otherwise interfering with your management's right to unilaterally initiate technological changes or to subcontract work during the contract term and constrains the shop steward to follow in the orderly way agreed upon—through the grievance procedure and arbitration, if provided for—his protest against your action.

Rule 22. In the absence of any contrary contract provision, a grievance that claims or alleges that management violated the contract by its unilateral action in making such changes or in subcontracting work during the contract term raises an arbitrable question under the customary arbitration clause governing grievances over the interpretation, application, administration or claimed violation of the contract or under any broader arbitration clause.

Rule 23. In such case the arbitrator has jurisdiction to decide the arbitrability of that grievance, that is, whether the parties agreed under their contract to make arbitration available for such a dispute, as well as to exercise his delegated authority to decide the case on its merits under the contract's set of working conditions.

Rule 24. Unless the contract provides otherwise, the arbitrator's award becomes final and binding upon the parties during the contract term.

References

The number preceding each reference, excerpt, or case refers to the page on which it appears.

The number following a reference, excerpt, or case cited more than once refers to the page where the full description of it appears.

The descriptive arbitration case heading used in the text precedes the full title of the case.

References to the unions' shop steward manuals appear in a separate section following this one.

Chapter 1

PAGE

3   THE CASE OF THE LAID-OFF SENIOR EMPLOYEES
Kidde Manufacturing Company, Inc. and United Electrical, Radio & Machine Workers of America, Local 437. Award October 7, 1955

17   THE CASE OF THE "RELATIVELY EQUAL IN ABILITY" CLAIM
Universal Atlas Cement Company and United Cement, Lime & Gypsum Workers Int'l Union, Local No. 189, AFL–CIO. Award June 24, 1958

22   Stern, James, in *Automation and Major Technological Change, Impact on Union Size, Structure and Function:* A Panel Discussion at a Con-

418

420

workers and Milltown Local No. 535, AFL–CIO & CLC, Grievance No. 6407. Award December 3, 1964

162   Warrior & Gulf Navigation Company. Page 137

163   THE CASE OF THE YEAR-END BONUS
Felsway Shoe Corp. (New York) and District 65, Distributive, Processing and Office Workers of America. Award October 17, 1951

168   Goldberg, Arthur J., "Management's Reserved Rights: A Labor View." Page 149

168   THE CASE OF THE NEW PLASTIC TANK LINERS
International Smelting & Refining Company, Perth Amboy, N.J., Refinery and United Steelworkers of America and Local 4985, AFL–CIO. Award August 21, 1964

172   THE CASE OF THE UNION'S PAST PRACTICE
American Machine and Foundry Company and United Automobile, Aircraft & Agricultural Implement Workers of Am., UAW–AFL–CIO and Local 116. Award March 12, 1963. Motion by the Union to vacate the award denied by the United States District Court 256 F Supp. 161 (1963); judgment affirmed, United States Court of Appeals, Second Circuit 329 F 2d 147 (1964)

Chapter 6

178   Goldberg, Arthur J., "Management's Reserved Rights: A Labor View." Page 149

183   Time Recording Form—Shop Steward Activities: Written Request for Permission to Leave Department. Industrial Relations Workshop Seminars, Inc., New York, 1962, 1966

186   Representative Form of Employee Report—Claim for Sick Leave Allowance or Other Benefit. Industrial Relations Workshop Seminars, Inc., New York, 1962, 1966

187   THE CASE OF THE AFTERNOON SHIFT BONUS
Universal Atlas Cement Company, Division of United States Steel Corporation, Hudson, N.Y., Plant and The United Cement, Lime & Gypsum Workers Int'l Union, Local No. 189, AFL–CIO. Award July 8, 1959

192   Personal Products Corporation. Page 158

Chapter 7

211   Labor Management Relations Act, Section 8 (d), 1947, 1959

References

References

PAGE

330   Brennan, Mr. Justice William J. Jr., Concurring Opinion in the 1960 Trilogy Cases. Pages 137, 313

331   Atkinson, Oil, Chemical & Atomic Workers Int'l Union, AFL–CIO–CLC. Page 325

334   Sinclair Refining Company vs. Atkinson, Oil, Chemical & Atomic Workers Int'l Union, AFL–CIO–CLC. Decided June 18, 1962; reported in 370 U.S. 195

334, 335   The Norris-LaGuardia Act (Anti-Injunction Act), 1932 (generally barring U.S. Federal Courts from issuing injunctions in a case involving or growing out of a labor dispute.)

335   Sinclair Refining Company. Page 334

336   Drake Bakeries, Incorporated. Page 325

338   "15,000 Strike Buick Over Job Standards." New York *Times,* January 9, 1964

339   Jones, David R. "Union Militancy Charged By Ford." New York *Times,* July 17, 1964

342   Burke, John P., quoted in "What Will Collective Bargaining Look Like in Twenty Years?" by George W. Brooks, *The Next Twenty Years in Industrial Relations.* Massachusetts Institute of Technology, Industrial Relations Section, Cambridge, Mass., 1957

343   "1,000 Walk Out at G.E. Plant." New York *Times,* July 24, 1962

343   Ford, Henry II, *Bargaining And Economic Growth,* Delivered at the Eighteenth Annual Meeting of the American Society of Corporate Secretaries, Coronado, California, June 22, 1964

344   Shultz, George and Robert P. Crisara, *Causes of Industrial Peace Under Collective Bargaining,* Case Study No. 10, The Lapointe Machine Tool Company and United Steelworkers of America. National Planning Association, Washington, D.C., 1952

344   Brooks, George W., "What Will Collective Bargaining Look Like in Twenty Years?" Page 342

347   Goldberg, Arthur J., "Management's Reserved Rights: A Labor View." Page 149

349   Enterprise Wheel and Car Corporation. Page 313

350   Fischer, Ben, "What And When And How To Arbitrate," *Proceedings of the Eighteenth Annual Meeting of the National Academy of Arbitrators,* 1965. The Bureau of National Affairs, Inc. Washington, D.C., 1965

424

Chapter 12

Chapter 13

References

Unions' Shop Steward Manuals Cited in Book 2

The commonly used abbreviated title of the union precedes the full name and address of the union. The numbers under each manual title refer to the pages on which the manual quotations appear.

AFL–CIO—American Federation of Labor and Congress of Industrial Organizations, Department of Education, 815 Sixteenth Street, N.W., Washington, D.C. Publication No. 75, December 1966
AFL–CIO Manual For Shop Stewards
   158

AFL–CIO—American Federation of Labor and Congress of Industrial Organizations, Publication No. 75, March 1962
AFL–CIO Manual For Shop Stewards
   154, 264, 346

AWIU—Aluminum Workers International Union, AFL–CIO, 818 Olive Street, St. Louis, Missouri
Shop Steward's Manual
   154, 184, 346

Brewery—International Union of United Brewery, Flour, Cereal, Soft Drink and Distillery Workers of America, AFL–CIO–CLC, Research and Education Department, 2347 Vine Street, Cincinnati, Ohio (Canada: 617 Ford Building, 193 Hastings Street, Vancouver, B.C., Canada)
Steward's Manual Know Your Union
   154

CWA—Communications Workers of America, AFL–CIO, Education Director, 1925 K Street, N.W., Washington, D.C.
CWA Steward's Manual—A Guide to Leadership
   153, 185

Glass-Ceramic—United Glass and Ceramic Workers of North America, AFL–CIO–CLC, Department of Research and Education, 556 East Town Street, Columbus, Ohio
So You're A Grievanceman!
   69, 154, 180, 194

IAM—International Association of Machinists and Aerospace Workers, AFL–CIO, Education Department, 1300 Connecticut Avenue, N.W., Washington, D.C.
Pocket Guide for Shop Stewards
   184, 194, 346

ICWU—International Chemical Workers Union, AFL–CIO–CLC, Research, Education, Health and Safety Department, 1659 West Market Street, Akron, Ohio
Handbook For Stewards
   154, 156, 184, 195

IUE—International Union of Electrical, Radio and Machine Workers, AFL–CIO, Education Department, 1126 16th Street, N.W., Washington, D.C.
IUE Leadership Manual For Shop Stewards
   156, 167, 310, 363

UAW—International Union, United Automobile, Aerospace and Agricultural Implement Workers of America, Education Department, UAW, 8000 East Jefferson Avenue, Detroit, Michigan
Steward's Guide—Hints on Bargaining and Grievance Procedure
   139, 152, 153, 154, 230, 346

UPP—United Papermakers and Paperworkers, AFL–CIO, CLC, Publications Department, Papermakers Building, Albany, New York
Successful Grievance Handling—A Manual For UPP Shop Stewards
   153

Pressmen—International Printing Pressmen and Assistants' Union of North America, AFL–CIO, Pressmen's Home, Tennessee
Shop Stewards and Committeemen
   184

URW—United Rubber, Cork, Linoleum and Plastic Workers of America, AFL–CIO, URW Education Department, 87 South High Street, Akron, Ohio
Manual for URW Shop Stewards
   136, 230

USW—United Steelworkers of America, AFL–CIO–CLC 1500 Commonwealth Building, Pittsburgh, Pennsylvania, Published by the Department of Education and Welfare, United Steelworkers of America, 1901 Yonge Street, Toronto 7, Canada
Job of the Steward A Manual for Shop Stewards
   156

Index